FROM ANGER TO APATHY

Mark Garnett is a lecturer in politics at Lancaster University. His books include *Splendid! Splendid! The Authorised Biography of Willie Whitelaw* (with Ian Aitken, Cape, 2002) and *The A-Z Guide to Modern British History* (with Richard Weight, Cape, 2003)

ALSO BY MARK GARNETT

Splendid! Splendid! The Authorised Biography of Willie Whitelaw
The A-Z Guide to Modern British History

MARK GARNETT

From Anger
to Apathy

The Story of Politics, Society and Popular
Culture in Britain since 1975

Printed and bound in Great Britain by
CPI Bookmarque, Croydon CR0 4TD

VINTAGE BOOKS
London

Published by Vintage 2008

1 2 4 6 8 10 9 7 5 3

Copyright © Mark Garnett 2007

Mark Garnett has asserted his right under the Copyright, Designs
and Patents Act 1988 to be identified as the author of this work

First published in Great Britain in 2007 by
Jonathan Cape
Random House, 20 Vauxhall Bridge Road,
London SW1V 2SA

www.vintage-books.co.uk

Addresses for companies within The Random House Group Limited can be
found at: www.randomhouse.co.uk/offices.htm

The Random House Group Limited Reg. No. 954009

A CIP catalogue record for this book
is available from the British Library

ISBN 9781844135325

The Random House Group Limited supports The Forest Stewardship
Council (FSC), the leading international forest certification organisation.
All our titles that are printed on Greenpeace approved FSC certified paper
carry the FSC logo. Our paper procurement policy can be found at
www.rbooks.co.uk/environment

Typeset by Palimpsest Book Production Limited,
Grangemouth, Stirlingshire

In memory of James and Mary Douglas, Ezio Rocca and
Zuzanna Shonfield – life enhancers, sorely missed

CONTENTS

ILLUSTRATIONS

Police shot of Fred West, 22 November 1995 (© *AFP/Getty Images*).

Joyce McKinney during her court case, 6 October 1977 (© *Hulton Archive/Frank Barratt/Getty Images*).

Mary Whitehouse with Cliff Richard, 1970 (© *PA Photos*).

Carl Andre's *Equivalent VIII* (© *PA Photos*).

Prince Charles and Princess Diana with Bob Geldof, David Bowie, Roger Taylor and Brian May at the Live Aid Concert, Wembley Stadium, 13 July 1985 (© *Hulton Archive/Dave Hogan/Getty Images*).

Alan Shearer being welcomed by Newcastle fans, 8 August 1996 (© *Rex Features*).

Tony Blair enters Downing Street, 1 May 1997 (*Hulton Archive/Tom Stoddart Archive/Getty Images*).

Pro-hunting groups protest against the hunting ban, Westminster, 15 September 2004 (© *Getty Images News/Scott Barbour/Getty Images*).

Anti-war march, 15 February 2003 (© *Getty Images News/Ian Waldie/Getty Images*).

ACKNOWLEDGEMENTS

After completing this book, I still couldn't say if it is harder to write biographies than general histories: but apparently the latter take longer. At times it has seemed as if I have been working on the manuscript for more years than the period under review. In part, the delay is due to the enjoyable and very instructive 'busman's holiday' I took in 2004-5, assisting Michael Crick on his biography of Michael Howard.

My immediate family has expanded somewhat while I have been working on the book. Millie and Ben have helped its composition, by keeping their demands for milk and amusement within reasonable bounds. Dili has been understanding and tolerant during the research, as well as being a wonderful mother. My own parents have always been marvellously supportive, and I hope that my appreciation is some return for their consistent kindness.

Even when surrounded by a special family, some parts of a writer's existence are bound to be solitary. In this respect, technological change has been a great help; and I should thank the 'regulars' on the Internet forums, aa606.co.uk and deathlist.net for their refreshing 'virtual' companionship after a hard day's writing. Thanks are also due to all of my colleagues at the Department of Politics and International Relations at Lancaster University, who have made me feel very welcome. In particular, I am grateful to David Denver and Patrick Bishop for their comments on specific chapters. I am also indebted to the late Lord Gilmour of Craigmillar, Sheila Harper and Francis Wheen, who read and reacted to individual chapters; and to my father, Allan Garnett, who ploughed through most of the manuscript. Naturally, the opinions expressed in the book are my own and any errors of fact are my responsibility. At Jonathan Cape, Will Sulkin gave me crucial encouragement when the idea for the book was first mooted. However, my greatest debt is to Jörg Hensgen, who always understood what I was trying to do with this book. As editor, Jörg has been patient and encouraging, even during phone calls at unseasonable hours. Without such friendly and positive input the task would have felt much more demanding, and taken even longer to complete.

INTRODUCTION: ANGER AND APATHY

You only have to move about Western Europe nowadays to realise how poor and unproud the British have become in relation to their neighbours. It shows in the look of our towns, in our airports, in our hospitals and in local amenities; it is painfully apparent in our railway system.

Sir Nicholas Henderson (1979)[1]

You hardly dare open a paper these days: the news is all of cataclysm and collapse. Tempers are threadbare; the yobs are winning; everybody accepts the fact that they've got to get nastier in order to survive. The world is going bad on us.

Martin Amis, *Success* (1978)[2]

IN the spring of 2004 considerable media interest was aroused by the report of an environmental think tank, the New Economics Foundation (NEF), into changes in the 'quality of life' in Britain over the previous half-century. In the study attention had been paid to material standards, conventionally measured by gross domestic product (GDP), but the Foundation had also examined social and environmental criteria, including crime, family breakdown, economic inequality, state welfare spending, pollution and the cost of commuting. Taken together, these indicators provided a more holistic 'measure of domestic progress' (MDP). On that basis, the NEF concluded that in the post-war period 1976 had been the best year to be alive in Britain.[3]

The analysts of the NEF were aware that their findings would surprise most observers – not least those who had actually been alive in the mid-1970s. As the *Guardian* accepted, the report gave 'a timely tweak' to forty-somethings who wanted to look back on days when their personal circumstances were relatively carefree. But it would be more realistic to see the study as a doleful verdict on subsequent developments, rather than a celebration of the real living conditions of 1976. A balanced reassessment of life in that distant year would require considerable effort; for understandable reasons first-hand memories had become imprecise by 2004. It was difficult to remember the kind of conditions which had vexed Sir Nicholas Henderson back in 1979. Many of his complaints – part of a leaked 'valedictory dispatch', written as he stepped down as British ambassador to France – seemed to have been addressed. If anything justified Tony Blair's short-lived rhetoric about 'cool Britannia', it was the new look of an old country. Britons no longer had to feel ashamed of their airports, and visitors could hardly miss the vibrancy of the capital city. Ambitious redevelopment was under way in many other parts of the United Kingdom. Victorian hospitals, in particular, were being replaced by gleaming modern buildings equipped with the latest technology, thanks to heavy government investment. Even the partly-privatised railway system *looked* less shabby, although performance was still nowhere near continental standards.

But Henderson had not just been complaining about Britain's material environment. He had added that 'A considerable jolt is going to be needed if a lasting attenuation of civil purpose and courage is to be arrested.' In this respect the years since 1979 had arguably marked a decline. The 2005 edition of the *Lonely Planet* travel guide claimed that Britons were 'uninhibited, tolerant, exhibitionist, passionate, aggressive, sentimental, hospitable and friendly'.[4] This enthusiastic portrait flew in the face of some long-cherished stereotypes, and was difficult for contemporary Britons to recognise. It suggested that the researchers had not extended their stay for long enough to consult a sample of the surveys which poured out of the press at the time, emphasising the fear and loneliness of the old, the heedless hedonism of the young and the growing inability of people of all ages to trust one another.

The sheer volume of such surveys was in itself sufficient to darken the national mood, particularly since the findings were often conflicting, if not contradictory. For example, in September 2003 *The Times* gave a positive spin to a poll about attitudes among twenty-somethings, arguing that people in that age group were generally happy about themselves, and with good reason. On the same day the *Guardian* gave front-page coverage to a study which suggested that behavioural prob-

lems among teenagers had steadily increased since 1974, while emotional
difficulties had 'shot up' since 1986.[5] As the journalist Nick Cohen
archly suggested, the experts themselves were hardly helping – 'we have
so many psychiatric problems because we have so many psychiatrists'.[6]
Yet there was good reason to suppose that demand was not entirely
the product of supply in this instance. And whatever they might think
of their own lives, Britons had plenty of grounds for complaint over
the state of public affairs when the NEF report appeared and the *Lonely
Planet* investigators were uncovering so much optimism. The aftermath
of the war in Iraq was only one among many problems facing the
country. Rightly or wrongly, Britons were convinced that crime was
lurching out of control; even the government acknowledged a growing
menace from 'anti-social behaviour'. Allegedly, woolly-minded judges
were handing out inadequate sentences to dangerous offenders;
paedophiles were roaming the streets and even finding work which
brought them into contact with children. The standard of public services seemed to be declining; even the National Health Service was the
target of critical comment, despite the huge increase in funding after
2001. Meanwhile, an already overcrowded country was continuing to
welcome unwanted outsiders – would-be welfare spongers, interspersed
with fundamentalist Islamic activists.

All this was bad enough, but were the mid-1970s really any better?
The NEF researchers certainly established that 'well-being' is about
more than bald economic data, supporting the eloquent arguments of
the LSE economist Richard Layard.[7]* But calculations that placed the
mid-1970s on top were still open to question. Henderson's views
cannot be lightly dismissed; after all, he had no professional interest
in talking Britain down. The poor conditions he reported could not
have come into being overnight, and national morale can take years
to crumble. One eminent historian, writing in the 1990s, went much
further than Henderson, recalling the five years after 1974 as 'a
dangerous, disorienting time when what counted most was to survive'.[8]

By coincidence, the idea of 'MDP' had been anticipated just when
it was supposedly moving towards its peak. Writing in the *New
Statesman*'s first edition of 1975, Mervyn Jones had given a cautious

---

* The academic debate, in fact, had been instigated in 1974 by the work of the American
economist Robert Easterlin, who showed on the basis of survey data that despite rising
living standards, perceived levels of happiness had remained stable over recent decades,
a phenomenon which came to be known as the Easterlin Paradox.

welcome to the prospect of a decline in the nation's wealth. As he put it, 'I never believed that human happiness can be measured in gross national product *per capita*.'⁹ A few months later Geraldine Norman took up the search for an alternative in a *Times* article. She unveiled her 'hedonometer' – a cheerfully unscientific way of gauging a nation's happiness. Six factors were listed, of which the most important was the 'Ability of an ordinary citizen to understand and control his environment'. On this score Britain fared very badly; on Norman's estimation it deserved no more than 50 out of 100. She argued that 'it is the very speed of change in his social and economic environment that leaves the ordinary [British] citizen at a loss'. As Mervyn Jones had suggested, Britons would indeed be better off if they were poorer; in 1975 Norman's hedonometer ranked Britain behind Botswana in terms of national well-being.¹⁰

The problem for commentators like Jones and Norman was that in 1975 very few Britons shared their enlightened view. Far from wishing for a return to a simpler life with less money and a more stable social environment, most people at the time were unhappy precisely because they felt that their living standards were on the slide. With inflation apparently surging out of control, people on fixed incomes had good reasons for fear. Others were beginning to brood over their job prospects, as the Labour government adopted tougher economic policies in the face of the inflationary threat. In this respect things certainly did not improve in 1976; unemployment rose, future public spending plans were curtailed, and the political outlook became increasingly unstable as Labour fought to stay in office despite the loss of its slender parliamentary majority. As the disgraced Labour MP John Stonehouse put it in one of his last speeches before being jailed for various financial offences, 'Although some material standards have been improved since 1946, it cannot be said that the majority of the citizens of England are significantly happier. Far from it. There is a tension, a disquiet and a dismay in the nation that can be seen on the faces of the ordinary people.'¹¹

If anything, 1977 was an improvement on the previous year, even if for a small minority the Queen's silver jubilee was notable only because it provided the Sex Pistols with a pretext for attacking the monarchy. By 2004 the punk generation was getting too old to pogo; bin-liners and safety pins were no longer fashion accessories, and the Mohican hairstyle was rarely glimpsed outside the postcards in London's souvenir shops. But popular music since the mid-1970s had been so formulaic and uninspiring that even those who disliked the Pistols and the whole New Wave movement now felt moved by the repetitive opening bars of 'Anarchy in the UK'. Punk rock, in short, had become a prime example of 'England's dreaming' – a profitable subsidiary of its nostalgia industry. Meanwhile other bands were still performing three decades after being written off as irrelevant relics. In August 1975 Roger Daltrey of The Who admitted that, 'We're getting old – to a seventeen-year-old we're old'.[12] Thirty years later his group (minus two deceased founder-members) performed at Live 8, the best-publicised concert of 2005. The popularity of such superannuated ensembles had not persisted merely because people who grew up in the 1970s now had plenty of money, and could shell out substantial funds for repeated 'reunion gigs'. They were still in demand because the songs they had written in the fast-receding past were good enough to thrill successive generations.

In 1980 Christopher Booker wrote that 'The seventies were scarcely a decade to cheer about, to quicken the pulse, to remember with excitement – hardly a time which in years to come is likely to inspire us with an overpowering sense of excitement.'[13] However, music fans are not alone in their retrospective relish for those years. Some television shows of 1975 were themselves products of nostalgia for an earlier time which is no longer so appealing; *The Black and White Minstrel Show* and *The Good Old Days* were popular enough to merit Christmas specials that year. But among the mediocrity there were several first-rate productions (like *Fawlty Towers* and *Porridge*) whose reputations have deservedly risen over the decades. It could be argued that the quality of entertainment in the mid-1970s was just an accident; equally, one could be over-schematic and describe it as a final cry of defiance against the dross that dominated the future. True, some of the more politically conscious artists who gave so much pleasure at the time – one thinks in particular of The Clash – did seem to detect a lasting downturn in the general quality of life rather than a temporary blip in the wake of the oil shock of 1973–4. But, if they thought about it at all, most performers assumed that they were contributing to a tradition of popular culture which would continue onward and upward, with or without their efforts.

Another assumption shared by most public entertainers in the mid-1970s was that their work should appeal across the generations. As a result, popular culture acted as a social glue at the time, rather than driving people apart. Even innovative comedies like *Fawlty Towers* could be enjoyed by viewers of all ages. The obvious exception was rock music, which had always been a vehicle for rebellion. But in 1975 the pop charts invariably included the kind of tunes which everyone could hum, providing adults with some understanding of the rising generation – even while they tutted over the 'teeny-bopper' adulation of groups like the Osmonds and the Bay City Rollers. The punk movement, of course, played a significant part in driving a wedge between the generations after 1975. But it did not create the conditions in which it thrived; its patrons profited from its ability to articulate an intergenerational conflict which already existed. Even so, it seems odd that so many people feel nostalgic about the mid-1970s because of punk rock, which was at least partly responsible for the subsequent cultural divisions within British society.

As a *Guardian* columnist quipped in April 2005, 'the main upshot of nostalgia is that it reminds you how much you can't remember'.[14] But regrets for the past may have more serious consequences. Richard Sennett has claimed that 'it induces resignation about the present, and so a certain acceptance of its evils'. On this view, there is a link between nostalgia and apathy.[15] Hopefully this book will act as an antidote to *unreflective* nostalgia about the 1970s – a mood which has become all too common, due to the prevalence of superficial television documentaries, the incessant reruns of vintage comedy episodes and emotional band reunions.[16] But this was not my main reason for undertaking the research. The original idea was to examine changes in British life wrought by Thatcherism. The Conservative-dominated 1980s, almost everyone agreed, seriously damaged the nation's social and cultural fabric. After becoming prime minister in 1997, for example, Tony Blair claimed that 'The 1980s were a time of "Who cares?"'[17] I saw no reason to dispute such generalisations. But the lamentable lack of broadly based studies in contemporary history meant that criticism of the 'Thatcher years' tended to be expressed in unsupported assertions. The book was originally intended as a means of supplying the necessary evidence for those who wanted to move beyond the familiar clichés. I was also hoping to satisfy my own curiosity, as someone who had become an adult at the dawn of the 1980s and held strong views at the time.

Although the study was intended to be about the 1980s, this was never going to be reflected in the chronological structure. Echoing Giovanni Arrighi and Eric Hobsbawm, I proposed to examine 'the long 1980s'.[18] It seemed to me that while most commentators were ready to condemn the 1980s – particularly since the polarising figure of Margaret Thatcher had dominated public affairs throughout the decade – they overlooked the possibility that the characteristics which disfigured those years might have outlived them. There was a tendency even for seasoned observers of the 1980s to look down on their previous selves, as if to say, 'That's how things were then, but we are so much wiser now.' So the narrative would carry the story right up to the present, to see if there really had been a decisive reaction against the 1980s which might justify such condescension. While some of the unpleasant stereotypes of that period now attract less media comment – one thinks in particular of yuppies – their bombastic successors are still around in substantial numbers. As the book shows, other deplorable trends which were supposedly unique to the 1980s have persisted, and even worsened, under 'New' Labour.

At the other end of the time frame, the purpose of starting in the mid-1970s was to give the book a 'before and after' feel. While not exactly sharing the NEF's implied view that it was great to be alive in 1976, I did expect to find that things *had* been better in crucial respects. In particular, at a time when left-wing ideas were apparently making progress within the Labour Party, there was reason to think that there would have been more evidence of *optimism* about the future (however naive) in the mid-1970s; at any rate, there would be much less *cynicism*. The NEF analysis, which appeared when research for this book was already well under way, made an interesting case for beginning the survey in 1976. But on reflection I saw no reason to change my hunch that 1975 – the year which saw Thatcher's rise to the Conservative leadership and the birth of the Freedom Association, David Beckham and the Sex Pistols – was a more interesting point of embarkation. This, after all, was the year in which Britain registered the full effects of 1973's massive rise in oil prices, with record inflation and soaring wage settlements. The psychological impact of those developments, arguably, was also greater in 1975 than it had been in 1974; as Britons began to adjust to the alarming prospect of rising unemployment, and a significant decline in general living standards.

Among numerous potential subjects for investigation, several outstanding themes suggested themselves. The obvious structure for the study was to make each of these themes into a separate chapter, which itself would take a roughly chronological approach. Taken together, the chapters would build an interlocking narrative of the last three decades, to help explain why Britain had moved from a time of anger to one in which apathy was pervasive. The book would start with anger because the mid-1970s were generally seen as a time of successful militancy, generated especially among people who thought that reactionary forces were standing in the way of progress towards greater justice and socio-economic equality. It would end with apathy, not just because of the dramatic decline in electoral turnouts over recent general elections, but because of a feeling that, whether or not they cast votes, the British are now passive *consumers*, rather than active *citizens*. This deeper sense of apathy, I believed, was shown in a resigned attitude towards injustice and inequality, at home and abroad; and I suspected that it would be possible to trace this attitude to the developments of the 1980s.

Although the original structure has been retained, further research has revealed a much more complex story. For example, far from advancing towards power in the second half of the 1970s the British left suffered a string of crushing defeats. The most important of these was the Grunwick industrial dispute of 1977–8, which ended in the failure of the Labour government and its trade union allies to enforce their interpretation of employee rights, against a combination of the police, the courts and the Freedom Association. The latter was the most vocal of many middle-class pressure groups which thrived at the time, expressing real anger at what was seen as the government's support for social justice at the expense of profitability and personal enrichment. Other right-wing bodies were more secretive, like the private armies which emerged to defend the constitution against the alleged British allies of the Soviet Union. Such organisations were rarely publicised by the media, while the microscopic Workers' Revolutionary Party and other left-wing groups were constantly reviled. Apart from its reliable friends in the press, the political right had the unwavering support of the police, which used National Front rallies as opportunities to pummel leftist agitators into a less radical frame of mind. If the left surmounted these orthodox constitutional obstacles, in the last resort the heavy artillery could always be wheeled out. As The Clash warned in 1978, 'The British Army is waiting out there / An' it weighs fifteen hundred tons'.[19] It was quite possible, in the volatile atmosphere of the mid-1970s, to imagine a scenario in which Britain's armed forces would be called upon to act against their fellow citizens.

Critics of the left in the late 1970s concentrated their fire on its attitude to freedom. Through its support for nationalisation and union power it was accused of wanting to extinguish free market activity, which had already been restricted by previous post-war governments. By contrast, in the social sphere it was working to extend liberties which had already become licentious. The left was slow to respond to these challenges, giving credence to the right's subsequent assertion that it had won a battle of ideas in those years (see Chapter 4). Whatever the truth of this claim, the left can certainly be accused of failing to rethink its attitude towards specific issues like pornography. As Chapter 6 argues, people on the left tended to retain the optimistic view that a relaxation in traditional morality would foster the creation of a more enlightened society. This argument, supposedly, had served the left well during the 1960s. Whether or not that was the case, by the mid-1970s the context was very different. Distracted by its passionate debate with social conservatives like Mary Whitehouse, the left failed to recognise that sexual liberation was being advanced by profiteers with a limited interest in promoting loving relationships of any kind. As a result, the left ended up being blamed for the practical results of permissiveness, even when these illustrated the capitalist system at its most exploitative. Although Margaret Thatcher agreed with social conservatives in blaming the rise of pornography on the left, her inability to translate her thoughts into effective action is suggested by the fact that this was one 'industry' which thrived during her years in office.

The subject of greed seemed more straightforward. Although many of her predecessors had spoken out in favour of material accumulation, Mrs Thatcher was the first prime minister openly to exult in the existing gap between rich and poor, and actively to promote policies which would make it wider. Given her steadfast belief in the (dubious) beneficial effect of financial incentives, this was only to be expected, and it would be a mistake to underrate the impact of her rhetoric on the validation of greed. However, on closer inspection (see Chapter 5) it is clear that Thatcher articulated views that were widely held *before* she became prime minister in 1979 – not least among trade unionists, who were supposedly progressive. In fact, the evidence of opinion surveys suggests that her unabashed advocacy of materialism actually inspired something of a reaction *against* greed, at least between 1979 and her third election victory eight years later.

After 1987 even the Labour Party made a concerted drive towards a reconciliation with the greedy. It seemed futile for remaining dissidents to persist in outspoken opposition to a new moral framework in which greed was 'good' – particularly since the greedy could entrench their values through constant repetition in the media, which was increasingly geared towards untrammelled consumerism. There were several public outcries against overpaid business executives in the early 1990s but the main targets for criticism were people who had worked for modest sums before their companies were privatised; sometimes even they seemed embarrassed by their sudden transition from a life of material comfort to super-affluence. No serious politician suggested any longer that such companies should be brought back under state ownership, even though they had signally failed to realise Thatcherite dreams of 'popular capitalism'.

Other manifestations of boardroom excess passed without critical comment, along with the soaring remuneration of sporting stars and other entertainers. By the 1990s, even supposedly rebellious rock musicians were openly bragging about their wealth without losing their credibility. As one aspiring star admitted at that time, 'At the end of the day, vast financial gain has got to be your main motive. I want a helicopter.'[20] Johnny Rotten of the Sex Pistols ended up as John Lydon, a successful property developer in the US whose remaining anarchistic impulses amused the public in the reality show *I'm a Celebrity, Get Me out of Here*. For idealists there was even something disconcerting in the fact that Joe Strummer, the epitome of an urban rebel during his time with The Clash, died peacefully in December 2002 sitting in his Somerset farmhouse.

Clearly the tolerance of greed was connected in some way to increasing apathy among the British public. But even this was nothing new. As Chapter 1 shows, there were plenty of complaints in 1975 that the electorate was too apathetic. This criticism could hardly have referred to levels of turnout in general elections, which remained respectable until 1997. Rather, the underlying argument about apathy at the time reflected the earlier assumption that a better-educated electorate would also be more public-spirited – and could force senior politicians to act responsibly in the national interest if they wanted to hold office. For many well-informed observers this hope was dashed in 1975, when the fleeting example of cross-party alliance induced by the referendum on membership of 'Europe' was instantly dissipated by the blinkered imperatives of partisan conflict. As the veteran Conservative politician Lord Boothby put it a few days after the referendum, 'We are not getting the government which the people want or deserve.'[21]

The inability of voters to force centrist politicians to contemplate the idea of cooperation on a lasting basis reflected a persistent belief that instead of being 'servants of the people', British political leaders were, and would always remain, their unloved masters. Although Britain had experienced the *form* of a full democracy since 1928, its political system remained irredeemably elitist. The referendum itself had actually been a triumph for apathy. Media coverage had focused on personalities rather than the issues, so that people like Edward Heath, who spoke honestly in favour of European integration, might as well have saved their breath. The anti-EEC campaigners were doomed before the campaign began, at least in part because they lacked celebrity support. After 1975 the British continued to vote in large numbers; but apart from a small minority of enthusiasts this mainly reflected the fact that participation had become an ingrained habit which would take at least a further generation to die away. This argument is supported by the fact that, rather than continuing a gradual decline, electoral turnout suddenly plummeted in 1997 and 2001. Only a country which was already well accustomed to apathy – in the fullest sense of an insufficient inclination towards civic engagement – could shrug off the horrifying figures of 2001, which cast doubt on Britain's credentials as a liberal democracy.

The apathy of 2001, then, can directly be traced to developments in the years *before* 1979. In fact an examination of contemporary reports shows some striking similarities between the perceived problems of the mid-1970s and the widely reported malaise of today. Not even the specific themes of the present study would have surprised the most concerned witnesses of 1975. At his enthronement in January of that year, the Archbishop of Canterbury, Donald Coggan (1909–2000), characterised his age as one of 'violence; materialism which shuts its eyes to extremities of wealth and poverty existing side by side; abandonment of the old gods and a pathetic inability to replace them with anything adequate for the needs of modern man; fear on every side; and because iniquity abounds, the love of many growing cold'.[22]

Far from being a professional doom-monger, Dr Coggan was normally the least pessimistic of prelates. In his new job he had every incentive to minimise the difficulties which confronted the majority of Britons. But the concrete evidence supports the tenor of his argument about the tendency of the times. As the research for this book developed, it became clear that instead of presenting a refreshing contrast to later trends, the 1975–9 period was an integral part of a problem which is too easily identified with the Thatcher years. Instead of being solved by Thatcher's downfall in 1990, that problem outlived her successor John Major and became if anything even worse after 1997. In itself, the end of a prolonged period of Conservative rule could hardly cure a distemper which had taken hold long before Mrs Thatcher took office; as it was, Tony Blair and New Labour did nothing of substance to reverse the trend. We are not living in the 'long 1980s' after all; rather, we are still stuck in the 'long late 70s'.

The present book begins with a review of leading events in 1975, based on a close reading of *The Times*. Even before it was taken over by Rupert Murdoch in 1981 that newspaper was not exactly a model of impartiality. Allowance has been made for its obvious preferences – for example, the unbalanced reporting of the 1975 referendum, which it shared with every other major national newspaper. Occasionally it provides unwitting testimony of the prejudices of the time,* but other publications were far worse in this respect. The most sceptical reading of this material still suggests that in 1975 Britain was an unpleasant place – especially when the actual conditions are compared to the potential of a relatively rich nation.

This leaves open the possibility that the impression of a decline in British life after 1975–6 only partly reflects realities on the ground. On this view, contemporary pessimism might reflect the media propensity to emphasise the negative. Undoubtedly since the mid-1970s this trend has grown, to the extent that cheerful people are best advised to avoid the television or the tabloid press. One can certainly argue that media influence has helped to make Britain a place of endemic

---

* A beautiful example of the unthinking racism of the time is a brief report of the January 1975 trial which followed a fatal stabbing at a football match in Blackpool. When it was still possible that the main suspect would be found guilty, he was described as a 'coloured boy'. When he was cleared, he suddenly became a 'Bolton boy'; *The Times*, 24, 27 January 1975.

incivility, where in some quarters the receipt of an anti-social behaviour order (ASBO) can be regarded as a certificate of street credibility. However, there were plenty of complaints about the general influence of the media in the mid-1970s. For example, in July 1975 the former Liberal leader Jo Grimond (1913–93) complained that 'Too often [the press] represents the trivial, the sensational and such persons and subjects which it, in its somewhat ingrown world, regards as newsworthy.'[23] The Chief Rabbi, Immanuel Jakobovits (1921–99), protested that the media was guilty of 'publicising the freak more than the common'; as such, it tended to 'amplify dissension and muffle the voice of stability'.[24] Similar sentiments were being expressed thirty years later, albeit in less elegant prose. Some allowance, though, has to be made for the relative standpoint of the critics. Grimond and Jakobovits were arguing that the media of 1975 was 'trivial' and 'sensational' by post-war standards; the critics of the early twenty-first century, by contrast, thought that the situation had deteriorated sharply *since* 1975.

Concrete evidence suggests that the later critics were right. Although the media of 1975 was often mischievous, it was malevolent only on isolated occasions (as in its coverage of the Stonehouse affair, discussed in Chapter 1). One way in which the post-1975 media excelled was its capacity to reflect (and stimulate) public fear. Chapter 3 shows that while this approach was known to be commercially advantageous, it was selectively deployed in the mid-1970s. Contemporary fears of Irish republican terrorism did not have to be exaggerated, since the threat was real. However, the tabloid press was not particularly anxious to inform its readers about the complicated history which lay behind the conflict. After 1979 the argument that Britain's continued existence was endangered by the presence of nuclear weapons within its territory was drowned out by the media's presentation of a justificatory menace – the Soviet Union, which was apparently run by homicidal maniacs who were willing to risk the destruction of their own homeland in their counter-intuitive quest for overseas annexations. Nowadays the creation and management of fear is a primary concern in the government's dealings with the media.

With hindsight, it looks as if the three decades after 1975 marked the period in which the influence of the mainstream media reached a height from which it is beginning to decline. Memories of the late 1970s are dominated by the disdainful coverage of a Labour government which, for all its limitations, was genuinely trying to work in the public interest. During the 1980s an increasingly shrill anti-Labour press bias was encouraged by Conservative politicians, who did not realise that the same weapons would be used against themselves if self-interest prompted a change of mind among the tabloid proprietors. This duly occurred after 1992. Once Labour had ceased to be the main focus of media muck-raking, public figures at all levels lived in fear of having their lives destroyed by newspaper stories, whether true or false. Afterwards, both John Major and Tony Blair were desperate to propitiate the most virulent media outlets. The main result was an increase in public distrust of the media, and opinion polls which showed that journalists were even less popular than politicians. The only upside, for the academic historian, is that during those years no one had to wait for the opening of government archives to gain an insight into the political process even at the highest level; the desire to be on good terms with the media ensured that one side or the other would always be ready to leak a detailed account in time to make tomorrow's headlines.

However, the advent of the Internet and satellite TV has sapped newspaper circulation and inspired increasingly desperate attempts to win the war between terrestrial television channels. Allegedly, this has inspired 'dumbing down' – a deliberate drive to pander to the perceived tastes of the lowest common denominator. Every established outlet has been affected by this tendency to some extent, but the problem can be exaggerated. For example, there is roughly the same amount of useful information in 'quality' newspapers as there was in 1975 – it is just harder to find among the instantly discardable supplements. High-quality radio persists, including such anachronistic BBC outposts as Radios 3 and 4. Television, though, is a different matter. The misnamed reality programmes are only entertaining or instructive by accident. Contemporary comedies like *Little Britain* are usually no more than a series of punchlines without any jokes; the most notable exception, Ricky Gervais's brilliant *The Office* (2001–2), was an exercise in the comedy of embarrassment and said nothing positive about the British work experience. This helps to explain the popularity of any show which features the cultural artefacts of the 1970s, the 1980s or even the irredeemably awful 1990s. Significantly, the 1960s have not featured so strongly in the nostalgia boom; no one wants to be reminded of a time when it really *was* quite easy to be optimistic. Even so, it is difficult to argue that the discerning viewer or radio listener is actually worse off now than in 1975. The difference, perhaps, is that in those days people who confined their attention to worthwhile broadcasting tended to be admired, whereas everyone is now pressurised into conformity with the tastes of the easily satisfied. Hence the repeated and unconvincing assertions that 'everybody' is watching shows like *Little Britain, Big Brother* and even the revived *Doctor Who* – which was popular enough in its first incarnation without the assistance of hype.

The multiplication of media outlets has made it more difficult to impose uniform views or tastes on the British public. The orthodox broadcasters and publishers enjoyed a dominant market position at the beginning of the communications revolution, and only began to lose it because their products were no longer attractive enough to command wide appeal. Instead of trying to raise their standards, long-established broadcasters like the BBC decided that it would be easier to make programmes which converted alienation from the modern world into a new form of entertainment. One result was the genuinely popular BBC sitcom *One Foot in the Grave* (1990–2000). But while the main character, the permanently dyspepsic Victor Meldrew, was in his sixties, his resentment of modernity was not restricted to a specific age group.* Life expectancy was increasing, along with the likelihood that people would spend an ever-larger proportion of their existence feeling disillusioned. This prospect, it seemed, was greatly enhanced among intelligent individuals who had been old enough to register the disenchantment of the late 1970s. In 2003 BBC2 began transmissions of a show called *Grumpy Old Men*. Alienation rather than age was the qualifying criterion in a show whose participants spoke out splenetically against a wide range of modern phenomena over which, as Geraldine Norman had predicted, people felt they had inadequate control. Among the first to get involved was Bob Geldof (born 1954), who had epitomised youthful energy as the lead singer of the Boomtown Rats in the late 1970s. But by his own testimony Geldof wrote the lyrics for the band's first hit single, 'Looking After Number One' (1977), because he was already growing tired of 'the pervasive selfishness of the time'.[25] Another early grumbler was the comedy writer John O'Farrell, who had been an idealistic seventeen-year-old left-winger when Mrs Thatcher entered Downing Street in 1979. Almost two

---

* Meldrew was a victim of 'involuntary retirement' and 'ageism'; he was made redundant when he was considered too old to begin a new career.

decades later O'Farrell had celebrated the end of Labour's years in the wilderness in his book *Things Can Only Get Better*, but his presence among the 'grumpy old men' suggested that they had not.[26] In contrast to the traditional view that people experience disappointment in middle age, by the early years of the twenty-first century it seemed possible to grow world-weary even in the womb.

Even from this brief survey, it should be clear that the period covered by this book did not see a straightforward transition from anger to apathy. One could even claim that these two traits have been wrestling for supremacy throughout, and the themes explored in the book merely explain why the latter has usually come out on top. Yet the initial sense of a crucial transition is still appropriate. In 1975, the perception that apathy was becoming a problem was reserved to a relatively small and arguably over-demanding minority. Thirty years later the feeling was ubiquitous; and it was recognised that apathy had extended beyond formal political participation to the general conduct of social life. Compared to 1975, more Britons today probably feel aggrieved for more of the time; but their feelings are much more difficult to mobilise into effective political protest. The main reason is that Britain is now dominated by individualistic consumerism. This outlook was noticed and often condemned in 1975, and at that time it did mark a significant change. Since then it has become so firmly entrenched that even those who complain about it are themselves individualistic consumers by the standards of 1975.

Obviously the impact of consumerism has not been confined to Britain. It might be the case that other countries have undergone broadly similar, and equally interesting, changes since 1975. A key underlying theme is the impact on Britain of its encounter with the United States, and this could provide interesting comparisons with, say, Germany or France. But ultimately these examples would only emphasise the extent to which Britain is different. No other country could match its mixture of gratitude, envy, contempt and meek compliance where the United States is concerned. Although politicians form only part of our cast of characters, their determination to make a reality of the mythical 'special relationship' is an important reason for Britain's endlessly ambivalent attitude to the US. Automatic and fulsome obedience to the foreign policy line laid down in Washington is actually a voluntary choice. In other respects, globalisation has meant that public and private decision-makers at all levels have been operating within new and tighter constraints since the mid-1970s. Even so, it is possible to cling to the view that, in Britain at least, choices and consequences could have been different.

This was particularly true after the 1997 general election. For the whole of our period until Labour's landslide win, the Conservatives were the only party to enjoy the kind of parliamentary majorities which offer some freedom of action. But a 179-seat margin of victory in 1997 gave Tony Blair an unprecedented mandate for change, even if his party had only secured 43 per cent of the votes. The new prime minister recognised that the dramatic swing in electoral fortunes since 1992 reflected a new mood in Britain. In his first keynote speech after the election, he accepted that, 'There is already a sense of hope and optimism in the country. People believe that there are new options, new possibilities.'[27] What the people did not know was that Blair had no intention of exploring these possibilities. His failure to break from the Thatcherite policy framework in any significant respect angered his critics, but it also reinforced the widespread, long-held view that voting was pointless because it never changed anything. Thanks to New Labour, the apathy which had existed since the 1970s at least became a regular topic for anguished public debate. But for Blair himself the decline in participation could hardly be a matter of regret; only apathy among Labour MPs and the public at large enabled him to cling to office long after he had forfeited the trust of his party and his country.

A final word needs to be added about the book's title. It is a common complaint that books about 'Britain' overlook the other component parts of the United Kingdom, and this study could also be regarded as unduly Anglocentric. On the other hand, according to the 2001 census England accounted for more than 83 per cent of the UK population (49 out of 58 million). Arguably its dominance is less than these figures would suggest, particularly since the successful implementation of devolution by the Blair government. However, this book is about general UK trends, and these are most likely to be identified in English developments. There is certainly no attempt to claim that the English have been any happier than their near neighbours since 1975.

BRITAIN IN 1975

Every time I buy anything I am astonished how much it has gone up since the previous week. I used to think I was well off. Now I do without all sorts of things and still seem to be in difficulties.

A. J. P Taylor to Eva Haraszti, 28 November 1975[1]

We have passed the stage when platitudes will placate, we are both frightened and furious, and we demand action.

Letter in *The Times*, 12 May 1975

Meanness has replaced generosity. Envy has replaced endeavour. Malice is the most common motivation. The current newspapers are the worst example of that.

Bernard Donoughue, September 1975[2]

To anyone earning over £7,000 a year: You qualify as a man [sic] who might drive a quite exceptional car ... The Peugeot 504 Superlative costs £3,484. We make it for people who've made it.

Motoring advertisement, 1975

I

DURING the CBS *Evening News* bulletin of 7 May 1975, the respected American journalist Eric Sevareid turned away from domestic happenings and permitted himself some personal reflections on the plight of one of his country's staunchest allies. Britain, he warned his audience, was 'drifting slowly towards a condition of ungovernability'. A recent visit had given him the impression that it was 'sleepwalking into a social revolution, one its majority clearly does not want but does not know how to stop'.

Sevareid's outburst was not unprecedented; the *Wall Street Journal* had just published an editorial with the headline 'Goodbye, Great Britain'. But when such views were aired on a widely watched news programme things were getting serious. Staff members at Britain's Washington embassy were disconsolate at this blow to their country's image and morale.[3] The prime minister, Harold Wilson, rebuked Sevareid at a press conference. But when it prepared its own editorial contribution to the debate the London *Times* found it impossible to dissent from the grim prognosis. Britain, it felt, was 'near the end of the line'. It lamented that individuals 'now look out for themselves because they despair of their country'. The situation could be remedied by 'nothing less than a revolution in the spirit of the nation'.[4]

On this occasion *The Times* could not be accused of fostering a scare story on the basis of random observations by foreign commentators. If anything, before May 1975 it had been playing down evidence of public pessimism and expectations of a dramatic upheaval; the most alarmist comments came from its readers, in the correspondence columns. The Christmas of 1974 had been marked by heavy consumer spending, and the New Year was celebrated in the usual style, with about 35,000 enthusiasts packed into Trafalgar Square. But although one curmudgeonly *Times* reader complained that the country was in thrall to 'fatuous optimism', apart from these festive spasms there was little evidence of escapism. A more cryptic correspondent confided that 'Disaster is stalking us in an invisible cloak.' The Gallup end-of-year poll had found that nearly two thirds of respondents expected 1975 to be even worse than the multifaceted miseries of 1974. In her Christmas broadcast even the Queen had referred to the danger that despondency might become a habit. From the safety of his London club, the historian Arthur Bryant tried to rally spirits in *The Times*'s first edition of the year. He accepted that 'There is plenty to be afraid of in our present situation,' but hoped that 'resolution, hard work, self-discipline and national unity' would see Britain through.[5]

On 17 January a much greater historian, A.J.P Taylor, warned his Hungarian lover that 'the entire Western world is approaching breakdown, with this country almost the first to go'.[6] For pundits like Taylor, the only question was whether the crisis would result in a dramatic swing to the right or the left in Britain. The correspondents of one provincial newspaper were split on this issue at the beginning of the year. A Nottingham man told the *Leicester Mercury* that a right-wing coup in March would displace Edward Heath from the Conservative Party leadership. His successor, Enoch Powell, would take over as prime minister from Harold Wilson in October. Another correspondent presented a contrasting scenario, predicting that Britain would become a communist state within twelve months.[7] Taylor's private view was that 'a modified Communist economic system, introduced by democratic methods' would emerge after a failed 'Fascist right-wing attempt'. However, 'the capitalist world may be frightened of this and come to our rescue'.[8] Even rock stars contributed to the convoluted guessing game. David Bowie thought that 'The best thing that can happen is for an extreme right-wing government to be elected,' and some of his later comments suggested that he would be interested in leading it.[9]

As Taylor recognised, Britain was not alone in facing serious difficulties at this time. All Western states were struggling to control inflation in the wake of a fourfold increase in oil prices after the Arab–Israeli Yom Kippur war of October 1973, combined with the dissolution of the Bretton Woods System which had ensured a degree of currency stability since the Second World War. In Britain the impact of these global developments was particularly severe because they followed a prolonged period of relative economic decline combined with a feeling of complacency about the country's prospects. All this accentuated an existing political problem. After 1968 both of the main parties had tried unsuccessfully to limit the power of Britain's trade unions. Labour's proposals, embodied in the White Paper *In Place of Strife* (1969), were dropped in the face of opposition which included senior cabinet ministers like the home secretary, James Callaghan. The Heath government at least managed to pass legislation, but its Industrial Relations Act (1971) was nullified by the unions' refusal to cooperate.

Before long, moderate politicians from both of the main parties had good reason to repent their failure to cooperate in this enterprise. In 1972 the government tried to resist a pay claim by the National Union of Mineworkers (NUM), but was forced to concede most of the demands in humiliating circumstances. Even before Yom Kippur, the NUM was preparing a new campaign in pursuit of a further increase. Industrial action by the miners, combined with the oil shortage, produced economic chaos in Britain over Christmas 1973 and the New Year: a three-day working week was introduced, there were regular power cuts, and petrol rationing was planned. Heath was eventually persuaded to call an early general election, but this led to his party's narrow defeat in February 1974. Even if its members had possessed the will or the means to drive a hard bargain with the unions, the incoming Labour government was weakened by its failure to secure an overall parliamentary majority in the election. The miners were bought off, and the Industrial Relations Act swiftly repealed. Opinion polls suggested that the electorate was unimpressed by the one-sided and vague Social Contract between the government and the unions, which was supposed to guarantee restraint in wage bargaining. Nevertheless, without an overall majority Labour could not delay a new election for long. When it asked the voters for an improved mandate in October 1974 the response was lukewarm; it emerged with a majority of only three seats.

By January 1975 the annual rate of inflation was around 20 per cent, and climbing. Pay deals tended to be even higher; increases of 30 per cent were not uncommon. Although economists disagreed about the precise relationship between wages and prices, few believed that present trends could continue for long. Left unchecked, they would lead to hyperinflation, mass unemployment and national bankruptcy. Already a favourite target for international speculators, the pound sterling came under new pressure at the time of Sevareid's remarks; the governor of the Bank of England warned ministers to expect further significant falls. In the first months of 1975 the currency duly established new record lows against the dollar on several occasions.

At a cabinet meeting in May ministers decided on a package of public spending cuts. The home secretary, Roy Jenkins, told his colleagues that 'The survival of society is threatened.' Echoing Sevareid, the left-winger Barbara Castle thought that 'we are drifting to catastrophe'.[10] Just a few days earlier in a speech to local authority representatives, the environment secretary, Tony Crosland, had announced that 'the party is over'. Like so many celebrated political remarks, this one has been distorted over time. Rather than calling for cuts in expenditure, Crosland meant that while the crisis lasted subsidies to local government would not increase as steeply as they had done in the past.[11] But something had to be done; by 1975 public spending had risen to an unsustainable 60 per cent of GDP.[12]

The government's measures suggested a significant shift in the priorities of post-war politics. Now the main aim would be the control of inflation rather than the maintenance of full employment. By July the jobless figure rose above one million, and was increasing at a rate of 15,000 per week. After difficult negotiations the government and union leaders agreed that for the next twelve months pay rises would be restricted to a maximum of £6 per week. In a gesture towards social justice, people whose earnings already exceeded £8,500 per year would have their salaries frozen; after all, advertisers considered that such people had made it already. But from the outset few believed that the wages policy would hold up for long. By the summer of 1975 even those who had begun the year hoping for the best were starting to lose heart. In January the right-wing *Spectator* magazine had published a front-page editorial under the headline 'No reason for gloom'. Six months later it had been forced to admit that 'for an objective observer it is impossible not to be profoundly gloomy'. 'The gloom industry,' wrote a *Times* economics correspondent in September, had become 'the fastest-growing sector of the British economy.'[13]

The idea that the political left would benefit from the crisis seemed counter-intuitive, since Labour was in office and not impressing many judges with its response to Britain's difficulties. Indeed, socialists tended to be sceptical about the future; after all, the capitalist system had survived many predictions of imminent collapse, and the British had proved resolutely unrevolutionary in the past. The typical left-wing prediction was that any additional move in their direction would shortly be followed by a rightward recoil; after all, as recently as 1973 this had happened in Chile, when Allende's socialist regime had been overthrown by Augusto Pinochet, a ruthless military dictator. The most ardent prophecies of communist advance came from the right. Some were genuinely concerned that traditional British liberties were threatened by doctrinaire Marxism; others, though, gave the impression of wanting to skip the revolutionary phase of the scenario and move immediately into a period of reaction.

A prominent member of the latter group was Lord Chalfont, born Alun Gwynne-Jones in 1919. A soldier who later took up journalism, in 1964 Chalfont was given a seat in the House of Lords by Harold Wilson and made a Foreign Office minister of state, with special responsibility for arms control and disarmament. His experiences during international negotiations convinced him that the Soviet Union was 'at the centre of a brutal, relentless tyranny; that it intends to spread that tyranny around the world; and that the only language it understands is the language of strength'.[14] Later Chalfont became increasingly disillusioned with Labour's anti-European stance after the 1970 general election. He resigned from the party in September 1974, leaving him more scope to engage in anti-communist agitation. Membership of the Lords gave Chalfont a permanent platform from which to air his conspiracy theories, which had become increasingly urgent and elaborate as Marxist ideology made inexorable strides in Vietnam, Cambodia and Laos, and even threatened to gain a foothold in Portugal.

On 26 February 1975 Chalfont instigated a debate in the House of Lords on 'subversive and extremist elements' within Britain. There was a bumper attendance, mainly from the Lords' resident army of ageing alarmists, who were grateful for the chance to frighten each other with their eloquence. In his opening speech Chalfont promised to 'take some account of extreme Right-Wing organisations and to consider the possibility of what is sometimes called a backlash against the activities of the extreme left'.[15] This would at least have given a semblance of even-handedness to his presentation. But he never got round to 'naming and shaming' Britain's prospective backlashers. Instead, thanks to parliamentary privilege, he was able to turn the debate into a witch-hunt, naming several individuals who 'constitute a very real and serious danger to our democratic institutions'. These included the actress Vanessa Redgrave, who added a dash of celebrity to the tiny Workers' Revolutionary Party (WRP). But Chalfont also listed several prominent trade unionists who were either members of the Communist Party of Great Britain (CPGB) or known sympathisers with its views. On the executive of the powerful Transport and General Workers' Union (TGWU), he claimed, at least fifteen out of thirty-nine members fell into that category. This figure was the more impressive because the Communist Party had been far less successful within the country as a whole. Chalfont estimated its membership at no more than 30,000 – fewer than the number of New Year revellers in Trafalgar Square. Only 32,000 had supported communist candidates in the general election of October 1974, which implied that the party's programme had limited appeal to floating voters. The overall number of 'extremists and subversives', Chalfont calculated, was no more than 50,000.

However, the national danger could not be judged on mere statistics. Chalfont claimed to detect a mood of 'apathy and complacency' which could allow a handful of determined fellow-travellers to extinguish centuries of British liberty.[16] He was certainly not alone in regarding this as a serious possibility. Lord Clifford of Chudleigh claimed that 'we are in a more dangerous position than in the 1930s', while Baroness Emmet of Amberley thought that the communist menace was the Devil in a new guise, and proclaimed, 'The enemy is at the gate.'[17] Several speakers quoted Edmund Burke's maxim, 'All that is necessary for the triumph of evil is that good men do nothing.'

Chalfont disclaimed any partisan intention before setting out his alarmist case, but he was well aware that it would be damaging to the Labour Party. The trade unions, after all, were Labour's paymasters. If they were falling under communist control, it was only a matter of time before official party policy would begin to reflect their subversive desires; indeed, many people thought that this had already happened. Equally, in a context of 'apathy and complacency' the communists could cut out the middleman and infiltrate Labour constituency parties. Before the end of 1975 Labour's national agent, Reg Underhill, had compiled a report about communist 'entryism'. Although he did identify one determined and well-organised Trotskyite group, the Militant Tendency, his findings also demonstrated the capacity of left-wingers for ludicrous factional disputes. For example, the International Marxist Group boasted, at most, 1,000 members. But it had already spawned two breakaway bodies, Big Flame and the Revolutionary Marxist Current. Neither of these organisations had any support outside Liverpool and Manchester; their combined membership was no more than 200.[18] The fissiparous nature of the left was even evident at Lancaster University, which was widely regarded as a stronghold of Marxist militancy. In its 1975 presidential election the Broad Left candidate beat off challenges from the International Socialists and the inaptly named Socialist Alliance.

Nevertheless, Chalfont sincerely believed that when the moment came the revolutionary left would suddenly pool its resources for a coordinated effort to seize power in Britain, backed by the military might of the Soviet Union. But what, exactly, could be done against such an insidious foe? Perhaps Chalfont thought that the KGB would abandon its schemes in the face of evidence that Britain's peers had inherited the martial vigour of their feudal forebears; or maybe the House of Lords debate could help to arouse some of the nation's sleepwalkers before it was too late. The most thoughtful contribution to the debate came from the former lord chancellor, Lord Hailsham, who would shortly propose a British bill of rights to defend the individual against an 'elective dictatorship'. But, as Hailsham's friend Ian Gilmour later remarked, written constitutions 'provide more of an illusion of safety than safety itself'. Even the Soviet constitution enshrined the right to free speech and freedom of assembly.[19] Another ominous example was the fate of the relatively liberal Weimar constitution, which had proved no defence against totalitarianism in Germany during the 1930s when that country was faced with economic collapse amid raging inflation. Though it was considered tactless to draw parallels in public, Weimar was certainly on the minds of Hailsham's shadow cabinet colleagues when they discussed the economic outlook in May 1975.[20]

Before the end of 1975 the police unearthed evidence of the left's bloody intentions. A raid was launched on the Revolutionary College of Marxist Education near Ashbourne in Derbyshire. Allegedly this was the venue for 'full-time indoctrination' of its recruits by the Workers' Revolutionary Party.[21] The seven-hour search by seventy police yielded a cache of nine .22 bullets. On the face of it this was a meagre arsenal for the vanguard of the proletariat, but those bullets could have made serious inroads into the higher echelons of the British Establishment; a skilful sniper could have accounted for the Queen, the Duke of Edinburgh, the Prince of Wales, the Archbishop of Canterbury, the prime minister and the leader of the Opposition, still leaving him with the luxury of three chances to bag Lord Chalfont. But the Director of Public Prosecutions decided not to proceed with the case. After all, it was not outside the realms of possibility that Special Branch had planted the bullets themselves.

Even if the WRP had really procured the bullets for a murderous purpose, it was hardly equipped for a full-scale encounter with the British army. This, at least, was one British institution which had proved invulnerable to Marxist propaganda. Indeed, judging from a recruitment drive of January 1975, it was prepared to act against the Labour Party if it should ever try to implement doctrinaire socialism through a peaceful democratic process. The advertisement which appeared in *The Times* of 10 January 1975 gives an insight into the mood among army chiefs: 'These days, it's not very trendy to declare that you're a patriot ... are you prepared to fight if necessary to prevent people taking control of this country by force or other unconstitutional means?'

These 'unconstitutional' methods were not specified, which was probably just as well because Britain's unwritten constitution had provided plenty of scope for innovation over the years. But would-be army recruits were left in no doubt that they might be called upon to use their skills against fellow citizens, rather than the rapacious Soviet enemy: after all, the advertisement warned, a country 'can lose its freedom little by little, without being overrun'.[22] In this context it is not difficult to believe the various rumours circulating at the time about plans for an armed coup which would impose 'a right-wing junta on the South American model', including the idea of using the luxury liner QE2 as an offshore prison for the displaced Labour cabinet.[23]

II

Even before the army advertisement and the Chalfont debate, it looked as if 1975 was going to be a very interesting year by post-war standards. The mood had been established by the antics of John Stonehouse, who had served with Chalfont as a junior Labour minister during the 1960s. Until November 1974 Stonehouse was barely known to the British public outside his Midlands constituency of Walsall North. But then he became a national celebrity, by vanishing entirely. He was facing bankruptcy after some ill-advised business deals. Some of his creditors were threatening to ruin his political career by exposing him, citing the recent precedent of an obscure Tory backbencher, Jeffrey Archer, who had been forced to give up his seat because of complications in his financial affairs. Stonehouse was also convinced that his telephone was being bugged by the secret services. Realising the game was up, he travelled to Miami and left his clothes on the beach in what he hoped would be accepted as clear evidence of death by drowning. Then he made his escape to Australia, with various forged papers in the names of two deceased constituents.

Stonehouse had taken out insurance policies which would have provided a nest egg of £125,000 for the wife who did not figure in his future plans. However, the ineptitude which had dogged his forays into business life continued to thwart him in simulated death. Not long before his disappearance he had submitted a written parliamentary question asking the home secretary to 'review arrangements for preventing drowning accidents'.[24] Even the most credulous were inclined to think that this sudden curiosity for aquatic mishaps was something more than a coincidence. Selecting Florida for his demise proved another tactical gaffe. The state's coastguards kept a close watch for night swimmers, and were certain that he could not have drifted more than fifty yards from the shore. If anyone drowned, the corpse almost invariably turned up within two days. Stonehouse was also well known to be a powerful and experienced swimmer. It was almost as if he actively wanted to be caught – a case of not drowning, but waving. As his erstwhile colleague Tony Benn recorded at the time, 'People don't believe he's dead.' Several informants alerted Whitehall officials to the possibility that the whole episode had been a hoax.[25]

Stonehouse's speedy apprehension, in Australia, owed something to bad luck. The authorities there were taking a closer interest than usual in mysterious newcomers in case one of them turned out to be Lord Lucan, who had gone to ground (in one way or another) after murdering his children's nanny and battering his wife in November 1974. The errant Stonehouse spent the next few months in prison fighting extradition to the UK, where multiple charges of forgery, theft and fraud had been compiled with suspicious rapidity. Unlike Lucan, Stonehouse had few reliable friends back home to protect him, and he promptly set about turning them into enemies, calling the leader of the House of Commons, Edward Short, 'a pusillanimous twit' and the party's chief whip Robert Mellish 'a crude bore'.[26] Back in 1968 the cabinet minister and pioneering diarist Richard Crossman had described Stonehouse as 'a kind of dangerous crook, overwhelmingly ambitious but above all untrustworthy'.[27] Harold Wilson, who had initially overlooked Stonehouse's foibles, belatedly recognised that he was a 'liar', and had decided not to offer him another government post after the February 1974 election.[28]

As soon as he resurfaced in Australia, Stonehouse's constituency party in Walsall disowned him and began the process of choosing a replacement. For a variety of reasons Wilson wanted the matter resolved quickly, but Robert Armstrong, his principal private secretary, advised that it would be difficult to expel Stonehouse from Parliament unless and until he was convicted; political sanctions, indeed, might prejudice his trial. 'If the House of Commons wishes to disembarrass itself of Mr Stonehouse at the earliest possible moment', Armstrong concluded, he should be persuaded to retire voluntarily.[29] At first Stonehouse seemed amenable to this suggestion, but then he stalled, sensing that his membership of the House gave him both a platform and a form of protection. His recalcitrance only hardened attitudes back in London. Increasingly desperate, Stonehouse wrote to several international political leaders, hoping that they would intervene in the judicial process and offer him a refuge. When this failed he argued for the right to return to the UK in order to save his seat by explaining his conduct. He sent an unavailing open letter to Harold Wilson, petitioned the Queen, briefly went on hunger strike, then published a self-justificatory book.

These escapades ensured that Stonehouse became a permanent fixture in the newspapers throughout 1975, and was often in the front-page headlines. Very soon, though, media attention centred on the nature of his relationship with his glamorous (and, like Stonehouse himself, married) secretary. Sheila Buckley had helped him prepare for his new life and was clearly hoping to share it; she had travelled to Australia and was also detained there. Romance was joined by comedy when David Nobbs's novel *The Death of Reginald Perrin* appeared while Stonehouse was still in Australia. Stonehouse himself was more inclined to compare himself with glamorous characters in Frederick Forsyth's popular thrillers, but, like Stonehouse, the fictional Reggie Perrin fancied his secretary and sought a new life by pretending to have drowned at sea. Those who did not read the novel certainly knew about the subsequent BBC dramatisation, *The Fall and Rise of Reginald Perrin*, thanks largely to Leonard Rossiter's superlative performance in the leading role.

Presumably the farcical overtones to the story have ensured that, while the Profumo affair still casts a dark shadow over academic histories of the 1960s, John Stonehouse hardly figures in serious assessments of the subsequent decade. It is almost as if mentioning the saga would be an improper intrusion into private grief.* However, the Stonehouse affair had very serious implications, for the Labour Party in particular but also more generally for the reputation of British political life in the mid-1970s. It was obviously galling for the government to receive daily bulletins about the ludicrous behaviour of a man who had recently been considered worthy of ministerial office. When rumours circulated that Stonehouse had been a communist spy, Harold Wilson personally announced that an inquiry had refuted the allegation. But to the paranoid spooks of MI5 – some of whom thought that Wilson himself was working for the Soviets – this was tantamount to an admission of guilt. In June 1975, when the Conservatives took the seat of Woolwich West at a by-election, Wilson's parliamentary majority was reduced to just one – and the member in question was in jail on the other side of the world.

---

* In this respect, academics have taken their cue from Harold Wilson, who mentioned Stonehouse's name just once in *Final Term*, his account of developments between February 1974 and March 1976.

After his return to Britain Stonehouse did attend debates in the House of Commons – even turning up in the evenings during his trial – but for two years his constituency effectively had not been represented. Back in 1974, stopping over in San Francisco on his journey to Australia in the borrowed persona of Joe Markham, Stonehouse had fallen into conversation with a taxi driver who told him that 'England sure is in a mess. What have you people been doing to it?'[30] Possibly this remark stuck in Stonehouse's mind because it could form the basis of an alibi if his planned disappearance should fail. But he had already begun to develop a narrative which explained his personal troubles as a tragic by-product of British decline. His last speech in the House of Commons before his disappearance had suggested both terminal disillusionment with Labour and a belated desire to be remembered as a notable orator. After his arrest he was examined by an Australian psychiatrist, who pronounced that he had committed 'psychiatric suicide'. The old John Stonehouse was well and truly dead – a point which the MP reinforced by referring to himself in the third person in future interviews. As he explained to a *Times* reporter in May 1975, 'The old personality has been enriched by the objectivity of the second personality.'[31]

In other words the new Lear-like Stonehouse was granted insights which had been denied to his previous self. This second Stonehouse was relentless in his disparagement of the media, which he blamed for his personal predicament. As he told Edward Short, 'Press freedom is a false God to worship; it has become a weapon in the hands of callous, cynical and completely irresponsible men . . . The negativism of such contemporary journalism is a cancer in the body politic and is gradually eating away at the vitals of British democracy.'[32]

Almost twenty years later, the Conservative cabinet minister Jonathan Aitken used very similar words when launching his ill-fated libel suit against the *Guardian*.[33]* By the mid-1990s it was possible to sympathise with the general gist of Aitken's remarks, even if the *Guardian* was wholly innocent in that specific instance; press standards were usually supposed to have deteriorated sharply since 1975. But during his own difficulties with the media Stonehouse could have drawn some grim satisfaction from the experience of Labour Chief Whip Bob Mellish.

---

*Aitken pledged 'to cut out the cancer of bent and twisted journalism in our country with the simple sword of truth and the trusty shield of British fair play.'

Reporters hungry for a quote laid siege to his house, keeping his family awake until 1.30 and resuming the assault six hours later. Mellish was forced to leave his telephone off the hook, despite the need to be in close touch with his colleagues. When the press finally caught up with him, he was asked whether he considered Stonehouse a 'bad apple'. Mellish made the mistake of muttering that 'He certainly seems an odd one,' which was used as the basis for some damaging reports about Labour's attitude to the affair.[34]

If in 1975 the press was getting out of control, its conduct was in keeping with standards throughout public life in Britain. In the book which he wrote in various Australian prisons Stonehouse recorded his impressions of the House of Commons in the last weeks of 1974, just before his disappearance:

Parliament had become a raucous rabble concerned only to shout the ephemeral slogans of the day. The few intelligent leaders cynically pandered to the appetites of their supporters so they could ride along on their unthinking support. Principle, except on rare and isolated occasions, was thrown out of the window. What leaders wanted was power; their political aims as politicians were subverted to this end, rather than power being seen as the means to achieve those aims. Power and office became the cruel masters of men as ends in themselves.[35]

In June 1975 the British public was given a chance to judge the 'raucous rabble' for themselves, when the proceedings of the House of Commons were broadcast on radio as a one-off experiment. The BBC received several complaints from listeners who objected to this frivolous disruption to the scheduled programmes, *Listen with Mother* and *Woman's Hour*. One outraged *Times* reader described the noisy conduct of the Commons as 'an affront to the British electorate, destructive of any lingering (illusory) respect it might have had for parliamentary procedure'. From his Parisian exile the former British fascist leader Sir Oswald Mosley wondered whether the microphones had been set up in London Zoo by mistake.[36] When MPs began to agitate for a substantial pay increase one *Times* correspondent asked, 'Is it too much to hope that they might now go on strike in support of their claim?'[37]

When describing his own experiences of parliamentary life, Stonehouse II constantly used the word 'humbug'. Now that the scales had fallen from his eyes, he could see his former colleagues as they really were. For example, he realised that Jim Callaghan was a second-rate careerist: 'a skilful politico, always with his eye on the main chance; a man without the impediment of strong convictions, so he is able to kick the ball in the prevailing political direction at any time'.[38] This judgement, at any rate, suggested that Stonehouse was indeed seeing things more clearly. Before long, Callaghan's sense of direction had enabled him to slam the ball into the net; before the end of 1975 Harold Wilson had singled him out as his natural successor in Downing Street. By the time he took over, however, it was doubtful whether the job would be worth its inevitable sacrifices.

It was not until November 1976 that the voters of Walsall North were given the chance to choose a new MP. By that time, thanks to more orthodox defections from Labour ranks, Callaghan was already running a minority government, dependent for its survival on the tolerance of minor parties. Meanwhile Labour activists were developing ambitious ideas for transforming the country. Shortly before the Walsall by-election the annual conference had endorsed *Labour's Programme for Britain*, which, according to the former MP Woodrow Wyatt, might as well have been cooked up in the Kremlin. The card vote in favour of the programme was 5,833,000, against just 122,000 opponents.[39] In the real world, though, it would be more difficult to implement the proposals, which included stiffer taxes on the rich, deep defence cuts and a radical extension of nationalisation. Advertising revenue in the newspaper industry would also be pooled, so that popular publications like Rupert Murdoch's *Sun* would effectively subsidise the communist *Morning Star*. The threat of this measure was not calculated to improve Labour's fraught relations with the press. Neither did the renewed gust of radical purpose in party ranks help the voters of Walsall North to overlook the Stonehouse effect. The Conservatives won the seat on a swing of 22.5 per cent.

III

On 5 June 1975 the people of the United Kingdom were invited to participate in a referendum. The proposition – chosen with the help of opinion pollsters, after some vigorous arguments between Labour's cabinet ministers – was, 'Do you think that the United Kingdom should stay in the European Community (the Common Market)?' The agonising over the wording was far from being a pedantic exercise; subsequent psychological studies showed that if people had been asked, 'Should Britain leave the Common Market?' the result would have been much closer.

However it was worded, campaigners on both sides agreed that this was a momentous question. While pro-Europeans insisted that Britain's economic prosperity depended on a positive vote, their opponents claimed that nothing less than national survival was at stake. But the method of decision was noteworthy in itself. Forty-seven years after the introduction of universal adult suffrage, this was the first time that the British public had been granted a direct say on a single political issue. The use of a referendum raised serious questions for a parliamentary democracy, and the Conservative Party was strongly opposed to this innovation. But in April 1975 the necessary legislation was passed, and Britain's politicians prepared for battle on unfamiliar territory.

Over the next three decades, 'Europe' would generate almost constant conflict between and within parties. In four separate incidents at the end of the 1980s it provoked the resignation of the chancellor of the exchequer, two other senior cabinet ministers and, in November 1990, the prime minister herself. Parliament had its 'Maastricht rebels' and 'whipless wonders'; among members of the public the same spirit of angry defiance produced 'metric martyrs', who insisted on using the age-old weights and measures of a proud island race in defiance of European dictates. In 1997 Europe played a leading role in bringing eighteen years of Conservative rule to an ignominious end. Subsequently Tony Blair and Gordon Brown found time amidst their personal feuding to pursue different agendas on the European single currency.

Compared to the level of feeling exhibited in future years, politicians and public behaved with surprising decorum back in 1975. There was a good deal of heckling at meetings but hardly any serious trouble.[40] Even the exceptional incidents seemed to be resurgences of the quaintly anarchic British electioneering tradition. In Lancaster on 27 May, for example, Edward Heath won a standing ovation for a passionately pro-European speech. But the chairman of the Blackpool Get Britain Out committee shouted that Heath was a traitor, comparing him to the wartime broadcaster William Joyce ('Lord Haw-Haw'). The heckler was promptly drawn into an exchange of facial slaps with a woman who turned out to be a member of the executive of Lancaster's Conservative Association. In contrast to this unseemly conduct by mature citizens, the students at the local university gave a respectful hearing to the former prime minister; indeed, one observer reported that 'most insults came from Heath himself'.[41]

Almost two thirds of the electorate – 26 million people – cast a vote in the referendum. The turnout was roughly equal across all the regions of the UK, and almost everywhere the result was similar. Overall, the vote in favour was 67.2 per cent. The pro-European campaign – Britain in Europe – could claim that the people had given 'full-hearted consent' because only the Western and Shetland Isles voted against Community membership. But was the public really aware of what it had done? A senior government policy adviser, Bernard Donoughue, visited several London pubs on the evening of the vote. 'The newspaper headlines were all about a landslide victory in the referendum,' he noted in his diary. 'No sense, however, among the people around of a great day of decision. They did not look as if they had voted!'[42]

As they enjoyed another brilliant sunset – the period from April 1975 to May 1976 turned out to be the driest thirteen months that Britain had ever experienced – Londoners could have been thinking that there was nothing special about visiting a polling booth. Some might even have been suffering from voter fatigue after the two general elections of the previous year. It was hardly surprising that the number of voters had dropped by more than two million (to 29.2 million) between February and October 1974, nor that there was a further fall at the referendum. The fact that the referendum turnout exceeded two thirds was in fact impressive testimony to the endurance of the British voting habit, which was clearly being absorbed by people between eighteen and twenty-one who had been enfranchised for the first time by the 1969 Representation of the People Act. After all, the overwhelming majority of Britain's senior politicians had asked the public to ratify a decision which had already been taken. On the face of it, 'Get to the polling stations to make sure things stay the same!' was not the most energising of battle cries. But it worked.

Over the years since 1975 opponents of British membership have persistently claimed that the politicians misled the public during the referendum campaign. Arguably, though, the greater danger was that politicians might be misled by the verdict delivered by the people. On the face of it the result could be taken as a vote of confidence in a particular style of government, and a generation of leaders which had dominated politics for more than a decade. A 1975 opinion poll did suggest a fair amount of goodwill towards the party leaders who had contested the two general elections of 1974; the prime minister Harold Wilson, his Conservative predecessor Edward Heath and the Liberal Jeremy Thorpe were 'respected and liked' by about 40 per cent of the electorate.[43] But as one Leicester resident wrote to his local newspaper at the beginning of 1975, 'Scepticism is the general attitude of the electorate towards their elected representatives. And who can blame them?'[44] 'Scepticism' was putting it mildly. The relatively positive response to the 1975 survey concealed the depth of feeling among those who neither 'liked' nor 'respected' senior politicians at the time. Of course, previous party leaders had been hated – indeed, in an adversarial political system this was virtually part of the job description. But in 1975 the mood of antipathy derived from something which was arguably more corrosive than hatred. More than ever before, members of the public felt – and were prepared to articulate – contempt for their democratic figureheads. Just two weeks into the New Year it became clear that this trend had also established itself among the politicians themselves. The posthumous serialisation of Richard Crossman's *Diaries* in the *Sunday Times* revealed the extent of fear and loathing within the Parliamentary Labour Party, and much of it revolved around the prime minister, Harold Wilson.

Wilson had been Labour's leader since 1963, and had fought five general elections in that capacity. His greatest achievement had been to keep his party sufficiently united to win four of those contests. For him the referendum was another ploy to contain the various Labour factions. The convention of collective cabinet responsibility was waived, giving ministers the chance to give full expression to their ill-concealed disagreements about Britain's future. Probably this helped to postpone a schism in the party, but not for long as it turned out. A vote on Europe in March 1975 showed that the parliamentary party was split almost exactly in half – 137 MPs for continued membership, 145 against – and a special conference the following month produced a big majority in favour of withdrawal, thanks to the trade union block vote. Wilson was already exhausted by his efforts to keep the party together, and he had no relish for the referendum. As Bernard Donoughue noted, when he spoke in support of the EEC the prime minister had to fight against his instinctive 'Little Englandism'. Wilson had always been accused of acting a part on the political stage, but this was a role too far. Once the disagreeable task was over, he could plan for retirement.[45]

At least Wilson was not expected to take the lead throughout the campaign, which meant that for much of the time he could revert to his favourite pose of serene statesmanship. The most prominent figures on the 'Yes' side were Roy Jenkins and Edward Heath. Jenkins had resigned from the Labour front bench when the party adopted the referendum as official policy back in 1972. When Labour returned to office in February 1974 he had agreed to serve a second term as home secretary, but with less enthusiasm this time round. In the 1960s Jenkins had felt that his task was to keep government legislation in line with public opinion which was changing in a 'progressive' direction. After February 1974 he was forced into a more defensive posture, pushing liberalisation where he could but also having to introduce measures which were disagreeable to him, like the controversial Prevention of Terrorism Act (1974). In itself, the lack of scope for progressive politics was suggestive of a new trend in public attitudes. In September 1976 – five months after Wilson finally left Downing Street – Jenkins resigned from the government in order to prepare for the presidency of the European Commission, which he took up in 1977. Despite the excitement of 1981, when he returned from Brussels to help found the breakaway Social Democratic Party (SDP), he never held government office again.

As the prime minister who had taken the UK into the EEC, Edward Heath was the natural leader for those who hoped to confirm the decision. Although he had bitterly opposed the referendum, the campaign was probably the highlight of his career; the subject, after all, was the greatest passion of his life. He ended up being chosen Britain's Man of the Year for 1975. But the referendum victory was bitter-sweet because he had already been displaced as Conservative leader by the Woman of the Year. A change in the party's rules had allowed a challenge to the incumbent, and a ballot was held in February 1975. Margaret Thatcher, who had served in Heath's cabinet between 1970 and 1974 as education secretary, was the only senior figure to contest his position. On the first ballot she beat Heath into second place, and although he could have fought on under the new rules the ex-premier promptly resigned. He would remain in the Commons until 2001, more than a decade after Wilson (1983) and Jenkins (1987) had departed to the House of Lords. But although he was never a negligible figure Heath was not recalled to ministerial office by his party or his country. His career in government had ended when he lost the February 1974 general election, before he had reached Wilson's chosen retirement age of sixty.

Wilson, Heath and Jenkins were talented individuals who would probably have thrived in politics at any time during the twentieth century, but their qualities were nurtured by the unique circumstances of the inter-war period. Wilson and Heath were born in 1916, Jenkins in 1920. Heath came from Broadstairs, Kent, and his parents were a carpenter and a maid. Wilson's father worked in a chemical plant in Yorkshire. Jenkins, from south Wales, was the son of a miner who became a union official and an MP. All attended grammar schools before progressing to Oxford University. Wilson was made a junior minister straight after winning a seat in the 1945 general election; when he was appointed president of the Board of Trade in 1947 he became the youngest cabinet minister since 1806.[46] Jenkins entered the Commons via a 1948 by-election, becoming the youngest member of the Commons at that time. Heath had to wait his opportunity until the 1950 general election, but was appointed Conservative chief whip just five years later. That post was no guarantee of further promotion, but relative youth and humble origins made Heath a remarkable contrast with previous Conservatives who had presided over the hierarchical and quasi-military whips' office.

Apart from home and education, politicians of this generation almost invariably cited two main influences on their thinking: mass unemployment and the Second World War. These could be formative factors even for those who had experienced neither at first hand. Throughout the 1920s and 30s, official unemployment never dipped below a million, and in 1932 it peaked at 2.95 million. It went without saying that a repetition of these figures was unthinkable. Similarly, this generation was determined to avoid another Europe-wide conflict. Harold Wilson had been a civil servant during the war, while Jenkins was recruited into the code-breaking team based at Bletchley Park. But whatever others might think of their non-combatant contribution, they rightly felt that they had been part of a collective endeavour; and, in spite of all contrary influences, that feeling never left them. The practical lesson, reinforced by the intellectual arguments of John Maynard Keynes and William Beveridge, was that social and economic problems were best solved by the state. In foreign affairs inactivity was equally reprehensible; the pre-war appeasement of Germany was regarded as an even greater blot than the refusal of successive governments to resist unemployment. The state should take responsibility, and the new generation of leaders was ambitious to take responsibility for the state. For Edward Heath, who did see wartime action, a further lesson was that intergovernmental cooperation across Europe was the best safeguard against future conflict, and would also have the effect of strengthening Britain's position vis-à-vis the great post-war powers, the Soviet Union and the United States. Hence Heath's enthusiasm for the EEC and his consistent belief that, in real terms, Britain's sovereignty would be enhanced by membership.

The initial prospects for their generation had looked the more promising because they were called upon to consolidate the work of others rather than introduce radical innovations. Academics still disagree about the nature of post-war politics, arguing about the true extent of the so-called consensus. But undoubtedly there was general agreement on broad principles among senior figures within the main parties. The central economic role of the state was widely acknowledged, and most of the industries nationalised by the 1945–51 Labour governments were kept in public hands when the Conservatives returned to office. The National Health Service was retained, along with Labour's range of benefits and services which promised a degree of security 'from the cradle to the grave'. This post-war settlement had been created in defiance of serious economic difficulties, but by the mid-1950s it seemed that the crisis had been weathered. In future, despite continued debate among radicals in all parties, it seemed that the tasks of political leaders would be essentially managerial. People like Wilson and Heath did not consider this an ignoble task. They were imbued with a (strictly secular) belief in human progress. If Beveridge and Keynes were seen as the inspirational architects of the post-war order, their work could not provide increasing benefits for all the people unless public servants were prepared to conduct day-to-day maintenance.

Wilson, Jenkins and Heath had embarked on political careers at a time when both main parties prized intelligence over any other qualification. After 1945 Conservative selection committees no longer plumped automatically for the richest applicant; and while Labour had never suffered from this self-imposed handicap, it was becoming more receptive to clever youngsters who (like Wilson) had only a limited acquaintance with the trade union movement. By 1975, though, the early promise of this truly meritocratic generation had dissipated. Jenkins had already become a convenient symbol for those who disliked the 'permissive' social legislation of the 1960s, which he had championed in his first spell at the Home Office (1965–7).* For his part, Heath was despised on the right for his failure to tame the trade unions

---

* Even his supposed friend Tony Blair thought it worthwhile to attack this legacy after Jenkins's death in 2003.

through the 1971 Industrial Relations Act; the left hated him for having made the attempt. Membership of the EEC, which Heath regarded as his greatest achievement, proved to be a more lasting source of loathing in some quarters – not least within his own party. Harold Wilson had faded into relative obscurity by the time of his death in 1995, partly because prolonged illness had forced him out of public life. But during his career left and right were united in reviling him as an unprincipled trickster. Some members of the publicly funded secret services were even more hostile to Wilson. In their view, the dedicated public servant who had been elected prime minister on four occasions was 'a crook, a red, a union stooge, unpatriotic, a Walter Mitty and a threat to the British way of life'.[47]

Why did these gifted and intrinsically well-meaning politicians incur such public odium at this time? A likely reason is suggested by the title of Douglas Hurd's insider account of the Heath government – *An End to Promises*.[48] The period between 1964 and 1974 was indeed a decade of unfulfilled promises, triggering the criticism that governments were trying to do too much, even if their intentions were benign.[49] But that begs the further question of why this generation of politicians should have felt *compelled* to promise too much at a time when the newspaper industry could be guaranteed to pounce on symptoms of failure in any pursuit. The answer was that the context of politics had been transformed since the early 1960s, when the American political scientists Gabriel Almond and Sidney Verba had depicted Britain as a country where a relatively high level of political participation was tempered by a strong tradition of deference.[50] The aggressive press helped to erode that tradition, but in doing so it was responding to existing social trends. By 1975 an increasingly acquisitive electorate had become too demanding for the comfort of politicians who had still been at school when Britain adopted universal adult suffrage (1928). The post-war consensus which they were happy to join in the late 1940s was explicitly anti-individualistic, but even before the fall of the Attlee government in 1951 the collective mood was starting to be undermined. It was no wonder that the party leaders of 1964–74 were uneasy about the new climate, and eventually floundered under the combined strain of electoral demands and adverse developments in the global economy.

The key factor here was the 1973–4 oil crisis. Among other things, this had the effect of making the EEC look less of an attractive proposition: it apparently tied the nation's economic fortunes to states with no oil reserves at a time when Britain was about to develop its own.* The first oil from the British sector of the North Sea was brought ashore just after the referendum. But the real benefits of this resource were not seen until after 1979, by which time it was too late for people like Wilson, Heath and Jenkins. The wonder is that their ethos had survived for so long. By the mid-1970s, when all three men finished their ministerial careers, the influence of television had lengthened the odds against them. Applicants for high office now had to be clever, conformist, charismatic and easy on the eye. The fact that Wilson was far more successful than Heath in mastering this new medium probably explains why he won three out of four of their head-to-head encounters; the narrow Conservative defeat of February 1974, in particular, could easily have been averted if the party had been led by a more effective small-screen performer. Yet even after this experience Heath continued to resist the image-makers, in the naive belief that crucial national decisions should not be swayed by gimmickry. It was not surprising that by 1975 many bright youngsters, who doubted that they could tick all of the necessary boxes which guaranteed political success, decided to channel their interest in public affairs into careers within the media.

The widespread feeling of contempt for the leading pro-Europeans makes the positive referendum vote more surprising, since personalities were more decisive than the issues in 1975. The outcome is partly explained by the fact that the most publicised of the anti-Europeans inspired even less public confidence. They tended to be dissenters from the centrist consensus, who disliked the idea of close European co-operation on the grounds that it would restrict the scope for radical initiatives of one variety or another. Tony Benn (born 1925), the left-wing secretary of state for industry, received the kind of newspaper coverage which made even Harold Wilson look like a darling of the press. In papers like the *Daily Express* and the *Daily Mail*, Benn was usually portrayed as an unhinged, pipe-sucking ideologue, incapable of resting peacefully until he had nationalised and/or bankrupted the whole of British industry. *The Times* was only slightly more subtle. In May 1975 it published an anti-European article written by Benn, and

---

* Another result of the new climate of financial stringency was the government's decision at the start of 1975 to abandon the construction of a Channel tunnel (much to the annoyance of the French).

illustrated it with a cartoon-caricature of the author. While other politicians featured in the series were depicted affectionately, the cartoon
of Benn made him look raving mad. Character assassination was one
thing, but at the time Benn was also the recipient of several written
death threats.[51]

While *The Times* posed as an open and honest advocate of a 'Yes'
vote, it smuggled in plenty of pro-European propaganda under the
guise of impartial reporting. Much was made, for example, of the fact
that the Soviet Union preferred Britain to withdraw from the EEC. On
13 May 1975 the newspaper's overenthusiastic Moscow correspondent
claimed that 'If the Soviet leaders were not atheists they would be
offering prayers for a majority in favour of Britain's withdrawal from
the EEC.'[52] Judging from *The Times* coverage, the uninitiated would
have supposed that Benn rather than Wilson was already the Labour
leader, and that such a change would have sparked off a comparable
bout of rejoicing in Moscow. Benn had publicly supported a referendum as long ago as November 1970, at a time when he had actually
favoured EEC membership. While Benn believed that such a major
decision required more than a simple parliamentary endorsement, others
(including Wilson) gradually realised that a referendum would offer
Labour the chance of neutralising an issue on which it was bitterly
divided. The difficulties had been cruelly exposed in October 1971,
during the five-day parliamentary debate which ended in an overwhelming vote in favour of membership.* When the shadow cabinet
finally agreed to his proposal in March 1972 Benn hailed 'a tremen-
dous victory', but he turned out to be the most notable victim of his
own initiative. He did make one serious tactical error during the referendum campaign, when he insisted that EEC membership had already
cost Britain 500,000 jobs, but he was not the only participant to
indulge in hyperbolic guesswork. Within a week of the referendum
Wilson took advantage of Benn's discomfort and demoted him to the
Department of Energy, where he worked until 1979 when his ministerial career came to an end, although like Heath he remained in the
House of Commons until 2001.[53]

While the press took the lead in vilifying Benn, its attitude to Enoch

---

* Labour had imposed a three-line whip, forcing MPs to vote against the principle of
membership. But sixty-nine MPs defied the whip and supported the government's policy.
By contrast, the Conservatives allowed their members a free vote, and only thirty-nine
broke ranks.

Powell (1912–98) was more complex and cautious. Although slightly older than Heath, Jenkins and Wilson, Powell can still be classed as a representative of their generation, and was enticed into politics by his experiences during the Second World War. Perhaps Powell was different because he had trained for an academic career in classics, while the others always had a more direct interest in politics. However, even if he had stuck to his original intentions Powell would have been a most unusual academic.

Having twice resigned from Conservative governments, in 1968 Powell had been dismissed from the front bench for rabble-rousing predictions about the impact of mass immigration. He had, however, remained a Conservative MP – with a burning sense of grievance and a realisation that the leadership would never dare to propose additional disciplinary measures against him. Before the general election of February 1974 he finally announced his departure from the party ranks, and that he had already cast a postal vote for the Labour candidate in his former constituency of Wolverhampton South-West. It was the most spectacular political defection in post-war politics. Powell's decision left many Conservatives disorientated – torn between their traditional loyalty to an incumbent leader and their feeling that Enoch was right on a range of crucial issues.* A considerable number ultimately decided that loyalty was less important than being right – thus destabilising their party for the next three decades.

Powell's impact on the 1975 referendum campaign was ambiguous. For Conservatives to follow his lead and vote against the EEC would mean defying not just previous leaders like Macmillan, Home and Heath; it would also present a horrifying early challenge to their newly elected successor. Margaret Thatcher had struggled to subdue her own Little Englandism and left some hostages to subsequent fortune in her support for the 'Yes' campaign. 'When we went in we knew exactly what we were going into,' she affirmed during the parliamentary debates on the referendum, and it was later reported that her first visit to the (unelected) European Parliament 'further strengthened her commitment to the European Community'.[54] While loyal Conservatives knew that a vote against Europe would be unwelcome to the party leadership, Powell's presence also caused complications on the left. Some Labour

* Such was the force of Powell's personality that his supporters were able to ignore his pronouncements on other subjects, like capital punishment and nuclear weapons, where his views were more compatible with the British left.

MPs, like Benn and Michael Foot, had mixed feelings about Powell, detesting his stand on immigration while continuing to admire the qualities of the man. But the level of unequivocal loathing for Powell among ordinary Labour Party members probably persuaded many of them to suppress their misgivings about Europe, and either abstain or cast a grudging vote for staying in.

To steady the nerves of wavering Conservatives, newspapers like *The Times* dealt with the Powell factor by reporting excerpts from his speeches but denying him the banner headlines which his eloquence deserved. Understandably frustrated, at West Bromwich on 18 May Powell claimed that the pro-EEC lobby was trying to 'chloroform the British electorate'. 'Now that the electors have the opportunity to decide,' he argued, 'the only way to prevent them from recovering their political rights is to persuade them that after all they have not got the power to do so.'[55] The newspaper which had given front-page coverage to an American commentator who claimed that the British were 'sleepwalking into a social revolution' was not prepared to give equal prominence to one of the country's best-known politicians when he made a similar warning about the EEC. Snippets from Powell's speech were relegated to *The Times*'s inside pages. The paper also published an article which depicted Powell as a busted flush – 'A would-be leader deserted by destiny'.[56]

On the day before the poll *The Times* did print a lengthy article in which Powell asked if the British people would 'perceive in time what is happening to them and where they are being taken?'[57] But from Powell's perspective, the answer was obviously going to be 'No'. When it came to voting, the public apparently decided that it disliked the mavericks more than the mainstream. By a comfortable distance, the most unpopular politician of the campaign was the stentorian oracle of inflexible Ulster Unionism, Ian Paisley, who saw the EEC as a Roman Catholic conspiracy. But this hardly affected the anti-EEC campaign, because (in an accurate snapshot of UK attitudes to politics in Northern Ireland) most voters disliked Paisley too much to notice which side he supported. Some members of the public were also unsure about the positions of Benn and Powell, but there was sufficient recognition of their views – and more than ample dislike for their characters in certain quarters – for them to be regarded as handicaps to their cause. According to one poll, 18 per cent of voters were so affected by the tirade of abuse against Benn that they would have been more likely to vote 'No' had he stood aside from the campaign.[58]

After the people had delivered their verdict, the anti-Europeans protested that their arguments had not been given a fair hearing. Even the official literature was loaded against them. Although voters were sent leaflets outlining the cases for and against, they also received a glossy government handout explaining why the renegotiated terms of membership had persuaded Labour that Britain should stay in the EEC when the party had previously wanted to pull out. In real terms, this counted as a second pro-European leaflet, specifically addressed to government supporters. Critics also claimed that the Britain in Europe campaign was far better funded, and that the press was heavily biased in favour of membership. They were right on both counts. Subsidies from the taxpayer had guaranteed £125,000 to each campaign.* But Britain in Europe had proved far more successful at independent fund-raising – unsurprisingly, since its cause was backed by almost all of Britain's wealthiest firms. Even before the vote, it emerged that Britain in Europe had lavished more than £100,000 on four ten-minute films and six radio programmes; their opponents, the National Referendum Campaign, had allocated only £3,000 to the same purpose. In the universities a previously obscure organisation called Young European Federalists suddenly emerged, flush with money. Britain in Europe was affluent enough to hire some slick public relations professionals; even if it had been equally well-endowed, the National Referendum Campaign probably would have spurned such assistance.[59] Among national newspapers only the *Morning Star* wanted the UK to withdraw; despite the vehement disagreement of some prominent columnists, the leading socialist journal, the *New Statesman*, came out in favour of continued membership. Even Rupert Murdoch's *Sun* had joined the chorus. After the result the *Daily Mail*, later the house journal of Europhobia, proclaimed that 'the effect of this thunderous Yes will echo down the years'.[60]

But in 1975 not even money and press support could guarantee success on a scale which would make the vote seem authoritative. In a survey just before the referendum more than half of respondents gave an incorrect answer when asked what the letters EEC stood for. Previous findings had suggested that a quarter of the population felt too ill-informed about the issues to cast a vote. Hugo Young has accurately characterised the public's attitude to the Community as 'changeable, ignorant and half-hearted'.[61] Clearly something new was needed to

---

* Coincidentally, this was the sum that John Stonehouse would have netted for his personal use if his insurance scam had succeeded.

make sure that both the turnout and the result were satisfactory when the voters made their decision. The obvious answer was to recruit the most popular Britons to the cause.

Ten years after Harold Wilson handed MBEs to the Beatles in a token attempt to make himself look modern, in 1975 the celebrity culture arrived en masse in British politics. Indeed, despite vigorous attempts to enlist them in future, celebrity influence would never again reach the levels of the 1975 referendum, because politicians were never quite so desperate for outside support. The pro-Europeans mustered a formidable roll-call of sporting stars and entertainers. The *Daily Mail* rounded up Yehudi Menuhin and Jack Warner, the avuncular star of *Dixon of Dock Green*. The eccentric actor Kenneth Williams was happy to record some supportive words on BBC radio although he was normally reluctant to perform without payment.[62] But while showbusiness contributed to Britain in Europe, it was overshadowed by the sporting world. The cockney boxer Henry Cooper and the gruff Yorkshire-born cricketer Brian Close both featured in television broadcasts. Scottish voters were presumably reassured by the recruitment of the football managers Jock Stein and Sir Matt Busby – both hard, shrewd men who could be expected to sniff out a bad deal for club or country. Another football manager, England's Don Revie, was brought in because of his previous record in charge of Leeds United rather than the plodding performances of the current England team. The ebullient scrum-half Gareth Edwards kept Welsh rugby fans onside, and the Olympic pentathelete Mary Peters furnished Northern Ireland with its own golden girl.* The jockey Lester Piggott was not renowned for eloquence; presumably his presence was supposed to persuade housewives to put their money on Europe. But perhaps the most astonishing campaigner was the showjumper Harvey Smith. Just four years earlier members of the Establishment had stripped Smith of first place in the British Show Jumping Derby because he had flashed a cheeky V-sign in their direction after completing his winning round. Now he was welcomed into the club, as long as he gave a thumbs up for the EEC.[63]

Although Paul McCartney supported withdrawal, the overall muster roll of nay-saying celebrities was much less impressive. It was symbolic of the campaign's disreputable image that its best-known showbusiness

---

* Peters had been the only Briton to win a gold medal at the 1974 Olympics – another shameful symptom of national decline.

spokeman was Kenneth Tynan, the theatre critic who was best known to the voting public for swearing on British television and profiting from his controversial revue *Oh! Calcutta* (now past its 1,500th performance in the West End's Duchess Theatre). Even if the National Referendum Campaign had been adequately funded, it is doubtful whether it could have emulated Britain in Europe's trick of making its preferred option seem both safe and glamorous.

Away from the claims and counterclaims about its economic impact, the most emotive argument against continued EEC membership concerned the issue of sovereignty. In hindsight it is surprising that the advocates of withdrawal made so little of this issue in their official literature.[64] But while the left believed that sovereignty had been lost already (to the United States), in the circumstances of 1975 it was easy to conclude that the country could hardly fare worse if control over its affairs was taken away from British politicians. Just in case the anti-Europeans tried to evoke historic fears of Germany, newspapers like the *Sun* and *The Times* ran articles which showed that expatriate Germans were already making constructive contributions in many areas of British life. From this perspective the worst incident for the Britain in Europe campaign was the European Cup Final, on 28 May 1975, when Leeds United lost to Bayern Munich in Paris. The Bayern side included Gerd Müller, who had orchestrated England's defeat in the 1970 World Cup – a blow which, in hindsight, seemed to have begun the prolonged slide in British morale. Although Bayern won 2–0, a perfectly good Leeds goal was disallowed by the French referee and the German team was accused of 'blatant cheating.'[65] After the game a group of Leeds supporters rioted, tearing out seats and throwing them onto the Parc des Princes pitch. 'My God, there goes half a million votes,' quipped one pro-European MP in response to the referee's decision.[66]

The prominence of celebrities in the referendum campaign can be taken out of context; after all, strategists on both sides were keen to stress that the vote would be very different from the usual inter-party battles. Nevertheless, in hindsight the campaign looks like another significant step into the media age, in which stars from the screen or the sporting world were regarded as more relevant role models than remote and outmoded politicians. Indeed, most voters thought that the non-partisan nature of the campaign was the best thing about it. The impression was that, if Britain's politicians could somehow disentangle themselves from the existing party system, the public might begin to respect them again. Obviously party conflict would not be abolished entirely, but there could be a realignment to provide a closer approximation to public preferences. The contending cross-party groups in the referendum battle suggested a way forward; the pro-European 'moderates' apparently had much more in common with each other than with their respective 'extremes'. Europe was virtually the only subject on which Tony Benn and Enoch Powell could agree, whereas Heath, Jenkins and Thorpe seemed to be natural allies on most issues of public policy. As *The Times* put it in an editorial a month after the referendum, general elections had become uninspiring because 'Since 1960 those who agree with each other have been forced to fight increasingly phoney battles in the name of party unity, supported by allies with whom they wholly disagree.' The newspaper argued that a new grouping that included Conservative and Labour moderates, as well as the whole of the Liberal Party, would mobilise what it called 'the Middle Majority' which more closely reflected new social realities in Britain. It also spoke out in favour of a system of proportional representation.[67]

Judging by its correspondence columns, *The Times* was undoubtedly speaking for many of its readers (although one outraged Liberal activist wrote to protest against the imputed moderation of his party).[68] The majority of MPs in the two main parties, however, were instinctively hostile. *The Times*, in its innocence, had urged that the economic situation demanded tough measures, and that these would have more chance of general acceptance if they were promoted by a government of national unity. To Labour MPs this was an exact replica of the scenario which had led to Ramsay MacDonald's apostasy and a disastrous party split in 1931. Just before the referendum Labour's education secretary Reg Prentice had talked of the need for national unity. Although he denied that he had been speculating about a coalition government, radicals in his constituency party of Newham North-East promptly began moves to deselect him. In December 1976 Prentice – who had once complained that the 1964–70 Labour government was 'not socialist enough' – resigned from the cabinet and a few months later joined the Conservative Party.*

The attitude towards proportional representation (PR) was broadly similar. An opinion poll of 7 October 1975 found that around two

* Anticipating a familiar trend of recent years, Prentice had released his text a few days in advance so that he knew how damaging his speech would be to his own prospects before he delivered it.

thirds of the public were in favour of electoral reform. Senior politicians were prepared at least to muse open-mindedly on the subject.
In September, for example, Roy Jenkins told Harold Wilson and Michael
Foot that 'electoral reform was likely to come, although perhaps not
for a decade'. Yet Foot was prepared to die in the last ditch in defence
of the status quo. In November he told Wilson that PR 'could be disastrous for our parliamentary system in general and the Labour Party in
particular'. It would condemn 'our descendants to a series of permanent coalition governments'.[69] This was a peculiar remark for a sincere
democrat like Foot to make, but it was a common calculation in both
main parties in the mid-1970s. When the cabinet finally discussed reform
of the electoral system in the spring of 1976, Jenkins's subtle idea of
convoking a 'Speaker's conference' on the subject, including outside
experts to counterbalance the self-interested arguments of parliamentarians, was squashed by Foot, Wilson and other ministers.[70]
Superficially, the last laugh was on Foot. Under his leadership, Labour
won just 27.6 per cent of the vote at the 1983 general election. In
combination with the Liberal/SDP Alliance vote of just over 25 per
cent, this gave the anti-Conservative parties a clear proportional
majority, and even if they had not formed a coalition they would have
been strong enough to bring down Mrs Thatcher. As it was, the
Conservatives stayed in office for another fourteen years. But in Foot's
eyes the 1983 election probably counted as a vindication of his stance
on PR. Thanks to the anti-democratic absurdities of the first-past-the-
post system, Labour won 209 seats, compared to just 23 for the Alliance.
Foot's party had thus triumphed over the moderation favoured by most
Britons, until the time came when Labour would allow Tony Blair to
transform it into a new version of the SDP.

IV

While very few Labour MPs were intrepid enough to nibble at *The
Times*'s gambit in 1975, the situation was even more delicate for the
Conservatives. If there was to be a coalition, the party could furnish
an obvious candidate for leader. But this unifying figure would be
Edward Heath, not Margaret Thatcher. If the situation arose, Heath
might have made the untypically tactful gesture of moving aside in
favour of the best alternative, Roy Jenkins. But even so, the suggestion threatened to expose divisions within the Conservative Party which

in any case were barely concealed from the public. A national government almost certainly would have tackled inflation by introducing statutory controls on both prices and incomes. But Mrs Thatcher regarded such a policy as an economic nonsense, and a direct threat to freedom. In her view inflation was purely a monetary phenomenon; that is, it arose from increases in the money supply which were unrelated to changes in the productive capacity of the economy. If governments kept a proper check on the money supply, firms which charged too much for their products or paid their workers too highly would ultimately be punished by the natural operation of market forces. In time, rational economic agents would learn to behave with discipline within a predictable monetary framework set by the government. From this viewpoint, increasing the money supply in response to inflationary pressures from outside (the oil price hike) was the economic equivalent of appeasement; in the short term it allowed workers and employers to behave irresponsibly, until the whole of society was engulfed in a general collapse.

Mrs Thatcher was convinced that monetarist policies were the right response to Britain's difficulties, and that they were unlikely to be applied with the necessary resolution if the Conservatives gave up their chance of governing alone after the next election. She was aware that her approach would lead at least to a temporary increase in unemployment, and expected people like Jenkins and Heath to flinch at this prospect. For her own part, although she did remember the 1930s her impression was that people like her father, a provincial grocer, had rallied round to support the 'worthy' poor through their temporary difficulties. Since then, improvements in state provision meant that no one would have to suffer too much while monetarism corrected the systemic defects in the British economy. She certainly did not anticipate in 1975 that her policies would devastate entire communities where manufacturing industry was the sole employer, provoking lasting antipathy towards her party. Before the leadership election she had argued that the Conservative Party 'must regain the ground we have lost in the industrial areas of the Midlands and North, in Scotland and Wales. This will be my priority if elected leader.'[71]

Mrs Thatcher had no illusions about the depth of her support within the Conservative Party. The majority of the shadow cabinet was sceptical at best, and instead of endorsing her ideas many backbench MPs had voted for her in the February leadership election merely because she was the most viable alternative to Heath. As Enoch Powell observed, Thatcher had beaten Heath – and Willie Whitelaw, who had been the main challenger on the second ballot – because she had been 'opposite the spot on the roulette wheel at the right time'.[72] Although her margin of victory in February's leadership contest had been unexpectedly comfortable – 146 votes to Whitelaw's 79 – she knew that she would be regarded as a provisional leader until she could claim the credit for a Conservative victory in the next general election. In private, some Conservatives were prepared to outflank Mrs Thatcher on the right. One journalist was astonished to hear a Tory MP arguing in a casual conversation that public spending on such amenities as playing fields and swimming baths was an appalling waste of money, that miners were invariably 'dirty, idle and unpatriotic' and that Britain was 'finished'.[73] But even if a significant proportion of Tory MPs felt like that, none was prepared to make their views public.

During the 1975 referendum campaign, Thatcher seemed content to let Heath monopolise the attention, but talk of a coalition after the referendum persuaded her supporters to hit back. It was reported that after Thatcher became leader she had been treated with scant courtesy when she visited Heath at his London home in Wilton Street with the intention of offering him a place in her shadow cabinet. In essence, the story might have been true. After all, it could not have been a pleasant encounter for the deposed leader, who had already made it known that he would not accept a place in Thatcher's team; and although Heath immediately issued a statement denying any rudeness, his grasp of social etiquette was flimsy at the best of times. However, the real significance of the story was that Thatcher and her supporters were clearly determined to use her sex as a weapon in what was really an ideological battle within the Conservative Party. If Thatcher had been male, her allies would never have thought of publicising the Wilton Street meeting to their advantage. As it was, Conservative supporters were left with the impression that a huffy Heath had been unmannerly towards a woman who had been willing to please. The Thatcherite version of the incident was generally accepted, eroding the vehement loyalty which many constituency parties had continued to show towards their previous leader. In later years, when the media manipulators had swung fully behind Thatcher, an incident which really was an unpleasant breach of confidence by her allies would be noted as the first symptom of 'the longest sulk in history' by Ted Heath – a politician who was just a bad loser.

It is often claimed that Thatcher's shadow cabinet colleagues found it difficult to accept her leadership because she was a woman. For some this might indeed have been a contributory factor, but undoubtedly she would have been accepted with more warmth had she not been an ideological dissident, who had run for the leadership on a platform which repudiated the record of the Heath government in which she had served. Also, Thatcher (born in 1925) had contributed nothing to the war effort and had now risen to the leadership of a group which included people (like Whitelaw and the future Foreign Secretary Francis Pym) who had not merely served, but had demonstrated unusual courage on the battlefield. Her hectoring attitude towards the shadow cabinet was understandable, given her lack of natural rapport with such people, but equally it was sure to be resented by men who felt that respect had to be earned rather than enforced. In this context her personal biography rather than her sex was the problem; as leader of a Conservative shadow cabinet she was hardly more acceptable than Tony Benn, who had seen some active service during a war which had claimed the life of his elder brother.

The sex factor might not have been an asset to Mrs Thatcher when she stood for the leadership of a chauvinistic party. But afterwards it became clear that it would help the Conservative cause, if only she could persuade people that she was anxious to uphold the interests of the nation as a whole. If the public had grown tired of the old, male faces and their factional battles, here was something completely different. After Thatcher won the leadership the traditionalist *Daily Telegraph* suggested that, among a certain section of the population, she would be allowed to get away with almost anything. The newspaper described her as a 'bonny fighter', an accolade which it would not have thought of extending even to her most pugilistic predecessor.[74] During the referendum campaign *The Times* published a profile which, one can assert with some confidence, marked a radical deviation from previous treatments of candidates for the office of prime minister: 'She is a trim and comely woman, quintessentially English in her features and manner. Her face is fine-boned, her eyes grey-blue, frank and alive. She was wearing a pinhead black and white Donegal tweed dress and jacket, the lapels and pockets braided, with black leather buttons and sensible black shoes . . .' The article went on to describe, at length, Mrs Thatcher's jewellery. She was happy to play along with the sexist timbre of the interview, admitting that her hair tended to become 'dishev-

elled' by about three in the morning when she was preparing an important speech.[75] No doubt the newspaper's readers were grateful to pick
up fashion tips from the new leader of the Opposition, and were not
surprised that the article had strayed so far from pressing political
issues. 1975, after all, was International Women's Year.

V

When *The Times* made its case for a coalition government it argued
that Britain's political institutions, rather than its people, had proved
unequal to troubled times. Once that deficiency had been rectified, the
situation could return to something like normality. Civil society, the
newspaper suggested, was fundamentally sound, despite recent stresses
and strains. 'The British people are in fact crying out to be properly
governed,' it declared. 'They do not believe that they are the most difficult people to govern in the world: on the contrary, they know that
they are among the most reasonable and the most resilient.[76] In August,
the Conservative MP David Howell acclaimed 'the hard-bitten common
sense of working people everywhere in Britain'.[77] Even three years after
the critical days of 1975 the author of a book about post-war Britain
found solace in the previous track record of the British people: 'In the
face of disappointment and sometimes cruel failures they have neither
panicked into reaction nor bolted after precipitate panaceas.'[78] This
sounds as if the wartime spirit was still thriving more than thirty years
after the return of peace in Europe, yet after the 1972 miners' strike
Edward Heath had tried to persuade the public to put aside its differences in the face of a national crisis, and the response had been tepid
at best. In early 1975 there were in fact numerous symptoms that
Britain's malaise went far deeper than its malfunctioning party system
and its economic weaknesses.

For anyone trying to capture the overall mood of a specific historical period, there are obvious dangers in focusing on contemporary
stories about law and order. However, in 1975 the reporting in newspapers like *The Times* tended to be muted; it is the weight of concrete
evidence that impresses the researcher. On 14 January, while the public
was still digesting the news of the joint disappearances of Lord Lucan
and John Stonehouse, a seventeen-year-old girl, Lesley Whittle, was
snatched from her home in Shropshire, and a £50,000 ransom was
demanded. Lesley was invariably described by the media as an 'heiress',

as if she had been a prize which no self-respecting kidnapper could spurn; actually, she had been left £82,000 in her father's will.[79] Subsequently it transpired that the girl had been murdered within a few days of being taken, but it was not until mid-March that her body was found hanging in a drainage shaft. The murderer, Donald Neilson (the 'Black Panther') had also robbed several post offices and was responsible for three additional deaths and several woundings.

Looking back over 1975 as a whole, even *The Times* thought that the year had been notable for its 'bizarre and half-pathological crimes', only a few of which made anything like the lasting impression of the Whittle case.[80] For example, in July 1975 a nineteen-year-old man from the Powellite heartland of West Bromwich was imprisoned for three years after attacking a girl who had met him while exercising her dog. The attacker, who had facial disfigurements, thought that the girl had mocked his appearance. In response, he dragged her into an empty house where he subjected her to a four-hour ordeal. He 'poured Brasso over her head and set her hair alight. He stripped and beat her, gagged and blindfolded her . . . He also beat her dog.'[81]

The protracted press coverage of the Whittle case – a result of the lengthy delay before her body was found – probably did something to encourage public perceptions that crime was getting out of control in Britain. In February, while the police were still searching for Lesley, the former home secretary and chancellor of the exchequer Reginald Maulding warned about 'the crumbling of discipline, the growth of crime, and the apparent erosion of the sense of personal responsibility'.[82] The increasing incidence of football hooliganism also contributed to this impression, and the violence after the European Cup final merely showed that British fans were now more willing to export a familiar domestic product. In other contexts – especially if it had occurred in a place like Brixton – the havoc wrought by football fans would have been described as a straightforward riot. In January 1975, after a League Cup defeat at the hands of Norwich, heartbroken Manchester United 'supporters' smashed shop and office windows before overturning several cars. Three months later United's away support caused more trouble during a match against Notts County. As a result, the Nottingham branch of the Police Federation proposed that clubs that failed to control their fans should be prevented from playing.[83] On several occasions in 1975, hooligans set fire to the buses or trains which had taken them to matches. The TUC urged that heavier sentences should be imposed on football hooligans who assaulted their members, especially bus drivers and railway staff. In August a judge expressed regret that he was unable to turn back the clock and sentence a group of Queens Park Rangers' fans to sit in the stocks, instead of just fining them. A few days later the 1975/6 season began, with about 200 arrests. At the fixture between Wolverhampton Wanderers and Manchester United fourteen stabbings were reported.[84]

Even sportsmen seemed more willing to engage in violence in 1975. On the same day in May courts in Birmingham and Bury dealt respectively with the cases of a cricketer who had used his bat to break the umpire's arm after being given out, and a footballer who had head-butted a referee. At least there was no evidence of hooliganism among cricket supporters. But a male streaker disrupted the second Test match between England and Australia, and the third game of the series was abandoned after the pitch was vandalised by a group campaigning for the release of George Davis, a London cabby serving a twenty-year prison sentence for robbery.* The poor performance of English cricketers and other representative teams undoubtedly added to the sense of national malaise, although not everyone turned to violence as a result. Earlier in the year no less a personage than Air Chief Marshal Sir Christopher Foxley-Norris had reflected a more general feeling of resignation by informing readers of *The Times* that 'on the playing fields of the world, we appear to have become the perennial losers, the predictable holders of all the wooden spoons.'[85] Nostalgic accounts of the mid-1970s tend to adopt the Foxley-Norris line, and regard the hapless performance of British sporting teams as a relatively minor matter at a time when the country faced much more serious difficulties. The reality was much nastier, suggesting a high level of underlying social stress. In football the World Cup-winning manager Sir Alf Ramsay had already been sacked, and after England lost the first Ashes Test in humiliating circumstances the team's affable (Scottish) captain Mike Denness fell on his sword amid a welter of venomous press comment.

Although the existing link between sport and crime was reinforced in 1975, the most spectacular advances were registered in the sexual field. In those days people who wanted to refute the Freudians by putting sexual activity into a rational perspective had some chance of

---

* Ironically, this was one game which England looked set to win, which would have levelled the series. Australia also knocked England out of the first cricket World Cup, held just before the European referendum.

succeeding without going to the lengths of throwing out the television set and refusing to buy any newspapers. But the impression that, in this respect, the mid-1970s was a relatively innocent time has prevailed at least in part because perverts like Frederick West, who was already active, were not brought to public notice until many years later. The British public in 1975 was exposed to public sexual displays to an unprecedented extent, backed by official tolerance in what was reputed to be a more liberal and responsible climate. In London theatres the Lord Chamberlain's censorious writ no longer ran, and productions like *Oh! Calcutta* were becoming more common. In August 1975 even the theatres which advertised in *The Times* were offering fare to satisfy the tastes of the most lascivious tourist. Paul Raymond, the sexual entrepreneur, was presenting *The Festival of Erotica* at his Revuebar in Soho; he was also responsible for *Let's Get Laid*. A new 'adult' attraction was the musical *Let My People Come*. These uninhibited exhibitions cast an ironic light on the title of another long-running theatrical attraction of the time – *No Sex Please, We're British*.

Sexual entrepreneurs, of course, angrily denied that their shows had anything to do with a rise in criminal activity. However, while Fred West remained at large in 1975, at the same time the courts were dealing with cases which were different only in degree. In June, for example, a father of seven children admitted 'debauching' each of them over a nine-year period. He had five daughters and two sons; the oldest of them was still only sixteen at the time of the trial. Nevertheless, this maniac was jailed for just fifteen years.[86] In the same month a child psychiatrist actually walked free when a jury accepted his explanation for touching the 'private parts' of a seven-year-old girl. He had claimed that he was 'only trying to teach her not to be ashamed of her body'.[87]

It was not just girls who were at risk from predators. In July 1975 an ITV programme, *Johnny Come Home*, highlighted the possibility of very young boys being enticed into prostitution if they ran away from home and headed for London. In various parts of the country young boys were found murdered in circumstances which strongly suggested a sexual motivation. But prosecutions of paedophiles who stopped short of murder were still relatively rare, though one notable exception in November 1975 forced the resignation of the Bishop of Llandaff, charged with gross indecency. The extent of abuse in a domestic setting can only be imagined, and children entrusted to social 'care' were at the mercy of their custodians. Even the more fortunate had to be warned not to 'talk to strangers', without being told exactly why such dialogue should be avoided. But they could hardly avoid absorbing the lesson that the outside world was full of nameless threats.

Heterosexual rape was rife in Britain during 1975 – although, of course, it remained grossly under-reported in International Womens' Year. The 'Cambridge Rapist', Peter Cook, was finally apprehended in June, after terrorising the women of the city for nine months and perpetrating at least eight serious sexual assaults. Having attracted excessive publicity by choosing to operate within an Oxbridge city, Cook was given a life sentence. Other rapists could expect much more leniency at this time because some members of the legal establishment clearly remained impervious to the arguments of the feminist movement. In February the director of public prosecutions ruled that *Forum*, Fred West's favourite pornographic magazine (claiming a 'readership' of five million), was not 'obscene'. At the same time the House of Lords ruled that a man could be cleared of rape if he 'honestly' thought that a woman had consented to sex. As interpreted by the courts, this meant that a man could argue that a woman had 'consented' if she had gone out for the evening wearing 'provocative' clothing. The House of Lords case raised even more troubling possibilities; a QC, Sir Harold Cassel, had told their Lordships that 'If a woman resists, the man may think that she is in fact consenting and is giving him the additional thrill of a struggle.' Until it was corrected by legislation championed by the Labour MP Jack Ashley, this constituted a rapists' charter. But even without the Lords' ruling, many judges were inclined to give men the benefit of the doubt. In June 1975, for example, an appeal was allowed on behalf of a convicted offender because 'the girl was not without sexual experience and the intimidation had been mild'.[88] This case made headlines because just a week earlier another rapist, who had menaced his victim with a knife, had escaped with only a suspended sentence. The judge had explained his decision by admitting that he disliked sending young men to prison if he could possibly avoid it.[89]

The ensuing furore rightly focused on the disregard shown by the judge for a woman's right to select a sexual partner without having to anticipate serious stab wounds if she withheld her consent. But indirectly it exposed another serious issue. At the time Britain's prison population was about 40,000, and this constituted the limit of existing capacity. This situation triggered a controversy which has been repeated at regular intervals over the next three decades. In April 1975 the liberal-minded

Louis Blom-Cooper, QC argued that the country faced 'a constant prison crisis compounded of overcrowded prisons and seething injustice to prisoners and their custodians'. It was a view which was fully shared by the much-mocked prison reformer Lord Longford (1905–2001). The experience of Brixton prison, where he had to share four working lavatories with 300 other inmates, had already made John Stonehouse into an ardent advocate of improved conditions.[90] From a different perspective, the president of the Justices' Clerks Society complained in May 1975 that 'Punishment for wrong-doing is condemned by progressives as something that does not work'. The lord chancellor, Elwyn-Jones, joined the chorus of calls for harsher prison sentences.[91] As always, the real argument concerned consistency of sentencing; while judges exercised mercy towards rapists, people could be sent to jail for refusing to take up work recommended to them by Job Centres.[92]

The value of a prison sentence either as a deterrent, a form of retribution or a means of protecting society has been debated back and forth between 1975 and the present – and continues to receive most media attention when the prisons are bursting at the seams. Other perennial topics which were debated in 1975 included dangerous dogs (several children were killed or maimed); the cleanliness of hospitals ('The Crimea is not a bad analogy to the conditions,' claimed one consultant in the specialist burns unit at Nottingham's City Hospital);[93] the danger that, apart from the effects on small business, the emergence of out-of-town 'hypermarkets' would increase 'the neurosis of modern living',[94]* and rationing within the NHS due to financial restraints. The Greater London Council (GLC) was trying to encourage car sharing in order to ease traffic congestion in the capital.[95]† It was also becoming increasingly difficult for first-time buyers to step onto London's property ladder; even young professionals wishing to rent a home were already experiencing some difficulties. From today's vantage point some of the properties on offer at that time look insanely underpriced. In the course of his travails

---

* The impact of these bloated boutiques on small businesses was particularly dramatic in the period of Conservative rule after 1979. As Elliott and Atkinson note, the number of family bakeries dropped from 5,000 to 3,500 between 1990 and 1995; over the decade after 1985 local butchers lost 16 per cent of their share of the meat market. Ironically, in view of Mrs Thatcher's family ties to the grocery business, corner shops fared particularly badly while she and her successor John Major were in office; see *The Age of Insecurity*, Verso, 1998, 129.

† The official forecast for registered vehicles by the year 2000 was remarkably accurate, although *The Times* thought it was far too high. The forecast was 28.6 million vehicles; the actual figure turned out to be 28.4 million.

it emerged that John Stonehouse had paid just £70,000 in 1972 for a six-bedroom country mansion near Salisbury.[96] In 1975 a six-bedroomed house in Notting Hill, 'scruffy but sound', with a sixty-foot garden, cost £32,500. A luxury three-bedroomed apartment in more upmarket Belgravia, covering two floors, was available for rent at £5,200 per year.[97] But the average annual London household income in 1975 was £2,000–3,000, and the average price of a house was £14,000, up from £6,000 in 1969. It was argued that inflated property values were pricing hard-working people out of the market and property was becoming more attractive as an investment for the rich, while savings accounts were progressively eroded by inflation. Credit cards were becoming increasingly alluring for the profligate; by August 1975 the pioneering Barclaycard (established in 1966) was gaining 40,000 new recruits every month, although thanks to galloping inflation and high interest rates neither it nor its rival Access was proving very profitable.[98]

Even the threats of imminent doom which so often feature in contemporary headlines were anticipated in 1975. The obvious parallel was the fear of terrorist attack. For most of 1975 the IRA was officially observing a ceasefire. In practice, this meant that Republican terrorists were less likely than usual to launch attacks on the security forces in Northern Ireland. Although secret contacts continued the ceasefire looked farcical in July 1975, when four soldiers were killed by a bomb in retaliation for the deaths of two Catholics. Other IRA operations continued unabated. On the other side, the British army was free to continue its clandestine preparations for a resumption of violence, although its numbers were reduced from a high point of around 14,000, and the government continued to release Republican suspects who had been detained without trial. In March 1975 civil servants canvassing ideas for a morale-boosting 'Brighten Up Ulster' initiative hit on the idea of dispatching entertainers like Morecambe and Wise to bring some sunshine to the population of Northern Ireland. However, it was never likely that the celebrity effect would be as salutory in Ulster as it later proved to be in the referendum campaign. The idea was dropped.[99]

Six years after the army had taken up peacekeeping responsibilities in Northern Ireland, the mainland population had become accustomed to the idea that the Republicans were the sole source of trouble across the Irish Sea. Only close and clear-eyed observers of newspaper reports would have realised that this popular impression was untrue. The main culprits in 1975 were in fact the so-called loyalist terror groups, like the Ulster Volunteer Force (UVF). On 31 July 1975 members of the UVF slaughtered three musicians from the popular group the Miami Showband. Five of the band's members were on a cross-border trip when they were halted by what they supposed was an army check-point. In fact, the men in uniform were UVF members. Two of them tried to plant a bomb in the van, probably in an attempt to make it look as though the musicians were attached to a terrorist organisation. The device exploded, killing two UVF operatives, whereupon the band members tried to run away. They were shot while they ran.

The IRA felt that it must respond to this surreal manifestation of sectarian hatred, and on 13 August four people were killed and more than twenty injured in a bomb attack on the Bayardo bar on Belfast's Protestant Shankill Road. Another victim of this fresh bout of killing was a four-year-old girl, shot by a sniper in Belfast. But the rising tide of loyalist violence convinced the IRA that it should escalate the battle in the enemy's heartlands. An IRA active service unit based in England had made its presence felt before the end of August, killing a bomb-disposal expert on London's Kensington Church Street. Then eight people were killed in Caterham, in a pub frequented by off-duty Welsh Guardsmen.

In 1975 the BBC screened a series of television programmes about the origins of conflict in Northern Ireland. But this balanced presentation was hardly likely to make a dent in public prejudices, which had been perma-nently fixed by the fact that only Republican groups were interested in attacking the British army or murdering people on the mainland. On 15 August six men were sentenced to life imprisonment for the November 1974 Birmingham pub bombings, in which twenty-one people had died and more than 150 were injured. The trial, held in Lancaster rather than the Midlands where feelings were running too high, took place amid tight security which cost an estimated £200,000 and greatly inconvenienced local residents. When the jury returned guilty verdicts after less than seven hours of deliberation, the judge declared that the evidence had been the clearest and most overwhelming that he had ever heard. Yet the only 'overwhelming' evidence was physical, showing that the suspects had been badly beaten by the police before they appeared in court. The Conservative spokesman on Northern Ireland, Airey Neave, promptly asked for an assurance that the convicted men would never be included in any amnesty which might follow a negotiated peace.[100] In October four defendants received similar sentences for their alleged bombing of pubs in Guildford and Woolwich, which had claimed a total of seven lives in the weeks before the Birmingham outrage. In 1991 all of the people convicted in these major trials were cleared on appeal, amid evidence that confessions had been extracted by force.

Apart from the fear of being caught up in an indiscriminate terrorist attack – or of being arrested by police desperate for a conviction – the public also had health scares to contend with in 1975. Despite the 1974 Rabies Act, which tightened regulations on imported animals, the disease seemed to be making inexorable progress towards Britain at that time. As *The Times* warned in July 1975, 'The rabies "frontier" is moving ahead at a rate of 30 miles a year, and is now not far from the Channel.' Rabies was the biological equivalent of communism, creeping ever closer while the country slept. But this was a scare story of a kind which became much more familiar in later years. The panic had been triggered by the deaths in London of two people who had contracted the disease on trips outside Europe.[101] Nevertheless, the newspapers and even the television news bulletins spelled out in detail the lingering, miserable death which could befall anyone who was reckless enough to befriend an off-colour kitten. While the scare lasted, young or impressionable people who made the mistake of listening to the news lived in the daily expectation of developing a sudden revulsion at the sight of water. But in 1975 neurotic reactions could still be evoked without media assistance. In August rumours suddenly swept the south of England about a potentially fatal intestinal disease affecting cats. Despite repeated assurances that there was no epidemic, vetinerary surgeries were besieged for several weeks by cat-lovers seeking vaccinations.[102]

Of equally enduring topicality were reports about the impact of excessive television viewing. In 1974 London had hosted the first international conference on obesity; the NHS was already spending more than £2 million on drugs to combat the condition. The following year another gathering of experts heard about the dangers arising from poor posture, which might result in the development of 'bulging "TV tummies."' Thanks to its addiction to the small screen, it was argued, Britain was in danger of becoming 'a structurally deficient nation'. Reassuringly, experts guessed that the unpleasant effects could be warded off provided viewers took a break every forty-five minutes and walked around the room.[103]

Actually, the quality of much television output in 1975 was sufficiently high to make the risk of 'TV tummy' seem worthwhile. Viewers were not immune from the effects of inflation, and just before the start

of the European referendum campaign the licence fee for a colour television was raised from £12 to £18.* But this was one of the more
justifiable price rises of the mid-1970s. Even political obsessives found
it difficult to resist competition from light entertainment beamed into
the living room. One anti-European, who had gone to the length of
writing and privately publishing a pamphlet on the need to withdraw
from the EEC, told Labour's Peter Shore that he was looking forward
to watching BBC coverage of the major set-piece debate of the referendum campaign, held at the Oxford Union. 'In fact,' he confided, 'I'm
giving up an episode of *Edward VII* on the other side!'[104]

Peter Hitchens has written that when people started to watch colour
television 'even the bad programmes looked good'.[105] This might help to
explain the impression of a subsequent deterioration, but in the mid-
1970s a decent proportion of the programmes would have looked good
in any hue, even though time has not added to the lustre of most evening
schedules. *The Black and White Ministrel Show* was still considered a
suitable vehicle for prime-time Saturday entertainment. *That's Life*, a
conduit for consumer outrage, made its first appearance in 1972, making
no apparent discrimination against the misdeeds of nationalised industries or private companies. In what was regarded at the time as a typical
British compromise, vituperative complaints about shoddy service were
interspersed with humorous poems, phallic vegetables and reports of rib-
tickling misprints from the newspapers.† The supposedly anti-enterprise
BBC also inflicted on the public a meretricious drama series called *The
Brothers*, about a family infected by material greed; this was quickly
succeeded by *Oil Strike North*, a show which somehow contrived to be
topical and turgid in equal measure. But in April 1975 the Corporation
gave a predictably cool response to the prospect of extra competition
from an additional terrestrial channel, which led to the establishment of
Channel 4 in 1982. Its argument that wider choice would turn out to be
an enemy of quality has not been refuted by subsequent experience.

Besides drama series, musical shows and consumer programmes, 1975
also saw *The Spirit of the Age*, an eight-part evocation of British architectural glories, and Jacob Bronowski's *The Ascent of Man*, which was

---

*And from £7 to £8 for black and white, the smaller rise being a flimsy gesture towards
social justice since even though the number of monochrome sets outnumbered colour
by more than two to one only the poor or the thrifty had yet to make the switch.
† In the very different atmosphere of the late 1980s this formula looked increasingly
tired, although the show limped on until 1994.

possibly the most erudite of all television series. But above all this was a golden age for British situation comedy, thanks to the BBC's commissioning policy. *Dad's Army* (first shown in 1968) had passed its prime, but new episodes were still being made and people did not seem bored by repeats. *Whatever Happened to the Likely Lads?* was only produced for television in 1973/4, but a new radio series was running at the time of the referendum. *The Good Life* was first shown in April 1975, and a second series began before the end of the year along with another dollop of the prison comedy *Porridge*. Although the team behind *Monty Python's Flying Circus* made no new television programmes after 1974, in the following year they released their wonderful big-screen spoof of Arthurian legend, *Monty Python and the Holy Grail*. September 1975 saw the first BBC episode of John Cleese's masterpiece, *Fawlty Towers*. *The Fall and Rise of Reginald Perrin* joined the mid-70s roll of honour in 1976.

Apart from the brilliant sitcoms, Britons could also laugh along with Eric Morecambe and Ernie Wise, and with Mike Yarwood, whose affectionate impersonations of politicians like Heath and Wilson earned him an OBE in 1976. However, the brittle nature of the nation's mirth at this time was reflected in the subjects chosen by the comic dramatists. *Dad's Army* was an exercise in pure nostalgia; it was reasonably safe to expose the incompetence of the wartime Home Guard three decades after the threat from the Hun had been repelled, even if Eurosceptics claimed that the EEC was a new version of the same project. Although *The Likely Lads* had a contemporary setting, the leading characters were obsessed with their previous lives; the theme song stated that the past was the only thing worth looking forward to. *The Good Life* was obviously pitched at a middle-class audience, but it was arguably the most subversive of all, depicting the attempts of a suburban couple to abandon materialism and embrace self-sufficiency. In a clever reversal of attitudes in the real world, their affluent, orthodox neighbours were obviously jealous of the impoverished, experimental couple.* As we have seen, Reggie Perrin took his

---

* As Larry Elliott and Dan Atkinson have noted, *The Good Life* was probably the only successful sitcom of the time which was still relevant to social conditions two decades later, when couples like Tom and Barbara Good could be taken as representatives of 'the downshifters, those fortunate enough to have made enough money in law or the City not to have to worry about money for the rest of their lives, who are now intent on "finding themselves"'. A survey of 2003 suggested that the number of 'downshifters' (more broadly defined) increased from 1.7 million in 1997 to 2.6 million five years later; *The Age of Insecurity*, 46–7; *Daily Telegraph*, 16 April 2003.

rejection of contemporary life even further; although the character was obviously suffering from a midlife crisis, his attempt to escape via a simulated suicide would not have seemed credible to a previous generation of viewers. *Fawlty Towers* transcended its times, but it did bear a few hallmarks of the mid-1970s. Those looking for hidden metaphors could interpret the character of the semi-senile, parasitic Major as a symbol of the bankrupt British Establishment. The rampaging hotelier Basil Fawlty certainly epitomised the general sense of things falling apart. In the episode 'Gourmet Night', first shown in October 1975, Fawlty's British-made car breaks down and he ends up attacking it with the branch of a tree. Many viewers would have sympathised with his frustration, although the form of road rage which the British eventually adopted would have less humorous connotations.

In *Porridge* the incarcerated villains were not just wittier than their gaolers – they were also more honourable at heart, if not more trustworthy. They also seemed happy enough to share a cell, which must have heartened hard-pressed Home Office planners. The main character, Norman Stanley Fletcher – played with unswerving skill by Ronnie Barker (1929–2005) – was more reminiscent of 'Uncle Jim' Callaghan than of an institutionalised jailbird. Kenneth Williams thought that the programme's 'romanticising of villainy' was 'sickening and disgusting', and he had a point; but this perspective went unnoticed by most of the audience, who, in the absence of first-hand experience, continued to feel that conditions in Britain's overcrowded prisons were too good for 'habitual criminals' like Fletcher.[106] Those who wanted a more realistic impression of crime and punishment in the Britain of 1975 could always tune in to *The Sweeney*, which was first shown under that title in January after a pilot programme the previous year. This gritty drama showcased the talents of John Thaw (1942–2002), beginning a body of work which would make him the nearest rival to Barker as the best British television actor over the next quarter-century.

Musically, the British were in an erratic frame of mind in 1975. But even without the distorting influence of nostalgia it is indisputable that the best-selling records were a marked improvement on the chart offerings of today. There were three novelty number one hits, marking the advance of the celebrity culture. The artists in question were Telly (Kojak) Savalas, the comedian Billy Connolly, and Windsor Davies and Don Estelle, whose cover version of the 1940 Inkspots hit 'Whispering Grass' had more merit than the regrettable programme (*It Ain't Half*

Hot, Mum) which spawned it. The Bay City Rollers were a reminder that, in this field at least, looks always had a chance of prevailing over talent; the intrusion of hysterical teenyboppers at their concerts added to the general feeling that British people were losing their grip on reality. But the same year saw three of the greatest pop singles of all time. 10cc's 'I'm Not in Love' and Queen's 'Bohemian Rhapsody' both reached number one. 'SOS', by the Swedish group Abba (who had won the 1974 Eurovision Song Contest) did not even make the top five, which showed just how stiff the competition was in late 1975.

The media hype surrounding groups like the Bay City Rollers gave serious music journalists plentiful grounds for complaint in 1975.* But the main critical targets were the bands who concentrated on albums and concerts rather than the singles market. Pink Floyd, Led Zeppelin and Genesis were already regarded as dinosaurs of rock, because of their lumbering music as much as the size of their following. Ironically, far from justifying the argument that the big bands had run out of ideas, in 1975 Pink Floyd produced the sardonically mistitled *Wish You Were Here*, which was even bleaker and more thought-provoking than their mega-selling *Dark Side of the Moon* (1973). In the song 'Welcome to the Machine' the group savaged the commercialisation of music more effectively than any of the punk bands which despised their alleged pomposity. The year 1975 also saw the release of Queen's *A Night at the Opera*, featuring plenty of innovative tracks in addition to the bizarre 'Bohemian Rhapsody', which dominated the chart at the end of the year. But that song and the accompanying promotional video (which cost less than £4,000 to make) would probably not have made such a strong initial impact had it been released at any other time. Although 'Bohemian Rhapsody' was a remarkable piece of work by any standards – and topped the charts again in 1991, after the death of Queen's lead singer Freddie Mercury – it says something about the general mood in the mid-1970s that this idiosyncratic, unnerving offering could be accepted as a classic so quickly.

But in 1975 the weirdness of the British was not simply registered by their ability to keep a straight face during a song which contained

---

* From the television coverage, it seemed that groups like the Rollers and the Osmonds were besieged whenever they showed their faces in public by a significant proportion of Britain's population of female teenagers. Looking at the reports thirty years later, it seems that the 'hysteria' was usually caused by a couple of hundred extremists – rather like the contemporary clashes between the racist National Front and its opponents, where the police would sometimes outnumber the demonstrators.

the line 'Scaramouche, Scaramouche, will you do the fandango?' In April 1975 an inquest heard that a man in Camberwell, south London, had jumped out of a window in his thirteenth-floor apartment. He had undertaken the leap in order to test his Christian faith, with fatal consequences. A more methodical but madder approach to the same end was taken by a man from West Bridgford, an affluent suburb of Nottingham. He carefully spread weedkiller on his sandwiches and munched them for two days before the chemicals did their deadly work.[107] And on 11 April 1975 Lady Lucy Russell, the twenty-six-year-old granddaughter of the famous philosopher Bertrand Russell, walked into a Cornish churchyard, doused herself in paraffin and burnt herself to death.[108]

VI

The macabre death of Lady Lucy Russell was rationalised by her radical grandmother Dora as a protest against America's bombing of Cambodia. In truth her troubles lay closer to home, and ultimately can be traced to the progressive educational theories of Bertrand Russell himself. The influence of Russell and other left-wing intellectuals in Britain during the mid-1970s tended to be exaggerated, not least by themselves and their opponents – who, like the egregious novelist Kingsley Amis, had formerly been on the left themselves. But education was one sphere in which their impact was indisputable. Not even Margaret Thatcher had been able to resist the trend towards comprehensive schools during her stint as education secretary. And the effect of radical ideas in the universities was registered during 1975 in regular reports of leftist-inspired sit-ins and rent strikes. There was nothing fanciful about the description of the unruly University of Rummidge in David Lodge's brilliant comic novel *Changing Places* (1975); as right-wing academics were keen to point out, the Polytechnic of North London was considerably worse.[109] On the assumption that the students of 1975 would provide political leaders at the beginning of the next century, it was particularly worrying to Middle England that the National Union of Students insisted on electing firebrands of the hard left as their presidents. The successful candidate in 1975 described himself as 'a Marxist to the left of Mr Benn'. As the son of one of Britain's greatest civil servants, even at such a tender age Charles Clarke should have been astute enough to realise that such comments might one day come back to haunt him.[110]

Compared to the later era of loans (rather than grants) and tuition fees, these were actually golden days for students. As for their teachers, in August 1975 an academic struck up what would become an over-familiar refrain by protesting that 'the present scandalous level of remuneration is threatening the distinction of British universities'.[111] David Lodge had already emphasised the gulf between their status and the conditions which existed across the Atlantic.

With the allegiance of future generations at stake, the ideological right correctly identified education as a key battleground. Its main contribution to the debate this year was the *Black Paper 1975* – the fourth in a series of critical essays, the first of which had appeared in 1969. In their introduction the editors, C.B. Cox (professor of English at Manchester University) and Rhodes Boyson (a former head-master who was now a Conservative MP) claimed that 'The educational scene is very sick indeed.' They pointed out that people under twenty-five made up half of the illiterate adult population in Britain: 'Industry complains of increasing innumeracy. Some 650,000 children play truant every day from our schools and teachers flee from city schools because of lesson-resistance and insolence by the pupils. Adolescent violence increases and universities show signs of a student and staff intoler-ance of free discussion which threatens a new dark age. Genuine cultural participation falls steadily and a non-value pop culture becomes dominant.'[112]

Even before the *Black Paper* was published, evidence had emerged in support of the editors' conclusions. In February Avon and Somerset police started special truancy patrols, linking abstention from school with a rise in juvenile crime. The problem was confirmed by figures from the London force, which reported that in 1974 it had arrested 32,000 young people between the ages of ten and sixteen; this repre-sented a 15 per cent increase on 1973. In April a survey of members of the National Association of Schoolmasters found that the previous term had featured more than 6,000 cases of classroom 'violence and disruption'. The following month a woman explained why she had left a job in a Paddington comprehensive school after just a few days. An experienced teacher who had returned to the classroom after a career break, she reported that her youthful charges 'ate crisps, read maga-zines and did their hair', making no attempt even to pretend to be heeding the lesson. In June the Sedgefield comprehensive school in Stockton-on-Tees was temporarily closed because the staff was no longer prepared to put up with a boy who had just received a suspended sentence for attacking a teacher.[113]

For those, like the present writer, who were just beginning their secondary schooling at the time, it is particularly disheartening to review the debate in 1975. By the early years of the twenty-first century the comprehensive vision had been attacked so often that its original ideals, upheld by enthusiasts like Tony Benn's wife Caroline, now seem like an historical curiosity, bereft of contemporary political significance. On paper it must have seemed plausible that mixed-ability classes drawn from diverse social backgrounds would produce an upward levelling of academic standards and an equalising of life chances for all students. In practice, though, they tended far too often to result in dumbing down. In the comprehensive environment peer pressure forced bright children to disguise their intelligence; the new classroom heroes were distinguished by their sporting (or fighting) prowess. Bullying of the gifted by the thick-headed, previously a feature of the public schools, was thus spread throughout the education system. By necessity, most teachers had to adjust to this pecking order – the alternative was to face continual disruption if they showed any signs of favouring the intelligent and well-behaved. In any case, the progress of the class had to be dictated by its slowest member – and given the lack of immediate reward for academic excellence, the slowest had no incentive to quicken their pace. The only way for a pupil to proceed satisfactorily in such an environment was to master in private the technique of passing examinations while behaving badly in public. Few were able to strike this unusual balance; and they should not have been forced to do so within institutions funded by the taxpayer supposedly in the national interest.

From this perspective, by far the best contribution to the 1975 *Black Paper* was Iris Murdoch's 'Socialism and Selection', previously published in the *Sunday Telegraph*. Although she associated herself with the left, Murdoch was sufficiently troubled to contribute her thoughts to what was already regarded as a right-wing propaganda sheet (the contributors included her renegade friend Kingsley Amis). But Murdoch's contribution provided good reasons why left-wingers should have rethought their commitment to comprehensive education in the context of 1975. She wrote that 'Those who are upset by the educational programme of the left are sometimes told: don't worry, able children will get their education somehow all the same. This may be true of middle class able children with moderately bookish homes and educationally ambitious parents behind them' ... but not of gifted children from disadvantaged backgrounds, who were left entirely unprotected under the new dispensation. Murdoch proceeded to argue that

Selection must and will take place in education and those who banish rational methods of selection are simply favouring irrational and accidental ones. The children who will be lost forever are the poor clever children with an illiterate background who on the 'chance' system are being denied the *right* to a strict academic education which can only be achieved on the basis of some sort of selection. Why should socialist policy, of all things, be so grossly unjust to the underprivileged clever child, avid to learn, able to learn, and under non-selective education likely to pass in relaxed idle boredom those precious years when strenuous learning is a joy and the whole intellectual and moral future of the human being is at stake?[114]

Since 1975 common sense in educational matters has been rare, and of course Murdoch could be accused of naivety, since middle-class parents had always proved adept at manipulating the selective system to their advantage. Even so, her contribution showed a willingness to transcend the stereotypes of left and right which dominated the political and social commentary of the time. Despite the obvious bias of most contributors to the volume, objective observers had to accept that something was going badly wrong. In August 1975 an official publication, *Trends in Education*, carried an article from a Post Office recruiter who complained that standards among school leavers were deteriorating in the basics of reading, writing and arithmetic. Furthermore, applicants for Post Office jobs had demonstrated a 'lack of knowledge and appreciation of what "work" is all about'.[115] It was almost as if Britain's schools had been preparing pupils for the prolonged period of youth unemployment which many economists were now accurately predicting. At this stage, and for many years afterwards, it was rare for anyone to suggest that the drop in standards might have something to do with inadequate parenting. Politicians would always be reluctant to suggest such a thing, since the nation's contingent of voters included rather more parents than teachers. Professionals within the education system were convenient scapegoats – all the more so since they included many would-be social engineers who had suffered from the delusion that comprehensive schools really could compensate for the unequal life chances of young Britons in the mid-1970s.

Since the end of the Second World War it had been fairly easy for Britons to retain an optimistic outlook. The figures in Gallup's end-of-year surveys fluctuated, but there had never been a crushing majority who expected life to get worse. Material standards looked set to rise indefinitely for most people, real poverty had almost been conquered, and – more important than these – it seemed that material comfort would be matched by a high level of spiritual satisfaction. Even amid the difficulties of the early 1970s the public retained a sense that things were likely to get better. But by 1975, as the true implications of the oil shock sank in, Britons were faced with many sources of disquiet. Certainly there was fear, inspired by terrorism, disease and a less tangible feeling that the country had become a more unpleasant place without anyone really noticing. Lust was prevalent, although older Britons who had been brought up before the war were anxious to deny it. Such people were more willing to acknowledge that their fellow citizens had been ensnared by greed; the evidence, after all, was ubiquitous in the new era of financial insecurity. Hope, faith and especially charity were obviously in shorter supply, particularly since inflation was cutting away at the real value of bequests from individuals who had denied themselves little luxuries in the hope of leaving something to a good cause.

Above all, for the first time in the democratic era British citizens were becoming more aware of the threat from apathy. The turnout in general elections might still be respectable by international standards, but nothing ever seemed to change for the better once the party battles were over. In August 1975 *The Times* reported that someone had written 'Apathy is the curse of Britain' in a north London public lavatory. Underneath, some wag had responded 'Who cares?'[116] In 2005 this inscription would hardly have been worth reporting among a group of friends down at the pub, but three decades earlier it seemed sufficiently original, witty and topical to find a place in a national newspaper. The problem of apathy was explicitly recognised in October 1975, when the Archbishop of Canterbury, Dr Donald Coggan, launched an appeal for national revival in conjunction with several other British churches. In a subsequent broadcast Coggan struggled to convince members of his flock that they were not powerless: 'Your vote counts. Your voice counts. You count. Each man and woman is needed if the drift towards chaos is to stop.'[117]* A few weeks earlier Harold Wilson's adviser Bernard Donoughue had privately branded Britain, 'A society of failures, full of apathy, and aroused only by the success of others.'[118] Even at Lancaster University, which in 1975 witnessed a well-supported rent strike followed by an occupation of the main administrative building, a letter in the student newspaper complained of the 'apathy and indifference of the student population and their so-called "leaders"'.[119]

Throughout 1975 inadequate public motivation was being cited by a variety of groups with diverse and often contradictory proposals for a recovery of national purpose. According to Lord Chalfont, public apathy could allow a communist takeover of Britain. From the communist viewpoint, apathy was the only thing that stood between Britain and a much-needed revolution. Enoch Powell argued that Britons had only endorsed EEC membership because the pro-European movement had lulled them into a false feeling of security. The mainland population was apathetic about Northern Ireland, combining a feeling that the problem would never be resolved with a rigid refusal to inform itself about the issues at stake. While commending the solid common sense of the British electorate, even *The Times*'s campaign for a moderate government of national unity implied that voters had been apathetic in the years leading up to 1975; if the conflict between parties was really so sterile, why had the overwhelming majority of citizens allowed elected politicians to get away with it, and turned out time after time to cast their votes in contests which would never provide the outcome that they really wanted? The argument for a wide-ranging coalition was never going to succeed, even in the context of 1975 when it seemed most plausible. One *Times* reader thought that rather than animating the electorate, a coalition would propel it into perpetual quiescence. 'Our problems arise out of apathy and selfishness,' he wrote. 'To seek a centre consensus is to accept this as normal.'[120]

By the end of the year, though, it proved possible to feel a little more optimistic about Britain's prospects. At 1.18 million, official unemployment was the highest at any Christmas time since before the Second World War, and Harold Wilson warned of some 'bleak' months ahead. But the government's pay policy seemed to be working; at least inflation was gradually declining. In its last issue of the year *The Times*

---

* On 21 January 2003, when it was trying to rally opposition to the war in Iraq, the *Daily Mirror* used almost exactly the same words on its front page: 'You are NOT powerless. You DO have a voice'.

editorial spoke of 'a recovery of self-control' and the glimmerings of 'a new realism'. The country still faced formidable challenges, but probably not an extra-parliamentary revolt from either left or right. This turned out to be an accurate prognosis; A.J.P. Taylor might have been a brilliant historian, but like almost everyone else in 1975 he proved to be a flawed prophet.

However, one part of Taylor's forecast turned out to be almost true. He had predicted that the capitalist world would be 'frightened' of developments in Britain and would 'come to our rescue'. By the end of 1976 a new succession of sterling crises had forced the government to ask for assistance from the International Monetary Fund (IMF). The terms of the subsequent 'rescue' were moderated by Jim Callaghan's adroit diplomacy, but they were still harsh enough in terms of public-expenditure cuts to ensure that the main guiding principles of the post-war consensus were now off the agenda. Yet, as *The Times* had consistently argued, despite the new electoral volatility those general principles, laid down under the almost-forgotten Clement Attlee, were preferred by most Britons who gave politics more than a modicum of serious thought. As a result, after 1976 the electorate was more disoriented than ever, and the gravest dilemmas were faced by those who were best informed and most open-minded. The only certainty was that Labour was too badly divided to be a safe vehicle of government for the immediate future; even senior figures like Callaghan and his chancellor Denis Healey failed to inspire confidence as they battled to secure agreement for policies which contradicted the beliefs they had upheld over many years before 1975. The Conservatives themselves were divided, and although their leader claimed to be in tune with the real convictions of the British public there was plenty of evidence to suggest that she was much more radical than her image-makers tried to imply. But at least the Opposition had a real appetite for office, which offered the possibility that the party would bury its differences if it won the next election; and whatever one thought of Margaret Thatcher, not even her worst enemy claimed that she would contradict all of her previous utterances if she ever made it to Downing Street. In short, she could be judged by her words as well as her deeds.

If there was not to be a violent overthrow of the British democratic system, there remained a possibility that the country would undergo an apathetic revolution – a radical transformation which very few people actively supported. In his end-of-year review of 1975 the editor of *The*

Times, William Rees-Mogg, reflected, 'The threat is not so much of successful frontal assault as of being compelled by slow degrees to surrender the values of toleration, truncate the formal procedures of justice and abandon the discreet methods of law enforcement appropriate to a free society bonded by consent.'[121] Rees-Mogg was still thinking of the communist threat, but his warnings seem prescient for critics of Thatcherism, almost thirty years after British politics took its decisive turn to the right.

As for John Stonehouse, in his own fashion he had anticipated the trend of the times by resigning from the Labour Party in April 1976 and joining the tiny English National Party. He conducted his own defence in his sixty-eight-day trial for fraud, theft and deception, but was found guilty in August 1976 and sentenced to seven years in jail. Compared to other white-collar criminals then and later, he certainly did not get off lightly. In 1977 he complained of heart trouble, but doctors assumed that his symptoms were psychosomatic. After Stonehouse had suffered the first of several heart attacks his brother appealed to the home secretary for early release. Despite his poor health he was still carrying out duties like lavatory cleaning. In September 1978 officials were aware that there was a good chance of him dying in prison.[122] Yet he was not released until the following year, being smuggled out earlier than advertised in order to avoid the media scrum. In 1981 he married Sheila Buckley, who had been given only a suspended sentence for her part in his various escapades. Meanwhile, a Department of Trade and Industry inquiry had denounced Stonehouse as 'a sophisticated and skilful trickster'.[123] His business career was ruined, and he had no chance of repaying debts estimated at more than £800,000. Like his former parliamentary colleague Jeffrey Archer, Stonehouse tried to recoup his fortunes from fiction-writing, but his thrillers enjoyed only moderate success. He never wrote *Murder by Media*, the book he proposed as an all-out attack on his persecutors.[124] Ironically, his final illness began during a visit to a television studio. When he died in April 1988 *The Times* covered the news as a brief item in one of its inside pages.

ANGER

Let fury have the hour
Anger can be power
Do you know that you can use it?
The Clash, 'Clampdown',
from *London Calling* (1979)

all the talk at the bookstall was about the utter hatred of unions and
strikes etc.: one day, I think this loathing will be channelled into action
Kenneth Williams, *Diaries*, 4 January 1979

I

JUST before 7 p.m. on 27 November 1975 Ross McWhirter was shot dead in the doorway of his home in the prosperous north London suburb of Enfield. He was a soft target, so the liquidation had required minimal planning. Knowing that their victim was inside the house, the killers hid in the garden until Mrs McWhirter arrived home from work. They forced her to open the front door and fired when her husband came out to greet her. Ross McWhirter was hit in the head and chest, and died soon after reaching hospital.

Within a few days the Provisional IRA had claimed responsibility for the murder. In the public reaction outrage was mixed with perplexity. McWhirter (born 1925) was well known throughout Britain, particularly to children, as the co-editor of the *Guinness Book of Records*. With his identical twin brother, Norris, he had appeared every week on the BBC programme *The Record Breakers*. Typically, they would loom up behind the ebullient host, Roy Castle (1932–94), to unleash a torrent of facts and figures concerning world-beating feats of skill or endurance. To juvenile viewers they appeared rather smug, but this hardly explained why either of them should be singled out for a violent death.

Many prominent figures from the worlds of sport and showbusiness had been recruited to woo the voters in the 1975 referendum on EEC membership. But even the celebrities who really cared about the issues at stake regarded their involvement in political controversy as no more than a temporary distraction. The McWhirter twins were very different. Both had been unsuccessful Conservative candidates at general elections in the early 1960s. After the pro-European Edward Heath became leader in 1965 they fell out of love with the party, but they lost none of their fanatical anti-communism. In their eyes even *The Record Breakers* could be regarded as a useful propaganda weapon in the ideological battle. At a time when comprehensive education was allegedly sapping the nation's competitive spirit, the programme preached a message of self-sacrifice in the service of the sporting ideal, exhorting young Britons to 'be the best' and to 'beat the rest'. For Ross and Norris McWhirter, the rest were the representatives of the Soviet Union and its eastern European satellites, currently producing a steady stream of successful Olympic athletes.

But the practical ideas of the McWhirters went beyond the physical reinvigoration of British youth. On 12 June 1975 – just a week after the referendum – they had lunched with the right-wing peer, war hero and former governor general of Australia Lord De L'Isle and Dudley at his home in Kent. The connection had arisen by chance, after Norris McWhirter and De L'Isle had sat next to each other on a plane and mutually mourned Britain's decline over the previous ten years. De L'Isle was delighted to meet a kindred spirit and invited the twins to lunch. Tony Benn and others had taken the referendum result as a symptom of a rightward shift in British politics, but the conclusions drawn by the luncheon party were directly opposite. The result of their deliberations was a decision to call a meeting of fifty prominent people at a London hotel at the end of July.

The list of notables was less glittering than the cast assembled so recently by Britain in Europe; the best-known person to show any interest was the chairman of the England cricket selectors, Alec Bedser (born 1918). The response, though, was encouraging enough for the organisers to start building a new campaigning group, the National Association for Freedom (NAFF). The advantage of NAFF was that it could pose as a respectable libertarian pressure group with no party affiliations. But although membership was open to all, it was unlikely that many Labour activists would be attracted. In the eyes of the McWhirters and their friends the elected British government had already undermined freedom and would make further inroads unless public-spirited people took a stand.

NAFF was just one of many organisations set up to combat the menace of socialism, and the indefatigable McWhirters were active in several of them. For example, they were associated with the myste-rious Unison Committee for Action (founded 1973) and the Anti-Dear Food Campaign. The latter was mainly concerned with keeping Britain out of the EEC; in 1972 Ross McWhirter had even started a legal battle to prevent Britain joining the Community, basing his argument on Magna Carta. He had also chaired a committee to fund the private prosecution of the Young Liberal anti-apartheid campaigner Peter Hain. More recently, he had set up a union-free publishing firm, the Current Affairs Press, which would ensure a flow of information to the public if the more reliable national newspapers were shut down by industrial disputes. In the meantime, the press issued a fortnightly news-sheet, *Majority*, which offered handy hints for aspiring strike-breakers.

In McWhirter's view none of these preparations was alarmist, and he believed that his views were widely shared. 'It's something the press are altogether missing,' he told a journalist. 'You haven't tapped it yet. People are beginning to see there is no end in sight, and they are very, very angry.'[1] For McWhirter, it was an anger which could not find adequate expression through the existing party system – indeed, the behaviour of the major parties only made people feel more aggrieved. *Majority* explained that parliamentary sovereignty was only acceptable 'so long as it is not manipulated, so long as it is decently and honestly run'.[2] If the democratic system could not articulate the views of ordi-nary, law-abiding Britons, freedom-lovers had a duty to associate in non-party organisations in order to press their views on political leaders.

Ultimately, in the interests of freedom, the results of democratic elec-tions might have to be overturned. In the mid-1970s several shady organisations were preparing to take action in the face of impending national emergencies. One such body, Civil Assistance (CA), led by General Sir Walter Walker, who had fought insurgents in Malaya and Borneo, was established as an act of 'self-defence against national suicide'; it improbably claimed 100,000 members in 1974.[3] Orthodox right-wingers were cautious about private armies like CA, which looked just as subversive as the groups they opposed; they also lent themselves to satire in programmes like *The Fall and Rise of Reginald Perrin*, which featured a character who constantly referred to secret paramilitary plans and kept a cache of rusty rifles 'in case the balloon goes up'.[4] Ross McWhirter, however, was glad to collaborate with people like Sir Walter.

It would be a mistake to assume that the extra-parliamentary 'new' right was working in concert. There were political differences, for example, between Sir Walter Walker and Colonel David Stirling (1915–90), who had helped to set up the SAS and was now organising 'apprehensive patriots' for the inevitable fight against the left.[5] But its members did feel that they were working against a common enemy, and they were less inclined than the left to expend their energy in ideological disputes. By the mid-1970s there was a network of individuals and organisations covering specific subjects, which could pool their resources when the crunch came. Thus Lord De L'Isle was something like an extra-parliamentary spokesman on home affairs; Mary Whitehouse was a freelance minister for morality; the monetarist Institute of Economic Affairs (IEA) was an unofficial Treasury; the authors of the *Black Papers* could have staffed a reformed Department of Education; and General Walker would have been delighted to stiffen sinews at the Ministry of Defence.

Ross McWhirter might have been an ideal minister for sport, but he had more lofty ambitions. The movement needed a philosopher-in-chief who would provide it with a manifesto of fundamental principles. Just before his death McWhirter had composed his fifteen-point Charter of Rights and Liberties, which was to be unveiled at the official launch of NAFF on 2 December 1975. Far from derailing the project, by killing McWhirter less than a week before the inaugural meeting the IRA ensured maximum publicity for NAFF. On hearing of McWhirter's death, the MP and *Black Paper* co-editor Dr Rhodes Boyson exclaimed that 'England should be weeping this evening for the death of law and order.'[6] In Parliament, McWhirter's political opponents lined up to deplore his killing; Roy Jenkins described him as 'outspoken and courageous'.

Naturally the most fulsome tributes came from the Conservative side. Margaret Thatcher, who had known McWhirter for more than a decade, acclaimed him as 'one of the finest people of his generation'. Anthony Berry, McWhirter's local MP, said that the assassination had 'added a new dimension of crime and terrorism to this part of the United Kingdom.'[7]* It was a pardonable exaggeration; callous as it was, McWhirter's assassination hardly ranked with the previous year's Birmingham pub bombings. But the sense of outrage was widely shared. NAFF soon had more than 10,000 members.

Ross McWhirter's political activities had made him an inappropriate host for a children's programme on the supposedly impartial BBC, but his role in establishing NAFF hardly explains why the IRA chose him as a target – especially since a successful mission would ensure that the children of mainland Britain joined their parents in hating the Republican cause. The motive arose from McWhirter's decision to offer £50,000 for any information leading to the arrest of IRA operatives currently engaged in a random campaign of violence in London. In its mixture of courage and folly, McWhirter's initiative epitomised the man: he was undaunted by the possibility that he might become a terrorist target, but it was difficult to see how the cash incentive would make London's public and police more vigilant when everyone was already aware of the threat. Probably McWhirter's real purpose was to win wider publicity for his ideas about confining the bombers to their country of origin. At a press conference on 4 November 1975 he proposed that all Irish people should ask special permission to enter or leave the British mainland and produce signed photographs of them-selves whenever they sought to rent a house.[8] Even if such measures were enacted, they were unlikely to be effective against a determined terrorist group. Nevertheless the IRA thought that McWhirter deserved to die in case anyone felt tempted to add to his £50,000 reward.

No bounty ever had to be paid for the apprehension of McWhirter's murderers. They were captured along with two other members of their active service unit on 12 December 1975 after a six-day siege in Balcombe Street, Marylebone. The gang had been involved in a shooting incident in Mayfair, before seizing the house and two hostages. They gave themselves up when they heard on the radio that the SAS was

---

* Berry himself fell victim to Republican terrorists, in the 1984 bombing of Brighton's Grand Hotel.

preparing to take action. Eventually they were charged with a total of ten murders, mostly of people whose deaths could only bring the Republican cause into further discredit. McWhirter was not the only individual they targeted. They also tried to kill Sir Hugh Fraser, who had stood against Heath and Thatcher in the first Conservative leadership ballot earlier in 1975. The bomb planted on his car did explode, killing a renowned cancer specialist who was out walking his dogs.

At his press conference of 4 November Ross McWhirter had suggested that terrorists should be brought under the law of treason, which still carried the death penalty. But it was unlikely that the Balcombe Street gang could be hanged under existing legislation, and McWhirter's allies believed that a Commons vote to restore capital punishment in terrorist cases would be a fitting memorial. However, on 12 December MPs rejected the idea by more than 100 votes, just as they had done the previous year. Whatever they felt about McWhirter himself, on this subject the overwhelming majority of British voters agreed with him. After his death Mrs Thatcher expressed her personal view that 'those who have committed this terrible crime against humanity have forfeited their right to live'.[9] With Mrs Thatcher's encouragement, Rhodes Boyson proposed that the public should be allowed a direct vote on the issue, but this was one referendum the government was unwilling to concede, rightly fearing an inconvenient result. Thatcher did help to establish a Ross McWhirter Foundation to campaign on law and order issues, and in December 1975 the dead man's friends gathered in St Paul's Cathedral for a memorial service, where Lord De L'Isle led the tributes.[10]

Before the end of the 1970s there would be several commemorations of that kind. Republican assassins gradually became more proficient than the bunglers of Balcombe Street, but their choice of targets was no more likely to win public sympathy. In March 1979 – just two days after the parliamentary vote of confidence that brought down Jim Callaghan's Labour government – the Conservative spokesman on Northern Ireland, Airey Neave, was killed by a bomb which detonated underneath his car as he left the underground car park at Westminster. This murder had a triple purpose for the Irish National Liberation Army (INLA) which carried it out. It showed that terrorists could strike even within the precincts of Parliament; it eliminated a politician who had advocated a more vigorous military strategy in Northern Ireland; and, since Neave had masterminded Margaret

Thatcher's leadership campaign in 1975, it signalled to the Opposition leader that her closest allies were in the firing line as the election approached.

However, Neave was a war hero who had escaped from Colditz, so his death increased the sense of anger and defiance among the British public. The next 'spectacular' was the killing of Lord Mountbatten of Burma and three others in his boat off the coast of County Sligo in the Irish Republic. Mountbatten was killed because he was the Queen's cousin; but as the viceroy who had steered India towards independence he could hardly be presented as a symbol of reactionary British colonial rule. While Neave had been important to Mrs Thatcher, for several years Mountbatten had been providing the Prince of Wales with (sometimes dubious) confidential advice.* After being informed of the murder, Prince Charles recorded in his diary an uncharacteristic 'fierce and violent determination to see that something was done about the IRA'.[11] On the same day in August 1979 eighteen British soldiers were murdered by booby-trap bombs at Warrenpoint in South Down near the border with the Republic. This operation was an unequivocal success for the IRA: sixteen of the victims were members of the Parachute Regiment, which had been on duty in Londonderry during 'Bloody Sunday' in January 1972.[12] For people on the mainland, those events had been obscured by many other bloody days, but the Republicans had longer memories.

II

As the reaction to Irish terrorism proved, antipathy to immigrants was not exclusively reserved for blacks and Asians.† But Roy Jenkins was a long-standing opponent of racial discrimination, and although his second spell at the Home Office was generally thankless it did give him the chance to build on his previous record in this sphere. The 1976 Race Relations Act made it much easier for people to take legal action in cases of discrimination, and created a Commission for Racial Equality (CRE) in place of the ineffectual Race Relations Board and Community Relations Commission.[13] The Act reflected considerable political courage – from Jenkins and from his Conservative opposite

* See Chapter 4 below.
† The former Sex Pistol John Lydon (Johnny Rotten) commemorated this discrimination in the title of his autobiography, *No Irish, No Blacks, No Dogs*, Plexus, 1994.

number William Whitelaw, who ensured that few members of his party voted against the measure. This was another subject on which a significant section of the public felt that Parliament had been opposing their wishes, even before the stiffening of the law. Enoch Powell's 1968 prophecy of civil strife in the wake of mass immigration was still a fresh memory, made more vivid by an hysterical press campaign against the Asians who had been forcibly expelled from Uganda in 1972, on the orders of the Sandhurst-trained dictator Idi Amin.

Powell's supporters had no personal affection for Amin, but his action was one which they would have liked to emulate. Instead, the Heath government had announced that it would honour its obligations to British passport holders, and around 27,000 of the expelled Asians were allowed into the country. At that time Powell had included government policy towards the Asians and the EEC in a general indictment, claiming to detect 'in Britain today a rising mood of cold anger, "not loud but deep", against decisions, policies and attitudes of government which ought to reflect the general will and command common consent, but manifestly do not'.[14] His personal pique after Margaret Thatcher's leadership election victory in February 1975 inspired a more direct foray into his favourite field. Addressing a meeting of the right-wing Conservative Monday Club, Powell foresaw 'an England rent by strife, by violence and by division upon a scale for which we have no parallel here and to which no ending that it is pleasant to contemplate can be envisaged'.[15]

Powell's inflammatory outburst was brought to the attention of the director of public prosecutions, who decided that no action could be taken under the existing laws on race relations. In the face of such rhetoric it was easy to forget that immigration had actually been controlled by successive Acts of 1962, 1968 and 1971 – particularly since the two main parties were reluctant to advertise their conscious attempts to restrict immigration on racial grounds. From this perspective, even the relatively progressive 1976 Race Relations Act looks like a mumbled apology to the immigrants who had already settled in Britain and raised families. Certainly that measure did nothing to muzzle Powell and others who thought like him; indeed, the British state seemed more determined than ever to *protect* those who promulgated racist ideas.

Since both Labour and the Conservative Party were afraid to tackle the issue of immigration head on, the main beneficiary of the Ugandan

Asian crisis was the National Front (NF), whose membership jumped to 14,000 in 1973 and reached 20,000 the following year. Since the Front was also anti-European, it had considerable scope for electoral advance at this time. Apart from its obvious attractions to right-wing Conservatives, it also picked up recruits in deprived inner-city areas which were natural territory for Labour. But the NF performed badly in the two general elections of 1974 – a year which also saw a major confrontation between members of the Front and left-wing students in Red Lion Square, central London. Kevin Gately, a Warwick University mathematics student attending his first demonstration, was killed by a blow to the head. It was the first violent death at a political protest in Britain for more than fifty years. Forty-six policemen were injured in the clashes.[16]

Although the police habitually argued that their priorities were to defend freedom of speech and to prevent street battles, their real intention was more aggressive.* The people who turned out to jeer at the NF were mostly members of left-wing groups, and as such were regarded as far more subversive than their racist opponents. In a typical battle in Glasgow on 24 May 1975, around 100 police faced 300 demonstrators, including many local trade unionists. There were sixty-five arrests and many allegations of unnecessary police violence. According to reports, only twelve people attended the planned NF meeting. The contingent included the fascist leader John Kingsley Read, who tried to incite the crowd with Nazi salutes.[17] Even by NF standards, Read was an unpleasant individual. In July 1976, when a Sikh teenager was murdered in Southall, west London, he had quipped, 'One down – a million to go.' As a hunting ground for the Front and its sympathisers, Southall was a natural venue for counter-demonstrations. On 23 April 1979 a thirty-three-year-old schoolteacher, Blair Peach, died there from head injuries administered by members of the Metropolitan Police's Special Patrol Group.

In the medium term the demonstrations probably damaged the NF, since an association with violence was likely to deter individuals who were otherwise attracted by racist policies. But in the mid-1970s the party's prospects looked bright, even after Kingsley Read's defection to establish a breakaway party at the end of 1975. In the Greater

---

* In May 1978 a speaker at the annual conference of the Police Federation claimed that training for riot control had become so intensive and enthusiastic that officers were running the risk of serious injury; *The Times*, 17 May 1978.

London Council (GLC) elections of May 1977 the NF won 120,000
votes – more than it had received from the whole British electorate in
October 1974. It also came third in three parliamentary by-elections
in 1977, including Birmingham Ladywood after a campaign which was
marked by brawls with members of the Socialist Workers Party (SWP).
The Birmingham by-election, held on 18 August, came five days after
fierce clashes in Deptford, south London, where the black and Asian
population was more than 10 per cent and racist candidates had
recently shared almost half the vote in a local election.[18]

The travel writer Jan Morris encountered some Front supporters just
before the Deptford riot. They were 'a clutch of short-cropped youths
in jeans, high boots and spangled leather jackets', singing 'Rule
Britannia' and evidently as keen on football as they were on beating
up 'nig-nogs'. Morris saw them as 'pure riot fodder, a demagogue's
dream, thick as potatoes, gullible as infants, aching for a fight.' These
semi-educated thugs were 'not without courage', Morris acknowledged.
But it is easier to put on a display of bravado in the knowledge that
the 'boys in blue' will fight on your side. At Deptford, for example, it
was estimated that around 3,500 police protected 800 Front supporters
– this despite a recent attempt by the Prince of Wales to improve relations between ethnic minorities and the police in the area.[19] There were
even more police in Southall when Blair Peach was killed. It was reasonable to expect trouble because Scotland Yard had decided to ban two
peaceful anti-racist demonstrations without adequate consultation; the
centre of Southall was cordoned off to ensure that the provocative
marchers could pass through unmolested.[20] Even on the assumption
that the left-wing protestors were just as unsavoury as the Front, this
was a disconcerting situation for anyone who regarded Britain as a
model democratic state in the mid-1970s. The passage of the 1976
Race Relations Act apparently made no difference. The autonomy of
local police forces meant that the Labour government had limited scope
for direct intervention. Even so, the suspicion remained that it would
have been hesitant to take effective action even if its powers had been
more extensive.

On this issue the overwhelming majority of the press sympathised
with the police and the racists. Although marches were deliberately
routed by the NF to cause maximum offence, the left was almost invariably held responsible for the ensuing trouble. After Southall, for example,
the *Daily Telegraph* described 'jeering, spitting demonstrators' hurling

pre-prepared weapons at the police cordons.[21] Yet under any rational interpretation of existing laws the NF marchers were clearly guilty of inciting violence – either by their very presence or by preaching hatred between races. Meanwhile, the arrival of any substantial new group of immigrants in the country was greeted with hysteria in most national newspapers. Even the liberal *Guardian* betrayed anti-immigrant bias in some of its coverage when Asians expelled from Malawi – formerly the British-run Nyasaland – were offered refuge in 1976.[22]

Race-related trouble could erupt without the intrusion of the NF. On 30 August 1976 a riot broke out at the annual Notting Hill carnival – the scene of serious trouble back in 1958 – after the police started to arrest suspected petty criminals. Although recent carnivals had been relatively peaceful, there had been ominous signs of rising tension between the London police and ethnic minorities. In July 1975, for example, plainclothes police were attacked in Brixton when they jumped out of an unmarked car to arrest a black youth. Reports in the popular press suggested that Brixton and other areas of south London were slipping out of police control. The 1975 carnival had produced very mixed reports. A local newspaper contained one account which boasted that there had been 'No arrests, no violent scenes . . . Pleasant smiles and good manners are the order of the day. It was the happy face of a people of great pride in themselves and their culture.'[23] But the numbers attending were estimated at up to 120,000 at their peak, and Notting Hill was not really suitable for such a crowd, given the very relaxed attitude of the organisers. A senior police officer gave a more pessimistic account of the 1975 carnival, reporting that 'The whole weekend was noisy, disorganised and potentially explosive.' The black revellers had intruded into 'an alien area whose inhabitants are not sympathetic to either the manner or cause of celebration'. Many local residents were indeed alarmed by the increasing size of the carnival and the criminal elements who inevitably homed in on the larger crowds. At a public meeting a local clergyman also complained that he had seen a couple 'fornicating under the bedroom window.'[24]

For the police, Notting Hill was now seen as an appropriate place for a show of strength to reassure the public that the ethnic minorities would be brought under control. Police numbers at the carnival grew from 200 in 1975 to 1,600 the following year. The chief constable of the Metropolitan Police, Sir Robert Mark, later claimed that this increase was nothing out of the ordinary. On his own account, indeed, law enforcement was still grossly inadequate, because the 1976 carnival

turned out to be 'like nothing so much as a return to the sordid celebrations attending the hangings at Tyburn Tree'. This evocative
comparison revealed Mark's antipathy towards the very idea of the
carnival, peaceful or not. He went on to claim that an early form of
political correctness meant that 'no one is prepared to tell the simple
truth when wrongdoing involves coloured people'.[25] This was a breathtaking assertion at a time when even respected newspapers invariably
focused on the ethnicity of blacks and Asians involved in crime, while
violence and intimidation against members of the ethnic minorities
went virtually unreported.

Mark's attitude shows that senior police were unable to distinguish
between people who attended the carnival with criminal intentions and
those who wanted to enjoy themselves but already felt alienated from
a police force which condoned racism. A modicum of sensitivity in
policing would have kept these groups apart. As it was, they found a
common cause. More than 450 people were injured during the 1976
Notting Hill riot, and there were fifty-six arrests. Although the protagonists in the battle with police were predominantly black, some white
youths tried to help them. Two members of the obscure London band
The Clash, Paul Simonon and Joe Strummer (born John Mellor, the
son of a clerk in the Foreign Office) were caught up in the riot unwit-
tingly. But they soon entered into the spirit, throwing various missiles
at the police and trying to set a car on fire before retreating when they
encountered the hardcore rioters. The song 'White Riot', which was
included on their band's debut album, expressed regret that white people
had not been able to take a full part in the proceedings.[26]

Another, much more prominent rock musician took a very different
view after the riot. Eric Clapton interrupted a concert in Birmingham
– heartland of the Powellites – to announce that Enoch had been right
after all, and that Britain was now 'overcrowded'. Clapton's outburst
provoked the formation of Rock against Racism (RAR), which was
soon joined in the fight for racial tolerance by the Anti-Nazi League
(ANL). In April 1978 an estimated 70,000 music fans marched from
Trafalgar Square to Hackney, in the key NF territory of east London,
for an RAR concert. The Clash – now widely regarded as the main
mouthpiece of the punk generation after the break-up of the Sex Pistols
in January – gave a memorable, committed performance which should
have laid to rest any ambiguity about the lyrics of 'White Riot'.
However, the playful imagery of punk had helped to make the swastika

respectable to a new generation of young people, and it was possible
to enjoy the songs while distorting their intended message.

According to the black union official and later Labour MP Bernie
Grant, the Anti-Nazi League 'forced the fascists off the streets'.[27] This
might have been true in the north-London area of Tottenham, where
Grant lived, but to neutralise the Front on a national scale required the
intervention of an organisation whose motives were very different from
the colour-blind idealism of the ANL or RAR. Reviewing the recent
activities and future prospects of the NF in 1978, one historian thought
that 'if the country seemed to be heading for really alarming chaos and
the Conservative Party threw up a strong leader promising order and
national revival – a de Gaulle – the kind of people who join the NF
would probably rally to *his* lead'.[28] In fact, the current leader of the
Conservative Party was a woman who felt that she was in touch with
public concern on the race issue. Interviewed on ITV's *World in Action*
in January 1978, Margaret Thatcher confided that 'people are really
rather afraid that this country might be rather swamped by people with
a different culture. And, you know, the British character has done so
much for democracy, for law, and done so much throughout the world,
that if there is any fear that it might be swamped, people are going to
react and be rather hostile to those coming in.' She was rewarded with
10,000 congratulatory letters, and in March the Conservatives won the
Labour seat of Ilford North in a key by-election.[29]

III

Despite her robust rhetoric on immigration, Mrs Thatcher still had her
critics on the far right. She offered NAFF – now renamed the Freedom
Association – a public endorsement by attending its first fund-raising
dinner in January 1977. The 500 guests returned the compliment with
a standing ovation. Ross McWhirter's Charter, which attacked 'unnecessary and confiscatory taxation' and proclaimed the 'Freedom to engage
in private enterprise', read like a Thatcherite wish list. But even in
April 1978 – after the 'swamped' remarks – a speaker at a Freedom
Association meeting claimed that Thatcher had been 'got at by the
trendy liberals in the [Conservative] Party'.[30] The chief concern was
that these do-gooders would prevent her from coming to grips with
the trade unions. In the last month of his life Ross McWhirter had
named Thatcher's employment spokesman James Prior in a list of

'political failures' who were nevertheless providing enough internal opposition to thwart her radical intentions.[31] Prior, and others who remained loyal to Edward Heath's 'consensual' approach towards industrial relations, agreed that the unions had to be reformed but advocated a gradualist approach.

In an essay published in 1977 the journalist Peregrine Worsthorne explained both the success and the current unpopularity of the British trade union movement. 'Unlike the leaders of every other institution in Britain,' he wrote, 'they, and they alone, have a clear sense of their own value and an unshaken faith in their own function.'[32] Union leaders like Joe Gormley (Mineworkers), Jack Jones (Transport and General Workers) and Hugh Scanlon (Engineers) seemed more powerful than the country's elected politicians and were obviously conscious of their influence. The interminable debates at the annual conference of the Trade Union Congress (TUC) ate into the television schedules by day, and preoccupied media commentators every evening. Deals were cut in 'smoke-filled rooms', while anxious politicians paced the floor outside. When the verdicts were unfavourable, governments tottered and fell. Edward Heath and his ministers had thought that the union leaders would acquiesce in their Industrial Relations Act (1971), but it was resisted and the miners claimed Heath's scalp in February 1974.* The incoming Labour government negotiated a 'Social Contract' in an attempt to secure amity in the workplace, but at best this was a truce rather than a final settlement. Infuriated Conservative supporters regarded it as a capitulation to Britain's true masters.

The TUC certainly had numbers on its side. In 1977 there was an affiliated membership of 11.5 million, and the tally was still rising. Of the total British workforce, about half were union members. Conservative critics emphasised the financial leverage enjoyed by the unions over the Labour Party; after the general election of October 1974 129 Labour MPs were sponsored by various unions. But when the Conservatives were in office from 1970 to 1974 Labour's parliamentary representatives were an irrelevance, sponsored or not. The trade unions beyond Westminster had provided the real political opposition.

---

* This outcome was anticipated in the lyrics of a successful 1973 pop single, 'Part of the Union' by the Strawbs – an unusual example of a protest song with a right-wing message. It included the lines, 'So though I'm a working man/I can ruin the government's plan'.

Peregrine Worsthorne believed that the trade union problem was so bad in Britain because the potential sources of opposition were uniquely ineffectual. In particular he claimed that the British middle class was 'much too nice' to take any direct action against the unions. In most other European countries, he wrote, 'management is backed by a middle class no less prone to explosions of militant anger, no more reluctant to take to the streets – yes, and to the barricades too, if necessary – than are the workers.'[33] 'Much too nice' was unduly flattering; more accurately, a residual feeling of deference meant that most representatives of the British middle classes were reluctant to engage in direct action on their own behalf. But they were increasingly content to look the other way if others took the initiative. If Worsthorne had investigated the situation more carefully he would have discovered that inhibitions were being eroded. As early as February 1975 the Thatcherite Tory MP John Gorst warned that the middle class would 'spontaneously combine and spontaneously erupt' if pushed too far by Labour tax increases. His remarks came just a few weeks after a lengthy *Times* editorial entitled 'The Anger of the Middle Class'.[34] In 1977 Patrick Hutber, a former Labour supporter who was now City editor of the *Sunday Telegraph*, asked a friend if he had any ideas for inclusion in a book of practical advice for the middle class. 'How to board up the windows and erect a barbed-wire barricade,' was the reply.[35]

In his counter-revolutionary handbook *The Decline and Fall of the Middle Class* Hutber conceded that this was a minority viewpoint. Like Worsthorne, he noted that the British in general were 'very slow to anger', but for his own part, he saw no reason as yet to give up on the democratic process. He was still optimistic about the Conservative Party under Mrs Thatcher's leadership. If the middle class kept up the pressure, it could hope for favourable measures when the Conservatives returned to power; the next government might even include a minister for the middle class. But it would be wrong to await the next general election in passivity. As a first step the middle class should employ accountants – not, of course, to practise illegal tax evasion but rather to ensure that they were not paying more than their true liabilities. Having defended themselves against the rapacious Treasury, they could move on to the offensive by campaigning on specific issues. For example, doctors could resign en masse from the National Health Service.[36] Others were even more outspoken. In June 1975 the National Federation of the Self-Employed threatened to withhold VAT payments, in order to strike back against a government which persecuted them because they were successful.[37]

Even at a time when traditional social boundaries were blurring, Lord de L'Isle was an unlikely champion of the middle class. His family tree included such non-bourgeois notables as the poet Sir Philip Sidney, Queen Elizabeth I's favourite the Earl of Leicester and an illegitimate child of William IV. But most of his colleagues in the Freedom Association, like Norris McWhirter, were recognisably bourgeois; and the organisation as a whole broadly shared Hutber's aims and outlook. Despite an occasional expression of impatience with Mrs Thatcher, the Freedom Association accepted that the Conservative Party looked more promising than it had done under Heath. It claimed that 'some 100 or more Tory MPs support our objectives' – a significant figure if true, since Mrs Thatcher won the backing of only 140 of her colleagues on the second and decisive leadership ballot in February 1975.[38] But the association also agreed that it was a mistake to sit back and wait for a general election, since it believed Labour was still capable of doing significant long-term damage to the national interest.

Although the Freedom Association believed that most of the Establishment was irretrievably lost to 'pink socialism', there was one institution which retained its confidence. Ross and Norris McWhirter had been familiar figures in courts of law since the early 1950s. Apart from their attempted use of Magna Carta to prevent EEC membership, over the years the McWhirters had brought cases against two home secretaries, the television authorities, trade union officials and the London Borough of Enfield. The letter of the law had favoured the unions ever since the 1906 Trades Disputes Act, but there was always a chance that a maverick judge would reach idiosyncratic conclusions if a suitable test case could be found. This kind of activity cost money, but the Freedom Association had attracted financial support from several business organisations, so it had much deeper pockets than the unassisted twins.

An opportunity arose in a dispute over union recognition at Grunwick, an obscure photo-processing plant in Willesden, north London. In August 1976, 137 workers – a third of the employees – were sacked after going on strike for the right to join the clerical union APEX. They won support from several local unions, and in November 1976 sympathetic postal workers became involved. This was a crisis for the management: without a reliable delivery service, the mail-order business would be strangled at a time of peak demand from returning holidaymakers laden with their Kodak Instamatics. The managing director of Grunwick, George Ward, was the kind of small businessman who appealed to the Freedom Association – he had worked his way up from the most unpromising origins, was well versed in the techniques of accountancy, and had no shortage of fighting spirit. When Ward started a High Court action against the postal union, the Freedom Association provided financial backing; later its members arrived in person to make sure that the post got through, following the late Ross McWhirter's advice by modelling themselves on the affluent activists who had helped to break the General Strike of 1926.

In the summer of 1977 Grunwick became one of the best-known firms in Britain. The media's interest was certainly not dampened by the fact that much of the workforce consisted of West Indians and Asians who had arrived in Britain via East Africa – like the Ugandan Asians. Ward himself had been born in India, though he was hardly a sprig of the colonial Establishment. His acquaintance with the subcontinent probably made him more aware that Asians were usually reliable workers, even for relatively low pay. The temperatures of the 1976 British summer were nothing new to them either. But many of his staff were students who objected to the working conditions and were confident and eloquent enough to act on their grievances. It was a sign that generational change was beginning to affect the established Asian population, at a time when white Britons were increasingly receptive to racist agitation.

Grunwick thus raised several complex and potentially explosive issues, and was treacherous territory for orthodox politicians. Yet the involvement of a powerful trade union with close links to the Labour Party created further complications. In May 1977 four APEX-sponsored Labour MPs, including the Secretary of State for Education, Shirley Williams, made sympathetic visits to the Grunwick picket line. The following month Jack Dromey, a local union activist, called for mass picketing of the plant. The response ensured a prominent place in the news bulletins for Grunwick, despite rival media attractions in the month of the Jubilee and the Sex Pistols. On 11 July nearly 20,000 pickets arrived from all over Britain, faced by 3,500 police. But although the numbers favoured the unions that day, they had already lost the battle for public opinion. During clashes on 23 June a policeman, Trevor Wilson, was struck by a bottle and knocked unconscious. The media seized on the image of the prostrate law enforcer with blood pouring from a head wound. At the time and even thirty years later allegations of brutality were levelled at both police and pickets. One senior officer is said to have remarked that the clashes were trivial compared to an average Saturday on the terraces at Arsenal Football Club. But the image of PC Wilson made the police look like plucky underdogs confronted by a revolutionary mob. In the climate of the mid-1970s this was enough for a majority of voters to cut through the complex and conflicting arguments about the right of a company to manage and the right of workers to join a union.[39] Mrs Thatcher's ideological ally Sir Keith Joseph proclaimed that 'The siege has suddenly shown us how far we have drifted, how far power in the Labour Party and unions has slipped into the hands of the authoritarians, the total-itarians, the men of violence for whom law and order are dispensable.'[40]

The troubles at Grunwick long outlasted the summer heat and the Jubilee celebrations. On 7 November 1977 more than 200 pickets were injured in new battles with the police. By that time the government's conciliation service, ACAS, and a court of inquiry under Lord Justice Scarman, had both found that the original strikers were more sinned against than sinning.[41] But the Labour government was deeply embar-rassed by the affair, and (more importantly) so were many union leaders. Ministers clearly hoped that George Ward would quietly capit-ulate, but stiffened by support from the Freedom Association he refused to do so. The Appeal Court made a ruling in his favour in July 1977, and before the end of the year this had been upheld by the House of Lords.

Despite these legal setbacks, the unions dragged out the dispute until July 1978. The right-wing historian Richard Clutterbuck thought that Grunwick left extremists on both sides looking 'nasty and stupid'.[42] This was a charitable judgement. If the press were to be believed, only one group of 'extremists' had been involved. Inevitably, Sir Robert Mark condemned 'the disgraceful behaviour' of left-wing activists at Grunwick, making no mention of the finely balanced issues at stake and congratulating George Ward for standing up against 'politically motivated violence'.[43] And the chief losers had actually been the advo-cates of industrial harmony. Having sided with the strikers, ACAS, which was supposed to prevent disputes from escalating, was terribly compromised. Shirley Williams would constantly be reminded of her visit to the Grunwick picket line, even after she had helped to found

the ultra-moderate SDP in 1981. Labour was supposedly on the side
of the workers, but when it came to a head-on collision almost all of
its MPs buried theirs in the sand. The government's agents, the police,
had been more proactive. They had suffered verbal and physical abuse,
but had not held back from retaliating in the same kind. After Grunwick
it was clear that they would be as willing to protect strike-breakers as
they were to defend the racist National Front.

IV

In November 1977, with the Grunwick dispute still at boiling point,
the BBC unveiled a new sitcom. *Citizen Smith* marked the television
debut of John Sullivan, whose next project, *Only Fools and Horses*,
made a more lasting impression. But *Citizen Smith* certainly had its
memorable moments. The episodes showed the central character, Wolfie
Smith, plotting the downfall of the capitalist system with his minuscule Tooting Popular Front. In the agitated context of the time the
programme was slightly surreal. In contrast to the fears of people like
Lord Chalfont and General Sir Walter Walker, it suggested that revolutionary posturing was harmless; the 'respectable' father of Wolfie's
girlfriend was concerned about the young man's attitude to work more
than any possibility of a proletarian uprising. At the same time, though,
there was little chance that the audience would sympathise with Wolfie's
ideas and objectives. This was a telling contrast to the general response
evoked by *Till Death Us Do Part*, a sitcom with a more serious satirical purpose which came to the end of its ten-year run in 1975. The
author, Johnnie Speight, had hoped to make racism look ridiculous
through his main character, the loud-mouthed working-class boor Alf
Garnett. Instead, Garnett's poisonous pronouncements about 'darkies'
had been widely regarded as profound social insights.

Wolfie Smith bore scant resemblance to Arthur Scargill, a union
agitator who was already one of the best-known figures on the British
left in the mid-1970s. Scargill's Marxism was not the product of youthful
rebellion; if anything he was less radical than his father, Harold, who
was a lifelong member of the Communist Party and rarely wavered
from the line laid down by Moscow. Arthur (born 1938) had a spell
in the Young Communist League but never joined the party himself.
He did follow Harold by starting work in the Yorkshire coalfields
straight from school, at fifteen. He was soon heavily involved in union

affairs, although at first he was frustrated by the moderation of Yorkshire leaders. By the end of the 1960s, however, the mood had become more militant and Scargill – a natural media performer – was often asked to explain his union's position on local television. He became a national figure during the coal strike of 1972, when he brought several hundred Yorkshire miners down to Saltley Gate, a well-stocked coke depot in Birmingham. Contrary to subsequent mythology the demonstration by these 'flying pickets' was largely peaceful – only thirty people were injured, including sixteen police, although Scargill himself was one of 180 pickets arrested.[44] But after less than a week of picketing the police were overwhelmed by numbers and decided to close the depot. This was seen as the decisive episode in the strike. The Heath government had already called a state of emergency, and the dispute was settled on the miners' terms within a few days of Scargill's triumph.

After Saltley Gate no picket line seemed complete without Scargill's hectoring presence, loudhailer in hand. In addition to his organisational skills he had a relentless, finger-jabbing style of oratory which no contemporary Labour politician could match. In May 1973, at the age of thirty-five, Scargill became president of the Yorkshire NUM in time to play a full part in the next miners' dispute, which helped bring down the Heath government. This time there was no need for a prolonged picketing campaign thanks to the helpful intervention of the Arab oil producers. Scargill's next battle honours were gained at Grunwick, where he led another large contingent of Yorkshire miners in solidarity with the strikers. In June 1977 he was arrested and charged with obstructing the highway outside the Grunwick plant but was subsequently cleared of the charges.

Scargill and the miners played no part in the industrial strife which discredited the Labour government in the winter of 1978–9. This infamous episode mainly involved low-paid public sector workers, whose relative living standards were declining at a time of government-imposed pay restraint. According to one lurid account, a strike by lorry drivers 'emptied the shelves in supermarkets while food rotted in the docks . . . Pigs, which will eat each other when nothing else is available, were reported to be resorting to cannibalism.'[45] Meanwhile, action by local government workers affected essential services like road gritting and rubbish collection. The most notorious incident, however, was grossly exaggerated by the right-wing press. A gravediggers strike in Liverpool meant that bodies went unburied, but the dispute only lasted a few days and involved a mere handful of workers. Much more serious was the picketing of some hospitals, causing delays even in vital surgical procedures. At its height the disruption involved almost a fifth of the British workforce; more working days were lost to industrial action than in any year since 1926. More than a quarter of a century later the episode could still induce hyperbolic reminiscences from right-wing columnists. In November 2006 one of them wrote that 'Britain was one big, open-air skip, carpeted in chicken carcasses, rotting vegetables and assorted household detritus.'[46]

The Conservative victory at the subsequent general election could be seen as both a challenge and an opportunity for the radical left. On the one hand, there was every reason to expect that Mrs Thatcher would try to succeed where Heath had failed, introducing tough legislation to curb union power and ensuring that it was fully implemented. However, at least this simplified the long-expected confrontation. Thatcher, it was argued, represented the true face of capitalism, whereas Heath and other 'one nation' Conservatives had thrown up a conciliatory smokescreen. Furthermore, as Labour returned to opposition it was demoralised after five difficult years when it had been in office but unable to exercise real authority. It had won four out of the last five general elections but had never really looked like a natural party of government. An inquest was inevitable, and so were its conclusions. The parliamentary party had failed the labour movement. There would have to be a new direction under a very different kind of leadership. Party members in constituency organisations and affiliated trade unions should enjoy much more influence over policy and personnel. At the 1979 Labour Party conference it was agreed that MPs should be subject to mandatory reselection by their members. The following year the conference voted in favour of unilateral nuclear disarmament and for withdrawal from the EC without a further referendum. An electoral college for choosing the party leader was not finalised until January 1981, but when the complicated system was settled it gave another boost to the radicals by handing the biggest say to the unions. This was the signal for Roy Jenkins, Shirley Williams, David Owen and Bill Rodgers to announce their defection from Labour and the establishment of a Council for Social Democracy, which became the Social Democratic Party (SDP) on 26 March 1981.

The emergence of the SDP created new schisms among those who regarded themselves as being on the left of British politics, although in many cases it merely allowed people who had hated each other for years to express their unfraternal feelings in public; and while they were not abusing the defectors, the remaining Labour loyalists sniped at each other. The former chancellor Denis Healey, who stayed within the fold, had been heckled savagely at the 1976 party conference as he explained the terms on which the government would negotiate with the IMF. In normal times Healey would have been the obvious candidate to succeed James Callaghan as party leader after the 1979 defeat. But as a former communist he had been regarded as a traitor on the left long before his tenure of the Treasury, while his inability to suffer fools caused resentment even among Labour's moderates. Callaghan resigned from the Labour leadership in October 1980, ensuring that his successor would be chosen by MPs rather than a reformed electoral college. But even within this narrow constituency too many people hated Healey. He won the first ballot – held on the day that Ronald Reagan became US president – but was overhauled in the final round by Michael Foot (born 1913), a romantic radical who had fought for party unity throughout the last difficult decade.

Unfortunately for Foot and his party, he proved an easy target for the right-wing press. He was sixty-seven years old at the time of his election and had neither the appearance nor the track record of an aspiring prime minister. According to one of his least reverential parliamentary colleagues, Foot 'epitomised and compounded all the problems of a party coming to be regarded as old, out of touch and irrelevant'.[47] He did his best to restore some unity among his colleagues but lacked the necessary personal authority. Probably in the early 1980s the task would have been beyond any Labour leader. The extent of the remaining divisions was cruelly exposed in September 1981, when Tony Benn challenged Healey for the deputy leadership of the party. This time the ballot was conducted under the complex new rules, which gave the unions 40 per cent of the vote while MPs and the constituency parties each had 30 per cent. This was still a long way from giving every member of the party an equal say – the formula favoured by Roy Jenkins and his allies – and while the influence of the union block vote was an affront to democracy, MPs were still over-represented. On this first occasion their input proved equally decisive and divisive. Healey scraped through on the second ballot – by 50.426 per cent to Benn's 49.547. Several figures associated with the left, including the young

Welsh MP Neil Kinnock, abstained in the vote, while others who supported Healey were on the verge of leaving the party for the SDP. Kinnock was branded a traitor, and some embittered delegates jostled and spat at him. Never one to shirk a physical or verbal confrontation, Kinnock had a public shouting match at the conference with Benn's friend and supporter Arthur Scargill.[48]

Three months after Healey's pyrrhic victory there was another crucial contest, which produced a more clear-cut verdict. Arthur Scargill was elected president of the National Union of Mineworkers, with 70 per cent of the vote. The NUM had already shown that it could be as effective against Margaret Thatcher as it had been against Edward Heath. In February 1981 the government had abandoned plans to close more than twenty pits on economic grounds, after the NUM threatened to call a ballot which seemed certain to authorise strike action. It was a humiliating climbdown. But, as Mrs Thatcher noted in her memoirs, 'it was really only a question of time' before a more decisive encounter.[49]

V

Despite Labour's problems after 1979, life was difficult enough for the Conservatives. They had divisions of their own; and if Foot was seen as an electoral liability even by many of his supporters, Mrs Thatcher soon became the most unpopular prime minister since polling began. In December 1981 she had the approval of only a quarter of voters, and no more than 12 per cent thought that the Conservatives would win the next election.

The negative attitude to Mrs Thatcher reflected more than disapproval. The feeling against her was unprecedented in its depth and longevity as well as its extent.* Mass unemployment was the main reason. At the Conservative conference of 1975 Thatcher had attacked those who accused her of wanting unemployment to rise, declaring

---

* The ill feeling was crystallised before Thatcher left office in Elvis Costello's song 'Tramp the Dirt Down' (1989), which looked forward to a time when the singer could pay an unfriendly visit to the prime minister's grave. In the same year Morrissey, the morose Mancunian ex-lead singer of The Smiths, chipped in with 'Margaret on the Guillotine'. In July 2002 a theatre producer attacked a £150,000 statue of Thatcher with a cricket bat, before decapitating it with a metal bar. Afterwards he said that it looked better in its headless condition; it certainly assumed a more classical look. Nevertheless, the assailant was jailed for three months.

that 'We hate the idea of men and women not being able to use their abilities. We deplore the waste of natural resources. We deplore the deep affront to people's dignity from being out of work through no fault of their own.'[50] Her message was prudent at a time of widespread anger against a Labour government which had been forced to take action against inflation at the inevitable expense of jobs. A Right to Work demonstration was held in Feburary/March 1976, with ninety people setting off from Manchester for a final mass rally in London. Before the marchers reached their destination there was a misunderstanding with police – one of a suspicious number of such incidents at that time. More than forty people were arrested after the clashes. That march took place when unemployment was just over one million, which was considered to be unacceptable in 1976. When the Conservatives came back to power they inherited an unemployment tally of 1.3 million, the kind of rate for which, Thatcher complained, her party would have been 'drummed out of office'. In September 1982, after three years of Tory rule, the total exceeded three million.

These figures were bad enough, and Mrs Thatcher would have been disliked whatever her reaction to the relentless rise. But her offence was compounded because in office Thatcher treated unemployment as a political embarrassment for which she bore no personal responsibility, rather than showing compassion, regret or understanding for individual cases. In opposition Thatcher had developed the argument that the unemployed had brought their plight on themselves, either by 'pricing themselves out of jobs' or by lacking the initiative to acquire marketable skills. Norman Tebbit's speech to the 1981 Conservative Party conference, when he compared the unemployed to his father who had 'got on his bike and looked for work' in the 1930s, was an invaluable supplement to his leader's rhetoric. Unlike Tebbit Senior, Mrs Thatcher's grocer father had never had to uproot or retrain in order to support his family.

Just before his death in January 1981 the political economist Andrew Shonfield dismissed the idea that Britain was 'in a situation of suppressed civil war'. But he thought that the Thatcher government was taking a risk by proceeding with its tough economic policies 'as if there were no possibility of violent opposition'.[51] Within a few months of Shonfield's death it looked as if such complacency had been based on a disastrous miscalculation. The inner-city riots which broke out in many parts of England during the summer of 1981 have often been explained as a reaction to unemployment, even by those who have no intention of excusing the disorder. The most popular music of the time conveys the same message. 'Ghost Town', by the Coventry band the Specials, is usually regarded as the soundtrack to the riots. The lyrics were certainly apposite when the single was released in the summer of 1981: 'Government leaving the youth on the shelf . . . No job to be found in this country . . . The people getting angry'. But the record had actually been cut early in the year, and the group's main concern had been violence at its own concerts. Even this phenomenon could be linked to high unemployment, or at least the prospect of lives blighted by economic deprivation; it was in the gloom of the mid-1970s that concerts began to be associated with fighting rather than drug-induced lovemaking.

The Specials were particularly sensitive to racially motivated violence, and their music had a cross-cultural flavour which was deliberately designed to transcend social divisions. Nevertheless, the Specials and similar ska-inspired bands such as Madness attracted shaven-headed racist followers. Sociologists could explain that such people only turned against immigrants because they were also victims of economic malaise who felt that their residual status was threatened. But this was scarcely a comfort when individual band members were beaten up and the National Front planned marches to coincide with their concerts. The Specials disbanded soon after 'Ghost Town' had climbed to the top of the charts. As it descended, another notable political song was still rising. 'One in Ten', by the Birmingham band UB40, ranged beyond unemployment in its diagnosis of society's ills. But the name of the group commemorated a bureaucratic form which was familiar to anyone on the dole at the time.

July 1981 was a surreal month. On the 29th – with the warnings of 'Ghost Town' still resonating from their radios – more than 28 million Britons suspended reality in order to watch the 'fairytale' wedding of the Prince of Wales and Diana Spencer. The ceremony at St Paul's Cathedral consummated the nation's love affair with the bashful bride. Just a few days earlier Ian Botham's batting had brought England's crick-eters from the verge of a crushing defeat in the third Test match of that year's Ashes series; then he and Bob Willis bowled the team to a stun-ning victory. At any other time the British (and the English in particular) would have been given a lasting fillip by these events. But they could never be more than temporary distractions. Charles and Di were unlikely to be married twice – at least not to each other – and it was hardly more probable that anyone would ever emulate Botham's heroics at Headingley. On the other hand, at the end of July 1981 it was easy to predict that riots would become a regular feature of English life.

The worst rioting was a response to heavy-handed policing. On 2 April 1980 a precedent had been established in a very different St Pauls – in this case not a cathedral packed with prosperous members of the Establishment but rather a run-down district of Bristol with a substantial immigrant population. The police had raided the evocatively named Black and White cafe on Grosvenor Road, in search of drug dealers. This action triggered off a four-hour confrontation with local residents, mostly black. Although police reinforcements were called in, the chief constable ordered a temporary withdrawal. The result was 'a night of looting and destruction as extensive as anything seen for two centuries'.[52]

The Bristol riot stunned Britain for a few days, but the trouble did not spread and even the home secretary, Willie Whitelaw, began to think that it was an isolated incident. Yet almost exactly a year later, on 10 April 1981, a sustained period of rising tension in Brixton erupted into a full-scale riot, after a police officer had tried to help the victim of a knife attack. The police had been clamping down on petty crime in an initiative called Swamp 81 (a tactless echo of Mrs Thatcher's 1978 interview on immigration). Within a week, a thousand residents – mainly black – had been stopped and searched by the police. This seemed to confirm the long-established suspicion among locals that the police were repressive intruders on community life rather than a protective force. In their 1979 album *London Calling* The Clash had anticipated a police assault on Brixton, and urged local people to retaliate with firearms. The situation did not deteriorate to this extent in April 1981, but for the first time in Britain Molotov cocktails were thrown. The disorder resulted in more than 300 injuries, many to the police; cars were set on fire, and properties were looted and burned.

There were further clashes between youths and police in April, while Lord Scarman inquired into the Brixton riots at Whitelaw's invitation. The other April outbreaks, mostly connected with fairs in various parts of London, were barely reported by the media. This was a rare example of responsibility, taking account of the danger that 'copy-cat' riots might spread further. But the media also failed to give adequate coverage to a rash of racist attacks throughout 1981, beginning with a suspicious fire at 439 New Cross Road on 18 January. Thirteen black people celebrating a birthday died in the flames. The incident occurred close to the scene of fighting between the National Front and anti-racists in August 1977. It was natural to suspect arson, but the police seemed anxious to exclude this possibility. More than 10,000 people marched in protest against the dilatory investigation, but even this demonstration was scarcely reported. Arguably, the blanket of media silence could be justified as an attempt to counter the possibility of racial violence on a greater scale. However, in the context of an overprotective attitude towards NF marchers, it was possible to argue that the forces of law and order were trying to provoke such a confrontation, and that the 'free press' was conspiring to ensure that immigrant communities would be viewed as aggressors rather than victims.

Surveying this evidence, some communities drew the conclusion that they would have to take the law into their own hands whenever they felt under attack. On 3 July 1981 there was a riot in Southall, London, where Blair Peach had been killed two years before. Several hundred skinheads, some of them carrying NF banners, arrived to hear one of their favourite bands. Their behaviour brought a violent reaction from locals, predominantly Asian. Barricades were erected – a sure sign that the rioters expected the police to turn on them rather than confront the provocative outsiders. The Hamborough Tavern, where the concert would have taken place, was burned down.

On the following evening rioting began in another area with a large immigrant population. Now the trouble had spread northward, to the Toxteth district of Liverpool, where unemployment among the black population was 60 per cent. The trouble caught police by surprise, and it took four days to bring the situation under a semblance of control. More than a hundred buildings were destroyed and almost 800 police injured in the clashes. Hard-pressed police used CS gas for the first time on the British mainland. Their inexperience, and the use of the wrong kind of gas canisters, caused injuries among protestors. The incident was followed by two nights of trouble at Moss Side, Manchester, centred on the police station, which was regarded by many locals as a citadel of NF sympathisers.

The initial riots all had a flashpoint of one kind or another, and were linked to real or perceived racial discrimination. To be black or Asian *and* unemployed was to be at two removes from what counted as 'respectability' in the Britain of 1981 – and doubled your chances of being treated as such by the forces which policed that society. But what happened afterwards could not be explained so easily. Trouble reportedly affected the London areas of Battersea, Dalston, Streatham, Walthamstow and Brixton (again); parts of Birmingham, Leeds and Leicester; Ellesmere Port, Luton, Sheffield, Portsmouth, Preston, Newcastle upon Tyne, Derby, Southampton, Cirencester, Nottingham, Hull, Slough, Keswick, High Wycombe, Bedford, Edinburgh, Wolverhampton, Stockport, Blackburn, Bolton, Huddersfield, Halifax, Reading, Chester, Cardiff and Aldershot. Some of these places contained sizeable ethnic minorities and pockets of unemployment which far exceeded the high and rising national level, but many of the rioters were not motivated by discrimination, deprivation or any other specific grievance. For some, the clashes with police offered an opportunity for looting, to satisfy their greed. Others, echoing the now-defunct Sex Pistols, were angry because they were bored. Clearly they would not have acted as they did in the summer of 1981 without some feeling of alienation from their communities. But this sense had not suddenly sprung up after 1979. It had been developing for several years, and only needed the stimulus of a practical precedent to provide an outlet.

Among other things, the riots exposed the fragmentation of the British Establishment. The instant appointment of the liberal-minded Scarman to examine the causes showed that Whitelaw and the Home Office wanted a thorough investigation rather than a one-sided report which would exonerate the police. Michael Heseltine, the environment secretary, undertook a first-hand inquiry in Merseyside; his findings, reported to cabinet in a lengthy minute entitled 'It Took a Riot', confirmed Mrs Thatcher's existing suspicions of her attention-seeking colleague. Among other things, Heseltine's minute included a barely coded appeal to 'the traditions of social justice and national even-handedness on which our party prides itself'.[53] These were decidedly *not* the elements of Conservatism that Mrs Thatcher was keen to perpetuate. For her own part, the prime minister was quick to claim that the rioters could not be justified by any circumstances. On one level she lost the argument, because the Scarman report did inspire a more sensitive approach to policing in difficult areas. Fire-breathing commanders like James Anderton of Greater Manchester were less likely to win promotion in future. But there was no concerted attempt to root out racism from British police forces; and whatever one thought of the activities which had produced the clampdown on black and Asian areas, no one could reasonably dispute the claim that police powers had been exercised with excessive gusto when the suspected offender was not white.

While changes in the police were subtle and unlikely to make much difference in the short term, other developments in the wake of the riots showed that Mrs Thatcher's authority had been undermined. A major cabinet revolt against further spending cuts in July 1981 left the prime minister isolated. She fought back by reshuffling her team in September, sacking her outspoken critic Ian Gilmour and demoting James Prior to Northern Ireland. Three rising Thatcherite stars, Tebbit, Nigel Lawson and Cecil Parkinson, joined the cabinet. The prime minister would have liked a more far-reaching reconstruction, but was much too weak to create a full cabinet in her own image. There was no move against her at this time, but in part this inactivity arose from the conviction that the Conservatives were bound to lose the next election even if they turned to a more conciliatory leader. At the time the most likely beneficiary was the SDP, in alliance with the Liberals. Within a few days of the riots in north-west England, Roy Jenkins almost snatched the Warrington seat from Labour in a by-election. In October the Liberals took Croydon North-West, and the following month Shirley Williams won Crosby.

But despite these significant political repercussions from the riots, at the level of underlying public attitudes they were probably helpful to Mrs Thatcher rather than otherwise. Those who shared her view that Britain had been swamped by alien cultures were bolstered by the fact that the most serious outbreaks had occurred in areas where the ethnic minorities were strongly represented. It was no surprise that Enoch Powell took this opportunity to claim that his prophecies were being verified. But while she could never displace Powell in the hearts of his admirers, Mrs Thatcher already enjoyed considerable public support on race and immigration. More importantly for her, the riots helped to foster a change of attitude towards unemployment, where she was much more vulnerable.

In the Autumn of 1982 the journalist Ian Jack visited Wigan, where around 20 per cent of the working-age population was unemployed. One jobless man explained that unemployment robbed people of their dignity, and that 'once you've taken someone's dignity away, they've nothing else to lose. That's when they'll fight the system we live under.' Yet there was no sign that Wigan was on the verge of an uprising.[54] By definition, the unemployed were far more difficult to mobilise for effective action than, say, workers in an important industry like coal mining. Their political leverage depended on public goodwill. This had tended to grow along with the jobless figures, since more people in work now had friends or relatives on the dole. But far from evoking additional sympathy for the long-term jobless, the link between civil unrest and unemployment only made it easier for right-wing Conservatives to claim that most if not all of them were 'undeserving'. Norman Tebbit recalled the exploits of his bicycling parent at the 1981 Conservative conference in order to rub in the point that decent people did not riot, whatever their economic circumstances. Michael Heseltine, speaking three hours earlier, attracted much less publicity with an impassioned and wholly sincere attack on racists who were trying to make political capital out of the riots by reviving Powellite visions of mass repatriations of non-white immigrants.[55]

Just before he was elected leader of the Labour Party, Michael Foot promised to organise 'the biggest protest campaign that this country has seen since the 1930s', and to 'rouse the country from one end to the other' against the 'atrocities' of unemployment. At the end of May 1981 a TUC-sponsored People's March for Jobs concluded with a peaceful and dignified rally in Trafalgar Square. But the riots in the next few weeks effectively erased public memories of that event, providing a helpful context for Tebbit's speech. Cruder right-wing propagandists discredited the march with irrelevant innuendo; one *Daily Telegraph* writer tried to draw sinister conclusions from the fact that Vanessa Redgrave had given signed T-shirts to the marchers on arrival in London, and that the Social Workers Party had 'distributed 50,000 leaflets on behalf of its Right to Work Campaign'. The clear inference was that any organisation which lobbied on behalf of the right to work, at the end of a march in support of the right to work, had to be some kind of Soviet front.[56]

Despite the continuing efforts of Foot and others, it was soon apparent that the country would not be 'roused' into forcing constructive government action to reduce the dole queues. Tony Benn blamed the long-term impact of the education system for the mixture of 'hopelessness, defeatism and bitterness' which he detected among unemployed youngsters.[57] As the unemployment rate continued to rise, some of his parliamentary colleagues became still more defeatist, and less bitter about what seemed to be a new fact of economic life. In May 1983 the Labour MP Giles Radice noted that although the unemployment rate amongst males in Stanley in Country Durham was about a third, at least the area boasted 'pretty villages and terrific views over the Derwent Valley and beyond'.[58]

According to most accounts, the British – or rather English – descent into disorder was brief, occupying just a few weeks in that strange summer of 1981 before normality was restored. There was another major outbreak in 1985, with riots in London and the Midlands, culminating in the murder of PC Keith Blakelock at Broadwater Farm, Tottenham, on 6 October. In fact there were several incidents in the intervening years, but they were less spectacular and barely reported. In part this was because the political climate was different and it was much more difficult to incorporate the rioting into a narrative about explosions of anger against a failing government. By the summer of 1982 Mrs Thatcher's public profile had been transformed. Her approval rating, which had been 29 per cent in February, had jumped to 52 per cent in July. Partly this reflected the government's success in its main objective, the control of inflation. The annual rate inherited by Mrs Thatcher and her first chancellor, Sir Geoffrey Howe, had been 10 per cent. By May 1980 it had more than doubled, to almost 22 per cent, mainly due to the government's own decisions. Afterwards the figure began to fall, moving back into single figures in April 1982. Another bonus was the impact of the 1980 Housing Act, which allowed council-house tenants to purchase their properties. In 1982 alone a record 215,000 tenants took advantage of the 'Right to Buy' at a massive discount.

But by far the biggest boost to Mrs Thatcher's personal popularity was the Falklands War of April–June 1982. This was ironic, given that the Argentine invasion would never have taken place if the 'Iron Lady' had not been so determined to trim the defence budget. Given Thatcher's familiarity with the psychology of deterrence, the cuts affecting British forces in the South Atlantic looked suspiciously like a preparatory move towards a decision to share sovereignty over the islands with Argentina. A group of MPs had already registered an angry protest against this approach. They were seething when the Commons met to discuss the invasion on 3 April, but the House was virtually unanimous in backing the firm action proposed by the prime minister. In the country at large, the argument about Thatcher's true role in the affair never really caught hold, at least in part because her backers in the tabloid press excelled themselves in providing an unprecedented level of post-war jingoism. The ever-faithful *Sun*, under Kelvin MacKenzie (editor since April 1981), proudly dubbed itself 'The paper that supports our boys'. It celebrated the sinking of the elderly cruiser *General Belgrano* with the immortal headline 'Gotcha!' Even MacKenzie realised that the miserable death of Argentine conscripts in icy waters was no real cause for gloating; the next day's paper actually celebrated the fact that hundreds of foundering 'Argies' had been rescued by 'our boys'.[59] But the paper had decided that the Foreign Office should carry the can for any blunders in the run-up to war, and the majority of MPs took the same view. The main political casualty was the foreign secretary, Lord Carrington, who was subjected to a vicious inquest at a meeting of backbench Conservatives in the wake of the invasion.

VI

MacKenzie stayed as editor of the *Sun* until 1994. His appointment, which came a few weeks after Rupert Murdoch had acquired the *Times* titles, was a masterstroke on the part of his proprietor. Early in 1981 MacKenzie had been lured away from the *Sun* by the offer of the night-editor's post at the ailing *Daily Express*. Murdoch not only forgave this disloyalty, but decided to reward it.[60] He knew a ruthless populist when he saw one. MacKenzie was particularly pugnacious in dealings with his colleagues. 'I'll shake your hand twice in case I miss you when you go,' he allegedly told new recruits when he met them for the first time.[61]

Under MacKenzie, the *Sun* adopted the technology which allowed it to print photographs in colour, but in moral terms it saw the world starkly, in black and white. It traded on anger – whipping up the emotions of its readers and smirking at the ineffectual protests of its critics. Apart from the editorials – which became more humourless, self-congratulatory and doctrinaire over the years – its contents were playful as well as provocative. Its staff always seemed to find the right phrases to produce maximum irritation among radicals who scanned its pages, almost as if the paper was being written by left-wingers with a cynical streak. This could never be said of the middle-brow tabloid, the *Daily Mail*, which was no fun at all. The *Sun* knew that some subjects would always provoke anger, but it was rarely repetitive and concentrated on topical grievances. The *Mail*, by contrast, was an active fomenter of infuriation. Supposedly the *Mail* catered for those who considered themselves to be middle class and wanted to stay that way, while MacKenzie worked hard to retain the working-class credentials of the *Sun*. The Murdoch-owned *News of the World* purveyed the same populist fare.

With *The Times* and its Sunday stablemate also in Murdoch's pocket, the government had covered all its social bases as a new election loomed. Long before the poll, on 9 June 1983, it was obvious that the Conservatives would win again. The only serious question was whether Labour – handicapped by weak leadership and a manifesto which was quickly christened 'the longest suicide note in history' – could hold on to second place with the SDP/Liberal Alliance challenging hard. In terms of seats, the result of this crucial contest looked one-sided; 209 Labour MPs were returned, compared to only 23 for the Alliance. But this merely reflected the eccentricities of the electoral system, which the Alliance wanted to change for understandable reasons. Labour had won just 27.6 per cent of the vote, only 2 per cent more than the Alliance. Could this dismal performance be attributed to the manifesto itself, or to the impression given by many Labour candidates that they did not believe in it? Labour's plight in June 1983 was bad enough, but it was made worse because it was possible to draw either of these conclusions. Tony Benn, who lost his Bristol seat, was convinced that the country was still angry enough to mobilise behind a radical programme.

Another Tony – a young barrister who entered Parliament for the first time at this election – took a very different view. Tony Blair had been a musician of sorts, but probably did not analyse this aspect of popular culture as a potential barometer of future political trends. Had he done so in 1983, he would have found some useful backing for his view that the future belonged to the right. At the time of the election, The Clash were on the verge of splitting up, thus silencing the most potent political legacy of punk rock. The initial energy of the New Wave had washed out long ago, and its most creative legatees (like Joy Division, whose lead singer committed suicide in 1980) tended to be introspective and gloomy. The mood even infected survivors from the 1960s. Having been slightly premature with their melancholy album *Wish You Were Here* (1975), Pink Floyd released *The Final Cut* (subtitled 'a requiem for the post-war dream') just before the 1983 election. Although they attacked 'Maggie' by name, it was evident that they were lashing out against a fait accompli. By this time, indeed, the members of the band were more interested in attacking each other than in expressing their anger about the state of Britain. Meanwhile the singles chart was dominated by consumption-conscious bands like Duran Duran, who reached the top for the first time in March 1983, and Spandau Ballet, who emulated the feat with their melodic but vacuous ballad 'True' in August. By contrast, Robert Wyatt's magnificent cover version of Elvis Costello's Falklands protest song 'Shipbuilding' fell short of the top thirty. Back in 1978 The Clash had fumed against people who turned 'rebellion into money'. In 1983 it was obvious that there was much more profit in acquiescence.

There was, though, one powerful movement which could be expected to resist the rightward trend in politics. There were several high-profile strikes during the first Thatcher government, notably by steel workers in 1980. The trade unions also took a leading role in organising demonstrations against rising unemployment. But there was nothing like the head-on clash which many people had anticipated when the union-hating Thatcher came into office. In part, this was because the government had advanced cautiously, making sure that it moved in tandem with public opinion when it introduced legislation to curtail union powers. This marked a triumph for the approach of James Prior. But the architect of the strategy had been removed from his post at the Department of Employment after just two years, and replaced by the more abrasive Norman Tebbit. Once the government was re-elected in 1983 there was good reason to expect more radical policies, and a stronger reaction from the unions.

However, the first moves towards conflict were taken by Mrs Thatcher's allies outside Parliament. In July 1983, a month after the election, Rupert Murdoch announced the appointment of the thirty-four-year old Andrew Neil as editor of the *Sunday Times*. Neil had been brought up in working-class Paisley and educated at Glasgow University. Despite his obvious intelligence and eloquence, Neil's background and lack of experience on a major British newspaper made him unduly defensive about his status; he was much more at home in America, with its 'dynamic, can-do culture' and its relative lack of snobbery.[62] Kelvin MacKenzie (born 1946, three years before Neil) had also been inspired by America, where he had worked for the *New York Post*. But, in direct contrast to Neil, MacKenzie had been brought up in the suburban middle class and his academic record was undistinguished. These experiences had not shorn him of self-confidence; in the words of Rupert Murdoch's biographer, 'His public persona was one of manic brutishness.'[63] In character, the two young editors were very different, but for their employer such traits were secondary considerations. Murdoch appointed people because of their attitude to the job, not their social bearing; and in this respect Andrew Neil and Kelvin MacKenzie had a great deal in common.

The appointment of these two iconoclastic outsiders was a symptom that change was coming to the British press, and not just in the content of the newspapers. Technological advance meant that much of the work performed by print workers could now be done by journalists. But in 1983 the Fleet Street unions were still powerful enough to protect the traditional production process, and most proprietors were reluctant to take them on. The union reforms of the first Thatcher government provided a platform for action, but even after the decisive Conservative victory in 1983 Murdoch continued with clandestine preparations rather than openly seizing the initiative.

The showdown began in the provincial press rather than in London. Back in 1974 Eddy Shah, an energetic businessman of Persian origins, had founded a group of free newspapers based in the north-west of England. Dependent on advertising revenue, Shah had an obvious interest in reducing production costs. He saw the new technology as an ideal opportunity for expansion, and by the summer of 1983 was ready to go ahead. But the print unions refused to cooperate. When Shah recruited new staff to operate the equipment the main union, the National Graphical Association (NGA), demanded that they should either join their ranks or be dismissed. Shah refused, so the NGA called a strike in one of his printworks. Shah's response was to sack the strikers.

In some respects the ensuing dispute resembled the battle over Grunwick. Like George Ward, Shah was a small businessman readily depicted as a plucky underdog. Mass picketing was organised against him involving several unions (including a contingent of miners from Scotland) and drawing in radical activists from outside the mainstream movement. But this time the protests were more violent. On the night of 29 November 1983 it looked as if Shah's Warrington plant would be overrun until the Manchester riot police intervened – apparently after Andrew Neil telephoned Leon Brittan, the new home secretary.[64] Neil was almost alone among London newspaper editors in supporting Shah. This was a telling sign of the power of the print unions, and very different from the situation at the time of Grunwick, when most of the press had lined up behind Ward. And while the legal wranglings over Grunwick had resulted in something like a score draw, on this occasion Shah emerged as a decisive victor thanks to the new union laws. The NGA was heavily fined, and when it failed to pay its assets were sequestrated by the courts.

Shah had not actively sought a confrontation with the unions, though after his victory it was convenient for the right to portray him as a self-conscious crusader. However, Rupert Murdoch had more grandiose visions, and welcomed the defeat of the NGA in the context of a wider struggle. In the summer of 1984 he told a gathering of his senior staff that the British trade unions were on the run: 'I hope Mrs Thatcher presses home her advantage. Now is the time to crack down on them hard.'[65] If Murdoch repeated his message to his friend in Downing Street, his words would have been superfluous. The 'crackdown' was already under way, with the prime minister's wholehearted approval.

Murdoch was not the only person making controversial appointments in the early 1980s. There was a considerable stir when, in April 1980, the secretary of state for industry Sir Keith Joseph announced that Ian MacGregor would be the next chairman of British Steel. The problem at the time was not so much MacGregor's qualifications for the job, but rather the terms of his employment, which would involve the payment of £1.8 million to an American investment bank in compensation for the loss of his services. Like Neil and MacKenzie, MacGregor was heavily influenced by American attitudes and practices; indeed, although he was born in Scotland his transatlantic dealings dated back to the Second World War. Though he was far from being an unfeeling hatchet man, he was resolute; and it proved easy for his critics to portray him in a negative light when he pushed through a programme of job-cutting and factory closures at British Steel. He took over an industry which was costing British taxpayers nearly £2 million every day and whose workers had just won a substantial pay increase after a four-month strike. In MacGregor's three years at British Steel the workforce was almost halved; more than 80,000 jobs were cut, at a high cost in redundancy payments. But productivity improved considerably, although the financial losses continued at a reduced rate.

In September 1983 the seventy-year-old MacGregor moved on to an even tougher troubleshooting job, as chairman of the National Coal

Board (NCB). Every day British Coal was losing £1.5 million – the equivalent of the total sum which the government had paid in order to retain MacGregor's services.[66] If he could reduce these losses, his appointment would truly be a bargain for the taxpayer. From the outset he made no secret of the fact that he was looking for significant savings. After his first meeting with Arthur Scargill he estimated that he would have to improve the annual balance sheet by £600 million. There was no reason to disguise his objectives, because both sides knew that a strike was inevitable, and a programme of pit closures had begun under the previous management. Scargill had called three ballots on industrial action since the strike threat which had forced the government to back down in 1981. On each occasion he was rebuffed by his own members; in October 1982 and March 1983 almost two thirds had voted against a strike.

The appointment of MacGregor changed the picture. In view of the developments within the steel industry, Scargill's repeated argument that the government had similar plans for coal now seemed much more plausible. MacGregor also insisted that he would not improve the below-inflation pay offer which was on the table; rather, he implied, the miners were lucky to be getting as much as 5 per cent. In October 1983 a special NUM conference responded by calling an overtime ban. But the strike itself did not begin until the following March, when the NCB announced the closure of Cortonwood pit in South Yorkshire. One of the major sources of contention between MacGregor's NCB and Scargill's NUM was the precise test of economic viability in an international market where relative costs were camouflaged by government subsidies. Scargill himself believed that pits should stay open until the last lump of fuel had been extracted. But whatever the criteria, Cortonwood should not have been a top target for closure. The NUM claimed, quite plausibly, that a pit which was far from exhausted but situated in Scargill's Yorkshire heartlands had been chosen as a direct provocation. The Cortonwood miners were not seen as a militant group, but they decided to fight the closure and neighbouring pits took sympathetic industrial action. Shortly afterwards, MacGregor disclosed the full extent of his plans. Twenty pits were to go, with the loss of 20,000 jobs. There was no point in further discussions with the unions. The long-expected nationwide strike began on 12 March 1984.

The usual explanation for the defeat of the miners is that they were 'lions led by donkeys' – and by one asinine figure in particular. Arthur

Scargill is held responsible for the decision to strike when coal stocks were high and demand for fuel relatively low. Above all, he is blamed for the union's refusal to hold a national strike ballot. These misjudgements reflected Scargill's idiosyncratic assessment of the prospects for revolution in Britain. His view is best characterised as an unstable blend of overconfidence, opportunism and pessimism. He believed that the Conservatives had no democratic mandate to govern because they had not won the majority of votes cast at either the 1979 or 1983 general elections. That was a respectable position for an advocate of proportional representation. But it was hardly the basis for revolutionary optimism, because more than two thirds of the voters had either backed the government or plumped for the SDP/Liberal Alliance, which was hardly less reactionary in Scargill's eyes. Yet Scargill believed that the impetus for a revolution could arise from 'things at the time not recognised to be important'.[67] This explained his participation in the Grunwick dispute, which began as a little local difficulty but ended up as a cause célèbre. Scargill had not been fooled by the government's climbdown in 1981. He knew that, compared to Grunwick, a new battle against the miners would make headlines from the start. The public might be passive at election time, but the coming struggle might be the moment when Britain's oppressed masses finally realised that they had the power to throw off their chains.

Yet even the NUM president had to recognise that many of his members were still opposed to a strike; several areas held polls of their own and voted heavily to stay at work. Thus, if a national ballot was held, serious divisions in the ranks were bound to be exposed, whatever the outcome. Scargill's best – or only – chance would come if a spectacular event could trigger off spontaneous industrial action. Then he had to hope that the course of events would sustain the momentum of the dispute, without anyone noticing the absence of a ballot. Such a scenario would give Scargill the platform he craved for his ferocious oratory, and hopefully this would awaken the latent revolutionary ardour of the British people. The closure of Cortonwood seemed to provide a suitable opportunity. What Scargill failed to appreciate was the main reason for the lack of revolutionary fervour in the ranks of his own union. Ironically, he was a victim of his own previous successes in prising above-average wage settlements for his members during the 1970s. In Nottinghamshire, in particular, many miners had now bought their own homes; and in accordance with the Thatcherite game plan, their new status was making them more inclined to vote Conservative than to plot the downfall of capitalism. One Nottinghamshire miner showed greater sociological insight than the NUM leader when he noted that 'Arthur Scargill's living in the age of the cloth cap and the greyhound on a piece of string, but the world's gone beyond that. The miners here have got washing machines, fitted carpets, and two tele-visions in their houses.'[68]

Thus, it was not that Scargill's tactics were wrong. Rather, they were based on an entirely mistaken analysis of British society in the mid-1980s. If he had been right on this crucial issue, it might not have mattered that the government was fully prepared for the struggle and ready on this occasion to beat the 'enemy within' into total submis-sion with every available weapon – along with other means which, on a strict view of previous constitutional practice, should not have been available at all. Since their climbdown in 1981 ministers had been building up coal stocks, which would ensure some breathing space even if a strike began during an arctic winter. It had equipped itself with tough new laws to prevent 'secondary' industrial action, and could coordinate police forces across Britain through the National Reporting Centre (NRC), to counteract Scargill's flying pickets. It would be an exaggeration to say that the police were spoiling for a fight, but at least recent memories of the inner-city rioting made them more resili-ent than their predecessors had been during the 1972 dispute. As in Brixton during Operation Swamp, they had no hesitation in using their powers to the full, stopping and detaining people on the slightest suspi-cion that they might be travelling to join a picket line.

The press, of course, was also more partisan on this occasion. The Daily Express fabricated a front-page scoop which claimed that Scargill had admitted the futility of the struggle. Not to be outdone, Kelvin MacKenzie seized on a photograph of Scargill in a pose which could be made to look like a Nazi salute, and provided it with the punning caption 'Mine Führer'. Outraged print-workers ensured that this did not appear, and they also spiked MacKenzie's editorial which stigma-tised the most militant miners as 'the scum of the earth'.[69] As MacKenzie understood, it was vital to deprive the striking miners of public support. Even many of those who wanted the government to prevail had a degree of sympathy for hard-working people fighting to preserve their communities; they wanted the impossible result of a victory for the miners which was somehow a defeat for Arthur Scargill. Yet even here the government had a propaganda card to play, arguing that the miners were as wrong as they were romantic in defending their old way of life. Why continue to risk disease, injury or death in the quest for such a dirty, loss-making mineral?

The dispute lasted a year, costing an estimated £6 billion. It ended in many cases with dignified marches back to the pits. However, the collapse of the strike did not heal the divisions which had emerged between and within the various mining communities. Friends and families were permanently estranged by memories of intimidation or 'class treachery'; even twenty years later some communities had separate pubs for strikers and strike-breakers.[70] The dispute induced another institutional split, like the formation of the SDP in 1981. This time a breakaway organisation, the Union of Democratic Mineworkers (UDM), was set up to represent miners in areas like Nottingham where support for the strike was always weak. Its members would still be regarded as strike-breaking 'scabs' two decades after the dispute.

The hatred between miners led to a tragedy in November 1984 when a taxi driver taking a 'scab' to his pit in south Wales was killed. Two striking miners had dropped a concrete post from a bridge on to his car. Another working miner was beaten with baseball bats in his own home.[71] Willie Peacock, who had returned to work after nine months instead of holding out for the whole year, was bullied so mercilessly at the end of the strike that he hanged himself.[72] But the victims were not all on one side, although elements of the press tried to present it that way. In the first weeks of the strike a picket was killed in an accident at Ollerton in Nottinghamshire, where the residents were often hemmed in by police roadblocks. However, there were no fatalities in the worst clashes of the strike, which took place at Orgreave coking works near Sheffield, in late May and June 1984. Scargill was determined to make Orgreave into a second Saltley Bridge, and the number of pickets peaked at above 10,000. But this time the police were too well organised and numerous. They poured into the area from all over the country, fully equipped with riot gear and backed by hundreds of mounted colleagues. Footage of the horseborne assaults on the massed ranks of pickets provided some of the most vivid images of the decade; miners argued vehemently that the pictures were doctored by the media in order to present them as aggressors. Whatever the truth of this allegation, there was still plenty of evidence of police brutality, particularly when the officers concerned were not local residents. Scargill himself was slightly hurt and (inevitably) arrested. It was rumoured that some members of the security forces had joined the operation in plain clothes, to act as agents provocateurs. Equally, it would be difficult to believe that there were no bona fide troublemakers among the thousands of pickets. But from a distance Scargill's friend Tony Benn had no doubt who was to blame. He recorded in his diary for 31 May 1984 that '7,000 pickets have been attacked by mounted and foot police with riot shields and helmets. It looks like a civil war.'[73] The scenes at Orgreave did bear an uncanny resemblance to the antics of the eccentric Sealed Knot society, which had been re-enacting battles between the Cavaliers and the Roundheads since the late 1960s. But there was very little chivalry on display at Orgreave, and the blood was real.

At the time Mrs Thatcher was widely believed when she declared that the Orgreave clashes represented 'an attempt to substitute the rule of the mob for the rule of law'. On two occasions it looked as if the challenge to the government's authority might prevail – in July 1984, when unrest in the docks threatened to open a second front in the industrial battle, and two months later, when the NACODS union, which represented pit safety workers, voted overwhelmingly to strike in support of its own grievances. The first problem was soon settled, but the government was still worried that safety cover would be withdrawn, and all the pits still working forced to close, when the Conservatives met for their 1984 party conference in Brighton. Just before three o'clock on the morning of 12 October a hundred-pound IRA bomb ripped apart the Grand Hotel where the prime minister was staying, killing five people. Among those who received terrible injuries were Norman Tebbit and his wife Margaret. Mrs Thatcher, who was fortunate to escape unscathed, lost little time in claiming a link between the terrorists and union activists who hoped 'to break, defy and subvert the laws'.[74]

A month after the attempt on her life, Thatcher paid tribute to the strike-breakers, declaring that 'The courage and loyalty of working miners and their families will never be forgotten.' The strike, she added, had been 'tragic', but it would have some beneficial long-term effects. She meant that the union movement would be more malleable in future. The NUM, at least, seemed slow to absorb the lesson. In January 1988 it re-elected Arthur Scargill as its president after he had submitted himself voluntarily for democratic endorsement. But if 'King' Arthur was still in place, he presided over an ever-shrinking castle. There were more than 250,000 members of the NUM in 1979; by 2000 the number had fallen to 5,000. The once-mighty miners were so enfeebled that even the *Sun* felt that it could afford to speak up for them in 1992, when Michael Heseltine announced a further round of pit closures in advance of privatisation. Tory backbenchers threatened to rebel against the plans, and Heseltine backed down. In an ironic coda to twenty years of angry confrontation, the last political victory for the miners was secured with the help of a few Conservative backbenchers who felt on this occasion that market forces should not be allowed to prevail. Some of them did, indeed, remember the 'courageous' and 'loyal' miners who had braved the picket lines and continued to work. But affectionate reminiscences did them little good in the end, as the collieries which had stayed open during the strike now closed down for ever and were turned to more useful purposes, like municipal land-fill sites.

VII

In February 1984 a new satirical programme was screened by ITV. *Spitting Image* was more directly political than its immediate predecessor, the BBC's *Not the Nine O'Clock News*, which had started just before the 1979 general election and finished its run in 1982. *Spitting Image* used puppets and impressionists to lampoon the leading politicians of the day, along with other celebrities. Despite its talented team of scriptwriters, it suffered from trying to be too topical; many of the jokes were unfunny at the time, and have certainly not worn well.

But even if the audience often struggled to raise a laugh at the sketches, the programme left a vivid impression. It was visually cruel to its subjects, since the puppets were brilliant, grotesque caricatures. The jokes, too, were merciless, usually focusing on some perceived defect in the victims. The most hurtful jibes were aimed at the Labour leader, Neil Kinnock, who had replaced Michael Foot after the 1983 general election. A gregarious man with an obvious relish for life, Kinnock had been born in 1942 and brought up 'in a prefabricated bungalow in Tredegar'. But his parents did their best to give their only child a platform for success in later life. As he famously declared in May 1987, he was the first in a thousand generations of Kinnocks to attend university, although his studies at Cardiff were subject to numerous distractions and he failed his exams in history and industrial relations at the first attempt.[75] University debating helped Kinnock to develop his style of oratory, which was often very moving. However, he was inclined to be long-winded when striving for effect, and in the Commons he was too verbose to land telling punches on the big occasion. This trait presented the gag merchants of *Spitting Image* with an irresistible target. Whether or not Neil Kinnock had the potential to be a national leader, his puppet was certainly not prime ministerial. It was always repeating itself, trying to express the same concepts in increasingly pompous prose. This was hurtful to Kinnock because it conveyed an essential truth. People who are genuinely angry rarely pause to polish their phrases. Instead of articulating the feelings of the people he had left behind in Tredegar, as he rose through the party ranks Kinnock often gave the impression that his main concern was to imitate the speaking style of the town's former MP, Nye Bevan.

Much of Kinnock's effort as leader was devoted to making Labour look more electable. Tragically for him, this process involved the abandonment of sincerely held views, notably the need for Britain to rid itself of nuclear weapons whether or not the Soviet Union followed suit. But a task he took on with much greater relish was expelling members of the Militant Tendency who had joined his party. Based around the newspaper *Militant* (founded 1964), the Tendency owed its inspiration to the teachings of Leon Trotsky, though few of its members could hope to emulate his analytical powers or his charisma. The organisation was candid about its desire to shift the Labour Party in the direction of its own brand of socialism, and rule changes that invited constituency activists to deselect unsatisfactory MPs offered it an ideal opportunity. A handful of Militant supporters were elected to Parliament, and in the early 1980s its representatives rose to powerful positions in Liverpool and in some London boroughs. The Militant Derek Hatton, who became deputy leader of Liverpool council in 1983, won extensive media exposure by virtue of his combative eloquence. Yet if Labour had been fit for office it would have dealt with Militant relatively quietly and quickly, as the Tories did in the mid-1980s with their extreme 'libertarian' infiltrators, the Federation of Conservative Students (FCS), who believed on free-market grounds that drugs should be legalised. Instead, there was a protracted and very public purge, which culminated in a defiant Kinnock speech at the 1985 party conference. That passionate oration was used by the party as the centrepiece to its campaign for the 1987 general election, but only reminded voters that Labour had been preoccupied with internal conflict instead of concentrating on its real job of opposing the government.

Arthur Scargill presented Kinnock with another serious dilemma. The party leader had to share a platform with Scargill at events like the annual Durham Gala, but he took pains to distance himself from the strike. This fence-straddling attitude was another disaster. Those who thought that the dispute was about the preservation of jobs and communities argued that Kinnock should have been more outspoken in his support; those who thought that the strike was an attempt to replace democratic government with mob rule were incensed that he had not disowned it more forcefully. The *Sun*'s usual tactic was to lump Kinnock together with the extreme left. Before the 1987 general election Kelvin MacKenzie ran a typical 'story' in which, via a medium, a range of dead historical figures revealed the way they would vote. Stalin turned out to be the only one to choose Labour. In its triumphalist mood the newspaper placed Henry VIII in the Conservative camp, even though some readers must have dimly recalled that the bearded monarch had been a home-grown psychopath who clearly belonged in the same stable as the Soviet dictator.[76]

Long before 1987, the *Sun* had been loathed by Labour activists; as one of them admitted, this was 'not just because it was so dishonest and debasing, but also because it was so infuriatingly effective'.[77] Whatever its readers thought of the *Sun*'s Stalin stunt, its proprietor had already struck a more effective blow on behalf of his friend Margaret Thatcher. After Eddy Shah's successful defiance of the print-workers, it was only a matter of time before Rupert Murdoch put his own plans into operation. He had already invested £100 million in new premises which could cater for all of his various publishing concerns. The Wapping plant was on the Thames, just east of the Tower of London. Its defences were equally forbidding, and during the strike it was appropriately dubbed 'Fortress Wapping'. It was also fitting that the *Sun* should move from Bouverie Street, not far from the traditional epicentre of the British press in Fleet Street, to the area of London which had been home to the fictional Alf Garnett.

Murdoch had left nothing to chance. Through the good offices of the ex-Labour MP Woodrow Wyatt – whose *News of the World* column 'The Voice of Reason' did not always live up to its billing – he made a deal with the electricians' union, which signed up to a no-strike agreement. In the weeks before Murdoch's deadline in January 1986 other

preparations were made; it was rumoured that the police had recon-
noitred the area, in order to second-guess the tactics of demonstrators.
The journalists, whose computers would in future do much of the work
currently monopolised by the printers, were offered incentives to stay
on (including, in a surreal echo of a *Not the Nine O'Clock News*
sketch about industrial negotiations, some fancy new chairs). Editors
like Neil and MacKenzie emphasised long-standing grievances between
writers and printers to undermine any new-found sense of solidarity.
This stratagem worked; a few of the more Quixotic writers found jobs
with other papers, but the majority stayed on board. The existing
printers took industrial action in protest, and were promptly sacked.
Murdoch had expected this; indeed, it promised to save him money
because the workers would have been entitled to greater compensation if they had called his bluff and pretended to accept the deal.

Thus it seemed that Murdoch had prevailed. He had the premises,
the printers and the prose-mongers to keep his newspapers in production. Customers kept buying his newspapers, although they would have
to look elsewhere if they wanted an impartial account of his ongoing
struggle. The *Sun* took a jocular approach, saying that its current
favourite topless pin-up Samantha Fox had joined the War of Wapping
and was 'pointing her bazookas at the enemy lines'.[78] However, the
print unions had two ways of firing back – by preventing workers
getting into Fortress Wapping, and stopping the printed papers getting
out. Normally they would have found it difficult to attract support for
their struggle, since most other workers regarded them as pampered
and arrogant; as John O'Farrell noted, it was also difficult to generate
much enthusiasm for people who had at any time taken wages from
the malignant Murdoch.[79] The travel writer Bill Bryson, who continued
to work for *The Times* during the dispute, had no sympathy for the
printers, although he felt very sorry for the 'hundreds and hundreds
of decent, mild-mannered librarians, clerks, secretaries and messengers'
who had also lost their jobs because they belonged to 'the most truc-
ulent unions'.[80] But even Eddy Shah had met fierce resistance, and the
'Dirty Digger' was a much more tempting target for activists. Besides,
this time the conflict was in the capital city rather than the north-west
of England. Wapping was far from being the most accessible part of
London, but there was every reason for the authorities to anticipate a
considerable attendance of assorted malcontents on the picket lines.

Like the miners' strike, the Wapping dispute lasted a year. Picketing was particularly heavy at weekends, when there would often be more than 5,000 protestors, and there were many violent skirmishes with the police. For witnesses who thought that the police had been unduly aggressive during the miners' strike, Wapping was a predictable repetition. Tony Benn, for example, reported on 3 May 1986 that after a signal had been given 'mounted police came out and charged in all directions and cleared the road'. He felt that the crowd was far less defiant than the miners had been, and had reacted with fear rather than anger. More than 200 people were injured on that night. 'I couldn't believe it,' Benn's diary records, 'the absolute horror of standing in the middle of the night in the middle of London, seeing the police flailing about with their truncheons at people who a moment earlier had been standing talking, and to know that it was authorised, planned.'[81]

It was indeed planned, with full cooperation from a government which pretended to be holding aloof; and the operation was successful, reinforced by legal action as in the previous battle with Eddy Shah. The unions and their allies launched one last assault at the end of January 1987; it was estimated that the streets around the plant contained about 10,000 demonstrators and 3,000 police. Andrew Neil was concerned that the complex would be overrun, but the police held firm despite more than 150 injuries in their ranks. Soon afterwards the dispute ended, and the print-workers eventually accepted Murdoch's terms.

The popular impression of the great set-piece industrial battles between the mid-1970s and the late 1980s is one of doctrinaire trade unionists launching unprovoked challenges against the 'system', and coming off second best. But closer analysis reveals a different picture. Between 1975 and Mrs Thatcher's third election victory in June 1987 there were three prolonged and bitter confrontations: Grunwick, the miners' strike and Wapping. In the case of Grunwick it might be argued that the original strikers were the aggressors, since they demanded a right to union recognition which the management had not previously conceded. However, in the context of 1977 this was not a radical position – certainly not in the eyes of a Labour government which usually gave a sympathetic hearing to any union request. Yet even the open support of Labour ministers could not force George Ward into submission. The other two drawn-out battles might have aroused revolutionary hopes among prominent players like Arthur Scargill, but they were really attempts to preserve the status quo, and both ended in morale-sapping defeats for the opponents of change. They resulted in the destruction of the mining industry and the transformation of newspaper production. Another defensive struggle, to keep the Greater London Council (GLC) and other metropolitan councils in existence, was equally unsuccessful. In 1985 the Tories simply used their parliamentary majority to abolish these institutions, which had tried to resist the rise of the ideological right. Instead of provoking violent resistance, the removal of an elected London-wide authority was marked by a costly fireworks display, followed by nothing more subversive than a chorus of boos.[82]

It would be tempting to say that Wapping marked a turning point, because after January 1987 industrial disputes became far less violent and politically charged. Alternatively, one might conclude that the fight against Murdoch was just a hangover from the miners' strike, which marked the real defeat for the union movement. But it can also be argued that the outcome of these celebrated disputes had been determined a decade earlier, when George Ward beat the Grunwick pickets with the invaluable assistance of the Freedom Association. At last friends of Ross McWhirter could toast his contribution to a posthumous victory over the forces of subversion.

FEAR

I

IN August 1981 forty-two people set out on foot from Cardiff, heading for the US airbase of Greenham Common in Berkshire. Calling themselves Women for Life on Earth – although the original marchers included a token male contingent – they targeted Greenham as the most suitable place to mark their opposition to a new generation of nuclear weapons. In December 1979 NATO had agreed that various European countries would host a total of 572 American land-launched cruise missiles with sufficient range to deliver their warheads to the Soviet Union. On behalf of Britain Margaret Thatcher had bagged more than a quarter of the consignment – 160 missiles in all. The first batch was due to arrive in 1983. Greenham, a former picnicking spot which had been turned over to the US military during the Second World War, was selected as an early recipient along with Molesworth near Huntingdon in Cambridgeshire.

When they arrived at the base – more than a hundred miles from their starting point – the protestors handed a letter to the American commander, expressing 'fear for the future of all our children and for the future of the living world which is the basis of all life'. They hoped that their demonstration would spark off a public debate, but the Americans simply ignored them. Instead of dispersing, some protestors chained themselves to the perimeter fence in a gesture which recalled the tactics of the suffragette movement. The authorities were wrong-footed, presumably thinking that the demonstration would be a transient publicity stunt. In fact, the last of the 'Greenham women' did not depart until the year 2000, outlasting the missiles themselves by a decade. Eventually nine separate camps were established, with different themes (and colour schemes) but all confined to women. The living conditions were austere, symbolising a rejection of the decadent Western lifestyle which the weapons were supposed to be defending. The residents lived under daily threat of police harassment or eviction; although they did have some local support, they encountered considerable hostility if they ventured into the nearby town of Newbury. Flagging spirits were sustained by songs and a sense of solidarity in sisterhood. Greenham also became the focal point for visits from sympathisers, notably in December 1982 when nearly 30,000 people (mainly women) responded to an invitation to make a human ring around the perimeter.

The Greenham protest attracted worldwide publicity, but it was just one manifestation of a much broader movement which sprang up in Britain in the wake of the 1979 NATO decision. The main beneficiary of this movement, in terms of membership, was the long-established Campaign for Nuclear Disarmament (CND). Founded in 1958, this organisation had declined since its heyday in the early 1960s, when annual marches from the weapons research facility at Aldermaston, also in Berkshire, could attract up to 100,000 people. In the mid-1970s it was widely assumed that the superpowers had entered a new era of sanity, including a negotiated disarmament programme that promised to resolve the problem without the need for public pressure. Foreign policy adventurism had fallen out of fashion, particularly in the US, which was chastened by its ignominious withdrawal from Vietnam in 1973.

The benign international outlook was transformed in December 1979 by the NATO decision to deploy the cruise missiles and the almost simultaneous Soviet invasion of Afghanistan. The increased likelihood of nuclear confrontation was officially recognised the following year when the British government reissued a civil defence booklet with the optimistic title *Protect and Survive*. This had first been published (after prolonged and understandable hesitation) by James Callaghan's Labour administration in 1976, despite the slight thaw in East–West relations at that time. Initial proposals leaked to the press had revealed that the public was to be kept in ignorance of a serious threat for as long as possible; just before the conflagration, a special broadcasting service would take over from the BBC, providing an element of entertainment 'for morale purposes'.[1] When eventually published, the leaflet provided advice to be followed when nuclear war seemed to be looming, including the idea that Britons should build makeshift 'fall-out rooms' – preferably in the basement of their homes – and stock up with food and water to last a fortnight.

The government decided to distribute *Protect and Survive* to libraries and bookshops; it would only be sent to every household in the UK if and when war seemed unavoidable. This was a wise strategy, because mass panic could easily have resulted from a general distribution. Those who did take the trouble to consult the document could only have their existing fears reinforced, particularly by its breezy imprecision. 'Everything within a certain distance of a nuclear explosion will be totally destroyed,' readers were notified. The authorities, of course, could not be sure where the incoming missiles would land in the event of an attack, and casualty estimates based on the carnage at Hiroshima and Nagasaki in 1945 were irrelevant because of subsequent improvements in the technology of death.

Even so, the booklet betrayed divided priorities. Although the public was presumed to be preoccupied with the task of self-protection in the event of conflict, the government was obviously concerned that it might have to protect itself against the public. The imminent threat of nuclear war might trigger an exodus of city dwellers to the countryside, but in the interests of rational administration it would be preferable for people to take their chances at their existing place of residence. To this end, would-be refugees were assured that 'No part of the United Kingdom can be considered safe from both the direct effects of the weapons and the resultant fall-out.' Those who decided that a temporary taste of the rural life might provide a picturesque refuge from the nuclear storm would be deluding themselves; the advice to anyone caught in open countryside was to 'lie flat (in a ditch) and cover the exposed skin of the head and hands'. Presumably they would have to assume this awkward posture for a considerable time.

The only rational response to *Protect and Survive* was a peal of cynical laughter. A Gallup poll in 1980 suggested that the public was unimpressed; 61 per cent of respondents thought that no conceivable strategy of civil defence could improve their chances of survival.[2] But in the circumstances of the late 1970s it was prudent for the British government to make at least token preparations for the unthinkable. International tension had been rising even before the Soviets moved into Afghanistan. Meanwhile the Americans were working suspiciously hard on the neutron bomb – a device which killed people while leaving property intact. This feature, critics argued, made the weapon particularly congenial to capitalists – or to American forces hoping to confine an atomic exchange to Europe. News of the weapon provoked demonstrations in several European cities, and in April 1978 the moderate US president, Jimmy Carter, announced that production would be delayed. But British opposition to nuclear weapons was re-energised, not least by the publication of *Protest and Survive* (1980), a collection of critical essays including a notable contribution by the historian E.P. Thompson.

With the election in November 1980 of the former actor Ronald Reagan – who had once been a progressive, but now followed a right-wing script on both domestic and foreign policy – the American presidency fell to an individual who regarded the Soviet Union as an 'evil empire' and freely linked the prospect of nuclear war to obscure biblical prophecies. Reagan pressed ahead with the neutron bomb, and in 1983 announced his commitment to the so-called Star Wars project – a shield of missiles which in theory could intercept any air attack. To critics of US foreign policy, this was not part of a defensive strategy as its promoters claimed; rather, it would encourage Reagan in his unnerving policy of nuclear brinksmanship. Fears were not allayed the following year when Reagan, warming up for a speech and thinking he could not be overheard, joked that he had signed legislation to outlaw the Soviet Union and that the bombing would begin in five minutes.

Whatever Reagan's foolish prattle did for the American public, it certainly scared many Britons. By 1983 CND's tiny band of national organisers was struggling to keep up with the influx of new members. It was estimated that 90,000 were fully paid up, compared to just 17,000 two years previously. In addition, an impressive array of local groups had emerged, along with bodies representing specific professions, like Members of Equity for Nuclear Disarmament which included young actors such as Ben Elton and Emma Thompson. CND enjoyed support from a wide range of established celebrities. When planning its national rally in October 1982, its list of potential speakers included the *Good Life* actress Felicity Kendall, the maverick football manager Brian Clough, and Paul Weller, frontman of The Jam (and erstwhile admirer of Margaret Thatcher).[3] For several years a large proportion of the profits from the Glastonbury rock festival was donated to CND. In 1982 25,000 music lovers paid £8 each to revel in the Somerset mud, well aware that they were also helping a greater cause. The same year, Raymond Briggs published *When the Wind Blows*, a poignant account of an elderly Sussex couple who passively follow the official advice when doomsday dawns. As the author of the famous children's book *The Snowman* (1978), Briggs was a potent recruit to the anti-nuclear lobby.

Another prominent author, Martin Amis (born 1949), became preoccupied by the nuclear threat in 1984, to the disgust of his Thatcher-loving father, Kingsley. In answer to the well-meaning advice of *Protect and Survive*, Martin Amis wrote that 'Nuclear civil defence is a non-subject, a mischievous fabrication.' He spoke for many when he voiced his fears of surviving a nuclear exchange.

Suppose my eyes aren't pouring down my face, suppose I am untouched by the hurricane of secondary missiles that all mortar, metal and glass have abruptly become: suppose all this. I shall be obliged (and it's the last thing I'll feel like doing) to retrace that long mile home, through the firestorm, the remains of the thousand-mile-an-hour winds, the warped atoms, the grovelling dead. Then – God willing, if I still have the strength, and, of course, if they are still alive – I must find my wife and children and I must kill them.[4]

Amis's grim prophecy picked up on a theme which *Protect and Survive* had made unpleasantly explicit. For various good reasons there was no point in planning for a network of huge underground bunkers to shelter the general populace – although there would be provision for the nation's leaders. So there would be no repeat of the Blitz, when Londoners of all classes could mingle in comparative safety at the local Tube station. In a nuclear war there would be no such thing as society – just millions of petrified individuals and their families, praying (like Amis) that if death could not be avoided, at least it might come quickly.

In this context, the idea of nuclear-free zones took on real ideological significance. By 1983, more than 20 million Britons were living in such areas, established by local councils. Obviously the label could offer no immunity against the random effects of atomic weapons, but it did offer local residents a way of combining in a single gesture their distaste for government defence policy and for the Thatcherite creed that society was a mere fiction. The Greater London Council declared that 1983 would be Peace Year, and funded its campaign against nuclear weapons with money allocated by the government for futile war preparations.[5] But the movement was not confined to big cities, or driven by politicians keen to strike anti-governmental poses.* Affluent Winchester, for example, had organised its own group opposing the introduction of cruise missiles back in August 1980.

In a constituency where the Conservative MP had won a majority of more than 20,000 in 1979, it was prudent for the Winchester activists to stress that their group would be non-partisan. In fact, there were opponents of cruise missiles in all parties. Both the Scottish National Party (SNP) and Plaid Cymru in Wales took strong anti-nuclear stances – Scotland was the unconsulted host to nuclear submarines in Holy Loch and Faslane – and the future Liberal Democrat leader Paddy Ashdown was committed to the cause. In 1984 a third of Conservative supporters thought that American missiles made Britain 'less safe'. Enoch Powell – still an object of veneration for right-wing Tories – consistently argued that the Soviet Union had no interest in invading western Europe, which meant that the weapons were useless or worse.[6] More predictably, a Church of England report argued that

---

* Years later, after sampling political life from the authoritarian side as home secretary, David Blunkett dismissed nuclear-free zones as an example of 'gesturist politics'. In the 1980s he had been happy to support the idea as leader of Sheffield City Council; see *The Blunkett Tapes: My Life in the Bear-Pit*, Bloomsbury, 2006, xviii.

the 'nuclear element in deterrence is no longer a reliable or morally acceptable approach to the future of the world.[7] Even the royal family included a vocal opponent of the NATO defence strategy – in Lord Louis Mountbatten, who spoke out forcefully against the concept of limited nuclear war just before his assassination in 1979.

However, the Labour Party was the natural home for supporters of unilateral nuclear disarmament. Its party conference had voted to adopt the policy back in 1960, although its pro-American leader Hugh Gaitskell fought successfully to reverse this decision a year later. In the early 1980s numerous Labour MPs and young parliamentary candidates like Tony Blair either joined CND or volunteered to identify themselves with its aims. By 1983 twenty-one national trade unions were affiliated to CND.[8] In these circumstances it was always likely that Labour would readopt unilateral nuclear disarmament as official policy. It was included in the manifesto for the 1983 general election, which Labour fought under the leadership of Michael Foot, a veteran of the 1960s Aldermaston marches and co-founder of CND.

More than twenty years after the controversy over cruise missiles, it is still difficult to comment on the quality of the rival arguments while retaining any vestige of objectivity. Those who supported the deployment almost invariably claim that their case was vindicated by the subsequent collapse of the Soviet bloc. On this view, resolute action by the NATO countries helped to expose the inherent economic weakness of the communist system. But it remains possible to argue that, at best, the diversion of Soviet resources into the arms race accelerated a process of decay which would have happened in any case – and that, in the meantime, the proliferation of deadly warheads on both sides increased the risk of a conflict that would have put an end to life on either side of the Iron Curtain.

Even if nuclear weapons did help to liberate many countries in eastern Europe from misrule in the name of communism, Britain's role in the process was ambiguous rather than pivotal – as Margaret Thatcher and her allies later claimed. The arrival of cruise missiles did not reinforce British claims to great-power status; rather, the weapons cemented the country's position as a client of the United States. Their arrival undermined the government's claim that its own American-made Polaris missiles represented a truly independent deterrent. Bizarrely, this arrangement was acceptable to many people who were genuinely frightened that Britain might be losing its sovereignty to the European Community. The deployment was consistent with US thinking about the possibility of a 'limited' nuclear war – one in which the carnage was kept on the other side of the Atlantic. It was precisely this scenario which had produced Mountbatten's eloquent warning just before he was killed by the IRA. If the Soviet Union really had aggressive intentions, the importation of cruise missiles made Britain a more urgent target than it would otherwise have been; and if cruise was such an effective deterrent, the time for the Soviets to strike would have been during the four years that elapsed between the publicly announced NATO decision and the first arrival of the missiles in Britain. Strangely enough, the Soviets made no attempt to take advantage of this window of opportunity, despite their widely advertised supremacy in conventional forces.[9]

However, while Enoch Powell had recommended 'the discipline of thinking logically about war', the British decision to accept cruise missiles was rarely defended on rational grounds.[10] The debate, if anything, fell short of the lamentable level established during the 1975 referendum, when the British public faced a question of comparable magnitude. Many CND activists genuinely believed that if Britain gave up its own weapons other countries would follow suit – a touching example of continuing faith in British stature on the world stage. Some, including senior Labour figures, believed that Britain owed a lasting debt of gratitude to the US for its (belated) assistance in two world wars; they asserted that the obligations of mutual defence in the NATO charter entailed acceptance of the missiles. There were others who really did believe that the weapons would act as a deterrent against a genuine threat. But this view implied a visceral hatred of communist ideology and a belief that the current rulers of the Soviet Union were psychopathic empire-builders comparable to Adolf Hitler. On this analysis, the refusal to accept cruise missiles would be a repetition of appeasement in the 1930s. Such a view, for understandable reasons, was most commonly encountered within the Conservative Party, whose pre-war leaders had tried to buy off Hitler. Margaret Thatcher, who took pride in having been dubbed the 'Iron Lady' by the Soviet Army newspaper *Red Star*, supported cruise for both of these reasons: she admired the United States and loathed communism in principle and practice.

Whatever the quality of its argument, the Thatcher government found it difficult to make headway on the subject of cruise missiles in the early 1980s. In early 1983 one opinion poll found that two thirds of voters were opposed to them.[11] Shrewdly, at the beginning of that year the prime minister appointed Michael Heseltine secretary of state for defence, knowing that his powers of persuasion matched his ambition to succeed her. With the first missiles due to arrive within months, Heseltine needed to launch a retaliatory verbal strike against CND without delay. The easiest course was to exploit hostility towards the Greenham women, who were, in Heseltine's words, 'living in indescribable squalor'. On one occasion the defence secretary was jostled by a crowd in nearby Newbury, which gave him an additional propaganda coup against people who were also open to criticism because many continued to claim state benefits during their protest. But the overwhelming majority of anti-nuclear protests were peaceful, including a torchlit procession by Durham students on an evening when Heseltine was due to speak to the university's union society. Apparently even Heseltine thought this an impressive demonstration.[12]*

In the absence of startling misconduct among protestors, Heseltine resorted to a style of argument which had proved very effective during the 1975 referendum campaign. At that time some pro-European newspapers had claimed that left-wing opposition to the EC was being dictated by Moscow. In the context of defence policy it was all too easy to depict the protestors as members of a gullible group playing into the hands of Britain's enemies. If this did not suffice, it could be suggested that some CND activists were active traitors to their country. In April 1983, for example, Heseltine argued that 'behind the carefully turned phrases about peace lies the calculating political professionalism of full-time socialists and communists'. CND had long been under public-spirited scrutiny by the secret services, and this internal espionage was stepped up after Heseltine took over at the Ministry of Defence.[13]

As the 1983 general election approached, it seemed that opposition to the American missiles had begun to soften. But this was not wholly due to Heseltine's vigorous campaigning. The Thatcher government had become more popular, mainly thanks to the refusal by the Iron Lady to appease the Argentine General Galtieri. At the time of Heseltine's appointment – six months after the end of the Falklands War – almost two thirds of voters already assumed that the Conservatives would

---

* The present author, who attended the demonstration, can vouch for that.

be re-elected. By contrast, Labour was widely regarded as being incapable of forming an administration, and few people saw Michael Foot as a prime minister in waiting. It was certainly a bonus for Heseltine that an Opposition leader who was ridiculed for a variety of reasons should be so closely associated with the anti-nuclear movement. After Labour's crushing electoral defeat in June 1983 Foot was replaced by Neil Kinnock, who was equally committed to the cause of disarmament. But whether or not Labour could win next time, the 1983 election result made it certain that Britain would get its cruise missiles; demonstrations, like a rally of 400,000 people in Hyde Park on 22 October, were unlikely to overturn the verdict of the ballot box. The weapons were flown into the Greenham base on 14 November 1983. A few days earlier a total of 102 'peace camps' had been set up throughout Britain, but this protest was to no purpose.[14]

This was not quite the end of the story, because the missiles were to be fired from locations outside Greenham Common (to make them more difficult to detect), and the military needed dress rehearsals for this procedure. On 8 March 1984 protestors gathered outside the main gate, where the vehicles were expected to leave the base. But the strong police presence there was a decoy, and the missiles were driven out of a side exit. As Heseltine reported in his memoirs, 'We had shown it could be done, and the propaganda victory was ours. We had relatively little difficulty thereafter.'[15]

It would be a mistake, though, to assume that opposition to nuclear weapons began to fade away from this point. In 1984 a survey found that more than half of the British public thought that their country was 'less safe' now that the missiles were actually in place.[16] In the same year the BBC showed its drama *Threads*, which gave the public a more realistic impression of the effects of an all-out nuclear war and would have made particularly uncomfortable viewing for the inhabitants of Sheffield. June 1984 saw the release of the single 'Two Tribes' by Frankie Goes to Hollywood, accompanied by a video which poked fun at superpower rivalries. The record proved even more successful than the group's chart-topping predecessor 'Relax', which the BBC had banned because of its sexual references. In July 1985 the corporation finally showed Peter Watkins's grimly realistic film *The War Game*, which had been made in 1966 but mothballed after political pressure. It included another imaginary scenario of events in Britain after a nuclear exchange, this time using Kent as the setting.

Yet it is difficult to resist the feeling that the BBC only screened *Threads* and *The War Game* because Mrs Thatcher's re-election had settled the question of nuclear weapons, whether or not the public felt happy about the outcome. Heseltine's successful dress rehearsal at Greenham had been another blow for the left, coming just two days after the meeting between Arthur Scargill and Ian MacGregor which triggered the year-long miners' strike. By the time of the 1987 general election the Conservatives felt that Labour was highly vulnerable on defence issues, despite continuing evidence of public support for unilateral disarmament.* The government's advertisers produced a poster which showed a surrendering soldier with the caption 'Labour's Policy on Arms'. The idea that the anti-nuclear lobby embraced the slogan 'Better red than dead' was genuinely believed by people like Lord Chalfont, if not by Heseltine himself.[17] Undoubtedly there were many people within the anti-nuclear movement who preferred the prospect of life under a communist regime to the destruction of the planet. However, the Conservative equation of support for unilateral disarmament with personal cowardice was a calculated slur against their political opponents. Neil Kinnock's argument that resistance would continue, even in the unlikely event of a Soviet invasion backed by deadly weapons, actually recalled Winston Churchill's defiant rhetoric during the Second World War. It reflected a tradition of active British citizenship which long predated the introduction of universal suffrage. The fact that Conservative strategists and their media allies saw no difficulty in presenting Kinnock's suggestion as a call for a ramshackle, *Dad's Army*-like guerrilla force is an eloquent testament to their own ideas about citizenship in a consumer society.

In all probability the Conservative attack on Labour's defence policy proved effective to the extent that it chimed in with general misgivings about the quality of Kinnock's leadership. The feeling that Kinnock would not be an effective spokesman for British interests, either at home or abroad, was enhanced before the election when the Labour leader was snubbed by members of the US administration on an ill-conceived trip to Washington. By contrast, during her own visit to Moscow in March 1987, Mrs Thatcher was treated with respect by her supposed foes in the Kremlin and acclaimed by the public on walkabouts.

---

* In 1986 Gallup found that a third of voters (compared to just 21 per cent in 1980) wanted Britain to renounce all nuclear weapons; see Wybrow, 144.

Whatever the personal qualities of Foot and Kinnock, they had been regarded as unelectable from the outset – whether or not they had supported the British nuclear deterrent. Yet after the 1987 general election Labour's leaders accepted the Conservative view that their policy on nuclear weapons had been a serious liability. Despite all the evidence from independent opinion surveys, Labour's own research apparently found no support at all for unilateral disarmament. As one senior adviser put it, 'People had a simple, common-sense view of the issue – if you have a dog, no one will attack you; if someone else has a knife, you should have a knife also.'[18] In the face of this irresistible logic, Neil Kinnock decided that the party would have to drop unilateralism – despite his own long-standing emotional commitment to the cause. Tacitly, he had now accepted a defence policy which, as he put it in June 1983, carried 'a risk and a price that passes all understanding'. Far from being a massive boost to CND, Labour's endorsement of unilateral disarmament had brought a respectable case into discredit.[19]

In its impact on British political culture, the defeat of the anti-nuclear movement ranks alongside incidents like Grunwick, the miners' strike and the Wapping dispute. It was no less significant although the effect on individuals was often unconscious or repressed. Fear of a nuclear holocaust was not confined to the left, as opinion polls had testified. Even those who accepted the government's argument about effective deterrence still had to live with the possibility of an accidental conflagration – a prospect which seemed more real in April 1986, when the nuclear power plant at Chernobyl in the Ukraine went into meltdown. This incident accentuated existing fears about the damage inflicted on the planet in the quest for economic growth, rather than war, which had been heightened by the discovery of the hole in the ozone layer over Antarctica in 1985. In 1974 Britain had produced the world's first avowedly environmentalist party – People, which became the Ecology Party the following year. In the wake of Chernobyl even Margaret Thatcher allowed a green tinge to feature in some of her speeches.

Over the years after 1975 environmental campaigners were able to build a convincing case for curbs on economic growth in the interests of long-term planetary survival. But although they urged immediate action to prevent the extinction of human life within a few generations, this message hardly registered outside the small minority of Britons who were not preoccupied with personal gratification. Even if the eventual effect would be similar the nature of the threat from nuclear war was very different, and was capable of terrifying even the most blink-ered consumer. Even public-spirited people were left, as Queen's Brian May put it, passively 'waiting for the hammer to fall'. Some wondered whether it was worth bringing children into such a world. When life could be extinguished with the flick of a distant switch by an unknown hand it was certainly not worth doing much constructive planning. Young people in the 1960s had embraced hedonism for positive reasons. Those who grew up 'in the shadow of the mushroom cloud' were more likely to live for the present because they preferred not to contemplate a fearful future.

II

Human fear is often aroused by an unknown or imagined 'other'. This was certainly the case among people who feared the Soviet Union. Few Britons had any idea what communism really meant. The present author remembers a lesson on the subject at junior school in the early 1970s. The teacher was a local clergyman – a perfect propagandist for impressionable young minds, since he was popular and normally very genial. However, for the purposes of the lesson he adopted a very sombre demeanour, and the class was left feeling that communists were an alien species who would stop at nothing to destroy Christian civil-isation. Their beliefs were left unexplained; we were not even given the standard warning that communism was seductive in theory but corrupted in practice. It was simply something to be feared without further investigation. For most of the class the lesson must have been like childhood inoculations against mumps or measles; they were most unlikely to catch communism even if they were exposed to it in later life. The risk, though, was that others might make inquiries for them-selves, and wonder why such a serious subject had been entrusted to a person who was so transparently partisan.

Possibly Soviet schoolchildren had the same kind of experience when they were taught about the evils of capitalism, but there was little chance of comparing the quality of lessons across the Iron Curtain in the 1970s. Largely thanks to official Soviet disapproval of meaningful cultural contacts, few British people had any knowledge of their supposed enemies. In the early 1970s the Soviet gymnast Olga Korbut created a highly favourable impression, but this elfin figure could not be regarded as an average representative of the 'evil empire'. Most of the well-known Russians were persecuted dissidents whose cases were raised by Western sympathisers – people like the great novelist Alexander Solzhenitsyn, who was admired by Margaret Thatcher, at least until he was expelled from Russia in 1974 and began to speak out against the spiritual deficiencies of the West. As late as 1986, Sting, the former teacher turned lead singer of The Police, thought it worthwhile to point out (somewhat plaintively) that the Russians 'loved their children too'. In fact most Russians were very like the British, but infinitely more stoical because they were less affluent. If more British people had known this, they might have been less willing to support the installation of missiles which had the potential to obliterate the unseen enemy.

For some citizens of the UK, the 'other' was not just someone living behind the Iron Curtain; there were plenty of strangers *within* the country's geographical boundaries. The most obvious example was Northern Ireland, where the new 'troubles' which began at the end of the 1960s reinforced traditional social, cultural and religious divisions. In Belfast, the estrangement between Catholic and Protestant was symbolised by 'peace lines', first erected in the early 1970s at the request of the British army. Residential patterns reflected the fact that Belfast was divided by class as much as religion; thus the poor Protestants of the Shankhill Road were near-neighbours of equally deprived Catholics in the Falls and the Ardoyne. The nature of the violence meant that fear was a constant factor in daily life; most victims were singled out by murderous strangers purely on the grounds of religion.

The IRA tended to be more selective in its targeting than the Protestant paramilitary groups, which featured sadistic maniacs like the 'Shankhill butchers'. But its use of bombs to damage property and morale could also result in random massacres. On 8 November 1987 one of its devices exploded without warning in Enniskillen, County Fermanagh while local people were paying their respects to the dead of two world wars. Eleven people who had been honouring the sacrifices of others were crushed when a wall collapsed. Even the leaders of the Republican movement were mortified by this 'accident', although it took ten years for them to issue a formal apology and they continued to plan attacks which had the potential to cause similar levels of 'collateral damage'. Just four months later an active service unit travelled to Gibraltar to prepare for a car bomb attack on the Royal Anglian Regimental Band. They were being watched by members of the SAS, who shot the three members of the gang. Subsequently the European Court of Human Rights ruled that the killings could have been avoided. Controversial as it was in itself, the incident had fearful consequences. During the funeral of the three IRA members at Milltown cemetery a loyalist gunman, Michael Stone, killed three mourners. One of them was another IRA member; when he in turn came to be buried, two young British soldiers who had driven close to the funeral cortège in an unmarked car were dragged out, beaten and shot dead. Amid the lurid media coverage there was little acknowledgement that the people who had attacked the soldiers might have been in genuine fear for their lives, so soon after the murders at Milltown cemetery.[20]

As Peter Taylor has written, 'The horrific pictures confirmed the majority of the British public in its view that republicans were savages.' This attitude had informed the response to developments connected with Northern Ireland since the IRA resumed its armed struggle. With the security of hindsight, it is easy to hail the British for their phlegmatic response to the threat from Irish terrorism. Londoners, in particular, were congratulated for emulating the spirit of the Blitz. However, the reality was rather different. For example, the IRA active service unit which killed Ross McWhirter and nine others in 1975 was widely feared because so many of its attacks were indiscriminate: 'workers went to their offices, fearful that they might be blown up on the way. Commuters shunned the Underground, suspecting it might be the next target for the bombers. Women refused to go shopping in the West End in case they never returned.' After the gang killed two people in a Chelsea restaurant with a ball-bearing bomb, 'London was on the verge of panic and its restaurants were virtually empty.'[21]

When a group of Republican prisoners went on hunger strike in Long Kesh jail (the 'Maze') in 1981, they won worldwide sympathy for their demand to be treated as political prisoners. Most Britons, though, supported Mrs Thatcher in her refusal to back down, even when eleven prisoners had died. The government succeeded in convincing the public that the dispute was about better living conditions for prisoners, rather than an attempt to gain recognition that IRA activities were not motivated by ordinary criminality. The fact that Bobby Sands, who was elected MP for Fermanagh and South Tyrone shortly before his death, was prepared to forgo food for nearly seventy days should have suggested that the prisoners were not merely campaigning for luxurious accommodation. His by-election victory underlined the extent to which the IRA was a real political force in Northern Ireland. But since most Britons on the mainland believed that people in the north of Ireland were crazy enough to kill each other without any reason at all, the hunger strikes were generally regarded as an outbreak of the old madness in a new manifestation. The subsequent decision of Ken Livingstone and the ruling Labour group on the GLC to hold talks with Sinn Fein, the IRA's political wing, was very helpful to the tabloid press in its campaign to portray prominent members of the left as 'loonies'. It was not so widely reported that the British government acceded to several of the IRA demands soon after the hunger strike was called off in October 1981.[22]

In the 1980s there were fewer attacks on the British mainland, but the IRA could still provoke fear and outrage. In July 1982 eleven soldiers were killed in two separate bomb attacks in London parks. In Hyde Park a nail bomb caused widespread carnage as the Household Cavalry passed by on their way to perform the Changing of the Guard at Buckingham Palace. Seven horses were also killed in the blast, complementing the horrific story with gruesome pictures which could not have been used if all the victims had been human. These, together with the higher death toll, overshadowed the other incident on the same day, in Regent's Park, but this was no less barbaric. The target was a military band entertaining holidaymakers and office workers with a selection of tunes from the musical *Oliver*. Some contorted logic might have portrayed the dead soldiers as enemy combatants, whether or not they were engaged in military operations when they were killed; but the bomb had been planted without any consideration for innocent onlookers. There was a similar outrage in December 1983, outside Harrods department store close to the site of the Hyde Park bomb. Three of the six people who died were policemen, who could be chalked up by the terrorists as active agents of the British state. Not even the criminally insane could deny that the other three victims fell into a different category. It was a reminder to the public that they would have to fear for their personal safety even when searching for Christmas gifts.

The bombing of Brighton's Grand Hotel in October 1984, which showed that the IRA was capable of wiping out half the cabinet with a little luck, understandably hardened Mrs Thatcher's resolve to defeat the terrorists. The Anglo-Irish Agreement, which she signed just over a year later, was certainly no gesture of surrender. Rather, it was a formal recognition by the British and Irish governments that armed Republicanism was a shared problem which could not be addressed without greater cooperation. However, Unionists in Northern Ireland and at Westminster regarded the agreement as a betrayal. Enoch Powell, still the Ulster Unionist MP for South Down, made a direct accusation of treachery against the prime minister in the House of Commons.[23] For several months Northern Ireland was subjected to a series of strikes, demonstrations and riots as the Unionists tried to repeat their success of 1974, when they had forced the British to abandon devolved government and restore direct rule from Westminster. This time they failed to secure a change in policy, thanks to the largely Protestant Royal Ulster Constabulary (RUC). For many years a prime target for Republicans, RUC officers were now subjected to intimidation by so-called loyalists but, with the help of extra troops from the mainland, they kept some semblance of order.

By the mid-1980s most Britons who followed the course of events in Northern Ireland acknowledged that the security forces were adopting 'dirty' tactics in the fight against the IRA. But the rulings of foreign bodies like the European Court of Human Rights made no impression on public opinion; if anything, people were glad that the terrorists were being made to taste some of their own medicine. Few were troubled by the possibility that the Gibraltar gang were killed when they presented no imminent threat either to the soldiers or the public, and without adequate warning. In 1984 Manchester's deputy chief constable, John Stalker, began an official investigation into allegations dating back to the late 1970s that the security forces had operated a 'shoot to kill' policy in Northern Ireland. Two years later, with his investigations almost finished, Stalker was suddenly removed from the inquiry. The official reason was that his association with a Manchester businessman had aroused suspicions, but if the politicians of the day had been subjected to the same test, most of the Parliamentary Conservative Party would have been debarred from office. The Stalker inquiry was completed, but no prosecutions resulted. Stalker himself became a media celebrity, particularly popular with advertisers who tacitly accepted that he was a decent man whose reputation had been smeared for political reasons.

Mrs Thatcher herself had few qualms about British tactics in Northern Ireland. In the words of the BBC's former political editor John Cole, she showed 'a total lack of feeling for a province that was remote from her own background'.[24] The continued British presence in Northern Ireland was the practical price which had to be paid for her theoretical attachment to the Union. But it is doubtful whether her outlook constituted a significant obstacle to real progress in the 1980s. If the people of Northern Ireland had to become war weary before a breakthrough, then she was the ideal person to preside over that decade. Since the mid-1970s there had been several impressive peace campaigns, but all had failed to move the advocates of violence. For Mrs Thatcher, there was a tragic personal postscript. Her close friend Ian Gow resigned as a junior minister in protest against the Anglo-Irish Agreement, and was still in the political wilderness when he was assassinated by the IRA in July 1990, by a car bomb outside his Sussex home. Thatcher had been mourning her ally Airey Neave when she became prime minister, and was still grieving for Gow when, four months after his murder, she was removed from office.

Under Thatcher's successor John Major there was a more concerted drive to find a settlement, after bombs in the City of London and in Warrington, where two children were killed on 20 March 1993. However, progress was hampered by Major's precarious parliamentary position, which made it vital for him to ensure at least the benevolent neutrality of the Ulster Unionists. The IRA showed that its patience was running out by breaking a ceasefire on 10 February 1996. Their strategy had the opposite intention of America's neutron bomb; this new campaign was designed to destroy property rather than to kill. Even so, there were human casualties. A half-ton lorry bomb in London's Docklands killed two people and caused almost £100 million of damage, affecting even the newly built Canary Wharf Tower a quarter of a mile away. The fact that the IRA had abstained from 'military operations' for almost a year and a half, persuading many Londoners that the threat was over, added to the impact of the Docklands bomb. Just eight days later an IRA operative was killed when the device he was carrying exploded prematurely on a London bus. In June a massive bomb devastated Manchester's city centre. The IRA shared the general expectation that Major would lose the 1997 general election, and a bomb hoax just a few weeks before the poll caused the Grand National to be postponed for a day, adding to the general sense of chaos under the Conservatives and reminding Labour that Republican terrorists were still in business.

Apart from this home-grown terrorism, Britain felt some shock waves from problems further afield. At the end of April 1981 six Iranian dissidents took hostages at their country's embassy overlooking Kensington gardens. After a siege lasting nearly a week one of the hostages was killed, whereupon special forces stormed the building. Five of the gunmen were killed, and dramatic television footage of the operation made the SAS into national heroes. Enthusiasm for their feat tended to obscure the unsettling proximity of the violence to such cultural landmarks and tourist totems as the Victoria and Albert Museum and the Royal Albert Hall. It also allowed most people to forget that the gunmen had been opposed to the revolutionary Islamic regime of Ayatollah Khomeini and would probably have been recipients of covert British aid if they had kept their activities at a safer distance.

Apart from the masked warriors of the SAS, the alarming embassy siege also produced a more traditional British hero in PC Trevor Lock, who had been captured at the outset but still managed to play an active role in the drama, tackling one of the gunmen as the SAS burst in. By contrast, another police officer caught up in an embassy siege in the early 1980s ended up being remembered as a tragic victim. On 17 April 1984 twenty-five-year-old WPC Yvonne Fletcher, who had been policing a small demonstration outside the Libyan People's Bureau in St James's Square, bled to death after shots were fired from the building. Diplomatic relations between Britain and Libya were severed. The country's leader, Colonel Gaddafi, became Britain's leading international hate figure during the 1980s. He was blamed, among other things, for having funded Mrs Thatcher's chief internal enemies, the IRA and Arthur Scargill's NUM. On threadbare evidence, a Libyan agent was eventually found guilty of the worst terrorist atrocity in British history – the bombing of Pan Am flight 103, which plunged into the Scottish border town of Lockerbie on 22 December 1988. All 259 passengers – who would have included the former Sex Pistol, John Lydon had he arrived on time for the flight – were killed, along with eleven Lockerbie residents.

Gaddafi himself had escaped an airborne assassination attempt in a US bombing raid of April 1986. The planes took off from British bases, with Mrs Thatcher's permission. She noted in her memoirs that the mission was a 'success', although residential areas were hit and one of the victims was Gaddafi's adopted daughter. Taking a view of human life which would become increasingly familiar when British politicians spoke about massacres in the Middle East, Thatcher complained that the television coverage 'concentrated all but exclusively not on the strategic importance of the targets but on weeping women and children'.[25] In fact the prime minister had serious reservations about the wisdom of the Libyan raid, which demonstrated that the imbalances of global power could not be redressed by her personal friendship with Ronald Reagan.

III

It was frequently remarked that the IRA terror campaigns made the British people more resilient, and it certainly prepared them for the shock of Lockerbie. However, every nation with a road network had grown accustomed to a regular toll of 'unnatural' deaths. In 1976 more than 6,500 people died in Britain as a result of road traffic accidents. Anyone who climbed behind the wheel of a vehicle had to be aware of some risk, and other road users like cyclists were especially vulnerable. More than 20,000 pedestrians were either killed or seriously injured in 1976, and almost 8,000 of these were under fifteen. By that time the number of dead and injured had actually been falling for ten years, and over the next three decades the death toll more than halved. The British record compared very favourably in this respect with the rest of Europe, but that was eloquent testimony to the capacity of Europeans in general to tolerate the waste of human life where cars were concerned. Certainly it was small comfort to the victims and their families, in what Mrs Thatcher once hailed as 'the great car economy'.

For the media, death on the roads usually merited little more than a brief mention in the local press. Incidents connected with the railways or the aviation industry were a different matter, because although the annual toll was invariably tiny in comparison the majority of deaths tended to occur in one-off 'spectaculars'. The result, though, was that people developed a fear of these means of transport which was out of all proportion to the relative risk. There was a terrible disaster at the beginning of our period on the London Underground. On 28 February 1975 a Northern Line train failed to stop at Moorgate station in the City of London. It ploughed into a blocked tunnel, killing forty-three people and injuring many others. London commuters were not even free from fear when they reached their destinations; on 18 November 1987 thirty-one people died after fire turned the wooden escalator at

King's Cross into an inferno. At least it could be assumed that British Rail's overground trains were safe – until a collision at Clapham in December 1988, which killed thirty-five passengers. After the railways were privatised in 1993 there would be further disasters, sapping the confidence of commuters at a time when policymakers were (belatedly and half-heartedly) trying to curtail the use of the motor car. In the late 1980s there was also a maritime catastrophe – the sinking of the ferry *Herald of Free Enterprise* at Zeebrugge in March 1987, with the loss of nearly two hundred lives.

If the travelling public felt more unsafe after 1975, Britons were no less vulnerable in their leisure activities. In August 1989 fifty-one people, mainly young partygoers, died after a collision between the pleasure cruiser *Marchioness* and the dredger *Bowbelle* on the Thames. Football spectators had learned to be more wary than pleasure-boat parties for a variety of reasons, but no one could have anticipated three very different tragedies within four years, which put the future of the game itself into serious doubt. On 11 May 1985, when more than 11,000 Bradford City football fans had gathered at the Valley Parade ground – not so much for the scheduled game against Lincoln City but rather to celebrate the presentation of the Third Division Championship trophy – a fire broke out just before half-time in the rickety wooden main stand, killing fifty-six fans. Just three weeks later, thirty-nine people died in the Heysel Stadium, Brussels, before the European Cup final. Liverpool supporters had rushed at rival Juventus fans and a wall collapsed. Terrible as these incidents were, before the end of the decade they had been overshadowed by the crushing and suffocation of ninety-six Liverpool supporters at the Leppings Lane end of the Hillsborough ground in Sheffield on 15 April 1989. Fans perished in front of the cameras while many of the police in attendance looked on.

Of the three football-related disasters only Heysel had been caused by aggressive behaviour, but football supporters had been a source of fear in Britain for many years. In September 1969 a *Daily Express* reporter had predicted that a repetition of the crowd trouble he had just witnessed could lead to more than ten deaths. By a terrible irony, he had been watching Liverpool play Sheffield Wednesday at Hillsborough.[26] In the same year a government working party had suggested that all-seater stadiums might help to reduce violence during the game itself, as well as reducing the risk of accidents. Nothing was done at the time, and incidents like the collapse of a staircase at the

Ibrox stadium, Glasgow, which killed sixty-six people in 1971, could be regarded as the kind of freakish accident which might happen whenever people were gathered together in large numbers.

The first murder directly related to football occurred in 1974 after a game between Blackpool and Bolton. By the mid-1970s, hooliganism was regarded as an inevitable accompaniment to professional football. But things only seemed to get worse after that. By 1985/6 – the season of the accidental Bradford fire – arrests at grounds had risen to a record 6,000. In this context trouble of any kind at football matches tended to be seen as a manifestation of the hooligan problem. In turn, this was commonly regarded as part of a more general indictment of British (male) youth, and often resulted in calls for the reintroduction of compulsory National Service. The tabloid press was always ready to express indignation, even when it had helped provoke the violence in the first place. Trouble connected with football matches was always guaranteed a prominent place in the tabloids, since it brought together the much-loved ingredients of violence and sport. The *Sun* came a cropper with its insensitive reporting of the Hillsborough disaster, which provoked a boycott of the newspaper in some parts of Merseyside, but it was far from being the only offender against taste and common sense. Typically, before a game involving the England team the tabloids would appeal to pugnacious nationalism; when England played Germany in June 1996, for example, the *Daily Mirror* previewed the game under the headline '*Achtung*! Surrender!' At the same time, the MP Alan Clark was rebuked by Conservative Central Office after publicly praising the 'martial spirit' of English hooligans, and describing football matches as 'the modern equivalents of medieval tournaments'.[27]

It was more difficult to produce even a spuriously romantic rationale for violence between supporters of rival British teams at this time. According to one combat-hardened Chelsea fan, 'Not wanting to fight at football matches seemed unnatural, almost un-British.' Allegiance to a particular team provided a source of collective identity, at a time when more constructive alternatives were in short supply. Membership of a violent gang was the ultimate proof of loyalty, and the aim of group activity was to win the fear and respect of rival hooligans. To back away from a fight was to bring disgrace on one's team and, by extension, to tarnish the reputation of the area which the team was supposed to represent, even when the entire playing staff (and manager) lacked any local connections. For some, indeed, the football was barely relevant; the whole point of the violence was to confront one's fear, which, as one hooligan put it, 'passed as soon as it arrived and became a good-time memory, like a horror movie where people are petrified yet come out of the cinema laughing'. However, the fear associated with football violence could not be confined to those who actively sought it. City centres on match days were always tense, and best avoided by non-combatants. The quest for the adrenaline rush of impending conflict could even inspire hooligans to intrude into more serious stand-offs. When visiting Manchester City fans failed to show up for a planned fracas in May 1981, the Chelsea Headhunters decided to check on the progress of the Iranian embassy siege. Several hundred Iranians were praying outside the building. To the astonishment of the police, the Chelsea fans charged into the midst of the worshippers, trampling on those unable to flee.[28]

By the mid-1980s, football hooliganism was widely regarded as the new 'British disease'. In fact, the problem was now almost entirely English; although Scottish supporters had shown their own 'martial spirit' by tearing up the Wembley pitch in 1977 and games between the Glasgow rivals Celtic and Rangers were always unsavoury sectarian occasions, followers of the national team behaved impeccably whenever they left the British Isles. As the reputation of English fans deteriorated, it almost seemed like a national imperative for the Scots to win the hearts of their foreign hosts. For Margaret Thatcher – whose sympathy even for peaceable football supporters was strictly limited – the hooligans were 'an alien breed, little better than the striking miners, another face of the "enemy within"'. As her best biographer notes, the problem furnished her with another opportunity 'to legislate on a basis of very little knowledge'.[29] She favoured a national system of identity cards for everyone who attended a match – a system which Luton Town had already introduced – but the idea was dropped as unworkable after she left office. The gangs preferred to identify themselves through calling cards, like the ones left on the beaten bodies of their victims by West Ham's much-feared Inter-City Firm. All-seater stadiums, though, were finally enforced for Premiership and First Division clubs after the 1990 Taylor report into the circumstances surrounding the Hillsborough disaster; the sale of alcohol 'in sight of the pitch' had already been banned. None of these measures could thwart the thugs who wanted to prove their virility in prearranged battles outside the grounds, but after the Taylor report, the corrupting

influence of money replaced violence as the main reason to stop taking
an active interest in the 'national game'.

In Alan Clark's complacent view, football hooliganism was something like a safety valve – a conduit for violent instincts which would
be expressed in other ways if the game was abolished. However, the
problem became more acute at a time when the public was expressing
a more generalised fear of violence. In 1981 a Gallup poll found that
83 per cent of Britons regarded violent crime as the main social problem
facing the country. At that year's Conservative Party conference a succession of speakers called for the return of capital punishment. This was
not a new development at that forum. But in 1981 the speeches were
applauded by the prime minister, and a motion praising the government's existing policy was defeated, provoking the home secretary,
Willie Whitelaw, to offer his resignation.[30] This was the year of inner-
city rioting, but other well-publicised incidents added to the sense of
personal danger and the desire for a return of the noose. Peter Sutcliffe
(born 1946), the 'Yorkshire Ripper', was caught in January 1981 after
at least thirteen murders, apparently beginning in 1975. Most of his
victims were prostitutes, who were usually treated by the tabloids as
being accessories to their own deaths. But in June 1977 Sutcliffe had
murdered a sixteen-year-old shop assistant, and a year later belied his
nom de guerre by crossing the Pennines to kill in Manchester. The
police broadcast a tape recording – later exposed as a hoax – which
suggested that the culprit came from the north-east of England. By this
time it was natural for women from Lancashire to Tyneside to feel that
it was unsafe to leave their homes unaccompanied after dark. They
were sharing the terror felt by women in Cambridge in 1974/5, when
a serial rapist was at large. In their anxiety to catch the criminal, police
began hiding up trees and behind dustbins.[31] Peter Cook, who committed
the offences, had taken to wearing a hood with the word 'rapist' written
on it; as he later explained, this was to 'save himself the bother of
introducing himself'. Understandably, this increased both the panic and
the publicity, and the shock value of the mask made it a desirable
fashion accessory for the Sex Pistols and their fans. Dennis Nilsen (born
1945), by contrast, was a London-based civil servant who quietly killed
fifteen homosexuals between 1978 and 1983, when he was apprehended because the drainage system at his home in Muswell Hill had
become choked with body parts. Before then, the disappearance of his
victims had attracted minimal public notice.

Sutcliffe's killings – inspired, according to his unoriginal claim, by the voice of God – spread terror because it seemed that he would never be apprehended. But another mass killer of the Thatcher years managed to generate lasting fear in less than one hour of a sunny afternoon. On 19 August 1987 Michael Ryan, a loner and fantasist who had been collecting weapons since the late 1970s, shot fifteen people dead and wounded fourteen others during a rampage around his home village of Hungerford, Berkshire. Whether strangers or neighbours, Ryan shot everything that came within his sights; he even executed his mother and his dog, before destroying himself in the local school. It was a fitting place to end Ryan's spree, since his behaviour recalled the school murders committed by Barbara Spencer in San Diego eight years earlier – the event which inspired Bob Geldof to write the hit single 'I Don't Like Mondays'. However, it was thought that Ryan had taken his ideas from the film *Rambo*. Whatever the inspiration, he had brought Britain a step closer to its nuclear ally across the Atlantic. The national murder rate might bear no comparison, but death by random shooting in a quiet village was now a possibility for Britons as well as Americans.

While Sutcliffe and Nilsen remained at large far too long, other killers enjoyed even more protracted careers. Fred West (born 1942), a semi-literate builder, murdered at least twelve people between the late 1960s and 1987, including his first wife, his natural daughter and two women whom he had made pregnant. The precise death toll exacted by West might never be known. His second wife, Rosemary, probably played some role in the hideous killings, but there was never any chance that she would replace the favourite tabloid poster-girl of fear, the 'Moors Murderer' Myra Hindley (1942–2002). Hindley remained newsworthy more than three decades after being jailed for life, mainly because of Lord Longford's unavailing attempts to win her release.

As in the West case, there is uncertainty about the numbers killed by the GP Dr Harold Shipman (born 1946). But he destroyed life on a scale about which West could only fantasise, and never had to adopt the latter's tactic of burying victims in his own cellar. Starting in the mid-1970s, by the time Shipman was apprehended in 1998 it was estimated that he had killed 236 of his patients – not far short of the number of deaths in the Lockerbie disaster. Based first in Todmorden, Yorkshire, then in the Manchester suburb of Hyde, Shipman had avoided being debarred from practising in 1975 when he was exposed as a drug addict and a fraudster. Unlike Fred West, Shipman did not manage to hang himself before facing trial; he had been convicted and was serving fifteen life sentences when he committed suicide in January 2004. His motivations remained obscure; apart from the occasional hope of financial gain, it seems likely that he wanted to reduce the number of patients under his care in order to make his professional life easier. While Shipman went about his business unobtrusively, the Lincolnshire nurse Beverley Allitt began harming young children in the hope of attracting attention to her caring qualities. Four died and nine more became seriously ill after Allitt injected them with insulin. Shipman escaped detection for so long because he preyed mostly on elderly people whose deaths could be attributed to natural causes. In Allitt's case the series of mishaps involving babies and children soon aroused suspicions, and she was arrested in 1991. As a child-killer who had abused a position of trust – and above all as a woman – Allitt was nicknamed the 'Angel of Death' and was sure to be remembered as one of Britain's worst offenders. But Harold Shipman defied easy categorisation, partly because the scale of his crimes was beyond comprehension but also because the public found it difficult to associate such barbarity with a middle-class professional.

Despite the extensive and sometimes hysterical publicity surrounding some murder cases, deliberate killing was still relatively rare in Britain. In 1980 the police recorded 620 instances of homicide – murder, manslaughter or infanticide – in England and Wales. Ten years later the figure had inched upwards, to 664. But one of the few things that made the 1990s notable was a significant increase in criminal activity as a whole. In 1995 the British Crime Survey (based on interviews with members of the public rather than police records) estimated that there had been almost 20 million crimes in the previous twelve months, and that about 40 per cent of the population of England and Wales had been victims during that period. Fear of burglary and vehicle crime was particularly strong. In the late 1980s and early 1990s there had been an upsurge in the theft of cars, sometimes for profitable resale but more often for the thrill of driving too fast. This 'joy-riding' brought a double fear – among motorists, whose cars could be stolen and very often crashed by uninsured thieves, and among other road users, who faced an additional hazard in the form of vehicles driven at high speeds and often with inadequate control. Sometimes the erratic driving was deliberate; 'ram raiders' realised that a stolen vehicle could be used to give quick (if somewhat messy) access to retail premises.

While the dangers posed by joy-riders could never be justified by any level of boredom, young people were also debarred from less destructive avenues of escapism. The 'acid house' craze, which reached its zenith in the so-called Summer of Love in 1988, spread from the outskirts of London to recession-hit northern towns like Blackburn, where abandoned warehouses were transformed from places of fruitless toil into venues for all-night festivals of hedonism. At first even the *Sun* welcomed this spontaneous movement, but when the tabloids realised the central role played by the Class A drug methylenedioxymethamphetamine – more commonly known as Ecstasy – they quickly changed their tone. Far from making users aggressive, Ecstasy usually created an impulse to embrace the whole world. But a few users did die after taking it – most notably Leah Betts, a policeman's daughter who fell into a coma during her eighteenth birthday party in 1995 – and its sudden popularity provoked a predictable panic. Adverse comments by Conservative MPs were followed by a ban by *Top of the Pops* on records which included the word 'acid', and a series of heavy-handed police raids on the spontaneous acid house parties.[32] The 1994 Criminal Justice and Public Order Act was drawn up with this movement specifically in mind, following a previous Public Order Act of 1986 and the ominously named Entertainment (Increased Penalties) Act, passed in 1990. Shortly afterwards a 'rave' party at Gildersome near Leeds was broken up by the police, resulting in more than 800 arrests. However, as Chas Critcher has written, Ecstasy was 'reviled in principle but condoned in practice'. Effective suppression of the drug 'would have required a mass mobilisation of the state against a substantial minority of youth'. Instead, restrictions on nightclubs were relaxed so that police could at least keep a closer eye on activities.[33] The intrusion into the rave scene of gun-toting gangsters, drawn in by the potent mix of illegality and profit, also helped to reduce the appeal of the spontaneous gatherings.[34]

The 1986 Public Order Act, which allowed the police to break up any gathering of more than twelve vehicles, was mainly aimed at new age travellers, who were a recurrent feature of tabloid journalism in these years. Almost invariably they were depicted as a disruptive, anti-social influence, descending uninvited on peaceful communities. Aggression towards the travellers was less widely publicised. On 1 June 1985 the Wiltshire police launched an all-out assault on a group heading towards Stonehenge for the summer solstice. Twenty-four

victims successfully sued the police for their brutal actions, which probably owed something to the euphoric mood after the recent defeat of
the miners. Measures like the 1994 Criminal Justice and Public Order
Act were designed to close down such avenues of legal redress for the
travellers, who numbered around 40,000 at the time.[35] It seemed that
the state was determined to extinguish even peaceful-minded noncon-
formism, backed by a public opinion which was being encouraged by
the tabloids to fear anything which it did not understand. In 1992 the
Daily Mail highlighted the case of a well-behaved middle-class schoolgirl who entered a 'dark tunnel of rebellion', deliberately failing her A
levels and becoming obsessed with the environment. After taking up
with a traveller she developed the 'eccentric syndrome which finds
something "wrong" in living in a centrally-heated, wall-to-wall carpeted
house'. Readers were left in no doubt that the young woman's subsequent death in a freak car accident was the direct result of her lifestyle
choice.[36]

The Criminal Justice and Public Order Act had already begun its
parliamentary passage by the time of the 1993 Conservative Party
conference, at which John Major launched a 'back to basics' initiative.
Major had embarked on his premiership in November 1990 by revealing
a vision of a nation 'at ease with itself'. When he made his ill-fated
conference speech, the statute book already bore testimony to the unre-
laxed state of the nation under his stewardship; indeed, it may have
dawned on him that continued Conservative success at the ballot box
depended upon the ability of his party and its tabloid allies to convince
the public that a vote for Labour would unleash the gathering forces
of anarchy. Fear could be a positive electoral force, if only the law-
abiding majority could be made to cling to the existing government
for physical protection.

Unfortunately for Major, his newly-coined slogan implied that for
fourteen years successive Conservative governments had been subjecting
the 'basics' to culpable neglect. In any case, Labour's home affairs
spokesperson Tony Blair had already put on record his own determination to be 'tough on crime, tough on the causes of crime'. After Blair
took the Labour leadership in 1994 his successor at home affairs, Jack
Straw, was careful to respond to public expressions of fear. When Thomas
Hamilton entered a school gymnasium in Dunblane on 13 March 1996
and shot dead sixteen young children along with their teacher, Straw
immediately called for a total ban on handguns in private ownership.

The Conservatives, who had much closer links with the British gun lobby, were divided and hesitant on this issue. A month after Dunblane, Straw spoke out against 'incivility and loutishness in town centres', promising to crack down on such antisocial behaviour when his party took office. He also supported moves by local councils to ban drinking in 'unauthorised areas', though he hastened to assure journalists that 'Your picnic with claret by the banks of the Thames will be safe in Labour's hands.'[37] This selective approach made New Labour appear even tougher on crime than the party of law and order. In March 1992 the Conservatives had enjoyed a 21 per cent lead over Labour when voters were asked which party would be best at tackling crime. By the time of the 1997 general election, Labour was ahead by 27 points (53 to 26 per cent).[38] It was not lost on the incoming government that they had achieved this remarkable turnaround by occupying natural Tory territory. In office they continued moving steadily to the right, for want of any bright ideas about tackling the 'causes of crime'.

New Labour's approach to crime was strongly influenced by the findings of its 'focus groups' – small panels of supposedly 'representative' citizens whose views were bound to be distorted by an unfamiliar group setting. At one such event in 1996 a woman compared British society to 'a black slime that could seep under your front door'.[39] In fact, the 'black slime' was already starting to recede. By 2003 the risk of being the victim of any crime had fallen to its lowest level for more than twenty years.[40] However, statistical findings were out of line with public perceptions. In 2003 almost three quarters of the public thought that crime was *rising*. In part, the discrepancy reflects the fact that criminal activity tends to leave an ineffaceable impression on its victims, so that for many years afterwards they will report an opinion that general levels are rising. But exaggerated fears were also generated by the interaction between the media and politicians. Sensational reporting of specific crimes made the public uneasy, and caused politicians to trade rhetorical punches on television in a way which offered minimal reassurance.

Apart from supplying an endless stream of criminal justice bills – and creating 700 new crimes during its first eight years in office – New Labour increased police numbers, which rose by 17,000 between 2000 and 2005.[41] The potential benefits of additional police were suggested in November 2003, when street robberies in London rose by 20 per cent while the Metropolitan Police was preoccupied with security provisions for George W. Bush's state visit.[42] But the new recruits were hardly more visible, and had to be supplemented by community support officers and special constables with more limited powers. In large part, the reduction in crime was due to a gradual resurgence of active citizenship, though this was a citizenship of fear rather than one of positive engagement. After 1982 local residents began to associate in Neighbourhood Watch schemes, of which there were more than 80,000 by the end of the decade.[43] But very often participation began and ended with the application of a sticker to a prominent window. Britons were more likely than their European counterparts to protect their family homes and cars with effective security devices, making burglary and theft more hazardous. The most prosperous communities could hire private security firms to exercise vigilance on their behalf. From June 1984 the BBC programme *Crimewatch* also enabled members of the public to identify some criminals. But while *Crimewatch* had to make do with reconstructions of criminal incidents, closed circuit television offered the chance of catching the original event on screen. CCTV became increasingly popular during the 1990s, partly thanks to government subsidies which boosted the profits of the thriving security industry. Politicians found it easy to conclude from the muted criticism of surveillance that the public feared crime more than an over-intrusive state. But in most cases people only saw footage which promised to lead to an arrest, so they still had little idea of the extent to which they were being watched in their lawful activities.

The combined effects of CCTV, security alarms, police computer databases, DNA testing and *Crimewatch* greatly increased the chances of detection in an increasingly anonymous society whose criminals could be miles away within minutes of committing an offence. Yet technological advances cut both ways; the Internet, for example, offered endless possibilities for fraud. Some serious crimes could never be deterred by the likelihood of being watched during the act. For example, in May 2004 a twenty-two-year-old was kicked and stabbed to death in Ilford by attackers blinded by 'road rage'. There were numerous witnesses, but when giving her story to the press one of them asked not to be named.[44] This reluctance to speak out – let alone to intervene at the appropriate time – was much more understandable when gang violence and guns were involved. Such incidents tended to be concentrated in the poorer areas of specific cities, notably Birmingham, Manchester and Nottingham, as well as London. This meant that the average citizen was unlikely to be affected, and even in 2002/3, when homicides in England and Wales reached a record high of 873, only 8 per cent of murders involved a firearm.[45] But despite the new measure introduced after Dunblane, gun-related offences doubled over New Labour's first two terms in office, allowing the Conservatives to claim at the 2005 general election that one such crime was committed every hour.

Fatal shootings were sure to win widespread publicity and to have a disproportionate impact on public opinion. The murder of the *Crimewatch* presenter Jill Dando in April 1999 had all the ingredients for a media sensation, not least because she was shot on her own doorstep in one of London's most salubrious residential districts. But even in those areas where gun crime had become relatively common, individual cases could terrify the public because the victims often had nothing to do with the dispute. Thus, for example, in January 2003 two teenagers, Letitia Shakespeare and Charlene Ellis, were gunned down outside a party in Birmingham. They died in an attack by a gang trying to avenge the murder of one of its members, who had been shot the previous month.

In view of the public notion that crime had continued to rise under New Labour, it was not surprising that its opinion poll lead began to slip away almost immediately after it took responsibility for the country's deep-rooted and complex disorders. By May 2000 the party was behind the Conservatives again on this issue. However, the Opposition had not done anything in the interim to rekindle public confidence; unlike New Labour, it even lacked a memorable slogan. While voters agreed that law and order was a crucial issue, it had a limited effect on either the 2001 or 2005 general election results. By that time most people had concluded that, for all their bluster, politicians would never make much difference on the ground. The best way to beat crime was to install the latest security equipment, pull up the drawbridge and mind one's own business.

IV

The fall in the official crime figures began under Major's tough-talking home secretary Michael Howard (1993–7), although few people were prepared to give credit either to the minister or the government. The last years of Conservative rule were overshadowed by fears which were invulnerable to rhetoric and even to legislation. Health scares were becoming increasingly common in Britain, and rivalled crime as a source of excitable tabloid headlines. In December 1988 the ministerial career of Major's former lover Edwina Currie was terminated because of a verbal slip which gave the impression that most eggs consumed in Britain contained the salmonella bacterium and carried a risk of serious food poisoning. Another bug, E. coli, caused no ministerial casualties but gave rise to similar scares on a recurrent basis. More worrying was the evidence that some bacterial diseases were becoming resistant to treatment with antibiotics. These illnesses were most likely to be passed on in hospitals, where sick people were gathered together; so that even before Beverley Allitt's crimes became common knowledge the place of healing was regarded with fear, particularly by elderly patients. The 'flesh-eating' bacterial infection, necrotising fasciitis, was a particular favourite with the tabloids when other news stories were in short supply. Methicillin-resistant Staphylococcus aureus caused more lasting fear in the form of its easily pronounced acronym, MRSA.

But in the mid-1980s Britons became aware of diseases which threatened deaths on an even greater scale. Acquired immune deficiency syndrome (AIDS) was only named in 1982, but there had been a few cases in the USA in the late 1970s. By the end of 1983 more than a thousand people had died in North America. However, it was still not known how the disease was transmitted; the connection with homosexual sex was clear, but haemophiliacs also succumbed and it was gradually realised that drug addicts could infect each other by sharing syringes. By 1985 the British public was beginning to panic, with the tabloid press taking its usual constructive part in proceedings. Pupils were kept away from schools by petrified parents when it was rumoured that the disease was present. There were predictable stories about people catching AIDS from coffee cups and toilet seats; firefighters were reluctant to give the kiss of life to victims of smoke inhalation. The veteran broadcaster Malcolm Muggeridge wrote to Mrs Thatcher, seriously suggesting that Mary Whitehouse should be brought into the cabinet to tackle the problem.[46] In March 1986 the British government began a public information campaign which was ridiculed by some but which certainly marked a major advance from the standards of *Protect and Survive*. By then work had progressed on isolating the virus (human immunodeficiency virus, or HIV) which caused AIDS, and drugs were already available which slowed its progress. By November 1991, when

Queen's flamboyant lead singer Freddie Mercury died hours after an announcement that he was suffering from AIDS, public alarm had receded as treatments improved and the real causes of HIV and AIDS were more widely understood. By November 2004 it was calculated that 53,000 Britons had contracted HIV, and there had been more than 7,000 new cases over the year. This was a worrying upward trend. Evidently young people now felt safe enough to disregard advice about safe sex. This also explains a dramatic rise in other sexually transmitted diseases (STDs), including gonorrhoea, syphilis and chlamydia. Overall, it was estimated that cases of STDs rose by almost 300,000 between 1995 and 2000. In boys aged 13–19, the rate of gonorrhoea doubled in just seven years after 1995. As fear receded, the old injunction that people could die because of ignorance became relevant again. It was reported in 2005 that when told that he had contracted HIV through sexual activity, a fourteen-year-old boy had protested, 'That only happens to older people.'[47]

While no one could be entirely safe from the threat of HIV – even those who abstained from sexual activity or intravenous drugs could catch it through a blood transfusion – the risks of infection in Britain were calculable with reasonable confidence. This seemed not to be true of the next big health scare, which had the potential to affect virtually everyone. Bovine spongiform encephalopathy (BSE) was first confirmed in British cattle in November 1986. 'Mad cow disease' attacked the nervous system of its victims, causing erratic behaviour and paralysis, and was invariably fatal. Worries about BSE turned into a panic in early 1996 when it was confirmed that the condition could 'jump the species barrier' and infect humans. Previously the British government had tried to reassure the public that beef was safe, and in May 1990 the Agriculture Minister John Selwyn Gummer had been photographed tucking into a hamburger with his four-year-old daughter, Cordelia. Not normally associated with photo opportunities, Gummer had volunteered for the starring role in one of the great British PR disasters.

After the announcement in March 1996 of a link between BSE in cattle and a new variant of the human Creutzfeldt-Jakob disease (CJD), British beef was placed under an international ban. Accusing European governments which had supported the ban of 'collective hysteria', John Major threatened to disrupt the decision-making processes of the European Union.[48] His gesture had a limited effect on his European counterparts, and he soon backed down. But this was little comfort for British voters, who were left fearing that new regulations concerning beef production had been imposed too late. In some respects BSE was like the nuclear threat writ large; there was absolutely nothing that the average person could do about it, and in 1996 many Britons felt that a bacterial bomb had already gone off without anyone noticing. To make matters worse, it was very difficult to be precise about the number of years that could elapse between exposure to diseased material and the first appearance of symptoms. But scientists knew that the disease had a prolonged incubation period, not least because long-term vegetarians had already succumbed to a slow and miserable death. By 1996 there had been a few deaths which could be attributed to CJD, but there was every prospect that this was the tip of the iceberg. If the early predictions were right, millions of Britons who felt completely healthy had reason to fear that they had already been condemned by an ill-advised visit to a fast-food outlet in the distant past. Cordelia Gummer might have looked fit and well for the cameras a few seconds after swallowing the burger, but the nature of the disease meant that she could not know if she had bitten off more than she could chew for at least a decade.

At the time of writing, it is still impossible to be sure that the early predictions about CJD were unduly pessimistic. However, the level of fatalities shows nothing like the leap that would have happened if the doom-mongers had been right. Yet in early twenty-first-century Britain it remains most unlikely that anyone will sound the all-clear – least of all the tabloid press. No one is ever going to sell a newspaper with the front-page headline, 'Relax – you haven't been killed by your lunch'.

V

The BSE affair reduced even further the fragile British faith in politicians of all parties, although inevitably its effect was greatest on the reputation of the ruling Conservatives, whose hostility to regulation, and relaxed attitude to money-making in general, could be identified as a key factor behind unhealthy farming practices. But it also raised questions of confidence regarding the country's scientific community. It had, after all, taken ten years between the first appearance of disease in cattle and the government's announcement of a hazard to human health. Having apparently left the public unprotected for so long, scientists subsequently failed to provide authoritative estimates of the likely death toll. There were good reasons for these omissions, but the episode suggested at the very least that the general public had become insufficiently sceptical when confronted with anyone who could demonstrate more than a nodding acquaintance with a laboratory.

One reason why the British public failed to reach a balanced perspective on scientific activity was that most people were only made aware of recent developments via the mass media. Despite the wild success of books like *A Brief History of Time* (1988) by the Cambridge cosmologist Stephen Hawking, modern science had never really been 'popularised'. Rather, an ignorant public took a free ride on the back of technological innovation, although it continued to assume that it could still exercise a veto if the scientists came up with anything it disliked. In fact the best-publicised discoveries left the public divided, with some always ready to hail a miracle and the rest vaguely fearing that science was meddling with matters beyond its competence. Fertility treatment, where Britain was a world leader, was particularly prone to polarisation. In July 1978, for example, Louise Brown became the first 'test-tube' baby. Sensational at the time, scientifically aided conception of this kind was passé by 1997, when British scientists unveiled the cloned Dolly the Sheep, who had actually been born in the previous year. The obvious inference that human cloning might be a viable proposition evoked nightmarish visions on the lines of Aldous Huxley's *Brave New World* (1932), but with the additional fear that unhinged dictators might use the technology to create hundreds of minions in their own images. While this prospect made everyone uneasy, men were particularly fearful that artificial conception could make them redundant, at a time when their non-biological roles were also coming under scrutiny.

In 1984 a committee headed by the Oxford philosopher Mary Warnock produced a report on the implications of new developments in human fertilisation. Seven years later the Human Fertilisation and Embryology Authority (HFEA) was established to oversee clinics and research centres. However, the public had reason to suspect that the regulators would always be one step behind the scientific community in this field, and even if most scientists stayed within the rules there would always be others prepared to break them either in the hope of being acclaimed as pioneers or simply for financial gain.

It was not that people thought that scientists were especially immoral. They were just like everyone else – only more clever and better resourced. Britons were aware that life had been transformed in the twentieth century, and that one effect had been to destroy any sense of a widely shared moral framework. Scientists could hardly avoid the impact of the revolutionary changes they had helped to instigate; neither, for that matter, could academics like Mary Warnock. The fragmentation of moral discourse was brilliantly analysed by the Glasgow-born philosopher Alasdair MacIntyre in *After Virtue* (1980). But one result of the moral relativism prevalent in the late twentieth century was that philosophy seemed to have little more to say, except (as in MacIntyre's case) to protest about it, or (like the postmodernists) to celebrate it with pretentious theorising.

The erosion of traditional morality in Britain evades concise explanations, which has not deterred politicians who want to attribute any problem that crops up on their own watch to the social developments of the 1960s. Tony Blair, who resorted to that tactic in a notorious speech of July 2004, might have enjoyed unimpaired first-hand memories of that decade, unlike others who had taken full advantage of the 'permissive society'; but then again he was only sixteen when it ended. In 1970 the American sociologist Alvin Toffler had offered plausible reasons for thinking that technological change was the real force behind developments in the moral sphere, and that far from beginning and ending with the social reforms of the 1960s the process would accelerate in the future. In particular, he envisaged individuals becoming increasingly rootless and more inclined to take a cavalier attitude towards people and property. In moral and material terms people would inhabit a 'throwaway society'. Although Toffler's main concern was America, his remarks also applied to Britain, the country with which the USA enjoyed the closest political and cultural ties, and his book was a best-seller on both sides of the Atlantic. Within a few years of *Future Shock*, consumers were introduced to numerous noteworthy technological innovations, ranging from conveniences like pocket calculators and digital watches (1971 and 1972 respectively) to the revolutionary home computer (1977). While it would be a mistake to think that his predictions were verified in detail, Toffler saw no reason to modify his general thesis in later books like *The Third Wave* (1980).

Toffler believed that successful adaptation was the only way to meet the challenge of the future. He estimated that at the end of the 1960s only 2 or 3 per cent of the world's population was really equipped to meet the shock of the future.[49] Even in the developed world, this left a very substantial residue of problematic people. They would be strongly affected by the outlook of society's pace-setters, particularly through the media. But if they lacked the necessary qualities to compete in the marketplace there was an obvious danger of disillusionment, as they were exposed to the fruits of success but lacked the means to enjoy them.

The people most likely to experience fear in the face of rapid change were the elderly. They could try to adapt by learning to use new technology, but they could not hope to realign their mindsets with every passing fad. The feeling of alienation affected even well-educated people like Tony Blair's ally the New Labour MP Giles Radice (born 1936). On 1 January 2000 he noted in his diary that due to the pace of change, it was 'the present, not the past, which is becoming another country'.[50] It was a damning admission from a politician whose party talked loudly of modernisation, and had recently used 'Things can only get better' as its campaign song.

Ironically, there was an echo of Radice's sentiment in a speech of March 2001 by the Conservative leader William Hague, who claimed that Britain had become a 'foreign land'.[51] Hague, though, was trying to distil a wide range of objections to modern life into an attack on Labour's policy towards asylum seekers and the European Union. The tactic was unlikely to inspire a major Conservative recovery, but it was cleverly designed to get older supporters of the party to the polling booths. By 2001 it was possible for them to feel that the wisdom which supposedly came from experience was discounted; in New Labour's Britain, it was folly to be anything but 'streetwise'. While other forms of discrimination gradually declined in the labour market, 'ageism' was more popular than ever. To the advertising industry, older people were increasingly irrelevant, obsolete; having grown up at a time when electronic gadgets really did save effort, they were far less likely than the young to invest in the latest equipment which merely performed the same tasks a little more efficiently. Since they were of limited interest to most advertisers, older people found that other media were increasingly uncongenial to their outlook. Because of greater life expectancy there were more of them than ever, but they were treated just like another minority market. Even marathon-running programmes like *Coronation Street* now included themes designed to appeal to the young, even at the cost of alienating the established audience. Older people had to make do with *Last of the Summer Wine*, offering viewers a world which shunned 'progress' and featuring the same innocent line in innuendo which had already seemed quaintly nostalgic when it was first screened in 1973. Significantly, *Last of the Summer Wine* was set in rural Yorkshire; it was quite unthinkable that the characters could have exhibited such continuity if they had inhabited a south-eastern suburb.

Conflict between generations was nothing new. But in the last quarter of the twentieth century it took on a new physical intensity, especially in areas of economic deprivation where social solidarity might have been expected at other times. Older people regarded the young with fear and suspicion, particularly after dark. Many decided that it was more prudent to stay indoors. But there were plenty of stories which proved that older people were not even safe at home. A Manchester woman of ninety-seven died in November 2003 after being beaten by a burglar who stole her Christmas savings. In March 2005 an eighty-four-year-old RAF veteran who had suffered three burglaries within a year hanged himself after saying that he no longer wanted to live in such a world.[52]

When daylight returned to many British housing estates, graffiti, smashed bus shelters and discarded condoms showed that the young had marked out their territory. At the 1997 general election New Labour included on its 'pledge card' a promise about speeding up the process of juvenile justice. This was unlikely to rebound on the party, since by definition juveniles have no votes. There were instances of very young children who constituted crime waves in themselves, like a ten-year-old boy from Blackpool who, with a slightly older accomplice, was responsible for more than forty thefts, assaults and other nuisances.[53] It seemed more practical to take a comprehensive approach and simply make it a crime to be young. Inter-generational antipathy even resulted in the coinage of a new word: paedophobia.[54]

There was also evidence to suggest that young people were becoming increasingly dangerous to each other at any time of day. Surveys suggested that the 16–24 age group was even more worried about anti-social behaviour than anyone else, including the over-sixty-fives.[55] Bullying was commonplace and sometimes led to tragic suicides, like that of the sixteen-year-old Kelly Yeomans, a member of the Salvation Army who killed herself at her Derbyshire home in September 1997.

In April 2005 a twelve-year-old Essex schoolboy hanged himself after being stabbed in the back with a compass at school. In the light of such episodes, it was easy to understand why truancy remained a serious problem, despite the expenditure of more than £1 billion between 1997 and 2005. Apart from those children who avoided lessons by preference, there must have been thousands who skipped school through fear. Absenteeism among teachers was also understandable. In April 2004 a woman who had taught at a boys' school in London explained that she had resigned from her job after just two years because she had been 'spat at, kicked and punched by pupils almost every day'. She had also been 'cut by glass, attacked with a fire extinguisher, urinated on and twice hit so hard in the face that she lost teeth'.[56] Workplace bullying also took its toll on young people. In December 2003 an eighteen-year-old who worked in a fast-food outlet in Manchester took a fatal overdose after persistent abuse and physical assaults by other members of staff.[57]

While such stories rarely made front-page headlines, the killing of the toddler James Bulger by two ten-year-old boys in February 1993 stunned a nation already well accustomed to stories of juvenile crime. In fact, just two months earlier a sixteen-year-old Manchester schoolgirl, Suzanne Capper, had been tortured for more than a week by a gang before being burned to death while her tormentors sang and laughed. But the fact that James Bulger's abduction from a Bootle shopping centre was captured on CCTV increased and prolonged the sense of shock and grief in this instance; Suzanne Capper was quickly forgotten. From the tabloid press coverage, it seemed that life for the average schoolboy in some parts of the country was a swift progression through truancy to shoplifting and murder. In the rush to inflict vengeance on the child-killers, few tabloid readers were bothered about the background circumstances that helped to explain the crime; it was as if Robert Thompson and Jon Venables had sprung fully formed from the Devil's mouth in order to commit the atrocity. Both in fact were products of deeply dysfunctional families. This hardly excused them, but it meant that, far from being a simple story about the frightening propensities of very young Britons, the case also highlighted serious adult failings, whereas the press and politicians like Tony Blair treated it as an incident that would presage an unprecedented wave of child killings unless urgent action was taken to remoralise the country.[58] This conclusion was also implied by a focus on the role of violent films, popularly known as 'video nasties', in the motivation of the crime. From the media treatment of these productions, one could be forgiven for thinking that they were made by the children who consumed them. Instead, like hard-core pornography, they were the work of older individuals who cared only for personal profit, whatever the age of the buyers and viewers.

It became clear during the trial of Thompson and Venables that many people had seen them mistreating James Bulger yet had decided not to intervene. This was not just because people were increasingly preoccupied with their own affairs. There was a growing fear that anyone who got involved in trouble could quickly turn from peace-maker to victim. In December 1995, for example, Philip Lawrence, the headmaster of a Roman Catholic comprehensive school in Maida Vale, was stabbed to death when he tried to protect a thirteen-year-old boy from a gang of young teenagers. Lawrence had recently stepped up security at the school, installing CCTV cameras. The headmaster was a spectacular example of an emerging trend in which people who would once have been symbols of authority and respect were now prime targets for violent assault. Health workers and firefighters were now often attacked as they struggled to serve an unruly society. The tabloid press had played an important part in undermining their status; rather than extolling people who worked hard for modest wages, it now appointed highly paid soap-opera stars and footballers as the nation's 'role models'.

The tabloids had no interest in helping to promote the kind of social tranquillity envisaged by John Major. In such circumstances they would have to change their ways or go out of business. Their main interest lay in stirring up fear against 'the other' – whether foreign nationals, criminals real or imagined, young people or a bacteriological infection. There was, though, one remarkable excep-tion in their lamentable record. On 22 April 1993 an eighteen-year-old was stabbed to death in Eltham, south London. The victim, Stephen Lawrence, was black, and his attackers were racially motivated. It was not an unusual killing in Britain – or even in Eltham, where two young men from ethnic minorities had recently been murdered. But the *Daily Mail*, of all newspapers, decided to take up the case. Stephen Lawrence also had tireless parents, whose dignity even won the admiration of Nelson Mandela. The *Mail* named the offenders, but on this occasion the British state failed to be tough on crime, let alone its causes.

No one was punished for the murder of Stephen Lawrence, but the incident and the publicity generated by the *Mail* suddenly highlighted the extent to which black and Asian Britons had been living in fear for many decades. Relatively few had died because of their skin colour, but the threat or reality of violence, intimidation and verbal aggression had been an integral part of their daily lives. The outcry over Lawrence's death prompted Labour to launch an inquiry into the Metropolitan Police soon after they came to office in 1997. The resulting Macpherson Report (1999) identified a worrying degree of 'institutional racism' within the police force. By extension, this was a damning verdict on the public as a whole, since few people doubted that the police reflected views which were more widely held. But despite some concern that Macpherson's recommendations would make the police more lenient when faced with real offenders from the ethnic minorities, there was a general recognition that both police and public would have to change.

Racial hatred in Britain was a classic example of fear being whipped up against 'the other'. Back in April 1968 Enoch Powell had quoted the claim of an unnamed working-class constituent that 'In this country in fifteen or twenty years time the black man will have the whip hand over the white man.' The fear of physical dominance by the 'other', the stranger, was Powell's best card. In the natural order of things, black and Asian people should have been cowering before a whip wielded by a true-born Anglo-Saxon; the prospect of role reversal provoked an understandable sense of unease, even among citizens of a country which had been active in opposition to slavery for more than a hundred years. Among the Powellites, fear of violent insurrection by unwanted intruders often mingled with the suspicion that black people were more virile, so that the eventual takeover would happen through peaceful, democratic (or demographic) means. This feeling was enhanced by the tendency of black and Asian families to congregate in specific areas of England; today's Brixton could be tomorrow's Budleigh Salterton, colonised by an alien people, 'wide-grinning piccaninnies' in Powellite parlance.

Although Powell himself faded from public view to some extent after leaving the Conservative Party in 1974, his warnings continued to be quoted with approval. The fear of being 'swamped', which Margaret Thatcher had recorded in January 1978, was real enough, even if most recruits to racist parties like the NF and the British National Party

(BNP) were primarily motivated by the excuse for some 'aggro'. But in November 1979 – less than six months after Mrs Thatcher was elected prime minister – the Nottingham Forest defender Viv Anderson became the first black player to win a full cap for the English football team. This development presented racist England supporters with a dilemma, which for many years was resolved by making monkey noises and throwing bananas when a black man played for an opposition club in domestic competition, and cheering the same people when they turned out for the national side. This attitude was too schizophrenic (or postmodern) to last for very long, but the first generation of black players had retired before it died away. Despite the cliché about footballers being role models, black celebrities in other fields probably had a greater impact on attitudes. The newsreader Trevor MacDonald (born in Trinidad) became a familiar and reassuring figure to television viewers in the late 1970s; early in the next decade Moira Stewart, born in Edinburgh to West Indian parents, won respect as the first black female to inform the nation of daily developments.

Enoch Powell's constituent had proved a poor prophet. In April 1988, exactly twenty years after the 'Rivers of Blood' speech, only 1 per cent of voters thought that immigration was the most urgent political problem in Britain. Between that date and Powell's death a decade later, the figure never rose above 2 per cent.[59] In the general election of 1997 the issues of race and immigration were barely mentioned.[60] Serious problems still remained, and anyone who thought that no major political party would ever again play the race card was quickly disabused by the advent of asylum seekers and Islamic fundamentalists as key topics in public debate. But it was reasonable to expect a lasting improvement in one respect. In the past, politicians of all parties had recommended stricter control of immigration on the grounds that a significant influx of non-white foreigners would tax the traditional tolerance of British people and endanger good race relations. Originally, this kind of talk had been a mixture of self-congratulation and hypocrisy, but by the end of the twentieth century it had become a fair reflection of reality. It was still possible to frighten the British with estimates of future immigration, and a lingering presumption against black or Asian people could easily be detected in the blanket antipathy to asylum seekers. Even so, overt racism was far less likely to be tolerated, whether in private conversation or in public, than it had been at any time in post-war British history. On this score, at least, Britain had to thank younger people for a gradual acceptance of more enlightened views.

VI

While the elderly had a generalised fear of change, for young people the greatest dread was a life of poorly rewarded labour – or even worse of long-term unemployment. Many observers predicted that the economic slump at the beginning of the 1980s would trigger an explosion of anger, and the 1981 inner-city riots were widely regarded as a foretaste of worse trouble to come. In part, fears of widespread disorder arose from a feeling that Britain was a more violent society than it had been in the 1930s – the last time that it had experienced unemployment on a similar scale. It was also felt that people would react more strongly because this time they had more to lose. From 1980 social security benefits were no longer uprated in line with earnings. The widening chasm between full-time wages and the dole meant that, for most people, redundancy enforced a dramatic decline in their quality of life. The unemployed were likely to have to sell their homes, give up their cars and retreat from their previous circle of friends – unless they too had lost their jobs.

Yet such misfortunes were just as likely to breed resignation among those who were already unemployed, and chronic, immobilising fear among those who felt that their own jobs were under threat. Research conducted in 1979–82 suggested that unemployed men were twelve to fifteen times more likely to attempt suicide than their contemporaries in work. Predictably, they were also much more prone to long-term illness as well as depression.[61] Fear of unemployment among those still in work was more difficult to quantify, but it can be detected in opinion polls at the time. In October 1985 MORI found that more than a third of people in work thought it quite likely that either they or a close relative would be made redundant within two years.[62] At the end of every year between 1978 and 1987 a majority of the British public anticipated a further rise in unemployment over the next twelve months. On this subject there had been a startling reversal of attitudes within a generation. In 1965 almost half of the respondents to a Gallup poll thought that it would be easy for the children of people like themselves to find employment; only 4 per cent thought that it would be nearly impossible. By 1984, with official unemployment at over three million, 39 per cent assumed that their children would find it impossible to secure a job; only 4 per cent expected that it would be easy for them. Such fears were well founded; by the following December more than a million men had been out of work for over a year.[63] Even those who felt reasonably confident that their jobs would survive were likely to experience fear at work, since the new climate in the workplace encouraged the importation of macho 'hire and fire' management styles from the US.

Despite the claims of their critics, the Conservatives had not actively sought unemployment on this scale. But they had hoped to inspire a new mood of 'realism' among workers; and as the official jobless figures climbed above three million in January 1982, they could tell themselves that they had merely underestimated the severity of the shock which had to be administered to Britain's recalcitrant workers. Perversely, many of the unemployed accepted their analysis; around a quarter of them voted Conservative in 1983. In that election less than 40 per cent of trade union members voted for Labour; support for the party had dropped by 12 per cent since 1979, even though it had developed policies in close consultation with the unions. After the 1983 general election union leaders were bewildered, and fearful, for the first time since the Second World War. They were trapped in a double bind, between a newly re-elected government which planned further curbs on their powers, and grass-roots members who seemed less likely to heed their calls for organised resistance.

Arthur Scargill of the NUM was almost alone among union leaders in refusing to recognise that things had changed; it is hardly surprising that he failed to muster the support he expected from the union movement as a whole during the miners' strike of 1984/5. Unions in the manufacturing sector had already decided that the future lay in single-union, no-strike agreements with individual companies. A few union leaders, like Frank Chapple of the electricians, actively supported the government's reforms. But the overwhelming majority were forced into acquiescence by fear; as Neil Kinnock had predicted, the 'gibbet of unemployment' made them obedient. Whatever ordinary union members really thought, they had to recognise that mass unemployment had created a vast pool of reserve labour for employers. At the first sign of militancy, workers could be sacked and instantly replaced by people who were equally qualified to do their jobs. Afterwards, they could stand on picket lines and shout 'Scab' or 'Blackleg' at their supplanters, but the temporary excitement generated by such confrontations could hardly replace the solid comforts provided by a regular wage packet.

Unemployment soared once more during the recession that began at the end of the 1980s, and the official figure again topped three million in 1993. Afterwards, though, it began a prolonged fall, which was still continuing when New Labour took office four years later. But this did not mean that fear of unemployment receded at the same rate. Memories of the last recession, in which many people had lost their homes as well as their jobs, helped to maintain discipline in the work-force. Like other sources of contemporary fear – nuclear proliferation, terrorism, burglary, mugging or assault, football supporters, the young, transport by air, water or land, threats to health and even the increas-ingly erratic weather – unemployment was attributed to forces outside the control of the average Briton. It was hardly surprising that they should become more inward-looking. But even then there were plenty of reasons to fear. In a superficial, celebrity-obsessed culture people were increasingly worried about their own perceived inadequacies. For some, the greatest dread of all was being judged by others as ugly, temperamental, unfashionable or nonconformist. During the miners' strike not even the most rabid left-winger could have predicted that two decades later there would be more registered professional coun-sellors than coal miners in Britain. But the British Association for Counselling and Psychotherapy (BACP), which was only founded in 1977, had 24,000 members by 2007, while the mining industry provided jobs for about 4,000 people.

From the media perspective, the best thing about the rise of neurosis was its potential to affect almost everyone. However, the most likely victims were affluent individuals in their early thirties – the favourite target of the advertising industry. This explains the vogue for programmes like *This Life* (BBC, 1996/7), a saga of dreary young self-obsessed professionals, and *What Not To Wear* (BBC, first broadcast 2001), which proffered advice to the insecure and assured them that there were people in the world more frumpish than themselves. In the press the phenomenon generated a plethora of 'lifestyle' supplements, debating the pros and cons of plastic surgery alongside more orthodox fashion tips for both men and women. To some extent the rich could escape the relentless propaganda about wafer-thin fashion models and super-fit footballers, since money provided the best assurance of respect from others. But in their exclusive circles there was always the chance of being upstaged by someone in the room with a bigger bank balance. For those lower down the social scale, there was a constant nagging fear of standing still while others were bagging bigger cars and more expensive houses. In many cases the attempt to assuage this feeling resulted in unaffordable purchases, creating the new fear of a knock at the door from the debt collector.

Unsurprisingly, among the many self-help manuals published during these years were books about coping with fear. In 1985 Dorothy Rowe, an Australian-born psychologist, offered her own solutions to the problem of *Living with the Bomb*.[64] Two years later – as Mrs Thatcher's Conservatives clinched their third successive general election victory – Rowe turned her attention to more mundane apprehensions, advising her jittery readers that 'To go beyond fear we have to accept ourselves and to let other people be themselves and to accept them as they are.'[65] In the context of Britain in the mid-1980s, this was well-meaning and important counsel. But only in a society which had veered away from any rational moorings could advice to 'accept oneself and others' have been regarded as anything other than a statement of the obvious. In such a society it implied that the best way to avoid fear was to remain passive amid many avoidable sources of outrage and apprehension – that to be 'fear-less' was to keep quiet and hope that the disagreeable things in life would happen to other people.

4

CHARITY, FAITH AND HOPE

my picture of Hell is complete with devils and tridents and burning lakes and darkness

Ann Widdecombe, 2000[1]

We don't do God

Alastair Campbell, April 2003[2]

I believe in the fundamental goodness of humanity. Sorry about that.
Ken Livingstone, 1987[3]

Superb wines (Corton Charlemagne '68 and Chambertin '64), fine Christmas food (oysters, Magdalen venison and Gateau Marjolaine*), followed by fierce debate between Kingsley [Amis] and myself about the future of socialism*

Kenneth Tynan, December 1975[4]

I

AFTER the speech, most observers agreed that it had been a great day for British charity workers. The Royal family had always been reliable supporters of the voluntary sector. But now one of the youngest – and certainly the most glamorous – members of the family had made a passionate public commitment to the cause at a time of economic depression when the charitable urge was sorely in need of prompting.

It was June 1975, and the Prince of Wales had been speaking in the House of Lords on the subject of voluntary service. He had focused on the need to prevent disadvantaged youngsters from falling into a lifetime of unemployment and/or criminal activity. Such people, he thought, could benefit from 'the challenge of adventure and hardship' – the sort of thing that he had experienced at his own Scottish public school. Prince Charles barely concealed his sympathy for the restoration of a form of National Service, but based on work within communities rather than military training.[5] He was already establishing an organisation which was formally launched in 1976 as the Prince's Trust. It awarded small grants to self-help groups and ran an annual week-long camp in Norfolk. The trust was far too modest to realise the Prince's ambitions – or even provide a small-scale prototype for a state-funded nationwide project – but in the trust's first thirty years around half a million young people got a taste of 'adventure and hardship' thanks to the voluntary efforts of the heir to the throne.*

To his detractors, it was hardly surprising that Prince Charles should be sympathetic towards the unemployed; for all his inherited wealth and social status, he shared their prospects of an indefinite period in enforced idleness. This jibe contained an element of truth. Even by 1975, the prince (born 1948) had become frustrated at the constraints imposed by his constitutional position. But he was far from idle – indeed, at the time of his speech he was serving in the Royal Navy. The impression of inactivity was at least in part the product of his own disposition and outlook. He was anxious to expand his constructive role beyond the inescapable ceremonial engagement, and the by-products of Britain's economic problems offered plenty of potential occupations. Unfortunately for him, his solicitude for the unemployed was not likely to please the Labour government, which had no desire to draw additional attention to the lengthening dole queues.

Prince Charles's chief misfortune was to be groomed for a life of public service in the era of consensus politics, and to start seeking a role just at the time when that approach was breaking down. Observers with a sensitive ear for ideological nuances could detect echoes of the Conservative One Nation tradition in his House of Lords speech, but in 1975 that position was quite compatible with a willingness to work with Labour moderates. Such centrist views were almost part of the job description for anyone who wanted to act as a figurehead for a harmonious

---

*Other initiatives included a £5 million scheme to help poorly qualified school leavers; see *The Times*, 5 November 2004.

society; despite her own obligatory reticence, it seemed reasonable to suppose that they were shared by Charles's mother. However, to the most dynamic politicians of the mid-1970s they were anathema – a symptom of the outdated, woolly thinking which had precipitated national decline. Queen Elizabeth herself might have been dismayed by this development, but over the years she had perfected a role which combined the appearance of political impartiality with iron-clad discretion. Amid the polarisation and anger of the late 1970s she was remarkably successful in creating an illusion of stability. As a result, outside a small republican minority, the British public was satisfied that in smiling, waving, opening public buildings and reading out 'her' government's parliamentary programme every year Queen Elizabeth was performing a useful function. Her son would never enjoy such a high level of uncritical approval and, to his credit, it was not what he wanted.

While the Queen's enduring popularity was not enough to protect her son from press speculation and intrusion, it certainly shielded her husband. Much more than the well-meaning Charles, the Duke of Edinburgh was a constitutional crisis waiting to happen. Although he was a representative of the consensus generation – he was born in 1921 – the fiery duke was anything but moderate in his political views. In his wife's jubilee year of 1977, for example, he contributed to a series of broadcasts on Radio Clyde, looking forward to the year 2000. Some of his predictions were remarkably prescient; for example, he foresaw an upsurge of interest in climate change and warned against international terrorism. But as his speech progressed, the Duke's real message became increasingly clear. His anti-communist zeal had inspired a vision of a totalitarian Britain by the year 2000. 'Judging by the experience of other countries,' he warned, 'individual initiative in commerce and industry will be considerably restricted.' There would be 'a gradual reduction in the freedom of choice and individual responsibility, particularly in such things as housing, the education of children, healthcare, the ability to acquire or inherit personal property, to hand on commercial enterprises, and the ability to provide for old age through personal savings and, perhaps, most important of all, the freedom of the individual to exploit his skills or talents as suits him best'.

If the duke imagined that he was obeying the constitutional niceties, that could only reflect the kind of company he was keeping.* While

---

* He had, after all, been mentioned in connection with plots for a dictatorship in 1975, and there was supposed to be a shadowy organisation called Philip for President (PFP). See Wheen, *Hoo-Has and Passing Frenzies*, 93.

few Conservative supporters would have disagreed with the detailed points he made, his argument added up to an uncompromising rejection of left-wing Labour goals in specific areas. For example, advocacy of 'freedom of choice' in healthcare and education at that time was a coded endorsement of private medical provision and public schools, neither of which had any place in a democratic society which wanted to see itself as genuinely fair and meritocratic. If anyone had missed the party-political point, the duke talked of state employees as 'zealous reformers and those who always know better', whose overriding ambition was 'to order the lives of their fellow citizens'. In his 1975 House of Lords speech Prince Charles had explicitly distanced himself from such attitudes, dismissing saloon-bar attacks on social workers as 'ridiculous generalisations'.[6] By contrast, the Duke of Edinburgh thought that his own pronouncements were sufficiently anodyne to allow their inclusion in a volume published by the Institute of Economic Affairs (IEA), a charitable body which just happened to be Margaret Thatcher's favourite think tank. His fellow contributors included the controversial right-wing ideologue Friedrich von Hayek, and the future Conservative Chancellor Nigel Lawson.[7]

Thus as Britain entered a period of radical right-wing government the father was much more in tune with the new mood than the son. Unsurprisingly, Prince Charles's semi-authorised biographer Jonathan Dimbleby allows himself to hint that the relationship was somewhat chilly and distant. According to Andrew Morton, Charles was 'intimidated' by his father.[8] Yet it was the Duke of Edinburgh whose counsel seems to have played a decisive role in persuading Charles to propose to Diana Spencer in February 1981. As Dimbleby has written, the duke probably intended to offer 'a piece of sound fatherly advice', but this was interpreted by Charles as an 'ultimatum', implying that unless he married Diana he would be accused of having 'callously exploited an innocent girl'. In reality, the primary promoters of the union were the tabloids, which had begun their fatal infatuation with Diana as soon as the friendship became public knowledge.[9] At most, the duke's intervention forced Charles to realise that in the media age he could no longer be master of his own feelings.

From one point of view his father's advice was indeed 'sound'. The fact that Charles had remained unmarried into his thirties gave the media an excuse for endless gossip about his activities and interests. If he set about the task of siring a legitimate heir, the press might even be less inclined to sneer at the lack of a fruitful occupation. The age difference was less of a problem than the totally contrasting contexts in which the couple had grown up. Born in July 1961, Diana had not even been old enough to vote when Mrs Thatcher won her first election. Even so, Prince Charles could convince himself that he might mould the character of a young girl of limited experience, who called him 'sir' and acted as 'his willing puppy who came to heel when he whistled'. The selection of such a bride fitted with the advice given by his beloved uncle Lord Mountbatten, who had told him to have as many affairs as possible before settling down with 'a sweet-charactered girl before she meets anyone else she might fall for'.[10]

If he had been alive in 1981, Mountbatten would surely have qualified his advice. The 'sweet-charactered girl' would also have to be steely and unquestioningly supportive. Neither of these things was true of Diana Spencer, who herself needed regular reassurance – not least because her parents had split when she was just six years old. Even if Prince Charles had been entirely devoted to her, her spontaneous emotional nature was likely to be stultified by the froideur of palace life. But while Mountbatten could not be blamed for the inappropriate choice of Diana, his cynical guidance had been based on an astonishing misreading of Charles's character. Unlike so many of his ancestors – both near and remote – the Prince was a hapless philanderer, more likely to lose his own heart than toy with the feelings of others. In the early 1970s he had begun a relationship with Camilla Shand, the daughter of a Sussex landowner and war hero. At that time marriage to a British commoner would have been unacceptable, not least to the press, which continued to speculate about possible matches with foreign princesses throughout the decade. In any case, Prince Charles had scarcely sown a single oat by that stage; marriage to Camilla would have to wait until he worked his way through the field. He was on a protracted voyage with the Royal Navy – his own version of compulsory National Service – when Camilla agreed to marry Andrew Parker-Bowles instead.

As the 'fairytale romance' between Charles and Diana degenerated into a blame game, almost every aspect of the story was contested by the rival camps. But whoever strayed first, it was clear to most objective observers that these were two decent human beings who ended up causing extreme misery to each other. It was typical of the couple that charity work became a major source of mutual annoyance; in this field, at least, their different personalities could have complemented each other. Diana's commitments often arose from the suffering of specific individuals, while the Prince took a more generalised view, in keeping with his 'One Nation' ideas. For Charles, this often meant working with unglamorous organisations which reflected the new climate of Thatcherite realism; a typical link was established in January 1985, when he became president of Business in the Community. Worthy as it was, this kind of activity was unlikely to win enthusiastic publicity. By contrast, even when Diana selected an unpromising cause – like the plight of AIDS victims – it tended to become glamorous overnight, thanks to her sponsorship. The disparity in the press coverage made it look as if Diana was the life-long champion of the underprivileged and outcast – exactly the role in which Prince Charles had cast himself. The overwhelming attention paid to his wife created the impression that the prince was back to square one, earnestly but ineffectually seeking purposeful employment.

The differences between the pair were brought into sharp focus by the Live Aid concert of July 1985. The event was inspired by the unkempt Irish rock singer Bob Geldof, who had been shocked by a BBC report of famine in Ethiopia broadcast in November 1984. It was already established that charity work was one area in which the burgeoning celebrity culture could be put to constructive use. Since 1976 the pressure group Amnesty International had benefited from a series of comedy shows which featured (among others) the Monty Python team; the charity Children in Need had started using marathon television appeals back in 1980; and the Prince's Trust was one of many organisations which raised money through pop concerts. But the best-selling Band Aid single 'Do They Know it's Christmas?' took the phenomenon to a different level. Thanks to Geldof's popularity within the music industry and his ability to hector recalcitrant recruits into compliance, the record featured contributions from most of the leading stars of the day, thus giving a wide range of fans a reason to buy it. All of the profits went to charity; even the record shops agreed not to take a cut. It made more than £8 million.

The day-long Live Aid extravaganza was an even more dramatic manifestation of the same formula. Geldof later asserted that 'We had got every major British pop artist of the last quarter of a century,' and there was also an American concert, linked by satellite from Philadelphia. The Wembley crowd of 80,000 included 'Chuck and Di' in the royal box. Prince Charles did his best to enter into the spirit, telling Geldof 'I think I've seen these chaps before' when Status Quo came on stage.[11] But while the prince vaguely recognised some of the participants, his wife was an enthusiastic fan of many acts, notably Duran Duran and Elton John.

In its review of Live Aid *The Times* claimed that it 'felt like the healing of our own nation' just a few days after the shame of the Heysel stadium disaster involving Liverpool supporters. There was certainly reconciliation for some – The Who appeared together after a long break, in what *The Times* mistakenly thought 'will probably prove to be the last word' for the ageing rockers.[12] Around £40 million was raised by the concerts; the worldwide television audience was estimated at 1.5 billion in 160 different countries. Briefly, it seemed that popular culture could bring the whole world together; David Bowie suggested that a similar festival should be held every year. In fact, the timing of Live Aid gave an illusory impression. It happened when long-established bands with devoted followers, like Status Quo, The Who and Queen, could still give dynamic performances, backed up by relative newcomers who looked set for enduring popularity, notably Duran Duran and George Michael. The future, though, would belong to 'stars' who quickly fell out of favour with the fickle public. As a result, attempts to resurrect the spirit of Live Aid would only combine increasingly weary veterans with one-hit wonders.

It could never be the same again for the music industry, but celebrity fund-raisers in other fields seized on Geldof's example. Comic Relief was first broadcast at Christmas in 1985, eventually generating more participatory spin-offs like Sport Relief (2002). In October 1985 the cricketer Ian Botham embarked on an epic walk from John o'Groats to Land's End, the first of several exploits on behalf of leukaemia research.* Even the venerable Children in Need refurbished its image to reflect the mood, adopting the familiar Pudsey Bear mascot in 1985.

Geldof himself was awarded an honorary knighthood, and persisted with his efforts to 'feed the world' despite tragedy in his personal life. However, Live Aid probably killed off his already-ailing career as a musician. The event also increased the estrangement between Charles and Diana. Having initially attracted press attention without wanting

---

* Botham had actually planned his journey years before, but the decision to go ahead in the charitable climate of 1985 probably ensured maximum publicity; he raised more than £1 million (see *Botham: My Autobiography*, CollinsWillow, 1994, 281–91).

it, the Princess of Wales now understood that celebrity status could have a constructive effect. This allowed her to increase her sense of self-worth while helping those who had lacked her advantages. By 1993 she was patron or president of more than a hundred bodies, including the National Aids Trust, Barnado's, the Great Ormond Street Hospital for Children, and (poignantly) Relate, which tried to help troubled couples. But Diana was only able to help such organisations while she retained her media stardom. She obviously relished many aspects of the role, but it meant that she had to endure the strain of excessive intrusion and much press ridicule as a prelude to posthumous adulation. Just before her death, for example, she attended the funeral of the murdered fashion designer Gianni Versace. Pictures of the princess comforting Elton John seemed surreal to one *Observer* correspondent: a person who could have been crowned Queen of England was 'consoling a weeping, defunct, re-haired Seventies glam-rocker about the murder of an Italian porno-frock-designing bondage freak by a Filipino-Californian gay hustler serial killer and/or Mafia hitman'. Nigel Fountain remarked that the tableau would have been 'quite unforeseeable and unbelievable two decades ago'.[13] That was very true. But if Diana's star qualities had been channelled more constructively the monarchy would have been safe at least for another generation.

In December 1992 the prime minister, John Major, told the House of Commons that the fairytale marriage was to end with a formal separation. Almost exactly a year later Princess Diana announced that she was cutting down on her charitable commitments and in effect would leave public life. In the previous month the *Daily Mirror* had published photographs of her exercising in a gym – a scoop which served no conceivable public interest. As Diana admitted in her speech, she had been unaware of how 'overwhelming' the media intrusion would become. By coincidence – or not – the venue for her speech was a meeting of the National Head Injuries Association. In October 1996 she confided her fears that her enemies were planning to silence her completely, by means of an arranged car accident in which she would suffer a 'serious head injury'.[14*]

---

* In 1991 Diana's advisers from the spirit world had apparently informed her to expect 'a problem involving a royal car'. Unhappily for conspiracy theorists, this piece of advice was probably inspired by a recent incident in which Diana and the Duchess of York had raced each other on the Balmoral estate in 'the Queen Mother's Daimler and a four-wheel drive state vehicle'; Morton, 139–40.

Although Diana was planning a drastic cutback on her charitable activities rather than a total withdrawal, her announcement was a serious blow to a voluntary sector which was already in trouble. After many lean years ushered in by the inflationary mid-1970s, charities had anticipated some concrete encouragement from Mrs Thatcher's governments. After all, the kind of philosophy espoused by the Duke of Edinburgh implied that the state should do a lot less in this area, leaving greater scope for private philanthropy if the right incentives were provided. However, tax concessions were not improved until 1986 – and even then they were severely limited.[15] Insofar as the government thought about the issue at all, it probably expected cuts in direct taxation to inspire a spontaneous increase in charitable giving, on American lines. When this did not materialise, ministers preferred to pass over the subject in embarrassed silence.

However, by the end of the 1980s a new way forward had been suggested. The last British state-run lottery had closed in 1826, since when the idea had been shunned because of its tendency to encourage 'immoral' gambling.[16] But the Thatcherite climate was more propitious. The share-buying boom fostered by privatisation had been a form of gambling – although the undervalued national assets had been a sure bet for investors – and many council-house buyers had also been banking on a rise in the market value of their properties. Viewing these developments in 1982, the jaundiced right-wing poet Philip Larkin told Kingsley Amis that Britain would 'soon be an off-shore gambling island supported by prostitution and exhibiting the Queen'.[17] Faithful in this single respect to her Methodist upbringing, Mrs Thatcher herself was hostile to the idea of a national lottery, but once she had left office the way was clear for lobbying organisations to foist the idea on publicity-hungry ministers.

For would-be lottery operators, the scheme was a guaranteed source of profit; they could dream up a percentage cut of any proceeds, sufficient to cover 'operating costs'. The trick was to convince the public that the main purpose of the scheme was to help 'good causes'. This would allow gamblers to imagine that their weekly investments were actually disguised donations to charity rather than desperate attempts to get rich quickly. It would also help if the government was prepared to promise that any funds distributed from lottery proceeds would be ring-fenced to ensure that they did not take the place of regular state spending derived from normal taxation. There were some inter-departmental disagreements, and the Treasury was opposed at first, but in 1993 the necessary legislation was passed, and the government duly set up five quangos to dish out the money. The five good causes were the arts, heritage, sport, the millennium celebrations and charity. As Simon Jenkins has noted, this represented a remarkable piece of nationalisation by a government which was supposedly a champion of the private sector. To the extent that lottery-players were actually motivated by charitable impulses, their donations were now under the control of bodies with an intimate connection to government. Among other things, the legislation would also allow governments to claim direct credit for the achievements of lottery-funded artists and athletes. Political parties had noticed the advantages of celebrity endorsement during the 1975 referendum on EC membership. Now many sporting stars would be permanent running, throwing and leaping advertisements for the benevolent British state.

For doubting Conservatives, one poetic advantage of the lottery scheme was that it would wrong-foot Labour – a party whose central philosophy had already crumbled after a decade of Thatcherism. Those MPs who did speak out tended to represent constituencies where existing gambling institutions, notably the football pools, were prominent employers. These Labour dissidents thus adopted the unlikely role of opposing nationalisation in the interests of private enterprise – an irony which greatly amused Conservative MPs. Predictably, though, the lottery did take a heavy toll on profits and jobs within the pools industry; it also hit bookmakers. For their part, most Conservatives saw the lottery as an embodiment of Bernard de Mandeville's proto-Thatcherite view that 'private vices' could result in 'public benefits.'[18] But even within the Conservative cabinet there were fears that most players (and non-winners) would be the poorest in society, grasping at the chance to become overnight millionaires.[19] Labour MPs were unwilling to use this argument, which implied that poor people were not rational enough to realise their minimal chances of winning anything at all.

Few MPs pointed out the danger to charities: they ran the risk of losing customers of their own small-scale lotteries and raffles to the state-backed leviathan with its enormous prizes. After his media-induced resignation, the former Heritage Secretary David Mellor let the cat out of the bag, admitting that charities were never intended to be *beneficiaries* of the lottery; rather, the sums they received were a means of *compensation* for their likely losses.[20] If it had been more widely publicised, this news might have unsettled many casual, well-meaning players. In 1995, according to a survey by the Charity Aid Foundation, most people thought that around a fifth of the lottery's takings went to charity, whereas the true figure was less than a tenth (overall, the five good causes received just 28p out of every pound spent). But when an additional midweek draw was introduced (February 1997) the decision provoked only a few muttered complaints, largely from the House of Lords.

Some estimates of the likely impact on charitable giving proved to be alarmist. In his memoirs John Major was able to dismiss the doom-mongers on the grounds that 'even before the lottery was launched there had been a long-term downward trend in charitable giving.'[21] In itself, this was a remarkable verdict on the Thatcherite notion that tax cuts would provide a massive boost to private philanthropy in Britain. The National Lottery Charities Board came in for sharp press criticism, for handouts to causes like the Scottish Prostitutes Education Project and a group which bred guinea pigs in Peru. The *Sun* ran a hotline poll which asked its readers if they wanted lottery funds to be allocated to overseas charities; only 630 approved, while more than 60,000 demanded that the money should stay at home.[22] In any case, charities hoping for matching funding from the lottery now had to devote much of their time to developing proposals which would impress the government quangos, thus adding to their bureaucratic costs.

The large number of lottery beneficiaries concealed the fact that, up to the beginning of 1996, almost a half had gone to a handful of major projects – mostly based in London.[23] One notorious award – more than £12 million to secure the papers of Winston Churchill – was even opposed by commentators who normally genuflected at the name of Britain's great war leader. But compared to the Millennium Dome, this outlay represented the bargain of the century. The much-cursed construction in Greenwich cost around £800 million to build and continued to be a financial drain; in the year after it closed to visitors maintenance absorbed a further £28 million. Elsewhere, large sums were invested in projects of marginal utility. Anthony Gormley's 200-ton creation the *Angel of the North* was surprisingly popular with many people who saw it on their way to Gateshead or Newcastle. But it is unlikely that this creation – compared by one commentator to 'a poorly designed scarecrow' – was the kind of investment that lottery players had in mind when they handed over their pound coins.[24] Another lucky fund-seeker wanted 'to convert an old Citroën car into a cinema for two' in the interests of art.[25] The lottery's Community Fund awarded money to the Coalition Against Deportation, which enraged ministers by campaigning against the removal of unsuccessful asylum seekers.[26] Perversely, such stories gradually helped to convince the tabloid press that the lottery was, indeed, a national asset. When they were short of real stories the papers gleefully exposed the secret lives of convicted criminals who hit the jackpot, like the so-called 'Lottery Lout' who scooped almost £10 million after serving a prison sentence for driving offences and criminal damage.[27] They could also rant against inflated payments to the executives of Camelot, the consortium which ran the state-supported game.

In hindsight, ambitious Labour MPs had reason to be grateful that they swallowed their misgivings and decided not to speak out against the lottery. The initial response defied all expectations. Nearly £50 million worth of tickets were bought in the first week – a sum which, allowing for inflation, almost equalled the proceeds of Live Aid. An estimated 22 million watched the BBC programme which featured the drawing of the winning balls – surely the dullest event ever to be put out on Saturday prime-time television. When, in December 1994, the ultimate game of chance produced its first millionaire, the *Sun* and the *Daily Mirror* offered £10,000 to anyone who could name the lucky winner, who turned out to be a man who had immigrated from Tanzania in the 1960s. To avoid applications for cash he changed his name, but this could not prevent the breakdown of his marriage. The 'Lottery Lout', Michael Carroll, also split from his wife and received death threats before resorting to cannabis and cocaine. An unemployed carpenter who netted £1.8 million bought a £500,000 mansion where he drank himself to death alone, living his last six weeks on an exclusive diet of whisky.[28] By comparison, more positive stories were rarely publicised, although in July 2003 sharp-eyed *Guardian* readers would have been heartened to learn that one couple had given more than two thirds of their £7.6 million winnings to charity.[29]

The advent of the lottery gave extra impetus to an existing trend within the charity world, which had finally been forced to accept the realities of post-Thatcherite Britain. Any self-respecting charity now had to present an image of sleek efficiency. The new dependency on government largesse meant that fund-raising skills owed more to the ability to bend ministerial ears than the rattling of collecting tins. As a result, charities came under the control of a new generation of sharp-suited executives, who demanded high salaries. By the late 1990s both Save the Children and Help the Aged were headed by 'social entre-preneurs' earning over £65,000 per year – more than the Archbishop of Canterbury.[30] Other positions emerged with titles jarringly familiar to students of the business world. In late 2006, for example, Oxfam advertised for a director of corporate communications with an annual salary of up to £50,000. The usual explanation was that charities were highly complex organisations, requiring specialised skills rather than selfless endeavour. After the passage of the 1992 Charities Act, they were obliged to submit annual accounts to the Charity Commission. Even so, the intrusion of 'fat-cattery' into this sphere presented an unpleasant contrast with the voluntary spirit, which was also being undermined by the increasing reliance of charities on paid persuaders – 'chuggers' as they were dubbed – to extract money pledges from pedestrians in shopping centres. Such developments understandably reinforced the well-founded suspicion that much of the money donated to good causes would never reach its intended recipients. This problem was particularly acute for organisations like Oxfam, which focused on overseas work. But even home-based bodies could be damaged by scan-dals, like the story of the fake 'Lady' Rosemary Aberdour, who swindled almost £3 million out of London's National Hospital for Neurology and Neurosurgery before being exposed and jailed. Down on the streets, tabloid newspapers were always keen to name and shame the few beggars who lived luxuriously on the proceeds – combined, in most cases, with fraudulent claims for state benefits. Even the *Big Issue* magazine, established as a monthly in 1991 and later a weekly publi-cation with a readership of a quarter of a million, was not immune from adverse publicity.[31]

Growing cynicism about charities in the 1990s meant that the sector was ever more dependent on the Princess of Wales. Although her repu-tation suffered wild fluctuations towards the end of her life,* in the eyes of her admirers Diana transcended the squalid spirit of the age; an endorsement from her was a certificate of sincerity. In January 1997

* The ups and downs of a super-celebrity were charted vividly in the correspondence pages of the *News of the World* during the summer of 1996, when Diana was portrayed either as a hypocritical parasite or a saint, depending on the publicity of the relevant week.

she had undertaken her most courageous campaign, against the use of anti-personnel landmines. Although the initiative infuriated the British government, the power of her name and image was signalled by the fact that even President Clinton was forced to take notice of the issue. Her death in August 1997 – almost exactly a year after her divorce from Prince Charles – seemed a shattering blow for charities. Yet her personal life had become increasingly erratic after the divorce. There were bound to be new revelations in future, but her tragic death meant that she would be regarded as an imperishable icon rather than a very frail human being. The right-wing journalist Paul Johnson, for example, improbably compared her to the Virgin Mary, and hailed the hysterical reaction to her death as 'a spontaneous religious act by the Nation'.[32]

Diana's death led to the establishment of a memorial fund which benefited to the tune of £37.5 million thanks to Elton John's tribute 'Candle in the Wind 1997', which became the biggest-selling single in history. As one of the few celebrities who took charity work seriously, the veteran singer was an excellent choice for the funeral service in Westminster Abbey.* But the hastily rewritten version of his 1973 classic ducked all of the interesting parallels between Diana and Marilyn Monroe,† replacing insights with 'bewilderingly mixed metaphors' and dubious clichés, like 'the wings of your compassion'.[33] While the lyricist Bernie Taupin had applied the line 'Never knowing who to cling to when the rain set in' to Monroe, for Diana this was changed to 'Never fading with the sunset when the rain set in'. The apposite observation, 'Even when you died/Oh the press still hounded you' was also airbrushed out, although Elton John himself knew what it was like to be hounded by the tabloids.‡ However, in hindsight these amendments were probably sensible; conspiracy theorists could already be trusted to claim that the two women were most alike because they had been killed to keep them quiet.

The memorial fund aimed to persevere with Diana's work, helping about 350 charities in her favourite areas. However, it became embroiled

---

* The Elton John AIDS Foundation, which later benefited from prunings of his over-capacious wardrobe, had been established in 1992.

† Eerily, in his notorious book about the princess, Andrew Morton had quoted her belief that 'Everyone said I was the Marilyn Monroe of the 1980s,' see *Diana: Her True Story*, 152.

‡ Although, unlike Diana, the singer was able to fight back through the courts, extracting £1 million and a grovelling apology from the *Sun* in 1987 and successfully suing the *Daily Mail* two decades later.

in several controversies. In theory it had good reason to defend Diana's likenesses against shoddy exploiters; just a fortnight after her death the *Sun* was complaining about the appearance of mugs, T-shirts and even pizzas, produced to cash in on her name.[34] Yet the fund took its custodianship too far in 1998 when it sued a US company making Diana dolls and plates. After fighting off the original lawsuit, the company launched its own claim for malicious prosecution. In the out-of-court settlement of November 2004 the fund had to pay out £13.5 million. This came a few months after the Queen opened a Diana Memorial Fountain in Hyde Park. The monument was supposed to reflect Diana's life and personal qualities. But it cost £2 million more than the original budget. In the first few days the waters were impeded by a blocked pump, then leaves caused a similar stoppage. Within a fortnight of opening three people had been taken to hospital after slipping on its granite floor.

At the first Labour conference after Diana's death Tony Blair spoke of fire rather than water. Britain, he claimed, could become 'a model twenty-first-century nation, a beacon to the world'. Although there was no reference to 'the wings of compassion', parts of the speech could have been adapted for inclusion in 'Candle in the Wind 1997'. 'Progress and justice are the two rocks upon which the New Britain is raised to the heights,' Blair exclaimed in Taupinesque mode. However, the speech is remembered for its peroration, which featured a maladroit shift from Marilyn Monroe to her lover, John F. Kennedy: 'There is room for all the people in New Britain and there is a role for all the people in its creation. Believe in us as much as we believe in you. Give just as much to our country as we intend to give, give your all. Make this the giving age.'[35] Even Blair's warm admirer Giles Radice had to admit (privately) that this was an 'embarrassing' effusion.[36] But the policy content of the speech exemplified Blair's ambition to get tough with the kind of people who had won Diana's sympathy. Shortly afterwards single mothers were invited to join the 'giving age' by surrendering 10 per cent of their state benefits.

By the beginning of the twenty-first century, an understandable reaction had set in against Blairite rhetoric and Diana mania. There was also a sense that the kind of television imagery which had moved Bob Geldof was beginning to lose its energising impact; the vivid depiction of suffering in so many places tended to make people feel apathetic. One polemical author, Patrick West, spoke of 'compassion fatigue', induced by the new trend of wearing ribbons and wristbands as marks of association with a variety of worthy causes. The rapid spread of these items was yet another by-product of the celebrity culture, but once they had become established they developed a momentum of their own. While the famous could rely on their publicists to broadcast their kind-heartedness, ordinary mortals had to wear visible tokens if they wanted to achieve the same effect. By 2005 the criminal fraternity had noted their money-making potential, and started flooding the market with fakes. Meanwhile a special black 'anti-band band' had been developed, to tell the world that the wearer was very witty.[37]

Patrick West rightly argued that 'Conspicuous compassion is a symptom of a fragmented society that has exchanged reason for emotion, action for gesture, cool reserve for mawkish sentimentality.' But he went too far when he claimed that 'We want to be seen to care because we are miserable.'[38] Overt identity with a cause is most likely to appeal to those who think they matter, and would like to matter a little bit more. However, few people are prepared to do good by stealth any more – except, perhaps, the Prince of Wales, and even he has been more charitable with his time than his money. Despite notable exceptions – like the Harry Potter author J.K. Rowling and the Pink Floyd guitarist Dave Gilmour, who sold his house for more than £6 million and gave the proceeds to charity – rich individuals and successful companies tend to shop around for the causes which offer maximum publicity for minimal outlay. The general level of philanthropy is indicated by the Per Cent Club set up by Business in the Community in the year after Prince Charles became president. Even this body was inaptly named, since for some years companies could be members if they committed less than half a per cent of pre-tax profits.[39] Even after fifteen years of cajolery from the prince, the top 400 British corporations were still giving less than a quarter of one per cent of their pre-tax profits to charity. In 2001 Marks and Spencer had a head of corporate social responsibility, but even this respected firm donated only £7 million. This measly contribution was ascribed to 'enlightened self-interest' rather than a straightforward desire to help the underprivileged. More than half of Sainsbury's £11 million gift consisted of handouts of unsold food. The supermarket's director of corporate affairs reportedly said that 'I'd be worried if a company was being over-philanthropic with shareholders' money, if there was no basic good for the business.'[40]

The votes stack up at Earl's Court Exhibition Centre, as Britain gives an overwhelming 'Yes' to Europe, 6 June 1975.

'We knew exactly what we were going into': flanked by Willie Whitelaw and Peter Kirk, Margaret Thatcher reaffirms her support for the European project, 3 June 1975.

John Stonehouse confronts his media tormentors, 28 August 1975.

'Black man gotta lot of problems/But they don't mind throwing a brick': the aftermath of the Notting Hill Carnival, 1 September 1976.

The trade unions provide moral leadership for the 'throwaway society': a street in Central London during the Winter of Discontent, February 1979.

The former picknicking site of
Greenham Common, Easter 1983.

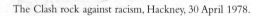

The Clash rock against racism, Hackney, 30 April 1978.

The Grand Hotel, Brighton,
after the IRA bomb, October 1984.

Catching the national mood, with a little help from his friends: Mr and Mrs Blair enter Downing Street, May 1997.

Poachers and gamekeepers: pro-hunting demonstrators taste their own medicine, September 2004.

'Not in my name': impotent protesters swarm past the most potent symbol
of British democracy, February 2003.

The growing cynicism about charity is unfortunate, since the phil-anthropic urge is already weak enough in Britain. The rich are not alone in their reluctance; although the poor were much more generous by comparison, in 2002 it was estimated that the average worker spared just 0.5 per cent of annual income for charitable causes. A 1998 survey found that two thirds of the population gave nothing at all, even though by that time there were more than 6,000 high street charity shops providing the chance of getting something useful in return for their donation.[41] The appeal after the Indian Ocean tsunami of Christmas 2004 gave a more positive impression, raising £300 million within two months – although a subsequent survey suggested that the generous response to that disaster diverted money away from other good causes.[42] On balance, if unsightly ribbons and bands were the best way of evoking a flutter from Britain's 'wings of compassion', they had to be regarded as a price worth paying when there were so many excuses for total inactivity.

II

In December 1993, just after Princess Diana declared her intention of cutting down on her engagements, the archdeacon of York declared that Prince Charles was not fit to inherit the throne. Strong rumours suggested that the prince had broken the sacred promises which he had exchanged with Princess Diana in St Paul's Cathedral: 'How can he then go into Westminster Abbey and take the Coronation vows?'[43]

This outburst provoked a period of media speculation about Charles's constitutional position. But it had been based on a naive reading of British history. If marital infidelity counted as a disqualification for kingship, few heirs to the throne would ever have been crowned. The whole subject was particularly embarrassing for moralistic Anglicans, since their Church had come into being as a result of a royal divorce.* If so minded, the Church of England might choose to cut up rough. But the Establishment looked most unlikely to close ranks against the next king as it had done against the uncrowned Edward VIII in 1935/6. The prince could avoid any unpleasantness by marrying Camilla Parker-Bowles in a register office, and then refusing to take the title Defender

---

* This awkward fact did not prevent the *Sun* – the true arbiter of the British consti-tution – from denying that Charles could become king if he chose to marry Camilla Parker-Bowles after both had been divorced; *Sun*, 29 February 1996.

of the Faith. In 1994 Charles indicated that this would not be a major
sacrifice for him, since as king he would see himself as the defender
of *all* faiths. Two years later the former Archbishop of Canterbury
Robert Runcie grumbled that Charles was growing distant from the
Anglican Church, preferring 'to be exploring Hinduism with people in
the inner cities'.[44] He was, in short, taking the Church for granted. If
so, this was one of the few things he had in common with his coun-
trymen in the mid-1990s.

The fact that the media was prepared to run with a story about a
constitutional crisis is eloquent testimony to its sales-driven preference
for Diana over Charles. The tabloid press was hardly the most pious
of institutions; normally its references to clerical life were confined to
sallies against left-leaning bishops and the exposure of sexual skulldug-
gery in the vestry. Had it not been for Diana, such newspapers would
have been urging the Prince of Wales to announce in advance his intention to rid himself of meddlesome priests, thus foreshadowing the final
separation of Church and state. The persistence of the link in the early
1990s reflected residual sentimentality about the union of 'the orb and
the cross' but it was mainly the result of institutional inertia.[45] The
Anglican Church had just sustained severe financial losses, thanks to
unwise property investments in the late 1980s. In their quest for profits
to subsidise clerical pensions, the Church Commissioners had borrowed
heavily. They had entered into some unlikely alliances, with worldly
figures like Sir John Hall, developer of Gateshead's Metro Centre.
However, they had called in the moneylenders just before a hike in
interest rates and a crash in the property market. Overall losses were
more than £400 million.[46]

This financial crisis coincided with a passionate and divisive debate
about the ordination of women as priests. This proposal had been on
the agenda for the Church since the mid-1970s; women were already
allowed to officiate at certain ceremonies in the capacity of deacons,
but they could not give communion. This compromise could not last.
A decision to go ahead with women's ordination was taken in 1992,
but only just gained the necessary two-thirds majority in the Church's
General Synod. There were apocalyptic warnings from traditionalists,
and two Conservative ministers were among those who broke ranks.
Ann Widdecombe, the outspoken under-secretary of state in the
Department of Employment, subsequently joined the Catholic Church,
ensuring maximum publicity for the schism. However, the predicted

disaster never happened. The first women were ordained in 1994, in time to enjoy the first episodes of *The Vicar of Dibley*, the BBC's gentle satire of what might have been an explosive situation. The next big question, though, was the official attitude towards gay priests. Given the entrenched attitudes in various parts of the Church, this endangered its existence as a worldwide institution.

Wavering clergymen probably thought that women's ordination was a gamble worth taking because the Church was already losing regular attenders at a depressing rate. A survey published in the year 2000 suggested that the proportion of English people who identified with the national Church had fallen from 40 per cent in 1983 to just over a quarter in 1999.[47] Informed guesswork put the number of 'usual Sunday attenders' at 1.5 million in 1970. By 1978 they had been whittled down to around 1.25 million, and before the end of the century the ranks of the faithful had fallen below a million for the first time. Turnout at festivals like Christmas and Easter Sunday was significantly higher and relatively stable over the years, but these occasional visitors were clearly not being inspired to adopt the churchgoing habit. In 2006 a Church of England spokesperson claimed that 'It is more difficult to go to church now than it was,' an explanation which worked slightly better in this context than as a reason for the fall in election turnout.[48] However, a growing number were couch Christians, tuning in every week to the BBC's long-running *Songs of Praise* programme – hosted for several years by Prince Charles's friend Sir Harry Secombe.* But in 2005/6 ITV reflected new commercial realities by halving the number of hours devoted to religious coverage, from 104 per year to just 52.

Faced with a prolonged decline rather than sudden collapse, senior clergy at least had time to consider their options for change. Unfortunately, none of these provided much prospect of a revival. The ordination of women could be presented as a step which (belatedly) brought the Church into the twentieth century. In reality, it just gave women an equal right to preside over increasingly anachronistic rituals. There were some more lively experiments, notably the Nine O'Clock Service in Sheffield, which suggested that the introduction of modern music, and a more 'youthful vibe' in general, could secure a devoted

---

*A brilliant *Not the Nine O'Clock News* sketch featured Rowan Atkinson as a clergyman whose congregation only turned up when the BBC cameras were in attendance.

following in some inner-city parishes. However, in 1995 the Nine O'Clock Service collapsed amid allegations of sexual exploitation. A more lasting initiative was the Alpha Course, a ten-week induction process headed from 1990 by a charismatic ex-barrister, Nick Gumbel. Originally based at the Holy Trinity Church in London's Knightsbridge, by 2004 more than 7,000 Alpha Courses were being held across the UK, and most Christian denominations had become involved.

The Alpha Course proved so successful because it mirrored secular trends. To outsiders, it was merely an alternative form of therapy, catering for the affluent and the anxious who wanted someone to tell them that they were special. Nick Gumbel's prominence within the movement invited comparisons with another Oxbridge-trained barrister, Tony Blair – with the difference that Gumbel's position allowed him to 'do God' on a full-time basis. His personal following was easily portrayed as a manifestation of the secular cult of celebrity; one jour- nalist sent to investigate the Alpha Course phenomenon quickly noticed that Gumbel was 'good-looking, tall and slim'. Adherents apparently included a former glamour model, an ex-captain of England's cricket team and the disgraced ex-Conservative cabinet minister Jonathan Aitken.[49]

Overall, the Alpha Course was catering for consumerist individuals in search of lifestyle choices, which was hardly in keeping with the Church's traditional mission. But its main offence in orthodox eyes was one of its few genuinely spiritual aspects – the encouragement of devotees to indulge in the theologically dubious practice of 'speaking in tongues'. Exploiting the psychology of mass hysteria, this practice was sure to alienate traditionalists, some of whom had never forgiven the Church for introducing the 1980 *Alternative Service Book*. This allowed fashion-serving clergymen to discard the 1662 *Book of Common Prayer* – one of the greatest achievements in English litera- ture – making the Church of England the first British institution to dumb down traditional culture. There was a new outbreak of shud- dering in the pews in 2002, when the Church gave its blessing to 'raves in the nave', the centrepiece of a 'national youth strategy'. These alter- native services would be a cross between discos and new age spiritualist gatherings. Church leaders were clearly reluctant to denounce anything which might swell congregations, but there was always a danger that their compromises with contemporary culture would turn away people who preferred their religious activities to be other-worldly.

Critics had identified a failure of leadership within the Church since the mid-1970s. The anonymous writer of the preface to the 1975 *Church of England Yearbook* had complained about the 'uniform middle-class niceness' of senior bishops.[50] They seemed incapable of showing anger, even when their calling seemed under explicit attack. For example, *The Life of Brian* (1979), Monty Python's superb satire on organised religion, provoked an outburst of censorious indignation from the devout in several parts of Britain. This pressure ensured that the film was banned in Surrey, in east Devon and in Harrogate.* However, these pyrrhic protests were instigated by the rank and file; religious leaders in the US were much more outspoken than their British counterparts. Those who did go public with their objections to the film, like the liberal bishop of Southwark Mervyn Stockwood, only made themselves look ridiculous.† It was no surprise that Church leaders proved even more reluctant to speak out in future, even under much greater provocation. Ten years later it was the freelance Mary Whitehouse who led the tirades against Martin Scorsese's *The Last Temptation of Christ*, which was held to be blasphemous even though it emphasised Jesus's ultimate triumph over fleshy delights.[51]

In 1999 the economics writer Dominic Hobson extended the indictment against the Anglican hierarchy, claiming that since the 1970s Church 'leaders have ceased to be men of holiness (or even learning) and become spokesmen of the public sector employees with whom they now share the burden of social work'.[52] There was much truth in this stinging allegation, but it is difficult to imagine the Church's fortunes improving under the direction of a brimstone-hurling evangelist in the mould of the Presbyterian Dr Ian Paisley. Within the Church of England in 1975 the alternatives on offer included an exorcising vicar in the London district of Hainault. In April 600 people turned up to witness a public display of his skills – an attempt to 'heal' a woman alleged to be a 'prostitute and alcoholic'. After a similar exhibition the previous October, a man had gone home and murdered his wife.[53] The vicar

---

* In Swansea the ban on the film remained in place for almost two decades; *Guardian*, 28 March 2003.

† At the time, the *Daily Telegraph* described the film as 'blasphemous as well as tasteless'; twenty years later, the polemicist Peter Hitchens claimed that it 'did more damage to faith among young Britons than every pamphlet and lecture which ever issued forth from the earnest spokesmen of rationalism and humanism'; *Daily Telegraph*, 9 November 1979; Peter Hitchens, *Monday Morning Blues*, Quartet Books, 2000, 155; Michael Palin *Diaries 1969–1979: The Python Years*, Weidenfeld & Nicolson, 2006, 594–6.

subsequently left the Church in order to work his miracles without fear of official reproof, but he was far from being alone in his diabolical fixation. In the summer of 1975 the crazed wife of a curate tried to cut the throat of her twelve-day-old son, believing that he was the 'devil incarnate'.[54] At the funeral of Lesley Whittle in March 1975 a local clergyman claimed that 'we are living in an age when demon possession is a reality'.[55]

Even in 1975 the Church was under the shadow of sexual scandal: the bishop of Llandaff was forced to resign in November after being charged with indecency. On balance, genuinely nice middle class candidates were probably the safest bet for promotion, and even they proved well capable of causing trouble. In 1980 Robert Runcie (1921–2000) took over at Lambeth Palace from the retiring Archbishop of Canterbury, Donald Coggan. Runcie was not just a very agreeable person, he was also a brave man who had been awarded a well-deserved Military Cross in the Second World War. But the archbishop's wartime nickname 'Killer' Runcie was misleading; his experiences had left him with a profound distaste for armed conflict.

In July 1982 Runcie delivered the main sermon at the thanksgiving service after the Falklands War, held in St Paul's Cathedral. He was indeed 'thankful' that the war was over, but he had no intention of celebrating the outcome, noting that 'It is impossible to be a Christian and not to long for peace.' He also reminded the congregation that Britain was itself the scene of ongoing conflict; the IRA had just killed a number of soldiers and horses in two London bombings. Runcie referred to these incidents as examples of 'mindless brutality' – an acceptable form of words for Margaret Thatcher. However, the rest of the sermon could be read as a coded attack on the prime minister. War was described as 'a sign of human failure'. In a different context this would have been an anodyne remark, but the alert would have been reminded that the Falklands conflict had arisen from specific failures by the British government. Another passage looked like a direct rebuke for the British Boadicea: 'It has sometimes been those spectators who remained at home who continue to be most violent in their attitudes, and untouched in the deepest selves.'

In fact these words were most applicable to the jingoistic *Sun*, which duly struck back against the presumptuous prelate; in a typically unamusing insult, the newspaper called Runcie the 'Archwimp of Canterbury'. But Thatcher was outraged by Runcie's sermon, and her instincts were reinforced by the views of equally bellicose backbenchers. Sir John Biggs-Davison thundered that 'It was revolting for cringing clergy to misuse St Paul's to throw doubt upon the sacrifice of our fighting men.' Of course, Runcie had done no such thing, but the anger was contagious. Julian Amery was closer to the mark when he denounced the Church's 'pacifist, liberal, wet establishment', although the Church had at least stopped short of endorsing unilateral nuclear disarmament. *The Times* defended Runcie in a measured editorial.[56] But this was drowned out in the atmosphere of overheated patriotism, and on balance it was a good thing that the service had not included one bright suggestion to symbolise the reconciliation between Britain and Argentina – otherwise the recumbent warriors in the cathedral would have had to endure the Lord's Prayer read in Spanish. As it was, Edward Heath was able to exercise his mordant humour by asking the Labour leader Michael Foot if he had written Runcie's script.[57]

Runcie also risked the displeasure of Downing Street by suggesting a less confrontational approach during the miners' strike of 1984/5. However, at least in this instance he was a secondary target. The main offender was David Jenkins, the bishop of Durham. Even before expressing sympathy for the miners – many of whom worked within his diocese, though not for much longer – Jenkins had caused apoplexy among the orthodox by questioning the literal truth of the virgin birth. Soon after his appointment in 1984 York Minster had been struck by lightning, setting off a serious fire. This celestial strike on behalf of the Conservative Party was not enough to silence Dr Jenkins or his fellow members of the 'liberal, wet establishment'. In December 1985 the Archbishop of Canterbury's Commission on Urban Priority Areas published a report, *Faith in the City*, which produced a list of detailed proposals for economic and spiritual renewal. While Thatcher privately protested that there was nothing in the report about the duty of self-help, one of her ministers claimed that the analysis was based on 'pure Marxist theology'.[58] That was pure Thatcherite nonsense. The report was actually a full-frontal assault on the government's philosophy from a liberal viewpoint which had much in common with the One Nation perspective – a point emphasised by a section headed 'Two Nations Recreated?' The need for urban renewal had been voiced from within Thatcher's own cabinet by Michael Heseltine, who could be accused of many things but hardly of Marxism. Even the most provocative suggestions in the report were not unprecedented. The authors pointed out that back in 1970 a commission on Church and state had named Anglican priorities as 'the poor and needy, whether in spirit or in body'. In the mid-1980s, it urged, the Church should 'by its example and its exertions proclaim the ethic of altruism against egotism, of community against self-seeking, and of charity against greed'.[59] But in the face of government hostility the Church's self-adopted mission to the inner-city poor could only have a marginal effect. As Jeremy Paxman put it in 1998, 'There *are* Anglican vicars heroically toiling away in poverty-stricken inner-city slums, helping people with their benefit claims, running soup kitchens and drop-in centres for the elderly or unemployed. But they are working as social workers – on half the pay.'[60] These exertions were a world away from the glamorous Alpha Course, which focused on the cities but generally ministered to the rich.

Runcie himself had been a wartime colleague of Mrs Thatcher's former deputy, Willie Whitelaw. After Whitelaw's death Runcie remembered with gratitude the occasions on which he had been defended by his friend.[61]* Whitelaw, of course, was a One Nation Conservative, or 'wet', who only stayed in the cabinet out of an ingrained sense of loyalty and social duty. Others of his kind were gradually removed from office, and joined a growing phalanx of discontented centrists. As Mrs Thatcher attacked other institutions which opposed her, well-meaning clerics in the Church became less tolerant of opposing views. Runcie's tendency to promote people who agreed with his outlook – a kind of clerical cronyism – was bitterly attacked in the preface to the 1987 edition of *Crockford's Clerical Directory*. The anonymous author depicted the embattled archbishop as the leader of a bishops' bench whose members exhibited typical 'attitudes of the bourgeoisie, both in its constant propensity to guilt and in its highly selective forms of liberalism'. Although the preface included some kind words about Runcie's personal qualities, it claimed that he usually 'nailed his colours to the fence', while his colleagues tried to stifle dissent. There was a harsher judgement on the bishop of Durham, who was accused of 'intemperate partisanship' based on incoherent thinking.[62]† A few days

---

* Inevitably, Runcie attracted little tabloid attention when he supported favoured Thatcherite causes. For example, in February 1986 he gave another sermon at St Paul's, this time at a thanksgiving service on behalf of industry and commerce; see Henry Clark, *The Church under Thatcher*, SPCK, 1993, 93.

† The jibe about sitting on the fence was attributed to the Labour MP Frank Field. Ironically, the author had been invited to contribute a piece which was a bit more lively than the usual offering in the *Directory*.

after the preface appeared, its author was revealed as Canon Gareth Bennett, a fellow of New College, Oxford, who promptly committed suicide.

The tragic and sensational conclusion to the *Crockford's* affair inflicted further damage on the Church. Even at the time of the Falklands sermon, questions were being asked about its continued link with the state because of its strident anti-Thatcherism. Government propagandists were trying their best to use the conflict as a springboard for national revival, yet the Church could only imply that the battle to recapture the remote South Atlantic islands had been a regrettable episode. Certainly the old jest about the church being 'the Conservative Party at prayer' was well out of date – Canon Bennett had been slightly closer to the truth when he called it 'the SDP at prayer'.[63] The controversy, however, merely drew public attention to the Church's problem in finding a role in the modern, materialistic world. In a sense it had become the institutional equivalent of Prince Charles. In 1982 the journalist Anthony Sampson produced a new version of his classic *Anatomy of Britain*; the Anglican Church barely figured as a footnote.[64] Mrs Thatcher could hardly punish her clerical enemies by disestablishing the Church; she contented herself by using her (limited) powers of patronage in a way which would upset Runcie, and by delivering periodic theological salvos like her 'Sermon on the Mound' of May 1988, which demonstrated that God was a sound Thatcherite.[65]

In one respect Runcie had the last laugh; his Church might be in trouble, but at the grass roots the Conservative Party was declining much faster. However, after Thatcher's departure from office her economic outlook became more influential among top Anglicans and more professional financial guidance recouped the losses of the early 1990s. Some clerics became well-versed in fashionable management-speak, hardly compatible with the delicious prose of the King James Bible. 'Our product is quite simply allowing people to move closer to God,' remarked a Lincoln cathedral canon. In 1991 St Paul's Cathedral started charging an admission fee; by the end of the century most of the nation's greatest ecclesiastical buildings had followed suit.[66] Many properties, like rural rectories, were sold off. But although the Church could practise self-help, it still required outside support to meet the crippling cost of maintaining its buildings. In 1977 the Victoria and Albert Museum had held an exhibition about the future of parish churches; its title, *Change and Decay*, suggested that all was not well.

The Historic Buildings Council subsequently agreed to help out.[67] In the 1990s the Church became another supplicant for lottery funding. The old spiritual and political bond between Church and state had dwindled into a cash nexus; and from this position, it was more difficult for the Church to obstruct the march of Mammon. In 1994 it had to acquiesce in the relaxation of restrictions on Sunday trading, after twenty-six previous attempts to change the law since 1950. As a grudging concession to clerical feelings, the legislation prevented shops from opening when the Church enjoyed peak demand – Easter Sunday and Christmas Day (if it fell on a Sunday). But the Church was not entirely defenceless; it could always resort to a form of blackmail to prise extra funds from the government. In 1990, for example, Hereford Cathedral was faced with a financial crisis which had not been rectified by a successful £1 million appeal in the mid-1980s. It decided to sell the *Mappa Mundi* – the finest mediaeval map of the world in existence. It would have been unthinkable to allow this treasure to leave Britain, so the National Heritage Memorial Fund provided a grant of £2 million. The British-based American philanthropist John Paul Getty Junior chipped in another million, for a new library.

Despite this largesse, individual clergy are now more dependent on their congregations for their stipends and pensions, and their numbers have gradually diminished to reflect their loss of custom. In 1978 there were more than 11,500; by 2005 this figure was down to 8,764 (including about 1,500 women). While they struggled to detain their straying flocks, they could at least console themselves that things were worse for their Catholic or Methodist counterparts. Between 1989 and 2005 Sunday attendance at Catholic churches halved, to just 875,000. Methodism – the church of Mrs Thatcher's childhood – lost more than 220,000 attenders over the same period, leaving it with less than 300,000 followers (which was still more than Thatcher's Conservative Party). In Scotland a survey of 2003 estimated that 300 people had stopped attending church every week for the previous eight years. The Church of Scotland and the Catholics fared equally badly in that period.[68]

In 2001 the national census included a religious question for the first time. Superficially, the findings revealed a fairly pious population. Apparently there were 42 million Christians in the UK. That figure fooled no one; it said nothing about the level of commitment, and even if it had done so, many respondents would have exaggerated the depth of their feelings. The survey showed that there were 170 different religions in Britain, thus apparently endorsing Prince Charles's self-description as a defender of faith in general, rather than the established Church in particular.* The diversity in part reflected a meteoric rise in new age superstitions. By the mid-1990s even sensible publications like the *Sunday Times* and the *Observer* had been forced to supply horoscopes for their more credulous readers.[69] Princess Diana was no stranger to the occult; even Cherie Blair, though ostensibly a Catholic, engaged in weird rituals under the guidance of her eccentric 'lifestyle guru', the former glamour model Carole Caplin. It was said that Caplin also advised the prime minister in his choice of underwear. Neither of Runcie's successors in the Canterbury see – George Carey (1991–2002) or Rowan Williams (2002–) – would have been entrusted with such a spiritual task. Fifteen hundred respondents to the census were prepared to say that they were Satan worshippers; insiders claimed that the true figure was closer to 3,000. The percentage of outright atheists was infinitesimal, suggesting that this status was still regarded as disreputable. The larger number of agnostics seemed to suggest that organised religion had failed to tap into a substantial pool of people who were prepared to think that there might be somebody watching over them from above, however they might fare in the National Lottery. About 16 per cent of the UK population were unable or unwilling to identify themselves with any religion – a stark contrast with the 2000 Social Attitudes survey, which indicated that the proportion of unattached individuals had risen from 31 per cent in 1991 to 44 per cent.[70] But whether or not people were being wholly frank in their census responses, its findings meant that there were at least nine million of no religion – three times the number of people who belonged to non-Christian faiths. There were only 1.6 million Muslims, although this made them the second largest religious community in the UK, and their numbers had increased from around 550,000 in 1981.

Islam was already attracting disproportionate attention before the terrorist attack on New York in September 2001. Prince Charles had been a close student of the religion for many years. The main source of fear and misunderstanding among Britain's nominal Christians was that sincere Muslims took seriously the idea of an afterlife. This idea clashed with the dominant consumerist ethos, which could normally

---

* The number would have been larger, but statistical killjoys refused to accept 'Jedi Knight' as a religion although almost 400,000 people responded to an Internet campaign claiming membership of the imaginary sect.

be expected to undermine the most fervent forms of religious belief; it was no accident that religious feeling was strongest among first-generation immigrants, whatever faith they happened to follow.* However, British Muslims were more likely than members of other religions to experience poverty and unemployment, thus compounding their sense of alienation from a Godless society.†

By 2006 more than 80 per cent of Britons regarded religion not as a source of solace but rather as a creator of 'division and tension' in society.[71] From this perspective, it was curious that New Labour took a positive interest in offering state funds to faith schools. In 2005 there were 7,000 of these, mostly in the primary sector. Only five of them were Islamic, although the media made it seem that there were far more. However, more than 120 independent Islamic schools were identified for possible future inclusion within the state sector.[72] The government's initiative gave the impression that senior figures were hoping for a religious revival in Britain, despite the mayhem that fundamentalist faith was currently causing throughout the world. From the agnostic viewpoint, young people offered the best hope of a peaceful future; according to a survey in the year 2000 two thirds of them had no religion. But Tony Blair took religion more seriously than political principle, straddling the divide between Catholicism and the Church of England in a theological version of his 'Third Way'. Briefly, his education secretary was Ruth Kelly, who sympathised with the controversial Catholic sect Opus Dei. Perhaps their own religious commitments – which set them apart from the country even more than their interest in politics – helped to convince Blair and Kelly that faith schools would invariably provide a better education than their secular counterparts. But almost certainly the real reason for the initiative was the familiar assumption that the government would be able to exercise more control if it took hold of the purse-strings. Once the Islamic schools were funded by the taxpayer, they might even stop being quite so Islamic.

---

* The 2001 census found that 54 per cent of Muslims living in Britain had been born elsewhere; *The Times*, 20 April 2005.
† In 2003 unemployment was 14 per cent among Muslim men compared to 4 per cent for Christians. For those aged between 16 and 24, the respective rates were 22 per cent and 11 per cent. Nearly a third of Muslim men of working age had no educational qualifications, compared to 15 per cent of Christians; *Guardian*, 12 October 2004.

III

A clergyman who knew Prince Charles during his time at Trinity College, Cambridge formed the impression that 'he was a deep person, that he wasn't taken in by the surfaces of life'. He had 'an openness of mind, a readiness to evaluate ideas, not taking things off the peg but thinking them out for himself.'[73] These qualities were admirably suited to his preferred academic subjects, archaeology and anthropology. In 1970 Charles became the first member of his family to take a degree, as befitted the heir to the throne of what was supposedly a meritocratic country; and in view of his numerous distractions, he did reasonably well to leave Cambridge with a lower second.

Unfortunately for Charles, his academic interests left him stranded between two vocal constituencies: the downmarket media and the intellectuals. In the one-eyed world of the popular press, a far-sighted man could never be king. By contrast, with barely anything to show for her own expensive education, and with her 'banal cultural pursuits',[74] Diana was admirably qualified to be 'the people's princess'. As the nation took sides over the troubled royal marriage, it might have been expected that intellectuals would rally behind Charles. However, even in these circles he was not taken seriously. It was all too easy to scoff at a prince who used his privileged position to promote his untutored architectural prejudices, including his 1984 description of the National Gallery extension as a 'monstrous carbuncle'. He was also an enthusiast for blood sports and was rumoured to talk to his plants. In short, despite his friendships with clever people like the South African-born writer Laurens Van Der Post – who took him on safari in Kenya in 1977 – Charles would always be rated as a dilettante. After 1997 not even his increasingly public disputes with New Labour ministers could overcome the traditional intellectual distaste for the hereditary principle.

It was scant consolation to the beleaguered prince that even the unanimous support of intellectuals would not have been worth much. In some ways the decline of intellectual influence on British life in the second half of the twentieth century was unexpected. In an increasingly secular society which retained glaring imperfections British intellectuals were a potential source of guidance for anyone who wanted to find a more secure form of happiness amid material abundance.

Their failure to provide compelling alternative visions suggests that there had been a kind of creative tension between the secular and the spiritual, so that they were predestined to decline together. A more plausible conclusion was that the forces of consumerism were powerful enough to subvert any opposition, whether based on rationality or religious faith.

In Britain – and particularly in England – intellectuals had always struggled to be taken seriously. Jeremy Paxman has written that 'if you are going to be an intellectual in England, you had better do it discreetly, and certainly not call yourself an intellectual'.[75] The stigma could apply to any calling. In June 2006 a *Times* columnist claimed that Rowan Williams was the wrong person to be Archbishop of Canterbury because he was an intellectual.[76] But it has been particularly dangerous for British politicians to be caught in the act of thinking. The Conservative Party is not the only organisation with an instinctive suspicion of people who seem too clever by half. Thus, although the Labour government which took office in February 1974 was one of the most intellectually gifted administrations in British history, casual observers could hardly have guessed it. Notwithstanding his pipe-smoking populist pose, Harold Wilson had been a brilliant Oxford student. His chancellor, Denis Healey, played along with the media image of a boneheaded bruiser with an irrational grudge against wealthy people. In reality, Healey was a profoundly cultured and multi-talented individual.[77]

Although Labour's leaders struggled to conceal their academic gifts, it was still natural for critics to accuse the political left of excessive intellectualism. Until the mid-1970s this charge was not too damaging, but the situation was transformed by the oil crisis and the subsequent polarisation of British politics. The notion that the post-war consensus had failed encouraged left-wing thinkers to examine more radical alternatives. The appearance of books like the widely discussed *The Socialist Challenge* (1975), by the Sussex University lecturer and Bennite MP Stuart Holland, allowed Labour's opponents to·claim that the initiative within the party was passing to impractical ideologues. Tony Benn himself was not really an intellectual and had a questionable roster of ideological heroes including long-dead libertarians like the seventeenth-century Levellers. This anachronistic view of Britain's ideological heritage was just about the only trait he shared with Michael Foot, who could certainly be classed as an intellectual, not least because he was one of the most brilliant essayists of the twentieth century. The choice of Foot as Labour leader in November 1980 was thus an uncovenanted boon for Thatcherites. Not only was Foot already beyond the official retirement age, but his intelligence made him so contemptuous of the image-makers that he was capable of turning up at official ceremonies in a coat which was considered to be insufficiently dignified.

Although Foot was an easy target for the Thatcherites, in 1980 they would have denounced any new Labour leader as a utopian follower of impractical theories. In their eyes the post-war consensus itself had been a rationalistic enterprise, inspired by the ultra-intellectual John Maynard Keynes (1893–1946). Actually this was an old argument, which had been perfected in the late 1940s by the Austrian-born economist Friedrich von Hayek. In 1949 Hayek had claimed that intellectuals – 'second-hand dealers in ideas', as he dubbed them – exercised an 'all-pervasive influence' on society through policymakers and opinion formers.[78] Hayek himself had hoped to rally like-minded intellectuals into a fightback against socialism, which he feared would take Britain down 'the road to serfdom'. Although Keynes was a Liberal, he was clearly included in this indictment because his ideas implied that the state was potentially a vehicle of human progress rather than a brutal repressive machine. Keynes also irritated people like Hayek because he approached economics with zest, while they thought that it should remain a 'dismal science'. Even worse, Keynes had 'warmed both hands before the fire of life' in a way which clearly mortified etiolated individuals like Hayek.

The attack on Keynes was taken up with enthusiasm by Margaret Thatcher, who spoke regularly about the need to win 'the battle of ideas' against socialists and Keynesian fellow-travellers. In the struggle to proselytise on behalf of economic freedom she was helped by enthusiastic right-wing think tanks like the IEA, the Centre for Policy Studies (established 1975) and the Adam Smith Institute (1977). Thatcher herself had few original thoughts on politics or economics, but once she had established herself as Conservative leader she became an inspiration for right-wing intellectuals because she shared their atavistic feelings about the effects of socialism, whether at home or abroad. After dining with Thatcher in October 1977, for example, Kingsley Amis crowed that she was 'bright and tough and nice, and by God she doesn't half hate lefties'.[79] This trait was particularly endearing to those, like Amis, who had once been committed left-wingers and had lost their faith over the years; and for Amis it undoubtedly helped that Thatcher was 'one of the best-looking women I had ever met and for her age, then over fifty, remarkable'.* The converts included the ex-Marxist Alfred Sherman and Paul Johnson, who had edited the *New Statesman* between 1964 and 1970. Another Thatcher-worshipper, Woodrow Wyatt, was a former Labour MP. Even Rupert Murdoch could be cited as a reclaimed sinner, having in his youth displayed a bust of Lenin – 'The Great Teacher' – on his mantelpiece.[80]

After Thatcher became Conservative leader the ideological distance between the official programmes of the two main parties was wide enough to offer such converts to the 'new right' plenty of scope for a critique. However, they insisted on taking Labour's arguments to the extreme limits of implied logic, exaggerating the extent to which the party had embraced rigid, doctrinaire ideas in order to justify their own abandonment of progresive thinking. This method of disputation quickly spread through Thatcher's entourage. Thus in 1979 Sir Keith Joseph, the new prime minister's ideological guru, happily put his name to a published tract on the subject of economic equality. The gist of his argument was that the complete levelling of incomes would result in a reduction of freedom. This was a reasonable proposition in itself. But it had no relevance to political debate at the time, since hardly anyone in Britain (let alone the senior ranks of the Labour Party) was putting forward a case for *absolute* economic equality.[81]

If the biggest brains on the right were prepared to tar all of their opponents with the same ideological brush, it was little wonder that amateur polemicists followed their example. One writer who contributed to this unjustly neglected genre was Minden 'Mindy' Blake, DSO (1913–81), a New Zealand-born air ace of the Second World War who went on to captain Wentworth Golf Club and pen such invaluable tracts as *The Golf Swing of the Future* (1972). In January 1979, enraged by the 'Winter of Discontent', Mindy decided to co-write a book entitled *Suicide by Socialism*. Even after Mrs Thatcher's election victory in the May of that year, the authors decided not to shelve their project. Socialism, they declared, was 'the basic cause of the country's

---

* Amis also experienced regular amorous dreams about Mrs Thatcher. He was not the only one whose ideological fealty was cemented by sexual attraction; when Friedrich von Hayek was first introduced to Mrs Thatcher soon after she became Opposition leader, he gasped, 'She's so beautiful.' Kingsley Amis, *Memoirs*, Penguin edn, 1992, 315–19; Richard Cockett, *Thinking the Unthinkable: Think Tanks and the Economic Counter Revolution 1931–1983*, HarperCollins, 1994, 176.

decline throughout this century'. Even if one accepts that 'socialists' had ever held office in Britain during those years – and it is doubtful that the label can even be pinned on the Attlee government of 1945–51 – this argument begged the questions of why Britain had been declining in relative terms even before Labour had emerged as an independent party, and why so many Conservative administrations had failed to rectify the damage. Presumably the authors thought that all of the ten Conservative premiers of the century up to 1979 had been socialists in disguise. From this vantage point they considered that James Callaghan and Margaret Thatcher merely offered a choice between 'a bit more Socialism and a bit less Socialism'.[82] They could not have been more wrong, on both counts.

Despite all the excited Thatcherite rhetoric about victory in the battle of ideas, it is unlikely that the intellectual arguments of the new right ever convinced more than a tiny handful of impressionable people. Ultimately, the Thatcherite case depended on practical example rather than theoretical reasoning. In a tight corner the new right could always hold up the Soviet Union as a warning to anyone who was tempted by left-wing ideas, although it was questionable whether the misfortunes of that state under decadent leaders like Leonid Brezhnev (1906–82) really disproved the humanistic visions of Karl Marx. The economic and social plight of the Soviet bloc certainly could not be regarded as a refutation of Keynes, whose theories about economic management were actually devised as a way of saving the capitalist system from its self-destructive tendencies. But in the gloomy circumstances of the late 1970s such nuances were easily overlooked by Britons who wanted a scapegoat for their problems. Intellectuals fitted the bill nicely, particularly since they could also be blamed for the decline in moral standards which had coincided with the political prominence of 'permissive' thinking in the 1960s.

Thankfully for Margaret Thatcher, the poverty of her thinking made little difference to her electoral fortunes. The Conservative Party would almost certainly have won the 1979 general election under any leader; and the Falklands War, rather than the cogency of Thatcherism, was mainly responsible for the revival of the prime minister's popularity which ensured her re-election four years later. Yet her acolytes continued to prosecute the 'battle of ideas'. As late as 1988 Paul Johnson thought it worthwhile to devote a book to an attack on the influence of subversive intellectuals, starting predictably with Jean-Jacques Rousseau. But

Johnson could end his book on a positive note. 'The belief seems to be spreading,' he wrote, 'that intellectuals are no wiser as mentors, or worthier as exemplars, than the witch doctors or priests of old.' He identified 'a growing tendency among ordinary people to dispute the right of academics, writers and philosophers, eminent though they may be, to tell us how to behave and conduct our affairs'.[83]

Johnson's book was a paradoxical exercise – an intellectual telling his readers that intellectuals were no longer worth heeding – but the collapse of the Soviet bloc the following year made his message seem prescient. In two respects the end of the communist regimes should have been liberating for left-wing British intellectuals. Instead of having to defend themselves against the allegation that they were stooges of hostile foreign powers, they could now present a more positive argument for radical change. At the same time intellectuals had played a significant role in the revolt against communism, often at considerable personal risk. The dissident playwright Vaclav Havel was even elected president of Czechoslovakia in recognition of his services to the democratic movement.

Opponents of Thatcherism had been quick to latch on to the underground style of writing favoured by the internal opponents of Soviet-style colonialism. In 1980, for example, the historian E.P. Thompson produced a volume of essays entitled *Writing By Candlelight*, entreating 'freeborn Britons' to fight for their old liberties even though the nuclear threat forced him to doubt that there would be 'a posterity to enjoy them'.[84] However, while their eastern European counterparts still had good reason to fear for their safety, British intellectuals had merely been trapped inside a gulag of public indifference. Whatever their real contribution to the fight against totalitarianism, the right-wing governments of Ronald Reagan and Margaret Thatcher received all of the public credit when the Berlin Wall came down. Far from permitting a re-evaluation of Marx's legacy in more propitious circumstances, the end of the regimes which had misruled in his name was quickly followed by the closure of the journal *Marxism Today*.[85]

On the face of it, the failure to exploit the new opportunities created by the fall of communism was a puzzle. One reason was the behaviour of the Labour Party, which had already embarked on the process of abandoning its traditional principles and was far too inflexible to think again. But while some intellectuals persisted in thinking that political change could improve their situation – and that Labour was still a worthy vehicle for their hopes – the response to the events of 1989 can only be explained as one result of a more general loss of confidence. Since the economic crises of the mid-1970s there had been a growing feeling that intellectuals were a luxury which the nation could no longer afford. Such sentiments were given scholarly support by the appearance, soon after Thatcher's first general election victory, of *English Culture and the Decline of the Industrial Spirit 1850–1980* by the American historian Martin Wiener.[86] Wiener attributed Britain's relative decline since its mid-Victorian heyday to a form of intellectual snobbery. Instead of teaching their children to follow their own example, entrepreneurs had tended to dispatch them to elite educational establishments, where they absorbed a supercilious attitude to the business community. A broadly similar message about the deleterious effect of perverse educational priorities was conveyed in a series of powerfully argued books by Corelli Barnett, notably *The Collapse of British Power* (1972) and *The Audit of War* (1986).

The practical effect of such writings was to question further the credentials of contemporary intellectuals as participants in British public discourse. Whatever one thought of their general role in political life, it had been difficult to deny intellectuals a say in the formation of education policy. But if their meddling really lay at the heart of Britain's economic weakness, they were the last people who should be consulted in future. The challenge was all the more effective because intellectuals had never been asked to justify their educational preferences. It had merely been taken for granted that Britain would benefit as a whole if its citizens were taught to think for themselves, and to appreciate 'high' culture. Thanks to Wiener and Barnett, Thatcherites could argue that this approach was bad for business, and that education at all levels should now be geared to more vocational subjects.

This was a tragic termination to the post-war dreams of intellectuals and educationalists. Most of them had taken it as an article of faith that the pre-war system had cruelly denied working-class children the chance to appreciate 'the best that has been said and thought in the world'. As Matthew Arnold had written more than a century before, 'the sweetness and light of the few must be imperfect until the raw and unkindled masses of humanity are touched with sweetness and light'.[87] Once their eyes had been opened to the glories of prose and poetry, young people from all backgrounds would leave the education system as enlightened citizens, rather than passive consumers with nothing more than a rudimentary acquaintance with reading, writing and arithmetic. Wherever their talents lay, in later life they would strike an appropriate balance between enrichment and spiritual fulfilment.

By the mid-1970s this roseate vision had already dissipated. If the project had succeeded, intellectuals would have been incidental bene-ficiaries; their productions would be bought, and talked about, even if people continued to patronise less demanding authors for light relief. But intellectuals discovered that they were unable to penetrate beyond the relatively small and select audience they had enjoyed before the advantages of education were extended to the poor. The British public as a whole concentrated its patronage on undeserving objects.

Those who denied that British culture was being affected by dumbing down could point out that although libraries were struggling badly, in 2004 almost two thirds of the population claimed that they read for pleasure, compared to just 55 per cent in 1979. On this basis, one commentator could claim that 'our intellectual life has never been so vibrant'.[88] But even if they could be taken at face value the statistics provided new reasons to deplore the conditions of the late 1970s, rather than praise later years. In any case, there was no quality control in such surveys, so that a person who read the premature, ghostwritten autobiography of a footballer would be counted as a leisure-time reader alongside someone who tackled War and Peace. With a little imagi-nation, the phrase 'reading for pleasure' could also embrace the perusal of celebrity magazines like OK!, Heat and Now, all of which usually sold more than half a million copies every month in 2004. For the same reason it was valid to question figures which showed an upward trend in book sales. Some charity shops had begun to open separate outlets devoted mainly to books. But once again it was difficult to take heart from this phenomenon without knowing exactly what kind of books were being bought. Instead of demonstrating the erudition of British readers, the results of the BBC's major survey The Big Read (2003) gave plenty of reasons for misgivings. Douglas Adams's The Hitch-Hiker's Guide to the Galaxy (1979) – a Monty Python deriva-tive with limited attractions outside its cult following – was ranked at number four in the list of all-time literary greats, while Wuthering Heights languished at number twelve, just above Sebastian Faulks's Birdsong (1993). As for War and Peace, it did sneak into the top twenty; but contemporary readers clearly did not understand that its shelf life of almost two centuries was certain to outlast the popularity of a current favourite among London commuters, *Captain Corelli's Mandolin* (1994, number nineteen in the survey).

Optimists could conclude that a taste for undemanding fiction might encourage Britons to move on to richer fare, but the results of The Big Read suggested otherwise. In an attempt to placate the new realities some intellectuals resorted to a cowardly subterfuge, arguing that in its own context *Coronation Street* was the cultural equivalent of *Coriolanus*. But even when expounding this unlikely thesis, intellectuals continued to *theorise*, thus betraying their estrangement from the popular culture of a consumer society. The most gifted, like Jeremy Paxman (born 1950) and Stephen Fry (born 1957), managed to retain intellectual credibility while contributing to the entertainment industry. But although they did produce work of enduring value among the ephemera, their careers left the unsettling impression that, had he been alive in their times, Voltaire would have hosted a celebrity chat show, while Rousseau would have been a regular on *Grumpy Old Men*.

Thus the attempt to raise cultural standards across the board through state education only resulted in the emergence of an increasingly resentful and irrelevant intellectual elite. Democracy had left them high and dry, and the results of near-universal literacy had only increased their despondency. Cheekily, after the 1992 general election the Oxford don John Carey reminded them that many of their heroes had fallen below the egalitarian aspirations of Matthew Arnold, making scathing comments about the 'masses' even before they had been given the chance to show their lack of taste.[89] In hindsight, though, it merely seemed that the snooty sentiments of Carey's subjects – people like H.G. Wells and George Orwell – had been far-sighted. Recognising that they could never fight back effectively, intellectuals exercised a private vengeance by making themselves ever more unintelligible to the general public, like a verbose version of the Freemasons. Hence, in part, the vogue for postmodernism and other abstruse academic fads. Like most minorities with a persecution complex, intellectuals also followed some senior figures in the Church of England by becoming more intolerant of dissent within their own ranks. In scholarly circles an interest in the history and ideas of the Conservative Party became as hazardous as the advocacy of armed insurrection in other walks of life; living representatives of the party, like Sir Keith Joseph, were either warned away from university engagements or pelted with eggs. When the university activism of the 1960s and 70s had died away, this intolerance was all that was left in the memories of former students who later graduated into government and imposed this style of thinking on the public at large under the umbrella term of 'political correctness'.

The chief dilemma for intellectuals after 1975 was that they were more dependent than ever on state subsidies. The more they defied popular tastes, the less likely it was that the public would pay the bills. For many good reasons, it was always likely that the confrontation would begin in the field of fine art, which had been threatened by film and photography long before the arrival of television. The lack of public awareness of British artistic endeavour was exposed in the BBC's Great Britons survey of 2002. No British artist – not even J.M.W. Turner – made the top hundred in the public vote, although the pop singers Robbie Williams and Boy George were included.[90] The lack of public recognition of earlier achievements meant that the visual arts were more vulnerable to counter-attack, and the economic problems of the mid-1970s gave the enemies of art an early incentive to strike. A telling symptom of the new mood came in 1976, when the Tate Gallery exhibited Carl Andre's *Equivalent VIII* (1966), a rectangular assemblage of 120 firebricks. Purchased by the gallery in 1972, this 'minimalist' artwork had attracted miniaturist attention when put on show in 1974 and 1975. However, in the following year a *Sunday Times* article about recent exhibitions at the Tate provoked an outcry from the self-appointed spokespeople of Middle England.[91] The *Daily Mail*'s front-page comment on the work was succinct: 'What a Load of Rubbish!' Predictably, the furore only increased the number of visitors to the Tate, until one protestor adorned the artefact with paint, causing it to be withdrawn from public view. The same year, the Institute for Contemporary Art also fell foul of the tabloids for displaying the feminist Mary Kelly's *Post Partum Document*, which included a selection of soiled nappies.

By suddenly taking an interest in contemporary art, the right-wing tabloids supposed that they were attacking intellectuals on their weakest flank. The media campaign might have attracted more people to look at the notorious *Equivalent VIII*, but only intellectuals could ever assign any meaning to it. The tabloids were trying to smoke such people out, inviting intellectuals to expose themselves to public ridicule by pontificating about the philosophical significance of a pile of bricks. However, once the dust had settled the incident suggested that the tabloids and the arts community could establish a relationship of mutual convenience. Avant garde artists could justify their state subsidies by acting as a harmless conduit for public anger, encouraging each other to produce works which seriously transgressed lowbrow tastes. The ensuing front-page stories would keep readers at boiling point during the periods when real news was rare; and once the furore had died down, artists could resume their habitual activities unmolested.

The problem was that the media had not anticipated the extent of the outcry against the bricks and the nappies, and it was difficult to guess when the next offending artefact would appear. A more predictable timetable of outrage was required. The art world obliged in 1984 by instituting the annual Turner Prize. From early on it was clear that the real purpose of this award was to restore the self-belief of artists by winning attention from the mass media. The victory of Gilbert and George in 1986 was a deliberate attempt to fling a paint pot in the face of Thatcherism; after all, this openly gay duo challenged traditional morality, as well as flouting conventional artistic standards with a body of work which included *Coming*, a bizarre assemblage of the artists being bombarded by female genitalia.

By 1995 the Turner judges had devised a new way of shocking the public. At least Damien Hirst's pickled animal remains were recognisable objects. But to the average tabloid reader it now seemed that worldwide acclaim awaited anyone with a chainsaw, plenty of formaldehyde and sufficient cheek to pass off a corpse as an example of creativity. Even this might not have secured the Turner Prize for Hirst, were it not for the high profile of animal rights in the mid-1990s. Thus for the tabloids the unfathomable fads of the art world could be used to provoke anger amongst tender-hearted intellectuals as well as their regular readers. The prize became such a big media event that it could be the making even of artists who did not win. In 1997 Tracey Emin attracted attention because of her drunken behaviour during a Channel 4 debate, 'The Death of Painting'. Her installation *My Bed* failed to secure the prize two years later, but the media-savvy Charles Saatchi reportedly paid £150,000 for the unkempt artefact.

For serious practitioners of literature, the dilemma was more acute. While a Turner Prize-winning daub (or 'installation') could be condemned by tabloid readers at a single glance, it was more difficult to irritate the same audience with a poem or an extract from a novel, which demanded more sustained attention. Furthermore, the main awards for literature, like the Booker and Whitbread Prizes (1969 and

1971 respectively) had been established at a time when the criterion of merit, rather than hunger for media exposure, was the chief consideration. As a result, fiction writers rarely hit the headlines after 1975 – except in the case of Salman Rushdie's *The Satanic Verses* (1988), when the attention was unwanted, and Alan Hollinghurst's 2004 Booker Prize-winning novel *The Line of Beauty*, which was bound to enrage right-wing tabloid editors with its tidings of gay sex and greed in the Thatcher era.

Far from being 'the unacknowledged legislators of mankind', serious British poets knew by now that they would only attract notice when they were touted as possible poets laureate, or (in the case of Tony Harrison) attacked by Mary Whitehouse. Probably the widest-read British poet of the time was Pam Ayres, the writer and performer of good-natured doggerel verse discovered by the ITV talent show *Opportunity Knocks* in 1975, who subsequently appeared on the BBC's consumer programme *That's Life* alongside misshapen vegetables. Overall, the only hope for intellectuals was that the publishing industry would persevere in its laudable practice of subsidising serious literary works from the proceeds of low- or middlebrow fiction and children's books like J.K. Rowling's highly profitable Harry Potter series, which began in 1997.

While the tabloids could afford to treat intellectuals with a mixture of amusement and disdain, politicians were less charitable. After all, intellectuals provided the main readership for the satirical magazine *Private Eye*, which acted as a merciless monitor of political morality, showing no favour either to left or right. In theory, politicians were committed to the principle of pluralism, but the *Eye* was one voice they could easily do without. The best long-term solution to the problem of intellectuals was to choke it off at its source – the universities. In this respect cultural philistines were well served after the mid-1970s. Harold Wilson's immediate successors in Downing Street had no need to play down their academic achievements. Indeed, James Callaghan and John Major were graduates of the university of life, and were unable to conceal their insecurity in the presence of people with more impressive formal qualifications. Margaret Thatcher used her Oxford career to advance her political and economic prospects, but there is no evidence that the experience expanded her cultural horizons. Tony Blair, who took his own Oxford degree in 1975, emerged from St John's College with deeper religious convictions, but in other respects his sojourn played a limited role in the formation of his mysterious character. He was at least sufficiently anti-intellectual to attract the fleeting admiration of Paul Johnson.

Only the worst kind of intellectual snob could assert that Britain would have been better governed after Wilson's resignation in 1976 if his successors had held All Souls fellowships. But in a period when governments of both main parties declared their commitment to the expansion of higher education, the universities might have hoped for some personal sympathy from senior policymakers and a recognition that learning could be valuable whether or not it led to material bene-fits. As it was, student numbers multiplied under the leadership of people who were at best indifferent to the universities, and at worst oblivious to the possibility that anyone could believe it worthwhile to pursue knowledge in isolation from the prospect of monetary gains. Typically, after 1975 they claimed that Britain would not be able to compete in world markets unless it nurtured a highly educated work-force, but they did nothing to maintain the quality of university education, shrugging off the inevitable protests with complacent refer-ences to the country's hard-earned reputation for academic excellence. Margaret Thatcher was the worst offender here, imposing a 20 per cent cut in university budgets between 1981 and 1984.[92] Academic pay fell further behind comparable professions, and security of tenure was abolished in 1988. Several of the older universities narrowly averted bankruptcy; newer institutions outside the Thatcherite heartlands, like Salford, Bradford and Aston, only survived by severely truncating their activities.[93] Elsewhere, departments were closed or merged, and student–teacher ratios increased. At the same time the government took closer control over the detail of university funding, scrapping the old, arms-length University Grants Committee and replacing it with a more subservient, business-oriented body. Like the Churches and charities, the universities were forced by their paymasters to realise that they could only escape from impoverishment at the cost of their autonomy. One lamentable effect of government interference was a ham-fisted system of research funding which meant that brilliant teachers who rarely published articles or books were driven out of the profession, to the obvious detriment of students.[94]

The assault on the quality of university education was based on a cynical calculation. By 1979 most middle-class parents had come to regard a spell in higher education as a natural extension of schooling for their children. However, the situation had changed since the mid-nineteenth century, when, according to Martin Wiener's thesis, successful entrepreneurs used the education system to transform their rough-hewn offspring into polished gentlemen. The student disorders of the 1960s – which actually affected Britain much less than the corresponding movements in the US and France – had given the universities a very bad name among their most valued customers. As a result, over the next decade middle-class parents faced the prospect of subsidising their children for a minimum of three extra years of reputed idleness which might leave them with a lasting addiction to hallucinogenic drugs or (even worse) a taste for radical politics. Despite these unpleasing possibilities, the British middle classes continued to send their children to university. Evidently the perceived importance of degrees to future career prospects had turned parents into semi-captive clients, who would tolerate slipping standards almost indefinitely and keep footing ever-expanding bills. Thus policymakers could expect to get away with a prolonged attack on the universities, while a similar campaign of cultural vandalism in the schools would have courted electoral disaster.

After initial resistance from middle-class parents, the Conservatives managed to replace student grants with repayable loans in 1990. It was left to Blair's New Labour to take the further step of charging tuition fees, in defiance of its own manifesto promises. Despite attempts to cushion the poor from the effects of these measures, access to higher education was now inextricably linked to the ability to pay. As elsewhere, this new climate brought to the fore a new generation of senior administrators who had mastered the vocabulary of management consultancy. After closing departments of chemistry, music and Italian, one vice-chancellor proclaimed that 'this is about the University of Exeter finding its place in the market'.[95] Simon Jenkins saw the parliamentary vote on tuition fees in January 2004 as a further erosion of university autonomy, without solving their funding crisis. 'They sold their souls to sup with the government Devil,' he wrote. 'Now they are covered in his vomit.'[96]

As an articulate community, academics were unlikely to accept these successive blows without at least going through the motions of protest. In January 1985, after a two-hour debate, Oxford dons rejected a proposal to give Margaret Thatcher an honorary degree, by 738 votes to 319. Thatcher thus became the only Oxford-educated premier to miss out on this award and apparently the only candidate to be voted down apart from Pakistan's President Bhutto, whose claims had been rebuffed in 1975 because of his alleged complicity in the mass slaughter of Bangladeshis. The decision to withhold the degree was hardly likely to rob the prime minister of any sleep, but the Thatcherite tabloids exploited the occasion to lambast academics for their treachery. John Vincent, a Bristol-based historian and unlikely *Sun* columnist, claimed that Oxford dons were greedier than the miners. Even *The Times* accused Thatcher's opponents of 'political spite'.[97] In fact, Oxford had suffered little damage from Thatcherite policies; as such, the vote was a more impressive example of solidarity than the current behaviour of the trade union movement towards the NUM. But after some reflection even some eminent intellectuals decided that it had been a counterproductive gesture. Lord (Noel) Annan, for example, deplored the vote as 'an unparalleled and mean-spirited snub'.[98] Paul Johnson's annoyance was surprising only in its durability. Almost two decades later he was still complaining that Thatcher's Oxford detractors had consisted of 'a pack of Left-wing laboratory assistants and other riff-raff'.[99]

Perhaps the Oxford dons should have chosen a tactic which made their point without exposing their lack of public support – perhaps by organising a mass boycott of the 1985 vote. However, short of emulating the spirit of their 1960s students and burning down the Sheldonian Theatre, there was little else that the outraged academics could do to register a protest against government policy on higher education. In 1981 364 economists had sent *The Times* a letter of protest against Geoffrey Howe's budget – a package which seemed to be inspired by a desire to contradict Keynesian theory rather than a concern for the real needs of the British economy. Their well-founded strictures were ignored, and when sections of the economy began their inevitable recovery from the self-inflicted trauma of the first Thatcher government, the 364 economists became another set of intellectuals who could be damned, along with the 'witch doctors and priests of old'. At the 1987 general election only 17 per cent of academics voted Conservative; even the unemployed looked more favourably on Mrs Thatcher.[100] However, this was not enough to prevent the government from winning a third term with an overwhelming parliamentary majority.

Against this background of impotent protest, Britain accidentally embarked on a period of rapid university expansion. Later this development was rationalised as an attempt to equip the workforce for the challenges of the twenty-first century, but initially governments were hesitant about allowing the rise in student numbers. Gradually they realised that this could be done without spending more money, and that it could also serve the useful purpose of keeping young people off the dole. In 1988/9, 15 per cent of 18–21-year-olds were in full-time education. By 1993/4, the proportion had doubled. A renewed drive under New Labour after 1997 took the figure to 44 per cent; its ultimate target (later downgraded to an 'aspiration') was to see half of 18–21-year-olds in higher education. Under the terms of the 1992 Further and Higher Education Act, the distinction between universities and polytechnics had been removed to make it look as if everyone was receiving education of a comparable quality. This was true, in a way. Outside a handful of favoured institutions, students could expect an educational experience which was uniformly mediocre and not far advanced from the provision in sixth-form colleges. This outcome could hardly be avoided, when between 1980 and 2002 the student–lecturer ratio doubled – from 1:9 to 1:18.[101]

Over New Labour's first term spending on higher education as a proportion of Gross Domestic Product (GDP) actually fell, compared to the Conservative years. Academics became atypically strike-prone – not through any exploitation of industrial power, but because they knew that their students would barely suffer from the withdrawal of their labour. Their grievances were only partly founded on their relative economic misfortunes over the years since Margaret Thatcher came to power. Compared to many professionals they still had a fairly easy life, although they were increasingly affected by stress-related illnesses.* More seriously, they had lost the spiritual compensation which arose from respect. In a neat reversal of Martin Wiener's thesis, academics could only advise their cleverest students to burn their books after graduation and look for a well-paid job in the City of London. A further degree, followed by a career in academia, would only make sense to first-class candidates when all else had failed.

IV

Intellectuals, of course, were not the only potential source of hope in Britain after 1975. But on balance they were the most likely to project their thoughts outside the consumerist cage. In this context it was telling that, when the universities wielded the axe on specific departments, philosophy tended to be a favourite target. The BBC did attempt

---

*Between 2000 and 2004 the number of Cambridge academics seeking emotional support from counsellors rose by 60 per cent; *The Times*, 18 August 2004.

to bring the subject to a wider audience; Bryan Magee (a Labour MP between 1974 and 1983 and later a supporter of the SDP) hosted two excellent series, *Men of Ideas* (1978) and *The Great Philosophers* (1987). The latter was particularly bold for its time, since it eschewed gimmickry and was broadcast when non-insomniacs were still awake. However, for many years British philosophers had given up any attempt to change the world; thanks largely to Wittgenstein, they now preferred to argue about the meaning of language. Later they would jump aboard the postmodernist bandwagon on its self-declared journey from nowhere in particular to oblivion. As a rule, when professional philosophers were given a public platform to pronounce on a subject of topical concern, it was only when the problem had already passed beyond remedy.[102]

Among contemporary political thinkers, the American John Rawls (1921–2002) held unrivalled sway. His *Theory of Justice* (1971) was an unconvincing use of social contract theory to suggest that excessive inequality was wrong. A significant symptom of academic morale, this ineffectual effort was hailed for many years as the centrepiece of a renaissance in political theory. Unsurprisingly, the revival was short-lived; the next author to cause any significant stir was Professor Anthony Giddens of the LSE, who struggled unsuccessfully to assert that New Labour was based on something more than electoral opportunism.[103] As Opposition leader, Tony Blair had hoped to 'start building a common thread between the ideas of academics, thinkers and intellectuals on what Labour is trying to do'.[104] No such 'thread' ever emerged. In a sure sympton of slumping morale, in November 2006 *Prospect* magazine published a list of the world's 'top 100 intellectuals', as nominated by its readers.

An understandable reason for intellectual defeatism was the sense that, even if ageing culture lovers and freethinkers clung to their outlook, they would have no legatees.[105] When the learned and staunchly liberal *Guardian* columnist Hugo Young died in September 2004, even conservatives lamented that he might prove to be 'the last of his kind'. The increasingly irascible Prince Charles had already risked a clash with the government by arguing that the constricting school curriculum could create 'an entire generation of culturally disinherited' young adults.[106] The feeling of impending loss pervades the melancholy character of Chief Inspector Morse, who first appeared in 1975 in Colin Dexter's novel *The Last Bus to Woodstock*. The novels were only moderately successful, but when they were adapted for television by ITV (1987–2000) they captured the public imagination, despite the demanding two-hour format which kept viewers guessing until the end; thirteen million people watched the final Morse episode, in November 2000. Morse himself became the best-loved intellectual of the period, but he was unlikely to raise the popularity of his real-life representatives. As triumphantly portrayed by John Thaw, he was prickly, morose and disgusted by the modern world. Incapable of finding a soulmate even in his beloved Oxford, Morse's solitary existence was sustained only by the cultural interests that alienated him from his colleagues. Above all, he was childless; his loves and his learning would die with him, along with his improbably cerebral methods of detection.

By the time that Morse embarked on his televised sleuthing, even some of Mrs Thatcher's allies were beginning to express quiet concern about the effect on the universities of the government's philistinism. Kingsley Amis, for example, lamented that the Thatcher governments undermined 'the free pursuit of knowledge and truth for their own sake', prioritising 'vocational training' instead.[107] For once, Amis was slightly unfair to his heroine. Even before Mrs Thatcher took office and began to drive higher education in her favoured, utilitarian direction, acute observers had noted a change in its ethos. In 1978, for example, the playwright David Hare detected in the universities 'a generation who are cowed, who seem to have given up on the possibility of change, who seem to think that most of the experiments you could make with the human spirit are likely to be doomed or at any rate highly embarrassing'.[108] No research grant was required to uncover the main reason for the apathetic mood. Despite the claims of Amis's allies that the universities were little better than outposts of the Soviet Union, staffed by humourless, doctrinaire academics in the *History Man* mould,* the campuses could not be insulated from the general loss of optimism in Britain since the oil crisis. Amid the ensuing economic mayhem, it was easy enough to defend the idea of a university education in the abstract – even Kingsley Amis had recognised its value, and had spoken out on its behalf for many years. But the British higher education

---

* In September 1977 a 'report' by some right-wing friends of Kingsley Amis asserted that Marxists were more active in academia than they had been even in the 1960s, and accused them of wanting to destroy 'a liberal, tolerant society'. Although the newspaper's editor characterised its findings as 'alarmist', he still considered that the report deserved front-page coverage; *The Times*, 21 September 1977.

system, as it existed in the mid-1970s, was much more difficult to justify on practical or principled grounds. As such, when the Thatcherites inherited it in 1979, they found it an easy target for public expenditure savings. For their own part, an increasing proportion of students realised that attendance at university was merely a way 'to prolong their youth and delay getting a full-time job'; in a nationwide survey of 2003 more than a third of students gave that as their main reason for persevering with the educational experience.[109]

In 1989, after a decade of Thatcherism, David Hare was still defiant. He observed that the *Sunday Times* tried repeatedly 'to inform what it calls the intelligentsia of the country that it is out of step with the – what is the word? – entrepreneurial mood of the times'. 'Well, for myself,' he retorted, 'I can only say these are fine times to be out of step with.'[110] But while Hare kept his composure, the feeling of being out of step evoked apathy in many intellectuals and a melodramatic form of misanthropy in others. In July 1989, for example, the novelist John Fowles compared human beings to a virus, or a 'ravenous self-destroying horde of rats'. Even Schopenhauer, or Jonathan Swift at his most splenetic, would have been hard-pressed to top that outburst; and since Fowles's fiction had sold well on both sides of the Atlantic, his feelings were not the product of disappointed material ambition. If there really was a God, he continued, 'I cannot imagine that we rampant, myopic and insatiably self-centred creatures should be allowed to survive a single day more.'[111] Fowles's disgust at the human condition conflicts with the private thoughts of the theatre critic Kenneth Tynan, who took delight in life as he found it while still hoping for something better. Despite being a notorious 'champagne socialist', Tynan was self-aware enough to consider whether he would be valued after the revolution. His answer was affirmative: 'I would not be as bereft of purpose, energy and ambition as I feel now in a world whose creed of personal fulfilment and gratification I have so lovingly embraced.' Those words were written in 1975; Tynan died in July 1980, before Thatcherism had really got into its stride. Before his death he was given a taste of what was to come when his attempt to persuade Kingsley Amis that it was possible to be a 'libertarian socialist' was met with the accusation that he was a spy for a future 'police state'.[112]

It was not the case that well-meaning individuals entirely gave up on visions of a better future after 1975. Campaigns to eradicate disease, for example, were based on the old-fangled notion that the world could still be cleansed of avoidable suffering; groups like Amnesty International, which tried to outlaw the use of torture, were deliberately flying in the face of time-dishonoured human practices; and those who claimed that animals had rights which ought to be respected were pushing the concept into new territory. But on balance the people who continued to hope were those who wanted to stop the world becoming appreciably worse than it already was – either by campaigning against nuclear weapons, expounding the case for environmental action, or trying to stop governments embarking on wars which would self-evidently cause additional suffering. For their pains, such activists were held up to ridicule as representatives of the 'chattering classes', 'do-gooders', or – worst of all – *Guardian* readers.

Taken together, these debate-quashing insults offered a useful insight into the nature of Britain in the early twenty-first century. They implied that people who were capable of pausing for reflection amidst the head-long race of contemporary life, and questioning prevailing orthodoxies, were irrelevant prattlers, devoid of common sense. Instead of commanding respect, their intellectual acquirements disqualified them as serious participants in public discussion. They verified Rousseau's accusation that 'a rational man is a depraved animal'. In practice, though, the hostility to intellectuals evinced by successive governments after 1979 was grossly unfair. They could hardly have been more useful and obliging enemies. They did not need to be intellectuals to understand that they had been beaten. Those whose ideas had been shaped by conditions prior to the oil crisis of 1973/4 had taken it for granted that history was on their side – that change might be incremental and uncertain, yet its general trajectory was sure to be 'progressive'. Intellectuals might never hold power themselves; but they could reconnoitre the ground as an advance party and later take the credit for having anticipated beneficent developments. Once the progressive trend was decisively reversed in the mid-1970s, British intellectuals were generally stoical in accepting their fate. They might talk treason at dinner parties, but they were only stirred to action by the most egregious government miscalculations (like Iraq), or when road-building programmes threatened neighbourhood property values. Ultimately, most of them were protesting against policies which padded their pockets even if they offended their consciences. Few were as candid as the comedian Michael Palin, who guessed that he would be about £10,000 per year better off after the 1979 budget, which featured a dramatic regressive shift from direct to indirect taxation. 'There is some inescapable lack of social justice in this,' he noted. 'But it doesn't keep me awake.'[113]

Although left-wing intellectuals had obviously lost the battle of ideas, it was difficult to say that the other side had won. Whatever its merits as an anti-socialist bludgeon, Thatcherism had limited attractions as a positive vision for the conduct of life. Ultimately its characterisation of human nature was derived from the favourite thinker of all anti-intellectuals, Thomas Hobbes (1588–1679). Anticipating consumer society and the rise of the commodified individual, Hobbes had written that 'the *value*, or WORTH of a man, is as of all other things, his price'.[114] Life, for Hobbes, was merely a succession of appetites, ending in death. Laughter arose from a realisation of the misfortune of others; love was indistinguishable from lust. For Hobbes's unwitting followers in the years after 1975, the life of man was undoubtedly 'solitary', 'nasty' and 'brutish'. But compared to the conditions of the seventeenth century, it was hardly 'poor'; and, thanks to modern medical science, it no longer had to be 'short'. Britons could keep on desiring and consuming for much longer than their ancestors; and in that expectation they found sufficient reason for considering that their earthly tenure could be tolerable.

5

GREED

Consumerism is castigated as greed, stupidity, and insensitivity to want. Every month a new book inveighs against overconsumption and its vulgar display. But what are we to do about it? If it is our moral responsibility to live more austerely, we are notably reluctant to do so.
Mary Douglas and Baron Isherwood, 1978[1]

Is it likely that Mrs Thatcher and her associates sat down and said to themselves, Now, how can we best go about promoting greed?
Shirley Robin Letwin, *The Anatomy of Thatcherism*[2]

I've got the best, I'll take all I can get
Killing Joke, 'Eighties', 1984

I

ON 11 July 1977 the *Daily Mail* broke away from its coverage of the Grunwick dispute to reveal the exclusive story that the England football manager, Don Revie, was leaving his position in order to coach another national side. In itself this news was not unwelcome to English fans. Their team was playing poorly, already looking sure to miss out on World Cup qualification for the second time in a row. Even worse, in June 1977 – just a month before Revie's resignation – England had lost at home to Scotland. The game was part of the 'friendly' Home International tournament, but after the final whistle some of the celebrating Scotsmen had departed from the spirit of amity. They invaded the Wembley pitch, broke down the goalposts and annexed large slabs of the sacred turf where England had been crowned as world champions in 1966.

In the month of Queen Elizabeth's silver jubilee, the disorderly scenes at Wembley were a powerful reminder of divisions within the United Kingdom. The rampaging Scots were the sporting equivalent of the Sex Pistols, whose snarling single *God Save the Queen* was number two in the singles chart when the match was played. The disaffection of youth which had fuelled punk rock, and the rising demand for devolution in Scotland (if not in Wales) were problems that could not be solved overnight. It was almost as difficult to see what could be done to improve the fortunes of the English football team; but at least in this case an individual scapegoat was available. Don Revie (born 1927) had been a very successful club manager but was never convincing in the England job. After the Scotland match his fate was inevitable, and he had good reason to seek employment elsewhere.

But while many fans had wanted Revie's removal, the circumstances of his departure made him the most hated man in England. He had been earning £20,000 per year – three times as much as his predecessor, Sir Alf Ramsay, who had actually led England to World Cup victory. In his new job, the *Mail* revealed, Revie would pocket £60,000 a year, tax free. Had his new team been an international giant of the game, like Brazil, there would still have been a roar of patriotic disapproval against the man who had encouraged the Wembley crowd to sing 'Land of Hope and Glory' during home games. But the *Mail* disclosed that Revie was leaving England for the Middle Eastern minnows, the United Arab Emirates (UAE). Once the story had broken, Revie told the press that 'This is an offer I cannot refuse . . . I had many offers to stay in England, but the tax structure, let alone the salaries available, make it impossible to earn this kind of money at home.'[3]

Revie's defection provoked a ferocious media outcry, reflecting a genuine sense of fury among England supporters as well as professional resentment of the *Mail*, which had scooped its rivals by getting the inside story. At that time, being picked for the England job was supposed to be the highest privilege in the game. Like civil servants and politicians, the occupant was expected to soldier on through the criticism which was bound to follow slipshod performances. When the evidence of failure had reached a certain level, an unworthy manager would fall on his sword – with a bit of tactful prompting from the English Football Association (FA), which had seen off Alf Ramsay in

1974. After reflecting on his shortcomings for a season or two, the substandard supremo might take up another job with a second-rate club side. The last thing he could do was profit from his ineptitude, selling himself to the highest bidder even before he had been handed his cards. Revie had broken all of these unwritten rules and seemed to be well aware of what he was doing; he had disguised himself when he flew to Dubai for talks with his prospective employers. To most England supporters, he was now the epitome of greed.

In fact, it seems that the *Mail* had only provided half of the picture. For many years rumours had been circulating about Revie's conduct as manager of Leeds. In some quarters he was known as 'Don Readies' because of an alleged habit of offering cash to rival teams who were prepared to let Leeds win. He was also accused of offering illegal payments in order to sign top players. According to the investigative writer Tom Bower, in 1977 the *Daily Mirror* was about to expose Revie's practices; hence his overhasty exit to Dubai. Although it had no love for Revie, the FA was anxious to suppress a story which was likely to inspire further speculation about football's shady practices. So it acted as if the official explanation was true, and Revie's only reason for leaving was his appetite for money.[4]

However, the FA had to satisfy the public's desire for vengeance, so it banned Revie from the management of any team under its jurisdiction for ten years. Revie appealed to the High Court, which eventually overturned the ban. But even when finding in his favour the judge, Sir Joseph Cantley, described his behaviour as 'a sensational and notorious example of disloyalty, breach of duty, discourtesy and selfishness'. By a pleasing quirk of chronology, the case ended in December 1979. Just a few days later Britain entered a decade which will always be associated with Justice Cantley's list of deadly sins – and, above all, with greed.

II

But were the 1980s really characterised by greed, in a way that was not true of the 1970s or of subsequent decades? What, exactly, constitutes 'greed'? The latter is an emotive and endlessly contestable question, but the most useful definition is 'a preoccupation with material acquisition, unrelated to physical needs'. The reference to 'needs' introduces a host of problems: does this term mean basic requirements like adequate nourishment and shelter (the view expounded by King Lear on the heath) or should we include additional facilities, without which human life would be a fairly dreary interlude between arrival and departure? Our definition is relatively restrictive and Lear-like, insofar as it omits *emotional* and *intellectual* needs. It runs against the ideas of Adam Smith and Karl Marx, who both understood that needs are socially constructed and relative rather than biological; it also contrasts with the more recent theorising of the American psychologist Abraham Maslow (1908–70), who portrayed love, esteem and self-actualisation as genuine human needs, no less than the desire for food and shelter.[5] But if such 'higher' motivations are allowed, the idea of needs becomes unusably elastic. For example, in 1989 the comedian Ken Dodd denied that he had hidden £336,000 in cash rather than banking it, because he wanted to avoid paying tax. Instead, he claimed that the physical presence of the money gave him 'a feeling of accomplishment' which other entertainers derived from the purchase of expensive cars.[6] Dodd's testimony helped to earn his acquittal on charges of deliberate tax evasion, but the verdict hardly amounted to an acceptance that his behaviour was 'necessary'. Other celebrities had a compulsion to cheer themselves up through wild spending-sprees. In another court case in November 2000 it emerged that Elton John had spent £293,000 on flowers in less than a year.[7]

Ideally, the question of needs would be omitted altogether. But the reference to *physical* needs has to be included in order to avoid counter-intuitive conclusions. For example, without this caveat a society in which most people face a daily struggle for survival could be judged as more 'greedy' than a country where the overwhelming majority has been liberated from worries about food and shelter. At the same time, it is possible to take a flexible view of physical needs, including technological innovations which make life more convenient. Greed should be distinguished from *affluence*, and our definition makes this possible by associating greed with the idea of material *preoccupations*. As we shall see, it is reasonable to expect manifestations of greed in an affluent society, but affluence relates to living standards while greed is a state of mind. So, for example, people who can afford a wide range of luxury items might be content with just a few of them, and donate the rest of their surplus income to charity. Greedy people, by contrast, continue to hunger for more even though they already enjoy an affluent lifestyle.

When people say that greed was a leading characteristic of British life in the 1980s, they sometimes imply that the whole population suddenly became pre-occupied with the quest for material gain. This is obviously ridiculous. A more plausible proposition is that there was something different about greed in the 1980s – that it was more widespread than before or afterwards, perhaps, or that greedy Britons were happier to flaunt their wealth than they were at any other time. But in order to justify even this modest claim, it would have to be shown that a significant proportion of the population wanted to improve living conditions which were already well above subsistence level, and that this was not true either of the 1970s or the 1990s. Unfortunately, this is a very difficult task. One objective measure could be levels of consumption, particularly of goods which no one could reasonably classify as necessities. But in isolation these figures cannot be used as proof of *attitudes*. Thanks to techniques of mass production, luxury goods tend to become cheaper over time, so that people who covet an item one year find themselves able to buy it the next without making compensatory sacrifices. The classic example of this phenomenon is colour television. In 1971 there were only 1.3 million licensed colour sets in Britain, compared to 15.2 million black and white. By 1976 there were more colour than black and white licences – 9.6 million compared to 8.4 million. One can argue that colour television falls into the luxury category, even though it took the viewer from a world of shadows into a closer approximation to reality; after all, a television of any kind (or even a radio) is scarcely a physical necessity. Even so, it would be hazardous to assert on the basis of these statistics that the number of greedy households in Britain rose from 1.3 million in 1971 to 9.6 million five years later. The bare figures tell us nothing about the outlook of the people who swapped black and white for colour at this time.

Apart from statistics about consumption, one can also draw on the findings of opinion surveys. However, on a subject like greed these sources have to be treated with more than usual caution. People are usually willing to identify greed in others – indeed, they might be tempted to exaggerate its extent. But they tend to be more hesitant in attributing it to themselves. In any case, qualitative surveys of this kind are difficult to frame in a way which avoids leading questions; and the results are more open to dispute when they are tailored to specific media tastes. Admittedly, some findings are more suggestive than others. For example, one study published in 2003 found that even among people who earned over £50,000 per year – more than double the average annual income – about 40 per cent felt that they could not afford to buy everything they 'needed'. The academic Clive Hamilton, who conducted the survey, concluded that 'The real concerns of yesterday's poor have become the imagined concerns of today's rich.'⁸ On the face of it, this evidence does provide significant support for the idea that greed long outlasted the 1980s. Even so, information from these sources should be part of an overall picture, rather than the single basis for argument.

Biographical studies can be useful, but there is a danger of confusing the antics of a few self-indulgent individuals with more general attitudes and trends. Media coverage, in particular, can be misleading. It is tempting to focus on the views of social commentators, and to judge the level of greed in a society in relation to the volume of complaint. But even columnists in the 'quality' press are prone to exaggeration. Shrill and persistent criticism across a range of newspapers and magazines can actually be taken as evidence of a revulsion against greed in a significant section of the general public. In a society where greed is most prevalent and commonplace, it is least likely to attract negative comment.

The views of people outside the world of professional punditry are potentially very useful, but allowance must still be made for factors such as age and social background. For example, Sir Joseph Cantley's attack on Don Revie could be taken as evidence of a more generalised hostility towards greed at the dawn of the 1980s. However, Cantley was almost seventy when he delivered his coruscating comments, and his moral outlook had been forged long before the 'age of affluence'. Even by the judicial standards of his day, Cantley was something of a maverick. During the trial of the former Liberal Party leader Jeremy Thorpe (which also took place in 1979) he made little attempt to disguise his antipathy towards the main prosecution witness, the 'male model' Norman Scott who claimed to have been Thorpe's lover. In his summing-up, Cantley told the jury that Scott 'is a fraud. He is a sponger. He is a whiner. He is a parasite. But, of course, he could still be telling the truth.'⁹ The fact that the majority of English football supporters applauded Cantley's remarks about Don Revie does not mean that he shared their general outlook or preclude the possibility that they would have forgiven the latter any symptoms of selfishness, if only he had proved to be a successful and long-serving manager of the national team.

The upshot of this preamble is that judgements about greed in the 1980s can only be based on a mixture of evidence of varying quality, combined with hypotheses and hunches. This would hardly be worth noting were it not for the fact that contemporary commentary on the decade rarely leaves room for scepticism. Such testimony might seem more persuasive because so much criticism of the 1980s has been generated by people with first-hand experience of the decade. However, even the most gregarious and perceptive observers could have been exposed to no more than a partial sample of life in Britain at that time, and their memories are bound to be coloured to some extent by hindsight.

The working hypothesis of this chapter is that greed, in our sense, was already a significant feature of British life *before* 1980. The main justification for exploring this suggestion is that several of the underlying factors which fostered greed in the 1980s were already present in the second half of the previous decade. The first of these we have already noted – the affluent living conditions of most Britons in full-time work. Affluence is usually assumed to have arrived in the 1950s, but the majority of adults in that decade had fresh memories of tougher times – wartime restrictions and the subsequent years of economic austerity, if not the mass unemployment of the 1930s – which, incidentally, affected Don Revie, whose father was out of work for two years. In many cases – though by no means all – memories of hardship produced an enduring distaste for conspicuous overconsumption, and in particular a dread of personal debt. By contrast, the generation of Britain's 'baby-boom', which began in the mid-1950s, could only imagine what rationing had been like. Brought up in a general context of rising living standards, most of them were likely to expect more of the same for themselves. By 1975 they were finding their way into the workforce, while their parents contemplated retirement.

As we have stressed, affluence is not the same thing as greed. But it provides a favourable context for the development of a greedy outlook, since acquisitions no longer have to be related to physical needs. Many of the products which became more freely available and affordable in the 1950s and 1960s, like cars and washing machines, were borderline cases; previous generations had got by without them, but they did make life easier. It could also be argued that some 1970s inventions, like the electric dishwasher and the Sony Walkman, either saved time and labour or enhanced leisure activities. But other new gadgets from this decade (like the television remote control) were of more doubtful utility. The burst of productive and innovative energies released after 1945 was beginning to run up against the law of diminishing returns; at best, most new products promised only fractional improvements on what was already available. By the late 1970s most Britons could watch television, listen to music whenever they chose, wash clothes and dishes in machines rather than by hand and keep their houses reasonably warm thanks to central heating. The majority of families were also mobile; in 1976 there were more than 18 million licensed cars in the UK as a whole, compared to 13.6 million ten years earlier. For the firms which manufactured such products, the average Briton already enjoyed all too many reasons for contentment: as the Chancellor Denis Healey put it in his 1975 budget speech, 'I recognise that very few classes of goods are now generally accepted to be luxuries.' The only solution was for manufacturers and retailers to make individuals feel inadequate if their car was 'old-fashioned' or their three-piece suite was starting to look a bit shabby. In other words, consumers had to be coaxed into the showrooms to buy something new, even if their existing possessions were still capable of performing their original functions. There was even a patriotic excuse for purchasing luxury items. As one reader of the *Leicester Mercury* asked in January 1975, 'If we no longer buy many so-called unnecessary goods how can the industries which manufacture them survive?'[10]

Advertising was the obvious medium for the manipulative trick of making luxuries seem like real necessities. By the 1970s, this 'industry' was well enough established to entice creative and resourceful people like the Saatchi brothers (Charles and Maurice, born 1943 and 1946 respectively) and Salman Rushdie (born 1947). While the advertisers drummed up new business, manufacturers were doing their bit to ensure that old customers came back for more. Cheaper goods often meant lower quality and built-in obsolescence, so that even those items which were not superseded by more fashionable models usually fell apart after a few years. This development meant that consumers came to regard purchases as provisional; instead of expecting their goods to last a lifetime, they knew that the relationship would be temporary. Clothes provided an admirable illustration of the new throwaway society. In the past most families had repaired them when they were damaged. The sewing machine was thus an important innovation; in 1946 they were found in 61 per cent of households. Despite decades of affluence and technological change, which made user-friendly machines easily affordable, this figure had actually *fallen* slightly by 1986.[11] Mending a pair of old trousers was too much like hard work, compared to a trip into town to buy something more fashionable.

Although this must have been disconcerting for many older people, it was easier to deal with when so many things were bought for show rather than for use. For the young, the contrasting ideas that possessions were important, but that nothing was built to last, helped to inspire a wave of vandalism. This was also fuelled by the tendency of rock groups like The Who to smash up their instruments on stage; but most vandals were sensible enough to target property which belonged to other people or to local councils – bus shelters being a particular favourite. The crime of vandalism had been given legal definition in the 1971 Criminal Damage Act, and by 1976 the problem had grown so acute that the Home Office produced a special film to reassure local residents that the police would act on their complaints.[12]

A preoccupation with material gain was also helped by the decline of rival distractions. Overall attendance at religious institutions in Britain had been falling since the Second World War, but there is every reason to suppose that 'the sea of faith' had been receding even faster, and that many people who continued to turn up at church on Sunday were not true believers. Organised religion had never been a safeguard against worldly thoughts, of course, but a decline in genuine belief meant that by the mid-1970s more people than ever rejected the idea of an afterlife, where self-denial was supposed to find an eternal reward. As we have seen (in Chapter 4) even secular beliefs were in retreat. The optimistic spirit of the 1960s can be (and usually is) exaggerated, but there is no doubt that many young people were inspired by the hope that the world could be made a better place. Even in the 1960s, a young hippy like Richard Branson (born 1950) believed that idealism could be yoked to moneymaking; he became a millionaire before the age of twenty-four. Once the optimism of the 1960s had dissipated, many people of Branson's generation transferred their ambitions for the world into a less elevated concern for their own interests. This trend was encouraged by the realisation that nuclear weapons could not be disinvented through the efforts of well-meaning campaigners, so that even worldly things might pass away sooner than expected. For many, the moral was that even if life was likely to be short it should be lived to the full; and the accumulation of material wealth was the most obvious way to secure short-term enjoyment.

In short, by the 1970s most Britons were already exposed to many factors which could lead individuals to set a high priority on 'material gain, unrelated to physical needs'. But something more was needed to overcome the feeling that the acquisitive impulse was morally wrong. After all, successive generations had inculcated this belief – partly, though not exclusively, for half-forgotten religious reasons. The crucial catalyst arrived in the last months of 1973, when the price of oil spiralled out of control. Inflation was already a problem in Britain and other developed nations, thanks to a general rise in commodity costs during 1973. But the decision of Arab oil producers to punish the West for its support of Israel by restricting supplies rapidly turned a difficulty into a crisis after the outbreak of the Yom Kippur war in October of that year. People who had grown accustomed to rising living standards suddenly faced the prospect of a return to wartime conditions; for a time it looked as if the government would have to introduce petrol rationing. To make matters worse, many of those who had lived through the Second World War were now pensioners who had good reason to feel unprotected from the effects of inflation. After the shock of 1973, even those brought up to spare an occasional thought for others were tempted to accumulate as much as possible for themselves, in case the whole edifice of post-war prosperity came crashing down.

One telling symptom of the new mood in Britain was the trade union response to the oil crisis. On most precedents a difficulty which had the potential to damage the prosperity of the whole nation would have impressed union leaders with a sense of public responsibility. In such grave circumstances even those who harboured the ultimate aim of destroying the capitalist system would have thought twice before exerting their full bargaining power. But in 1973/4 the National Union of Mineworkers (NUM) exploited its advantage to maximise short-term economic gains for its members. The Conservative government led by Edward Heath tried to accommodate the miners' claims within the terms of its pay policy, acknowledging that people who worked in such hazardous conditions deserved to be classed as a special case. Even so, on 4 February 1974 members of the NUM voted to convert their ban on overtime into an all-out strike. Shortly afterwards, Heath called a general election at which the Conservatives lost their overall majority.

The miners' dispute of 1973/4 is still regarded in some quarters as a magnificent victory for the trade union movement – not least because subsequent trade union history is dominated by demoralising defeats. In reality, the outcome was a victory for greed. Had the miners used their moment of overwhelming influence to demand concessions for other workers, things might have been different. But, along with the power workers who also took opportunistic action at this time, they treated the rest of the public with contempt. Electricity supplies were regularly cut off in the winter of 1973/4, regardless of the effects on the poor and the frail. Even the revolutionary socialist Paul Foot

noticed the effect on attitudes towards the NUM, without relinquishing
his romanticised view of the 1973/4 dispute:

I remember reporting the TUC conference of 1976 for *Socialist Worker*, and
being astonished when a delegate from the miners' union was openly jeered.
What had only two years previously been a spirit of solidarity with the miners
had changed into a spirit of hostility. The miners were suddenly envied for
what they had achieved. The feeling that all workers were in the same boat,
and that the strongest should break their employers on behalf of the weakest
– all had gone as early as 1976.[13]

Foot's idea that the miners had done a favour to the weaker unions
by 'breaking their employers' was particularly ironic, since coal mining
was a nationalised industry and the employers were ordinary
taxpayers. The change of mood he detected among other workers in
1976 was almost certainly a delayed response to the events of 1973/4,
when the NUM had utterly failed to demonstrate a 'spirit of solidarity'. It was particularly significant that Foot considered the miners
to be objects of envy, overlooking the possibility that they were also
resented because of their selfish behaviour. Other observers had been
quicker to notice the difference. In May 1975 the former editor of
the *New Statesman* Paul Johnson had claimed that 'Trade unionism
is killing socialism in Britain.' His analysis reinforces the view that
the economic crisis of the mid-1970s was a crucial stimulus to greed:
'wage inflation is the very worst kind of rat-race. It sets group against
group and makes self-interest the guiding principle of life. It makes
money seem the only social nexus, and the sole criterion of well-
being. It forces on us all the aggressive posture of comparative envy
. . . It makes the young predatory, the middle-aged apprehensive, the
old fearful.'[14] In 1975 Johnson sensed that greed had become 'a vora-
cious moral corruption eating at the heart of society'. According to
Paul Foot, the new outlook only came to a head in the strikes of
1978/9 – the 'Winter of Discontent'. These disputes, he felt, were
nothing more than 'bloody-minded expressions of revenge and self-
interest'.[15] In fact, most of the strikes were conducted by low-paid
workers sick of the new dispensation under which the most powerful
unions (like the NUM) could hope to get everything they were asking
for, while others had to accept pay settlements which barely kept
pace with inflation.

Looking back on the Winter of Discontent, the former Labour cabinet minister Peter Shore felt that it was 'as though every separate group in the country had no feeling and no sense of community, but was simply out to get for itself what it could'.[16] The scale of the action was certainly new. During 1979 as a whole, nearly 30 million working days were lost thanks to more than 4,500 industrial disputes. These were record figures, but there was nothing original about the callous spirit which characterised the disputes. Workers such as lorry drivers, refuse collectors and even hospital workers were determined to show that they could cause as much disruption as the miners. The secret, they had learned, was to act as if members of the public were enemies rather than fellow citizens who also happened to pay their wages. One striking ambulance driver in that inclement winter made the view of his union perfectly clear: 'If it means lives must be lost, this is how it must be.'[17] It was like the spirit of the Blitz in reverse.

The Winter of Discontent marked the democratisation of greed, fifty years after the arrival of universal suffrage in Britain. In retrospect, some observers identified the union militancy of the 1970s with a more general (and laudable) decline in deference.[18] More accurately, feelings of deference were as powerful as ever, but they were in the process of being transferred to the rich, whatever the source of their wealth. It is doubtful whether this was a change for the better. Even at the beginning of our period it was possible to encounter specific criticisms of greed and its likely effects on society. For example, the first edition of the *Leicester Mercury* in 1975 included a letter which lamented that 'we are all brought up to believe that we are entitled to much more than we receive; thus we have a grabbing instead of a giving society'.[19] Admittedly, this witness might have been an oddball, although the editors of correspondence columns in provincial newspapers can be expected to winnow out wholly unrepresentative expressions of opinion. The Liberal chief whip (and later leader) David Steel certainly concurred. He claimed in January 1975 that 'the motivation of greed is year by year taking a greater grip on our society'.[20] The industrial relations expert Professor Hugh Clegg warned that there was every prospect of 'the destruction of the democratic and civilized way of life in this country by the continual rending of competitive greed at the fabric of society'.[21]

In this context it was telling that the 1975 referendum on Europe was dominated by materialist arguments, with both sides claiming that

Britons would be better off provided that they took the right decision, whether or not they increased their exertions. Other observers, with very different outlooks, provided unwitting confirmation of greedy attitudes at this time. In 1976 the journalist Patrick Hutber published a book which included letters from his readers. His intention was to illustrate the grievances of Britain's middle class, but the actual effect was to reveal a 'preoccupation with material acquisition'. One of the responses quoted by Hutber included biographical details which record the dramatic change in expectations over the years. His correspondent had been born in 1930, when both of her parents were out of work through no fault of their own. Life was hard, but the family survived, mainly because the parents had been prudent in more prosperous times. Now in her mid-forties, their child was a teacher, married to a company director. She lived in 'a nice house in a nice neighbourhood' and evidently enjoyed comforts beyond the most avaricious dreams of her parents at the time of her birth. However, she still felt it necessary to protest that 'The human urge to better oneself, to improve on previous generations, is at present being stifled.' This allegedly universal 'human urge' was not a post-war invention, but it would certainly have mystified the overwhelming majority of people who lived before the industrial revolution and considered themselves fortunate if they were as well off as their parents. Not content with this anachronistic pronouncement, the writer became more specific, claiming that the phrase 'If you can get on – good luck to you!' embodied an 'old Elizabethan ethic'. Hutber's correspondent taught history; for the sake of her pupils, one can only hope that sixteenth-century Britain was not part of the syllabus. But the real value of her detailed testimony was that she had already satisfied 'the human urge to better oneself' in material terms – and still wanted more.[22] In her case, clearly, pre-war attitudes had been washed away by the subsequent consumerist tide.

The plight of Britain's middle classes had also been examined by *The Times* at the beginning of 1975, provoking many readers to send in their thoughts. The correspondence suggested a schism in Britain at the time, between those who thought that people should be grateful for the improvements which had occurred since 1945, and others who had assumed before the oil shock that living standards would keep on rising. One reader argued that the desire to better oneself 'becomes tarnished and even squalid when it is alloyed with greed and envy', and this was increasingly the case when 'most of us, I guess, live under conditions with which we ought to be content'. Another correspondent attacked the views of a new pressure group, the Middle Class Association, as 'a good indication of the greed which pervades this country'.[23] Judging by their Home Counties addresses (not to mention their choice of daily newspaper), neither of these readers was on the breadline. But they were certainly in the minority among the well off in the mid-1970s. Most people at the time probably recognised that wealth is no guarantee of personal happiness, but they acted as if acquisition was the only thing that could make life tolerable. The impulse was particularly strong among the newly prosperous. In 1980 Owen Reynolds, a Welsh steel worker who had been born in 1928 (a year after Don Revie) shed some light on the process. As he explained, 'in the old days you felt differently. There are no poor people if you're all poor people. It's only when you see the rich that you realise "God, I'm poor."' Television had exposed people like Owen Reynolds to the lifestyles of the rich, and now their antics were 'continually flaunted in glowing colour on 21-inch screens in every Port Talbot house'. Presumably Owen was referring to imported American programmes like *Dallas*, an improbable saga of the dysfunctionally wealthy. First screened in 1978, the soporific soap opera peaked with an estimated viewing public of 21 million in November 1980.[24]

The millions of people who watched *Dallas* on that winter evening in 1980 tuned in to discover the identity of the person who had shot an unpleasant, greedy individual called J.R. Ewing. But although Ewing was a fictional character – and a Texan to boot – it was not as if harsh practical lessons about the effects of greed closer to home had been unavailable in the late 1970s. The history of the Sex Pistols was one lurid and widely publicised example. Malcolm McLaren, the group's manager (born 1946), had dabbled in radical philosophy as a long-serving art student in the 1960s, but later tried to marry his sense of mischief with moneymaking. Whatever McLaren's true intentions, the Sex Pistols tapped into a real mid-70s sense that materialism was contemptible and (what was worse) boring. However, by the beginning of 1979 the Pistols had split; the bass guitarist Sid Vicious had died of an overdose after killing his girlfriend; and the band's royalties had become yet another subject for litigation, in a year of remarkable court cases. In the film *The Great Rock 'n' Roll Swindle* (1980) McLaren presented the Sex Pistols as a kind of postmodern joke, in which a bunch of talent-free adolescents had managed (thanks to his guidance) to extract money from a series of greedy and gullible record companies. However, not everyone appreciated McLaren's sense of humour, since the people being exploited were not just the executives of multinational corporations. Within a few weeks of Sid Vicious's death, Richard Branson's Virgin record company released a single with the deceased musician on lead vocals. It was an excellent commercial decision; the mundane cover version of Eddie Cochran's *Something Else* sold more copies than the Pistols' incendiary single *God Save the Queen*, helping Branson to develop the Caribbean island he had just bought for $300,000.[25]

As early as the summer of 1977 – at the time that Don Revie was negotiating his exit to the Middle East – The Clash had warned against commercial exploitation of punk rock in their classic single, 'White Man (in Hammersmith Palais)'. 'Ha! You think it's funny,' the lead singer Joe Strummer had snarled, 'Turning rebellion into money?' However, even the politically committed Strummer was compromised by the fact that The Clash had signed a long-term deal with the US media giant CBS. At least The Clash could argue that their contract never stopped them from purveying a truly rebellious message, unlike the Sex Pistols whose output became increasingly puerile after the cash started flowing in. Even so, the influence of the money men ensured that the explosive force of punk was contained within a few short months.

Despite this evidence, the 1970s are rarely associated with greed. One explanation for the omission is that the most influential (and quotable) critics of British life at the time were aiming their fire elsewhere. As usual, politicians were blaming each other for the country's economic problems. Academic commentators who claimed that Britain was becoming 'ungovernable' usually traced the problem to inadequate political institutions. For their part, the non-parliamentary left blamed the Conservatives when they were in office, then turned on Labour with equal savagery after 1974. Even if Paul Johnson was clear-sighted enough to identify the early symptoms of unmitigated self-interest within the union movement, most revolutionary sentimentalists refused to accept that they could be anything other than altruistic. The government, by contrast, was allegedly stuffed with 'class traitors' who spent their time resisting reasonable pay demands. While the left accused Labour of being insufficiently socialist, from the opposite flank the government was pilloried for its supposed addiction to that outdated philosophy. If the right was to be believed, the British people were being prevented from earning a decent living (or satisfying 'the human urge to better oneself') by a government which peddled 'the politics of envy'. And the right enjoyed a significant advantage over 'socialists' in the second half of the 1970s; there was one party leader who shared their outlook and promised to put their ideas into practice.

III

When commentators discuss the alleged greed of the 1980s, Margaret Thatcher's name is invariably invoked. To her critics she was the personification of greed. In 1989, when an ambitious Labour front-bencher, Gordon Brown, wrote a critique of the Thatcher governments, it was given the title *Where there is Greed*, with a picture of the prime minister on the front cover. No further commentary was needed.

Fittingly, in view of what was to follow, greed played a part in Mrs Thatcher's successful campaign for the Conservative leadership. In the run-up to her contest against Edward Heath, held in February 1975, Thatcher's opponents had alighted upon a magazine interview in which she advised elderly people to stock up on tinned food as a safeguard against the effects of inflation and temporary shortages. The idea of hoarding food might be sensible for those who could afford it, but it would be impossible for people living on subsistence incomes, and could encourage panic-buying, transforming real necessities into luxuries for the majority. However, instead of harming Mrs Thatcher, the resulting publicity raised her public profile in a positive way. She invited the media to inspect her own larder, which was spartan enough to suggest that she had not been following her own advice.[26]*

Probably Mrs Thatcher's chances would have been badly damaged if the inspection had revealed a mountain of bread and sugar. Party leaders, like football managers, were still expected to keep their greed within limits. But it was no longer certain that such restrictions were recognised by the public at large. One of the candidate's constituents, for example, claimed that 'If Mrs Thatcher can hoard, so can we,' as she stuffed her shopping bag.[27] Mrs Thatcher's victory over Heath

---

* In those innocent days no one seemed to suspect that a helpful Thatcher aide might have smuggled out her surplus foodstuffs before the journalists arrived.

certainly proved that it was no longer suicidal for a senior politician to empathise with the increasing number of voters preoccupied with their material interests even at the expense of their fellow citizens.

In many respects Mrs Thatcher was an unlikely High Priestess of Greed, and the state of her larder at the beginning of 1975 was not very surprising. She was born in 1925, into a fairly prosperous provincial family. Her father, a Lincolnshire grocer, was also a Methodist lay preacher who tried to follow his precepts in practice. Together with his mother-in-law, he introduced the young Margaret to 'Victorian values'. Almost sixty years later Mrs Thatcher was anxious to promote this moral code. In January 1983, for example, she proclaimed that 'Honesty and thrift and reliability and hard work and a sense of responsibility for your fellow men are not simply Victorian values. They are part of the enduring heritage of the Western world.'[28]

For Mrs Thatcher's critics, such remarks exposed reactionary longings for a return to the conditions of the nineteenth century. However, as so often they misjudged their opponent. Given an entirely free hand, Mrs Thatcher might have explored the possibility of restoring some Victorian instruments of social control, like the workhouse, and she would hardly have objected if Britain had regained its nineteenth-century power and prestige on the world stage. But as Matthew Parris has pointed out, in the nineteenth century Mrs Thatcher's gender and socio-economic background would have prevented her from entering politics, let alone becoming prime minister. She would not even have been able to take a degree from Oxford University, saving the rebellious dons of 1985 the trouble of denying her an honorary award.[29] This was not the only way in which she offended against the Victorian world view. Far from casting adulterers and homosexuals into outer darkness, she was happy to employ them. She even married a divorced man without suffering any recorded struggles of conscience.

As Mrs Thatcher acknowledged in January 1983, thrift was a key Victorian value. For her father, this demanded self-denial – an avoidance of unnecessary expenditure, even if the family could afford it without falling into debt. The money which could have supplied the household with convenient gadgets had to be saved instead, as a matter of duty. From an early age, his daughter decided that this approach was wrong-headed. After she had been prime minister for six years, and won two general elections, she remembered that she had 'kicked against' the lack of modern appliances in her childhood home. For all

his preaching, Alf Roberts could not save his child from the contam-
ination of the world outside, and the feeling of restraint drew her
towards un-Victorian models of behaviour. In the first volume of her
autobiography she confessed to feeling 'entranced with the romantic
world of Hollywood', and she clearly resented the contrast between
that glamorous existence and her humdrum life in Grantham.[30]

In some children these stirrings would have resulted in a serious
rebellion against parental authority. But Margaret had absorbed her
childhood lessons, at least to the extent of deciding that she must
always treat her father (if not her obscure mother) with respect. Her
solution was to devise a new interpretation of thrift. In her own mind,
this meant that a family must live within its income. It was still virtuous
to save money, to ensure that one never became dependent on the state;
but in her eyes excessive self-denial was no better than thoughtless
overindulgence. For the rich, at least, the idea of deferred gratification
was simply absurd; why delay a purchase if one could easily afford it?
However, Thatcher continued to commend thrift as if the Victorian
formulas still applied – not least because as prime minister she wanted
to apply the same logic to state expenditure, in order to justify the tax
cuts which would make it easier for her supporters to spend freely as
well as to save.

It was not surprising that Mrs Thatcher's critics overlooked her deviation from Victorian values. In this crucial respect some of her better-off
supporters were equally bamboozled. The right-wing poet Philip Larkin,
for example, defined Thatcherism as 'Recognising that if you haven't
got the money for something you can't have it.'[31] Patrick Hutber gave
the impression that nothing had changed since the days of Samuel
Smiles and Mr Pooter, writing that 'If a single word had to be found
to sum up the characteristic middle-class virtues, middle-class aspirations and middle-class attitudes, I would choose a relatively
old-fashioned one: thrift. Put in a slightly longer, slightly more up-to-
date phrase, it could be called the readiness to postpone satisfactions.'[32]

For Margaret Thatcher herself, Hutber's 'up-to-date phrase' had
been redundant since December 1951, when she married a wealthy
businessman. Although he had been born in London, Denis Thatcher's
parents were New Zealanders; and although he did absorb some of
the characteristic views of the British Victorians, these were chiefly
restricted to the subject of the natural inequality between races. He
shared Margaret's views about living within one's means, and was able

to combine her new understanding of thriftiness with the possession
of a sports car and a London flat. His second wife would never lack
the latest contrivances and would not have to waste too much time
looking after the children. To Margaret, Denis must have seemed like
a cross between Santa Claus and her father. Her description of life
after her marriage in December 1951 is highly revealing, and deserves
extended quotation.

To be a young married woman in comfortable circumstances must always be
a delight if the marriage is a happy one. But to be a young married woman
in those circumstances in the 1950s was very heaven. I am always astonished
when people refer to that period as a time of repression, dullness or conformity
– the Age of Anxiety, etc. The 1950s were, in a thousand different ways, the
reawakening of normal happy life after the trials of wartime and the petty
indignities of post-war austerity. Rationing came to an end. Wages and salaries
started to rise. Bananas, grapes and fruits I had never heard of suddenly
appeared in the shops . . . Ordinary homes began to accommodate fridges,
Hoovers and electric washing machines. Billboards sprouted fewer Government
notices and more commercial advertising . . . Although I might have been
perhaps rather more serious than my contemporaries, Denis and I enjoyed
ourselves quite as much as most, and more than some. We went to the theatre,
we took holidays in Rome and Paris (albeit in very modest hotels), we gave
parties and went to them, we had a wonderful time.[33]

The last sentence proves that her post-marital exhilaration was fuelled
at least in part by a sense of liberation from the Victorian view of
thrift. In an interview many years later she recalled that in her childhood 'it was rather a sin to enjoy yourself by entertainment'.[34] It was
obvious that she had never shared that opinion. But even Aristotle
would have been impressed by the moderation of her self-indulgence;
she and Denis spent much more than her father would have done but
were still most unlikely to upset the bank manager. The passage is also
notable for its uncritical attitude towards 'commercial advertising',
which Mrs Thatcher always regarded as a great asset in any free society.
    Thus while Mrs Thatcher was obviously influenced by Victorian values,
she would have to be classified as a radical revisionist in that camp. The
hoarding incident typified this outlook: it might have been prudent (even
'thrifty') to buy up food in advance of a possible shortage, but from the
strict Victorian perspective it was thoroughly bad form to recommend

the same course of action to others who shared her financial advantages, at the expense of the less fortunate. For the rest of her political career Mrs Thatcher remained sensitive to allegations of personal greed. After becoming prime minister, she refused to draw her full salary – no great sacrifice for a millionaire's wife, perhaps, but still a gesture which cost around £10,000 per year. In 1985, when she and Denis selected a house for their eventual retirement, they opted for convenience rather than grandeur; the property in Dulwich, south London, would allow Denis to pursue his fanatical golfing hobby. Indeed, it was so unsuitable as an ex-prime minister's residence that the Thatchers hardly used it. It was sold in 1992 at a respectable but not exorbitant profit.[35]

In short, Mrs Thatcher thoroughly enjoyed the trappings of wealth, but a verdict of 'greedy' could only be brought in by a jury which was biased against her for other reasons. Ironically, her outlook bears comparison with that of her outspoken critic and predecessor as Conservative Party leader, Edward Heath, who also relished the good things in life while making sure that he never paid too much for them. The difference, though, is that Heath was a practical politician who was instinctively disinclined to moralise. By contrast, Margaret Thatcher was a moralist by nature; and, as such, she should be judged by her message as well as her behaviour.

For fervent Thatcherites like the late Shirley Robin Letwin, it was ludicrous to suggest that the prime minister and her allies set out to promote greed.[36] Yet this argument missed the point that for Mrs Thatcher the acquisitive impulse did not require much active promotion. Mrs Thatcher never said that 'greed is good': that aphorism was used by the fictional American financier Gordon Gekko, paraphrasing the real American financier Ivan Boesky.* But when her ideas about human motivations are taken together, it is certainly possible to construct an argument that greed is *natural*. For Thatcherites, individuals are naturally acquisitive, and governments should do nothing to obstruct the exercise of this healthy instinct. In many of her speeches, in opposition and in government, Mrs Thatcher tried to play down any suggestion that life was all about economics. But this was rhetorical window-dressing. Her political outlook was informed by an assumption that individuals are preoccupied with their economic interests. She

---

*In September 1985 Boesky told an audience at the University of Berkeley, 'I think greed is healthy. You can be greedy and still feel good about yourself.' He was jailed for insider dealing the following year.

once explained her political purpose in terms which sounded more like a summary of Marx's dialectical materialism. 'Economics are the method; the object is to change the soul.'[37]

In fact, there were at least two crucial respects in which Mrs Thatcher certainly did promote greed. A central Thatcherite proposition was that before 1979 Britons lacked adequate incentives to work as hard as their overseas competitors. Under Labour, the Conservatives claimed, too much of their gross pay was being confiscated by the state. This was a simple message which could easily be understood by the average taxpayer (and used by Don Revie as an excuse for resigning as England manager). For example, from 1975 to 1977 the basic rate of income tax was 35 per cent. When indirect taxation was added, the fiscal burden became even greater. The Thatcherite Adam Smith Institute calculated that in 1978 people would have to work until 21 May before they started to earn money for themselves rather than for the state. According to some calculations, in 1955 the average earner, with a partner and two children, paid less than 4 per cent in income tax and national insurance; by 1975 the corresponding burden was 25 per cent.[38] But the top rate of income tax – for those earning more than £24,000 in taxable income – was 83 per cent. The highest rate of tax on investment income was 98 per cent.

The levies on the super-rich made sensational headlines, but they were seriously misleading. While the Conservatives used them to scare the average taxpayer, they only affected people who could avoid their impact by employing an accountant. But whether or not the level of taxation in Britain was too high at this time, the incentives argument was bogus as it applied to individual effort. For a Marxist the obvious rejoinder was that ordinary workers were never recompensed to the true value of their work, even before tax; the excess was creamed off by the employer in the form of profits. But even ardent supporters of the capitalist system should have found the logic difficult to swallow. A reduction in the basic rate of income tax would mean that people in work would be awarded a pay increase, whether or not they worked any harder; and since the highest rates were levied on people who were very rich already, a tax cut for them would be even less invigorating. In fact, if they wanted to make people work harder Mrs Thatcher's Conservatives should have proposed that taxes should be *raised*; and if they had been interested in social justice, they should have used the proceeds to help people on fixed incomes, who really did suffer from the combined effects of tax and inflation. A more pertinent argument for the Thatcherites was that the brightest Britons would take their talents abroad if they continued to be penalised by higher tax rates.* But those who failed to emulate Don Revie, and refused to join the so-called brain drain between 1975 and 1979, managed to muddle through despite the excessive demands of the Inland Revenue.

Mrs Thatcher's second positive contribution to the cause of greed was her insistence that the rich should not feel guilty about their circumstances. This argument, in its different way, was as doubtful as her claim about incentives. Some of her senior colleagues within the Conservative Party – the so-called wets – might have felt guilty about the wealth that they had inherited, but they represented a minuscule proportion of the electorate. In the late 1970s those who had made money for themselves – by fair means or foul – showed little sign of self-hatred. As Patrick Hutber's correspondents showed, far from being apologetic many of them were very angry indeed.

The assault on the much-exaggerated phenomenon of bourgeois guilt represented Mrs Thatcher's second front on behalf of greed – her attempt to denigrate any viewpoint from which greed could be attacked. In particular, she heaped scorn on politicians who traded on their social compassion – those who 'drivelled and drooled' about the underprivileged. This Thatcherite argument was another deviation from Victorian values, which (on Mrs Thatcher's own account) included 'a sense of responsibility for your fellow men'. In her mind, this sentiment could become a vice if taken beyond the limits of prudence. The impression of her speeches was that those who could not support themselves by their independent efforts ought to eke out a living through charitable donations – and that the prime minister herself would be disinclined to make a contribution.[†]

---

* In a significant sign of the nascent celebrity culture, those who publicised this phenomenon tended to concentrate on names rather than brains. A typical example was a 1979 book which singled out 'Sir Billy Butlin, the holiday camp millionaire; former Open golf champion Tony Jacklin; actor Sean Connery; former world racing champion James Hunt; the singers Tom Jones and Englebert Humperdinck; and [somewhat incongruously, in this company] Lord Cromer, former Governor of the Bank of England'. It was not explained why the departure of these individuals from British residence was likely to cause undue suffering to the people they left behind; Blake and Weaver, 69.

† After leaving office, Lady Thatcher established a charitable foundation. But this was mainly concerned with the task of taking the free market message to those parts of the world which remained benighted, like Russia which after 1989 passed from extreme communism to rampant capitalism without an intervening period of common sense.

Mrs Thatcher's main target, of course, was socialism. Thatcherites argued that this was the main reason for the high level of taxation in Britain, and they were not afraid to claim that their own party had flirted with the doctrine in the past – especially under the recently deposed Edward Heath. As a result, substantial sums of money had been confiscated from decent, law-abiding taxpayers and lavished on unnecessary bureaucracy. But the real sin in Thatcherite eyes was an alleged socialist project to eradicate economic inequality. By the end of the 1970s, Thatcherite propagandists were accustomed to fulminating on this subject; Mrs Thatcher herself published a volume of speeches under the title *Let Our Children Grow Tall*, which implied that socialist Britain aimed at levelling everyone down to a common standard of living.[39]

Of all Mrs Thatcher's rhetorical attacks on post-war politics, this was probably the most effective. Far from thinking of the 1970s as a decade of burgeoning greed, many people who were alive at the time probably suppose that it was dominated by misguided attempts to make people more equal in their economic circumstances. Yet even before Mrs Thatcher took the Conservative leadership, the Marxist sociologists John Westergaard and Henrietta Resler were using government statistics to show that although the richest people in Britain had lost some ground since the Second World War, the poorest 30 per cent had also fared badly, especially in recent years.[40] The beneficiaries of Britain's economic growth had been the 'middling sort' – those who were in quite well-paid work rather than being dependent on welfare benefits of various kinds or investment income. These findings cast an ironic light on the campaigning efforts of Patrick Hutber, who urged that such people should fight back after decades of decline. But to do justice to Hutber's memory, he was talking about a different group – the dwindling band of individuals who continued to follow Victorian values in their original spirit. By the mid-1970s British class boundaries, as traditionally understood, were breaking down. The real middling sort were not the thrifty; they were people with a lot to spend who would have liked to be able to spend even more. They were the greedy, like the relentlessly vulgar characters in *Abigail's Party*, Mike Leigh's 1977 play about suburban lust. They were the people for whom Margaret Thatcher felt a special affinity, although in truth she had left them far behind when she escaped her father's clutches and married into serious money.

Only after Mrs Thatcher left Downing Street did right-wing commentators realise that the old-style British middle classes had vanished. Indeed, the insight tended to be granted to them after 1997, when the political dominance of New Labour made them more sensitive to adverse social developments. Once the penny had dropped, they were plunged into fury and despair. Digby Anderson, formerly director of a Thatcherite think tank, the Social Affairs Unit, declared that the decency of 'Middle England' had been replaced by the hegemony of the 'oik', a development which occurred 'quite quickly, sometime in the years between 1975 and [2004]'. People of all ages now behaved in public in a way which would not have been tolerated by previous generations. In its attitudes and vocabulary, Middle England betrayed everything it once stood for: 'It now rarely talks about right and wrong, it favours prizes for all and talks of "moving forward",' just like 'its old lower-class enemies.' Another author spoke of the self-destruction of the middle classes as a 'great abdication' which underlay Britain's decline. To complete the miserable picture, a study conducted by academics at Keele University suggested that the middle classes were responsible for forgeries and frauds which cost the UK a total of £14 billion every year – more than the bill for burglaries.[41]

As Anderson emphasised none of these developments was new. In hindsight, it looked as if Mrs Thatcher had been a tactical genius, somehow contriving to construct and maintain a coalition of the thrifty and the reckless. In truth, her electoral success was down to luck more than judgement, and it would never be repeated. Her spiritual successors, New Labour, paid much closer attention to social trends and had no illusions about the true nature of their target audience in Middle England.

IV

In the spring of 1981 the journalist Ian Jack interviewed some students at Oxford University. One of them claimed that all the students, regardless of their social origins, 'are out for themselves. If you're at all bright you know you screw other people before they screw you.' There were some dissenting voices in the survey. One student explicitly rejected the idea that life was about 'money and reputation', preferring, 'Beauty, love, success, respect.' However, he admitted that he was 'very, very, very rare indeed'. More typical was the student who confided that his ambition was to be 'Very very rich. As rich as one could possibly be.'[42]

The students of Oxford University might be regarded as unrepresentative of society as a whole. However, they constituted an elite group which was likely to have a wider influence once its members had permeated the workforce. Jack's interviewees probably found their way into the ranks of the 'yuppies' (young, urban professionals) who played a prominent role in the social and cultural discourse of the 1980s. The acronym originally appeared in America in 1984, but like so many similar terms it proved readily amenable to a transatlantic voyage. Yuppies, with their designer suits and well-thumbed Filofaxes, found their natural habitat in London, and the best place to spot them was the City. As the stock market soared, upward mobility could be attained with dazzling speed by any young person who was prepared to forgo sleep and treat other people as 'contacts' rather than friends.

But while the yuppies left their grubby fingerprints all over the popular image of the 1980s, their precise role must be interpreted in its true context. Although would-be yuppies could be found in all sizeable British cities, they attracted disproportionate attention because the most unsavoury exemplars were located in the capital, rubbing shoulder pads with copy-hungry journalists from the Sunday supplements. It could be argued that the manifestations of greed were genuinely newsworthy in Britain after 1980, catching the eye of insightful commentators like Ian Jack as well as journalists desperate to fill their columns. But there is every reason to suppose that they attracted undue attention because the party of government changed after 1979, and the country had a new prime minister with a more aggressive attitude to the question of economic inequality. The gap between rich and poor was not invented at the dawn of the 1980s, and greedy people did not spring to life at Mrs Thatcher's beckoning. They already existed; but thanks to the media's obsession with Westminster politics, it was only in 1980 that they started to be discovered.

Superficially, Ian Jack's book *Before the Oil Ran Out* can be seen as an early assessment of Mrs Thatcher's impact on British life, and for critics of the Conservative Party the results are suitably unedifying. But the first-hand testimony in the book is open to a different interpretation. Certainly the reported attitudes of Oxford students in 1981 are consistent with our definition of greed. However, even the youngest of those individuals would already have been well into their teens when Mrs Thatcher came into office. Unless the 1979 general election caused a universal conversion among such students, one can only suppose that their attitude to life had been forged earlier, when Labour was in office (1974–9). Similar things could be said of the steelworker Owen Reynolds (who was also quoted in Jack's book), and the residents of Port Talbot with their 21-inch colour televisions. Margaret Thatcher certainly had an impact on these people, even in her first months in Downing Street. But their general outlook on life could not be regarded as an exclusive product of 'Thatcher's Britain'.

Perhaps the most arresting testimony to the change which overcame Britain in the late 1970s is the remark which 'Uncle Jim' Callaghan supposedly made just before the 1979 general election: 'There's a sea change in politics.'[43] Callaghan was well placed to detect a new mood among the voters, having tried and failed to persuade the unions to stick to his policy of pay restraint. Like Heath, he had hoped to rally support by appealing to the national interest, and his reward was the Winter of Discontent. But it would be a mistake to accept Callaghan's judgement of national trends at face value; more likely, the 'sea change' had happened before 1979, and Callaghan only noticed it when he realised that he was about to be swamped. There were pressing reasons for him to identify dramatic and very recent social changes as the true reason for his impending electoral defeat. He had, after all, built his career on the appeasement of the trade unions; the Winter of Discontent thus suggested that a lifetime of work within the Labour Party had been wasted. Callaghan had also missed the chance of holding the election the previous autumn, when his party was narrowly ahead in the polls. The miscalculation was a bitter personal blow. Although he remained more popular than Mrs Thatcher, defeat would ensure that he was the only post-war prime minister apart from Alec Douglas-Home to fail to win a general election.

Despite Callaghan's verdict, the result of the 1979 election looks far more significant in hindsight than it did at the time. Mrs Thatcher's Conservatives achieved a lower share of the vote than the party had managed under Heath in 1970; Labour actually received more votes in 1979 than it had done in the election of October 1974, which it narrowly won. During the campaign Mrs Thatcher was advised to disguise her intention of breaking radically with the post-war consensus. She was right to take the hint; Labour's only chance of distracting the public from its unimpressive record was the possibility of carrying the attack to the Opposition. The most popular Conservative policy of the campaign was the proposal that council tenants should have the right to buy their properties. In 1979 its main attractions were that it would satisfy the British preference for ownership rather than tenancy, and allow existing occupiers to alter their homes as they wished without having to ask permission from unyielding bureaucrats. As such, the right-to-buy policy actually had the potential to revive a more healthy and responsible attitude to property ownership, and offered people a chance to exert greater control over their circumstances. The problems arose in implementation, as councils were forced to sell off their housing stock at ludicrously low prices, allowing Thatcher to build a constituency of Conservative-voting clients. Between 1980 and 1989 1.3 million tenants took advantage of the offer. But instead of acting as a bulwark against greed, the Englishman's home became a casino chip rather than a castle, triggering violent fluctuations between booms and busts in the housing market.

As we have seen, during the first Thatcher government (1979–83) some journalists who understood Mrs Thatcher's real message began to pay attention to greed for the first time. But critical commentary concentrated on other subjects, such as unemployment (for under-standable reasons), renewed fears of nuclear war (see Chapter 3), and the fragmentation of the left which resulted in the formation of the SDP in 1981. The most notable attacks on the culture of greed came from the arts world, but even there the response was fairly muted. John MacKenzie's *The Long Good Friday* was not just a brutal portrait of greed amongst London gangsters; it suggested that public servants, like police and councillors, were driven by the same motives as the men of violence. However, as an attack on Thatcher's Britain the film has to be classed as a piece of prophecy; it was made in 1979, but placed on general release only after a delay of two years because of fears about its violent content. Its searing critique thus belongs to pre-Thatcherite days.

While *The Long Good Friday* suggested what might happen to society if greed became ubiquitous, Martin Amis's breathtaking masterpiece *Money: A Suicide Note* examined its effects on an individual character. The novel appeared in 1984, but its events were set in 1981 (around the time that the Oxford students were discussing their ambitions with Ian Jack) against the background of rioting in many English cities. As one reviewer rightly observed, the misadventures of Amis's central char-acter, John Self, present 'a rancid and punitive vision of mankind'.[44]

Self arrives in America with access to apparently limitless funds, and his character disintegrates as he runs through an exhausting routine of expensive indulgences. Despite a series of humiliations and the realisation that he has been defrauded by people even greedier than himself, he remains in thrall to money at the end of the book.

Money was an uncomfortable read, not for its obvious distortions but rather because of its merciless presentation of painful truths about Britain during those years. John Self describes himself as one of 'the new kind, the kind who has money but can never use it for anything but ugliness'. But he is of the 'new kind' without being particularly young; he depicts himself as 'an obedient, unsmiling, no-comment product of the Sixties'. His big break came when he created a series of dubious advertisements in 'the flaming summer of '76'. Whether coincidentally or not, Amis had dated the rise of John Self to the brief heyday of punk rock rather than the election of Margaret Thatcher.[45]

To most readers, the character of John Self must have seemed a grotesque caricature. However, some aspects of his outlook were represented in contemporary life. Malcolm McLaren, for example, was another unsmiling (though hardly a no-comment) product of the sixties. Like McLaren, Self wants to make as much as he can from the entertainment industry, through flashes of creativity rather than sustained effort. But Self's attitude to money bears an even closer comparison with that of the prime minister's son, Mark (born 1953). One of his mother's aides reportedly remarked that 'Mark Thatcher is a twit. In my view, he has nothing to offer the world.' The *Daily Telegraph* was more polite, but given its habitual obeisance to the dynasty its editorial verdict that Thatcher was 'not possessed of the most obtrusive commercial qualifications' was equally damning.[46] Nevertheless, Thatcher was accepted as a useful middleman in a series of international business deals during the 1980s, and while Margaret Thatcher claimed to be 'batting for Britain' by attempting to secure lucrative contracts abroad, her patriotic endeavours coincided with her son's elevation to multimillionaire status. Financially, at least, this was another success story of the 1980s whose origins lay in the previous decade; Mark Thatcher had begun his attempts to cash in immediately after his mother became Conservative leader in 1975. The result of the 1979 general election had no effect on his outlook, and merely inflated his ambition; he declared that he wanted to become a millionaire in his own right before the age of thirty. Five years later concern about

Mark's business activities had grown to the extent that even his father, Denis, thought it necessary for him to pursue his profits abroad, away from the over-inquisitive British media.[47]

Despite the fears of senior Conservatives, Mrs Thatcher's reputation was not seriously tarnished by the activities of her son. Her party had been re-elected in 1983 largely because of the 'Falklands Factor' and the inadequacies of the Labour Opposition. Given these advantages, the most notable thing about that general election was the 1.5 per cent fall in the Conservative vote share compared to 1979. Clearly the British electorate remained unconvinced by the Thatcherite message, but re-election gave the prime minister a chance to press ahead with her policy agenda. The main theme of her second term was the privatisation of state-owned industries. The sales of British Telecom (BT, 1984–6) and British Gas (1986–8) provided opportunities for small investors to participate in the great adventure of capitalism. Lavish advertising campaigns like the 'Tell Sid' series produced by Saatchi and Saatchi for the gas sell-off helped to generate public interest. But a more effective enticement was the knowledge that the shares were massively undervalued. Contrary to Thatcherite rhetoric about the buccaneering spirit of capitalism, these were no-risk investments for people who were already well off. More than two million people helped themselves to BT shares, and twice as many subscribed to British Gas. Over the Thatcher years, the proportion of Britons owning shares increased from 7 to 25 per cent. In one sense Mrs Thatcher was right to hail the privatisations as instances of 'popular capitalism'; giving money away is rarely unpopular among the recipients. However, the country had scarcely become a 'share-owning democracy'; after all, even a minuscule stake in a privatised company was beyond the means of the poorly paid and the unemployed. In any case, by 1989 some 2.7 million of the shares in BT and British Gas had been re-sold to the big investment houses. Against these super-rich companies, there was little chance that the voice of small shareholders would ever prevail.[48] The main beneficiaries of the policy, ultimately, were the organisations' senior managers, who were now free to award themselves massive pay rises for doing exactly the same jobs.

One effect of the privatisations was to consolidate the self-interested constituency of reliable Conservative voters. Those who retained their shares had a material incentive to vote against Labour, which had promised its own supporters that the privatised companies would be returned to public ownership. Mrs Thatcher also settled her party's old score with the NUM in the ill-fated strike of 1984/5; she was treated with grudging respect by most world leaders, and with something approaching awe by Ronald Reagan; and just before the 1987 general election the official unemployment count finally dropped below three million for the first time since 1983. So everything pointed to a third decisive Conservative victory when the prime minister called an election for 11 June 1987. The outcome could be hailed as an historic achievement for Mrs Thatcher: her party secured an overall majority of 102. But this was less than the Conservative lead before the election, and its share of the vote fell again, albeit only fractionally. At times the prime minister genuinely feared that she might lose the election, and there was friction amongst her leading advisers.[49]

The most significant lesson of the 1987 general election was that a majority of British people was still opposed to Thatcherism. Indeed, some opinion polls suggested that the practical experience of life since 1979 had alienated the public from the prime minister's views. For example, in 1977 Gallup found that 35 per cent of their sample thought that poor people were probably responsible for their own plight. By 1985 this figure had fallen to 22 per cent, and in November 1987 only 13 per cent thought that unemployment was the result of individual failings. Other polls suggested that the government should prioritise the fight against unemployment rather than tackling inflation; higher spending on public services was preferred to tax cuts; and the trade unions became popular again.

Some of these findings obviously registered the effect of previous government policies: people were less bothered by tax because of previous cuts, and the trade unions were more popular because government measures had curbed their powers. But more detailed surveys told a similar story. In the summer of 1988 MORI asked respondents to compare their ideal society to current conditions in Britain. The electoral system had just delivered a third successive victory to a party led by an unquestioning capitalist, and in the opinion poll 77 per cent agreed that Britain was 'A mainly capitalist society in which private interests and free enterprise are most important'. However, while 43 per cent said that this statement came closest to their ideal state of affairs, 49 per cent would have preferred its opposite – 'A mainly socialist society'. Only 16 per cent wanted 'A society in which the creation of wealth is more highly rewarded'; by contrast, 79 per cent hoped for 'A society in which caring for others is more highly rewarded'. As usual, there were some mixed messages, and Thatcherites could take heart from the finding that 53 per cent approved of the idea that people could 'make and keep as much money as they can'. Yet the egalitarian argument, that people should receive broadly similar rewards, was approved by 43 per cent – after more than a decade of scoffing attacks from the right.[50]

As always, the results of that poll have to be seen in context. There had been a stock market crash after the 1987 general election, which suggested that the foundations of Britain's 'economic miracle' were insecure. This was also the year of Oliver Stone's film *Wall Street*, a vivid indictment of money-mad culture with the odious Gordon Gekko as the asset-stripping anti-hero. Unusually for an American film, *Wall Street* implied that Britain was morally superior to the US; Gekko's main opponent is a British industrialist whose lust for money is checked by residual feelings of human decency. But even if Britain was still different in 1987, it was catching up with the Gekkos of this world. The former cabinet minister Sir John Nott, who took a highly paid banking job in 1985, was disgusted by the greed of his Wall Street contemporaries, but even he noticed after his retirement that the City of London was 'no longer a nice place at all'.[51]

Before the 1987 general election even the normally loyal *Sunday Telegraph* suggested that the Conservative Party was in the grip of a distasteful 'bourgeois triumphalism'. Its editor, Peregrine Worsthorne, warned that 'yuppies feel confident enough to shed all inhibitions about enjoying the spoils of the class war which they think Mrs Thatcher has fought on their behalf'; later he accused them of behaving like 'vulgar, loud-mouthed, drunken yobboes, scarcely better, if it all, than football hooligans'.[52] Yet within a year of the election the government delivered more of the spoils to their natural supporters in the City. In the 1988 budget Chancellor Nigel Lawson cut the highest rate of income tax from 60 to 40 per cent. Lawson's speech was greeted by outrage on the Opposition benches and semi-concealed gloating among the wealthiest Thatcherites, for whom the budget would ensure a substantial and wholly unearned pay rise. Lawson justified his deci- sion with the usual argument about incentives, although the Treasury had just received a report which cast understandable doubts on this overused proposition. Under the new tax regime a person earning £200,000 per year would be more than £33,000 better off without any extra exertion. Overall, the value of the tax cuts was £6 billion; and 40 per cent of this sum was bestowed upon the top 5 per cent of earners. It coincided with the government's announcement of a £1 billion cut in social security.[53] Labour's John Smith described the budget as 'immoral, wrong, foolish, divisive and corrupting'. Addressing Lawson, Robin Cook claimed that 'long after the Minister's and my names are forgotten, the budget of 1988 will be remembered. It will be remembered as a Budget for the greedy paid for by the needy.' Gordon Brown claimed, 'No Budget this century has so offended the decent instincts of the majority of people, who are far more altruistic and far less selfish than the faction that now rules over us.' Lawson's proposals, he stormed, were 'born out of greed' and 'founded on indifference to the poor'.[54] For Brown, the passage of time brought more prudent reflections. In December 2005, amid stories of unbridled boardroom excess, the *Guardian* noted that although Chancellor Brown still spoke about 'fairness', a higher income tax rate of just 50 per cent on the superrich 'would be dismissed as unthinkably revolutionary by New Labour'.[55]

Mrs Thatcher herself had initially queried the scale of Lawson's handout, but soon reassured herself that it would provide 'a huge boost to incentives, particularly for those talented, internationally mobile people so essential to economic success'.[56] Presumably in her own mind this indispensable group included her son. However, Mark Thatcher considered even the new reduced tax rates too punitive. Fortunately for him, in 1990 the Inland Revenue decided that for tax purposes he could be considered non-resident in the UK over the previous six years. The same year he treated himself to a £2.1 million property in Kensington.[57]

The 1988 budget, announced just a couple of months before the MORI poll, probably affected its findings. The survey also coincided almost exactly with the final passage of the Local Government Finance Bill, which introduced the community charge or poll tax. This measure heaped further financial gains on the beneficiaries of income tax cuts and privatisation. Like most Thatcherite measures, the poll tax had the effect of making the rich better off at the expense of the poor. But unlike previous decisions, such as the near-doubling of VAT in 1979, the poll tax arrived in British households in the form of a printed demand for money; and non-payment would be followed by a court summons. Although reform of local government finance was badly needed, in the 1970s even right-wing agitators had favoured a local income tax – which would have a strong correlation with the ability to pay – as a replacement for the rates.[58] The implementation of the regressive poll tax suggests that the Conservatives felt invulnerable thanks to their self-interested electoral support. At this time the same logic was inspiring the Conservative-run Westminster Council, led by Mrs Thatcher's friend Dame Shirley Porter, to bolster its own electoral position by selling council houses in key marginal wards at knock-down prices. This practice was subsequently found to be illegal, but no one was ever prosecuted for pushing the poll tax through Parliament.

After the 1988 budget even Mrs Thatcher began to realise that her party might be damaged by allegations of greed. In May she addressed the Church of Scotland's General Assembly and argued that money-making was compatible with Christian ethics. Before her speech at that year's party conference she told her friend Woodrow Wyatt that 'We've got to deal with this materialistic attack.'[59] She responded with typical pugnacity. 'What we are actually encouraging,' she told the conference, 'is the best in human nature . . . The fact is that prosperity has created not the selfish society but the generous society'.[60] This statement shows the extent to which Mrs Thatcher had become isolated from the world outside Downing Street. The earlier decision to preach in favour of greed in Edinburgh was a remarkable example of self-delusion. At that time Scotland was experiencing the first stirrings of revolt against the poll tax, which was to be introduced there a year ahead of England and Wales. The level of popular enthusiasm for Thatcherite values in the country could be measured by the fact that the Conservatives had lost more than half of their Scottish MPs in the 1987 general election.

When the poll tax was implemented in Scotland in April 1989 the response was a mass campaign of non-payment, leading to legal proceedings of various kinds against 38 per cent of the registered Scottish population.[61] Despite panic-stricken attempts to cushion the impact of the new tax with subsidies, it proved equally unpopular in England and Wales. Yet Mrs Thatcher rejected any radical change to the system, clinging to the belief that people would accept it in time. However, Conservative MPs were less sanguine. The widespread displays of dissent – notably riots in London at the end of March 1990 – gave them a taste of the job insecurity which many fellow Britons had been feeling since 1979. Although Mrs Thatcher's failure to win re-election as Conservative leader in November 1990 was triggered by internal party disagreements over Europe, it was also provoked by the knowledge that the poll tax would cause an electoral disaster. Her successor John

Major expressed his hope that Britain would become 'a nation at ease with itself'.[62] Since there was ample evidence to associate greed with social tension, his words gave the impression that the age of 'bourgeois triumphalism' had ended with Mrs Thatcher's tearful exit from Downing Street – the first time that she had cried in public since 1982, when her son Mark temporarily went missing while competing in the Paris–Dakar motor rally.

V

Despite Major's warm words, the Labour Party remained the chief hope for people who continued to resist the message of Thatcherism. On the bare evidence of the 1988 MORI poll it had every reason to stick to its traditional values. The message of the survey was reinforced by the 1990 volume of the *British Social Attitudes* series. Its findings inspired one contributor, John Rentoul, to predict that 'the politics of the 1990s are likely to be shaped by a reaffirmation of collectivism' – the apparent precondition for a Labour resurgence.[63]

Although the 1987 result was a serious blow for Labour, the party had increased its vote by more than 1.5 million – its biggest numerical improvement since the crushing victory of 1945. A sober analysis would have acknowledged that the Labour governments of 1974–9 had been unusually unproductive, so that a return to office was always likely to take time. Internal dissent was also to be expected, given Labour's past history. But there had been serious wrangling in the late 1950s, and this had not prevented Labour's return to office in 1964. The period between 1983 and 1987 had been marked by some bruising battles; but the Militant Tendency had been beaten and its best-known supporters expelled from the party.

If Labour wanted to change anything, it should have looked at its current leadership. Neil Kinnock had shown courage during the recent battles with Militant, but he had also revealed his limitations in the parliamentary debates of January 1986, on the Westland Affair. This self-induced crisis, concerning the future ownership of a struggling West Country aviation firm, cost the Conservatives two gifted cabinet ministers. It might have toppled Mrs Thatcher herself if Kinnock had made the most of the ammunition at his disposal; after all, the prime minister was clearly implicated in attempts to undermine her own cabinet colleague, the Defence Secretary Michael Heseltine, who wanted

Westland to join forces with a European-based consortium rather than the American option favoured by Thatcher.[64] But Kinnock blew the opportunity with a speech more notable for rhetorical flourishes than the close forensic argument which the circumstances demanded. This concrete example of Kinnock's shortcomings was backed by polling evidence which suggested that the public did not regard him as a potential prime minister. Although Kinnock had often secured better approval ratings than Mrs Thatcher, the margins were never wide enough. In its much-praised 1987 election campaign Labour had made every effort to repackage Kinnock, but the voters remained unconvinced.

At this point, a party which was seriously preparing for a speedy return to power would have thanked Kinnock for his services and looked for a more convincing replacement. To his credit, Kinnock himself considered stepping down.[65] Instead, the party decided to keep its leader and ditch its principles. In the course of a wide-ranging policy review before the 1992 general election, Labour abandoned its plans for a wholesale renationalisation of the privatised industries, accepted Conservative trade union reforms, promised that the higher rate of income tax would only be raised to 50 per cent, and scrapped its unilateralist approach to nuclear disarmament.

A party which truly believed in alternative principles would have taken the opinion poll findings of the late 1980s as an invitation to develop an updated radical agenda rather than a reason for immediate surrender. There was a remarkable glimpse of what might have been achieved in 1989, when the Greens won 2.3 million votes in the European parliamentary elections. Although the public never treated these contests very seriously, it was a remarkable outcome for a party which was more like a pressure group than a vote-winning organisation. But by that time Labour strategists had already decided to abandon any radical policies which might frighten the public. They had conducted their own research and duly found what they were hoping for – conclusive evidence that Mrs Thatcher really had won the 'battle of ideas', and that policies based on an alternative vision of society could only be electoral liabilities.[66] In a foretaste of the spin that would dominate the 'modernised' party, one of the most supine policy documents was entitled *Meet the Challenge, Make the Change* (1989) – although the contents showed that Labour was determined to *duck* the real challenge of the times.

Kinnock and his modernising allies within the party offered a plausible rationale for their approach. In order to win power, they argued, Labour would have to attract support from floating voters. These were assumed to be people who lacked firm political loyalties and would choose the party which offered the greatest material benefits. In other words, the key voters in Britain were Thatcherites, like the people who kept returning a Conservative candidate for the marginal Essex seat of Basildon – a constituency which always declared its result early, and tended to be an accurate litmus test for the country as a whole. Logic suggested that the party would have to accept Thatcherite policies if it wanted to win a general election. Furthermore, after a future victory Labour would have to govern in accordance with Thatcherite principles. Otherwise it would face concerted opposition from powerful interest groups, notably financiers in the City of London. Without their cooperation, the modernisers believed, Britain could be made ungovernable. Significantly, this scenario had been used as the basis for a 1982 novel – *A Very British Coup* – by Tony Benn's ally Chris Mullin. The book was adapted as a Channel 4 television series in 1988 – exactly the time when Labour was at its most defeatist.

Despite the resemblance between the message of Labour's modernisers and the Thatcherite approach, there were some respects in which their policy programme would still be distinctive. In particular, they would pay some attention to the demands of 'social justice', and spend more money on the public services. If anyone asked where the necessary cash would come from, the modernisers could play their trump card. Labour no longer wanted to hamper the vital work of Britain's 'wealth creators'. Instead, it would actively help them, by rewarding enterprise through the tax system and investing in research and development. The next Labour government would preside over an 'enabling state', and the resulting prosperity would bring in ever-increasing revenues without any need for a substantial rise in tax rates.

It is difficult to uncover the real motives which propelled Labour towards acceptance of the 'modernisation' project. Although the main players have attracted interest from numerous biographers, few of these have penetrated behind the carefully cultivated, media-friendly images. At the top, a hunger for office obviously played a part in the creation of New Labour. Generally speaking, these were not politicians who had entered Parliament because they wanted to serve their constituents. They believed that they had the ability to climb the increasingly greasy pole, and reach the cabinet. After 1987 they were increasingly impatient at their lack of progress. This made them quick to identify and condemn any policies which seemed to be holding Labour back, and they also tended to exaggerate Mrs Thatcher's real impact on the outlook of British voters. In this respect they were not alone on the left. The appeal of Thatcherism was also overrated by some left-wing intellectuals who had no ambition even to serve as parish councillors. One influential group, associated with the magazine *Marxism Today*, saw Thatcherism as a 'hegemonic project' which cunningly exploited the breakdown of traditional class divisions. Immediately after the 1979 general election, for example, Martin Jacques argued that Mrs Thatcher's brand of individualism had struck a chord 'well beyond even the traditional areas of Tory support'.[67] Only a serious case of revolutionary defeatism could have inspired such an analysis. In terms of vote share, Mrs Thatcher's Conservatives hardly fared better in 1979 than Alec Douglas-Home's party had done in 1964; and Mrs Thatcher had been fighting a disheartened Labour government, while in 1964 Douglas-Home was the much-ridiculed leader of a scandal-rocked administration. The pertinent question after 1979 was to ask why, despite all her tactical advantages, Mrs Thatcher had failed significantly to improve on the electoral performance of her predecessors. The most likely answer is that the crude message of Thatcherism had forced the British public to look at what it had become in the last years of the 1970s – and it did not particularly like what it saw.

If even Marxist intellectuals were prepared to distort recent history, it is hardly surprising that ambitious Labour MPs accepted a similar view after the 1987 defeat. Yet this does not explain why the rest of the party acquiesced in the proposed changes to Labour's policies and institutions. Ian Aitken, a veteran observer of the Labour movement, thought that he knew the answer. He detected a 'profound, genuine and largely spontaneous change of mood in the grassroots' after the 1987 general election.[68] No doubt the increasingly desperate constituency members thought that their decisions would help to bring Labour back to power at the first opportunity. In reality, the headlong plunge towards modernisation was making the party unelectable in the short term. The modernisers had forgotten that a new Labour Party would sound wholly unconvincing if it retained its old leader. As it was, Neil Kinnock had to spend much of the 1992 general election campaign explaining why he now advocated policies for which he had previously expressed personal loathing.[69] His undisguised opportunism prompted, and partly justified, some savage media attacks before polling day. In this, as in so much else, the *Sun* led the pack, and Kinnock played into its hands by acting like a rock star at Labour's eve of poll Sheffield rally.

When the results were in and Labour had lost yet again, Kinnock announced his resignation and launched a passionate counteroffensive against the media. For his fellow modernisers this was a mistake which showed that he lacked full-hearted commitment to their project. In their eyes, the *Sun* had proved itself to be a formidable enemy with substantial public backing. As such, Labour should make even more strenuous efforts to appease its strike-breaking, tax-allergic owner, Rupert Murdoch. Looking for an explanation for the defeat which would clear them of any blame, the modernisers concentrated their fire on the party's moderate plans for income tax increases directed at the rich. This was potentially awkward for them, since Kinnock's obvious successor was John Smith, who had designed the offending tax policy as shadow chancellor. However, Smith was well aware that his position would be unsafe if he excluded the chief modernisers from his front-bench team. The price of keeping people like Tony Blair on board was a tacit acceptance of their analysis of the 1992 defeat. This was hardly the basis for an harmonious relationship, but up to Smith's death in 1994 the underlying cracks had not been exposed in public, and Tony Blair could give the impression that he was the natural custodian of the old leader's legacy.

Yet while Kinnock and his friends had been fighting to reposition their party in the years after 1987, the acceptance of a political programme based on the philosophy of greed was looking increasingly unwise. Nigel Lawson had felt confident that his 1988 tax cuts would not have damaging effects on the economy as a whole, partly because he sincerely believed Thatcherite propaganda about a sustainable revival in British fortunes, if not an economic 'miracle'. The reality was somewhat different. Overall, economic growth in Britain between 1980 and 1989 was identical (2.2 per cent) to the figure achieved in the much-derided, oil-starved 1970s.[70] But after the initial period of deep recession under Thatcher the period 1984–8 saw growth which matched the best of the post-war era. Thus Lawson's tax cuts added further impetus to an economic boom which in any case was unlikely to last. Ironically, though, the most culpable error in the 1988 budget was a concealed tax *increase*. Tax relief on mortgage interest had previously been available to individuals, so that, for example, a married couple could each claim up to a limit of £30,000 when they bought a house together. After the 1988 budget the tax relief applied to the property instead of the purchasers, so that for many married couples, mortgage tax relief was halved. In a rare tactical misjudgement Lawson decided that the introduction of this measure should be delayed for several months. As a result, many couples were induced into panic-purchases in a housing market which was already overheated, taking out increasingly expensive mortgages. Thanks to fears of rising inflation, interest rates, which had fallen to 7.5 per cent in May 1988, had almost doubled by October 1989. People who had bought their homes at the wrong time found that their mortgages were now greater than the value of their property – the new phenomenon of 'negative equity'. Others simply found the newly raised interest rates too onerous. In 1989 it was estimated that 380,000 people were in arrears with their repayments. Many thousands eventually had to give up the struggle, and their homes were repossessed by the mortgage companies. In 1979 only 2,530 families had suffered this misfortune. By 1989 the figure had risen to 16,000. But the worst period was 1991–3, when almost a quarter of a million houses were repossessed.

In part, these figures were the miserable symptoms of rising unemployment. By November 1989 it looked as if the Conservatives had finally brought this problem under control, but under the impact of high interest rates the boom ended and jobless figures began to rise again, topping three million in January 1993. If the effects of the recession had been confined to the victims of 1982–5 – mainly people in the north of England, much of Wales and many parts of Scotland – this would have been a terrible blot on the government's record; but not necessarily an electoral disaster. However, on this occasion the impact was also felt in southern England. For the first time since 1979 Conservative policies were causing hardship in their heartlands.

A general election held in such circumstances was the political equivalent of a penalty kick for Labour; but the party still managed to blaze the ball over the bar in 1992. The fact that the modernisers were able to convert that conclusive public rejection of recent policy U-turns into a vindication of their project is, in part, a testament to their flair for media manipulation. However, many Labour supporters were distracted from the real reasons for defeat in 1992 because right up until the end the opinion polls suggested that the party would finally make it this time. In hindsight it almost looked as if the British people had deliberately cheated Labour out of its victory by misleading the pollsters about their attitudes and voting intentions. As one long-suffering activist later complained: 'For some reason, when people were asked what they considered to be the most important issues, no one volunteered the true answer, "my wallet", or "how rich I am", or "keeping an extra few pence back from the tax man and living in a shitty run-down country as a result". People felt so guilty about the way they were voting that they lied to the pollsters *and even lied to themselves* in the secret ballot at the exit polls'.[71] The writer, John O'Farrell, was connected to Labour's new elite because he had helped to write speeches for Gordon Brown. But even he seemed to forget that his party had lost its fourth successive election *in spite of* a concerted drive to appease the greedy. Labour's most controversial proposal in 1992, after all, had been to lift the highest rate of income tax back to a level which would have satisfied Mrs Thatcher herself if Nigel Lawson had not chosen to be even more radical in 1988.

After their patchy performance before the 1992 general election, many polling organisations felt it necessary to build into their published findings a degree of deception on the part of voters who intended to support the Conservatives, but were too ashamed to say so. There is good reason to suppose that this phenomenon – which became known as the 'spiral of silence' – must apply with additional force to surveys concerned with attitudes on economic and moral questions. Confronted with such questions, it was even more tempting to express abstract agreement with 'enlightened' views which were at odds with the respondent's day-to-day outlook and conduct.

The tension between what one would *like* to think – or what one supposes that one *ought* to think – and the practical outlook enforced by the social context of the period was accentuated by the recession which began soon after the 1987 general election. Like the oil crisis of 1973–4 – but not the slump at the start of the 1980s, which followed years of economic malaise – this sudden and severe downturn generated deep insecurity among those who had begun to feel that increasing prosperity was guaranteed. Such individuals had borrowed heavily on the strength of their future prospects, and not just for house purchases. Credit card debt, in particular, had burgeoned in the second half of the 1980s. The number of cards in circulation had risen from 10 million in 1980 to 27 million before the close of the decade: 13 million of these were issued by stores, which invariably asked for repayments at rates well above the bank level. The reality or prospect of crippling debt was bound to induce in many people a fixation with economic self-interest, no matter what they might say in attitude surveys.

On this subject concrete evidence is extremely elusive. Yet there are some signs that resistance to Mrs Thatcher's philosophy was beginning to subside even as her own popularity plummeted. It was only in 1989, for example, that the *Sunday Times* started to publish its Rich Lists for readers to drool over – or curse, according to taste. Rupert Murdoch launched his long-contemplated satellite broadcasting service, Sky, hoping to cash in on rising demand from a viewing public with full pockets and limited cultural tastes. Murdoch's media rival Robert Maxwell stepped up the illegal exploitation of his own company's pension fund which had begun on a modest scale three years earlier.[72] A jury believed Ken Dodd's explanation of his secreted fortune, and acquitted him on charges of tax evasion. The year 1989 also saw the publication of Peter Mayle's wildly popular *A Year in Provence*, which showed how people who had made money in Britain could escape from the tawdry scene of their material success and carve out a more meaningful existence where the people were authentic and as warm as the weather. The migration of affluent Britons to sunnier climates had been used in the 1970s as a means of attacking Labour. By the end of the following decade a brain drain inspired by the same motives was more commonly regarded as an understandable exercise of the 'freedom to choose' which came from being rich.

Eloquent testimony about changing attitudes can be drawn from contemporary depictions of greed. The comedian Harry Enfield's vulgar braggart 'Loadsamoney' was a cockney plasterer, who first appeared in the Channel 4 comedy programme *Saturday Night Live* in 1988. The character was an overnight sensation, and Enfield achieved a chart hit with a spin-off single. At that stage, there was every reason to think that young people in Britain were taking the joke in the intended spirit, but the *Sun* editor Kelvin MacKenzie guessed that many of his readers would see Loadsamoney as a *positive* role model. Much the same thing had happened in the 1960s, when the repellent racist Alf Garnett had been hailed as an astute social commentator in some quarters. Enfield was angry enough to contemplate legal action when MacKenzie used the Loadsamoney catchphrase to advertise his newspaper. Realising that a courtroom victory would do nothing to change the minds of the millions who had misunderstood him, he took the alternative course of dropping the character from his act.[73]

But this circumstantial evidence does not amount to a validation of Labour's change of course after the 1987 general election. That defeat, after all, persuaded party strategists to accommodate changes in British attitudes that, in defiance of much evidence, they thought had already happened, during Mrs Thatcher's first two terms. The logic of Kinnock's policy review suggested that 'pocket book' voting was rampant in Britain in 1987, and explained why Labour lost for the third time in a row. The party's decision to strike a partial compromise with Thatcherism just at the time when the government's 'miraculous' economic record was beginning to unravel must itself count as a crucial reason why voters reluctantly opted to follow Labour's example between 1987 and 1992 – even if a considerable number still found it impossible to admit the enforced change in their views.

VI

To summarise a complex argument, according to our definition most Britons were 'preoccupied with material acquisitions, unrelated to physical needs' by the time of the 1979 general election. Instead of *making* people greedy, Margaret Thatcher's blunt advocacy of materialism made them think twice about their existing attitudes and lifestyle. However, after the third consecutive Conservative victory, in 1987, it was much easier to conclude that there really was 'no alternative' to Thatcherism. The severe economic downturn after 1989, combined with avoidable errors by the government, provided the conditions in which the leading Opposition party (Labour) could have capitalised if they had carried conviction, given that the Conservatives had been in office for a decade and had now presided over two serious recessions. But by that time Labour's most influential figures were people who (for one reason or another) had accepted the Conservative premise about the acquisitive nature of the British people. After its subsequent defeat in 1992, despite a deliberate appeal to 'Thatcherite' voters, the Labour Party decided that its most promising course of action was to persuade the public that its conversion was sincere.

Although the popular notion that Mrs Thatcher somehow caused the greed of the 1980s is untenable, this does not mean that politicians cannot help to shape public attitudes – only that they tend to do so inadvertently. Thus, initial exposure to the practical effects of Mrs Thatcher's philosophy actually increased public support for the values she hated. But Labour's response to its 1987 electoral defeat was even more significant. Because of the peculiar British first-past-the-post system, it is natural for voters to understand democratic politics as a confrontation between government and Opposition; and at the time this tendency was accentuated because the third party, which subsequently became the Liberal Democrats, was undergoing its own period of self-induced turmoil. The fact that after 1987 the main Opposition party decided to minimise the difference between itself and the government robbed millions of voters of any chance to enforce a decisive change at the top. For the majority it looked as if greed was the only show in town, for better or for worse. Alternative attitudes, as expressed in the late 1980s by the travelling community, were quickly stamped out by police action, with popular support from a public which was increasingly intolerant of people who acted as if Thatcherism had never happened.

From a narrowly partisan perspective, of course, Labour did very well to lose the 1992 general election. Initial expectations that John Major would break with Thatcherism proved unfounded, partly because the new prime minister lacked boldness and imagination but also because he had a slender parliamentary majority and the Thatcherites soon made it clear that they would vote him out of office at the first serious sign of heresy. As a result, the Conservatives hung on for five years after an election that they should have lost. This gave them time to bring Thatcherism into further disrepute, notably through their ill-conceived privatisation of the railways. Major also presided over the introduction of the National Lottery, which Baroness Thatcher regarded as an unforgivable breach of Victorian values. When the lottery was launched in November 1994 she was horrified to see a young mother buying a ticket in a local shop. 'Don't do it!' the ex-premier cried. 'Invest that pound instead! Invest it. Invest it! Watch it grow. Invest!' Alf Roberts would have been very proud.[74] Even those who felt that state-sponsored gambling was permissible, provided that a proportion of the proceeds went to genuinely good causes, had reasons for unease about the way in which it was run. Britain's National Lottery was a game designed for the greedy, organised by profit hunters. The odds against winning the jackpot were nearly 14 million to one, but it was felt that the British would prefer an infinitesimal chance of winning a huge fortune rather than better odds for a lesser sum.

Between 1992 and 1997 the Conservatives fell apart over the issue of Europe. But internal conflict did not absorb all of their energies; they also gained a new reputation as the 'party of sleaze'. This was a spectacular instance of life belatedly imitating satire. Laurence Marks and Maurice Gran had already attacked Thatcherite philosophy in their ITV series *The New Statesman*. The manic main character Alan B'Stard (brilliantly realised by Rik Mayall) was rather like Gordon Gekko transplanted to Westminster and injected with greed-enhancing drugs. The series was successful and, unlike Harry Enfield's Loadsamoney, the central character was unambiguously hateful. But although he must have amused many Labour supporters while he was on screen between 1987 and 1992, B'Stard obviously did not convince many floating voters to switch away from the Conservatives. It was only after the series had ended that people began to realise that he genuinely bore a resemblance to some of the nation's legislators.

In hindsight, the sleaze was hardly spectacular. In July 1994 the *Sunday Times* revealed that two Tory MPs had agreed to be paid £1,000 in return for tabling parliamentary questions. At the centre of this 'cash for questions' scandal was the controversial businessman Mohamed Al Fayed, who was allegedly told by a lobbyist that MPs could be hired just like taxicabs.[75] Even for a taxi journey in London after midnight, £1,000 is an exorbitant fare, but in the world of business it was a petty sum, which suggested that MPs' services were not rated very highly. Further revelations of subsidised stays at the Ritz Hotel in Paris, by Jonathan Aitken (born 1942) and Neil Hamilton (born 1949), fell into the same category. Taken together, these incidents suggested that Conservative MPs were prepared to commit constitutional improprieties in return for relatively trivial sums, and few of them believed that they had actually done anything wrong.[76] This was not surprising in the context of the government's financial misdeeds. In November 1994, for example, the High Court ruled that ministers had been wrong to contribute £234 million to Malaysia's Pergau Dam because the project did not meet the official requirements of Britain's overseas aid programme. Whether or not the dam would help local people, the Malaysian government was not exactly strapped for cash; it had recently placed orders worth more than £1 billion with British arms manufacturers.

Significantly, the Pergau affair attracted far less attention than the errant MPs. This suggested that public outrage against financial malpractice was being manipulated by the media in association with 'spin doctors' whose priorities were dictated by political calculation rather than moral considerations. Between the fall of Mrs Thatcher in 1990 and the 1997 general election, there were several stories about greed which focused on individuals rather than institutions. An early target for criticism was Iain (later Sir Iain) Vallance, the first chairman of the privatised British Telecom. In 1991 he was awarded a six-figure bonus on top of his £450,000 salary at a time when the company (now rebranded as BT) was laying off thousands of workers. The shadow trade and industry secretary, Gordon Brown, described the deal as 'scandalous', and proposed that privatised companies which offered excessive boardroom pay increases should be forced to cut their prices. Vallance, who protested that he earned far less than a successful pop star, decided to make a sizeable donation to charity.[77]*

It was probably no accident that Vallance had worked his way to the top from within the nationalised British Telecom. Such people endured the harshest criticism on the assumption that they had once rubbed along happily enough on modest salaries and were now struggling to think of ways to spend their exorbitant earnings. The classic example was Cedric Brown, an employee of the nationalised British Gas who became chief executive after the company was sold off. In the same month as the High Court ruling on the Pergau Dam, Brown's salary was doubled, to nearly £500,000 per year. After a media outcry Brown became a public hate figure, portrayed as a pig with his head in a trough. This threatened to draw attention to the more general phenomenon of extravagant boardroom pay, and even to provoke a revolt among small shareholders. As a result, the Confederation of British Industry (CBI) set up a commission on pay under Sir Richard Greenbury. Before he delivered his report, Sir Richard's annual salary from Marks and Spencer rose from a meagre £779,000 to more than £900,000, which left his impartiality on the subject somewhat compromised.[78] The commission left things much as they were, allowing top management to help themselves to huge salaries, backed up by lucrative share options. This was a world in which failure could be a good

---

*In a way, Brown followed up his suggestion when he became chancellor of the exchequer in 1997, penalising privatised firms with a 'windfall tax.'

career move, because inept chief executives were still able to dictate their own pay-off packages when they were sacked. Almost invariably, they found themselves new jobs afterwards. Cedric Brown, in contrast, opted for a quiet retirement in 1996. Compared to his pay rise, his departure was a one-day wonder in the eyes of the media; the Greenbury commission had done its job, and 'fat cats' were no longer newsworthy.

It was ironic that these scandals damaged John Major, since their origins clearly lay in Margaret Thatcher's 1980s. Neil Hamilton's notorious visit to the Ritz Hotel, for example, had taken place shortly after the 1987 general election. By the mid-1990s, when the most damaging scandals were exposed, explicit declarations of greed could pass without much press comment, provided that they were not uttered by Conservative supporters. At the 1995 Brit Awards, for example, Noel Gallagher of the 'Britpop' band Oasis announced that 'I've got nowt to say except I'm extremely rich and you lot aren't.'[79] However, Major had left himself unprotected against the whirlwind, because of his inability to change the Thatcherite course he had inherited in 1990. The public outcry against cash for questions and fat cats was genuine enough, but it was a sudden burst of flame from dying embers. Once the media had made an example of Cedric Brown, Britons had to accept that he was only a symptom of a perverse and pervasive boardroom culture which nothing could shift. The public still expected higher standards from its MPs. But the cash for questions case actually proved that elected legislators *were* better than businesspeople, because the *Sunday Times* had approached twenty MPs, and only two had fallen headlong into the trap. Yet thanks to other scandals at this time, the public had good reason to suppose that if MPs were not receiving clandestine payments in brown envelopes, they were having sex with people to whom they were not married. Or rather, Conservative MPs were either making love or taking money. Fortunately for the new party leader Tony Blair and his fellow modernisers, none of the ten Labour MPs approached by the *Sunday Times* accepted the bribe, and no major sexual scandal involving a Labour MP was publicised between Blair's rise to the leadership and the 1997 general election.*

---

* In February 1994 it was revealed that the veteran left-wing MP Dennis Skinner was conducting an affair. However, Skinner's high and generally favourable public profile meant that there was no question of giving up his seat, much to the regret of the modernisers.

By 1994 sections of the media felt that the Conservatives had been in office too long and pursued alleged cases of sleaze with vigour in the expectation that the public would not condemn the intrusions if concrete proof was lacking. By that time the Tories had already been rocked by Black Wednesday (16 September 1992), when violent movements of the currency markets forced the UK to leave the Exchange Rate Mechanism (ERM) of the European Monetary System (EMS). Desperate and doomed attempts to shore up the value of the pound cost the taxpayer at least £3.3 billion; interest rates were briefly raised to 15 per cent.[80] It was obvious that the government would never recover from this blow to its reputation for economic competence, so even media outlets which had previously concentrated their fire on Labour felt free to take pleasure in Conservative misfortune. This episode was a peculiar comment on the assumption that individuals vote out of economic self-interest, because the departure from the ERM which made a Labour victory inevitable actually ushered in a prolonged period of stable economic prosperity which began under a Conservative chancellor of the exchequer, Kenneth Clarke.

VII

The case of Cedric Brown and the establishment of the ineffectual Greenbury commission provide excellent symbols of the wider public mood in the 1990s. People were still vaguely uncomfortable about greed, so individual exemplars had to be identified and punished, someone safe had to be asked to look into the problem, and then everyone could continue to be as greedy as they were before.

Anyone who is misled by the isolated attacks on fat cats and sleaze merchants during the 1990s should examine the extent to which the British were now prepared to let greed invade their favourite pastimes. In April 1989 ninety-six football supporters were crushed to death before an FA Cup semi-final at Hillsborough, Sheffield. Later that year – almost exactly a decade after a former colleague had denounced Don Revie – Lord Justice Taylor produced an interim report into the implications of the tragedy. Taylor thought that the danger of similar incidents would be reduced if those who came to watch football matches were in future forced to be seated, rather than standing on terraces. This suggestion was prompted by humanitarian considerations; many of those who had died at Hillsborough had been trapped by the cages erected to prevent hooligans invading the pitch – like the Scottish fans who had torn up Wembley in 1977.

Unlike Sir Joseph Cantley, Taylor was sensitive to more general developments within British society, and he was careful to stress that his recommended changes should not lead to a significant rise in ticket prices. But his cautionary words were thrown away in a society which was no longer resistant to Thatcherite greed. Although everything else in Britain (even water) was now regarded as a potential source of profit, investors had previously shied away from football because of its association with violence. The prospect of all-seater stadiums changed everything; it opened the possibility that the middle classes would flood back to football grounds, and that they would be happy to tolerate prices which were high enough to drive away the potentially violent poor.

Despite Taylor's laudable intentions, his report removed the final buttress which had been holding back an influx of greed into English football. In 1992 the top twenty-two teams broke away from the rest of the league to form the Premiership. The emergence of satellite broadcasting meant that there would be fierce bidding for the right to show live matches on television for those who could not afford the new ticket prices – or were too inert to travel – and the top teams wanted to keep most of the proceeds. Rupert Murdoch's Sky duly won the first auction with a bid of £305 million. Back in 1965 the BBC had paid just £5,000 for the right to screen its package of highlights, *Match of the Day*. At that time fans had been quite happy to wait until the evening to see the action, but the supply of live pictures created its own demand. Sky, which initially incurred heavy losses, had become another source of profits for Murdoch by 1993. Since then the broadcasting rights have been the subject of frantic bidding in which the interests of ordinary fans are ignored. Meanwhile, the cost of watching one's heroes in the flesh (albeit from a sedentary position) has increased out of all proportion to the cost of living. In 1991 the average price of a ticket to a Newcastle United match was £5.26. Just six years later it was £16.

The new money from the broadcasters transformed Britain's favourite game overnight. Football had always been a business of sorts, but the wealthy local businessmen who ran the clubs were not primarily motivated by economic self-interest. This mood had already begun to change when Murdoch set up Sky. Boardrooms began to be infiltrated by people who had done well out of the Thatcher years, and even when such individuals were genuine supporters, they brought their moneymaking ethos with them. Even Robert Maxwell dabbled, at Oxford United and Derby County. Existing board members took the hint, and their salaries began a resolute upward march. At several clubs there was a struggle between the new breed of business people and the old guard. The Thatcher-worshipping Sir John Hall, who had made millions from the development of the Metro Centre in Gateshead, invested in Newcastle United in 1988. Three years later, just before the official launch of the Premiership, he took overall control of the club. Jack Walker made his capital gains from steel, and it has been estimated that his tax-efficient desire to reside in Jersey cost the British Treasury more than £130 million.[81] In 1990 Walker put about a quarter of this sum into a trust fund for the benefit of Blackburn Rovers, whom he had continued to support from afar. His generosity paid off, and Blackburn won the Premiership title in 1995. But as David Conn has noted, '"Uncle Jack's" charity was applied with a sharp commercial edge.'[82] He was determined that after his initial cash injections, the club should be self-supporting. Blackburn was not a prosperous area, and although ticket prices soared, the team could not sustain its success. In July 1996 its greatest player, Alan Shearer, was bought by Sir John Hall's Newcastle for a world record of £15 million. Despite this sensational outlay, Newcastle never quite managed to win the Premiership. Nevertheless, Hall had no reason to regret his involvement; David Conn estimated that he and his family received a capital gain of £100 million in just five years from share transactions.[83] It was no wonder that Hall's son Douglas held Newcastle supporters in contempt, as a clandestine *News of the World* investigation made clear in April 1998. Another timely investor was Alan Sugar, a businessman whose company Amstrad manufactured Sky's satellite dishes. He had not previously shown an obsessional interest in the sport, but became the biggest shareholder in Tottenham Hotspur just before the TV deal with Sky.

However, people who were already rich were not the only beneficiaries of the football boom. Before the birth of the Premiership footballers were well rewarded compared to the average workers. But, as the entertainers who actually drew in the dupes, they were well placed to absorb much of the television money. This seemed only fair; after all, Sky's viewers were not tuning in to watch a kick-around among the fat cats in the boardroom. Like the miners in 1973/4, the players (abetted by their agents) were not slow to exploit their bargaining position. At Blackburn Rovers Alan Shearer was earning around £500,000 per year. After the move to Newcastle United – the club he had worshipped as a child – his annual salary plus various advertising endorsements was worth about £5.5 million.[84] Players also took a slice of their transfer fees, which in those years were outstripping even house prices in their inflation-busting capacity. Back in 1981 Manchester United had broken the British transfer record when they snaffled Bryan Robson from West Bromwich Albion. They had paid £1.5 million, so the price of bringing Shearer back to his home-town club represented an increase by a factor of ten over fifteen years.*

Multi-million-pound transfer fees opened the way for greedy managers to negotiate a percentage for themselves, and in the 1990s there were several allegations of corruption involving thousands of pounds and brown envelopes left in improbable places like motorway cafes. But although the more knowing fans realised that their heroes were on the make, a mixture of passion and passivity prevented them from taking effective action. The Arsenal supporter Nick Hornby admitted that he was umbilically linked to the club, though he knew that it 'exploits me, disregards my views, and treats me shoddily on occasions'.[85] The greatest exploitation was the flotation of several clubs on the stock exchange. Fans were encouraged to invest in order to have a real involvement with their beloved teams, but the result was much like Conservative propaganda about popular capitalism – with the crucial difference that on this occasion the shares were massively *over*valued when trading began.

By the beginning of 1995 even Tony Blair thought that the effect of money on the national game was worthy of public comment. An article under his byline in the *Mail on Sunday* attacked football's 'growing obsession with money-making'. The interests of smaller clubs were being ignored; ordinary fans were being ripped off and taken for granted. Sport in general was in danger of being corrupted by 'the get-rich-quick, something-for-nothing philosophy'.[86] The analysis was accurate, but it was strange that Blair should put his name to

---

* In 1975 the British transfer record was £350,000, which had taken the striker Bob Latchford from Birmingham to Everton in the previous year. Shearer himself had previously set a new record, in July 1992 when he moved from Southampton to Blackburn. At that time the market value of his services had been £3.2 million.

it. The top football teams were indeed taking their supporters for granted, guessing that a sense of irrational loyalty would make them scrape together the money for exorbitantly priced season tickets. But New Labour was doing roughly the same thing, hoping that the party faithful would stay true despite all the changes since 1987 – because their loyalties were too ingrained to allow them to switch sides. An FA report of June 1991 had noted that in a consumer society the tendency of the leisure sector had been 'to move upmarket so as to follow the affluent middle-class consumer'.[87] Modernisers within the Labour Party had already noticed (and exaggerated) the same trend.

Blair was certainly right to extend his critique to other sports. The bonanza for football players had an understandable knock-on effect, and resistance from fans or administrators was equally unavailing, even if money transgressed the original spirit of the game. In 1992, for example, the amateur ethos still prevailed in Rugby Union. On the face of it this was a bizarre survival from pre-Thatcherite days, made even more surreal by the fact that Denis Thatcher was an enthusiastic unpaid referee. The Five Nations tournament between England, Scotland, Wales, Ireland and France was already a major televised event, and after 1987 there was a World Cup, which drew in the rugby-mad nations of Australia, New Zealand and post-apartheid South Africa. But Rugby Union had prided itself on its freedom from the commerical spirit; this, after all, was the reason for its break from the more materialistic Rugby League at the end of the nineteenth century. It was not until August 1995 that the dam finally burst, and open payments to players were allowed. The strict principle of amateurism had already been breached through over-generous expenses and benefits in kind. After the official end of amateur Rugby Union – at least at the top level – Rupert Murdoch's money was soon flowing into the game.

However, the impact of television on sport had been felt long before the 1990s, and Murdoch was not the main offender. In May 1977 – two months before Don Revie's desertion of the English football team – the Australian media tycoon Kerry Packer attracted thirty-five prominent cricketers from several countries to play in a new World Series. One of the key figures in Packer's 'circus' was Tony Greig (born 1946), the incumbent English captain. In that role Greig had been earning little more than £1,000 per season. Packer offered him twelve times that amount on a guaranteed three-year contract. Not only did the

England captain accept the offer, but he also acted as Packer's recruiting sergeant. Greig was promptly sacked from the England captaincy for this 'breach of trust'. For English cricket fans the blow was softened by the fact that only three of Greig's colleagues followed his lead; by contrast, the Australian team was decimated. The player who took Greig's place as all-rounder in the England side was Ian Botham, who proved more than adequate. The new captain, Mike Brearley, turned out to be one of the most successful leaders in the history of Test cricket. England retained the Ashes in 1977 and crushed their deadly rivals on their home soil the following year. While they celebrated these events, England fans could even see Greig's departure as a blessing in disguise. The only mystery, for them, was why the authorities had ever entrusted the captaincy to someone who had not been born in England.

After Kerry Packer's death in 2005, almost all of his obituarists argued that World Series cricket had brought lasting benefits to the game. The element of personal greed, which had dominated critical comment at the relevant time, was barely mentioned. Don Revie could be defended on similar grounds: apart from feathering his own nest, he had introduced financial incentives for England players, with £200 for a drawn game and £300 for a win – a bonus which was all too infrequently collected. He also generated extra income by allowing a sponsor's name to appear on England shirts for the first time. The former England player Jimmy Greaves thought that this was 'commercialism gone mad', but it was no more than a tentative step towards the full-scale merchandising ethos which pervaded every marketable sport by the end of the century.[88]

Don Revie himself did not live to join the Premiership's profiteers. He died in May 1989 after a long and dignified struggle with motor-neurone disease. Fans of Leeds United draped the team's Elland Road stadium with tributary shirts and scarves. This kind of gesture was already losing its poignancy; it had become part of the compulsory ritualism of grief, and the death of every club stalwart set the tills ringing in the souvenir shops. But on this occasion the feeling of loss was genuine in Yorkshire. By 1989 most Britons would have joined the mourning, had it not been for Revie's old offence against patriotism. His mercenary nature was no longer an issue. After all, as the former Leeds player Johnny Giles put it, 'Who isn't greedy? The people who write the stories in the tabloid newspapers might be the greediest in the world.'[89]

6

LUST

---

there is no escape from having pornography brought to one's notice
The Earl of Halsbury, 1976[1]

*My own deepest fear is that the young growing up in a culture soaked
in coarseness, crudity and cruelty, may react against sex, and therefore,
against life and the God who gave it; that we shall, between us, raise a
generation which either grasps at sex as a physical lust or treats it simply
as a passing fancy.*

Mary Whitehouse, 1993[2]

*We all have our faults, but mistakes which involve a betrayal of trust
are especially worrying ... It clearly can't be right for a politician to
say one thing and do another in his private life.*

John Major, 1996[3]

there is nothing so unattractive to a man as strident feminism
Helen Fielding, *Bridget Jones's Diary*, 1996[4]

I

NOVEMBER 1977 was a memorable month for British journalists. For
decades the legal system had been a reliable source of salacious stories;
even lofty publications like *The Times* felt that they had a duty to
inform their readers about the details of messy divorce proceedings
when adultery was involved. But two sensational cases of November
1977 went way beyond the usual tales of furtive extramarital fumblings

in hotel bedrooms. Even better, the star courtroom performers were attractive young women with no sexual or verbal inhibitions.

The first case provided the tabloids with an irresistible tag line – 'Sex in Chains'. On 22 November, in Epsom magistrates' court, Joyce McKinney was accused of kidnapping a young Mormon missionary, Kirk Anderson. It was alleged that after ending a brief affair Anderson had fled to England to avoid the infatuated McKinney. However, she had tracked him down and, with the help of a male accomplice, a replica gun and some chloroform, bundled him into a car on 14 September 1977. He was taken to a rented cottage in Devon, where he was held for three days. As Anderson explained in court, the last night brought his ordeal to a climax. 'When she came into the room there was a fire in the fireplace and she put some music on. She was wearing a negligee . . . She came to me as I lay on the bed. I said I would like my back rubbed.'[5] This kind of scenario is rarely encountered in kidnapping cases. But although she was quite happy to provide a relaxing massage McKinney was determined to take things much further; and since Anderson was chained to the bed at the time, he was in no position to resist.

If the gender roles had been reversed in the McKinney case, even the British tabloids would probably have withheld some of the details and called for judicial vengeance. But the alleged aggressor was an American woman who had been attractive enough to win the title of Miss Wyoming, so little was left to the reader's imagination. As a result, the victim tended to be treated with envy rather than sympathy, especially when McKinney claimed that she would have 'skied down Mount Everest in the nude with a carnation up my nose' in order to win his affections. McKinney was bailed by the magistrates to stand trial the following May. To the regret of the tabloids, she failed to answer the charges and was duly sentenced in her absence to one year's imprisonment.

It was easy for the public to treat the case of the manacled Mormon with levity because both of the primary actors were foreigners and the incident could have happened anywhere in the world. As such, the reaction in Britain was far more relevant than the facts of the case. But the other courtroom drama of November 1977 was more directly concerned with the state of British morality and its relationship to the law. This time the case was heard at the Old Bailey rather than an obscure magistrates' court. The defendants had published several magazines which were held to have breached the 1959 Obscene Publications Act. It was a crucial case for the Metropolitan Police, whose reputation for high-minded law enforcement had been dented over the previous year by three high-profile trials resulting in the conviction of several senior officers for running something akin to a protection racket on behalf of selected Soho pornographers.

Having ignored serious breaches of the Obscene Publications Act for many years, the police were in need of some headline-catching convictions. The Old Bailey case of November 1977 was a partial success; although six of seven charges were dropped, the publishers were found guilty and fined on the remaining count. However, contrary to police intentions the case became something of a cause célèbre for critics of censorship. Their most effective mouthpiece was Mary Millington (née Quilter, born 1945), a blonde model and actress involved in the management of the magazines, as well as appearing on (too) many of their pages. Millington could be described as Britain's first sexual superstar; many of her predecessors had evoked the same adulation, but no one had been quite so free with her favours. During her stint in the witness box on 30 November 1977 she declared that 'Sex is beautiful and in no way obscene.' She was found not guilty, but the judge clearly disagreed with his jury and with Millington's claim that she was 'a person with morals . . . and not a raving nymphomaniac'. In his summing-up, he had compared 'sex without love' to the behaviour of monkeys. After the verdict the furious actress reiterated the principle underlying her work. 'I don't do this for the money any more,' she told the eager pack of reporters. 'I do it to get the law changed.'[6]

Mary Millington was not alone in thinking that the laws relating to obscene publications were in need of revision. Even those who accepted the argument for censorship thought that the terms of the 1959 Act were inadequate. It outlawed publications which 'tend to deprave and corrupt persons who are likely, having regard to all relevant circumstances, to read, see or hear the matter contained or embodied in it'. But as far back as 1857, when the first legislation on the subject was debated, it had been pointed out that people were likely to differ in their view of what counted as obscenity. The tendency 'to deprave and corrupt' was also a matter of opinion. Judgements could differ between generations; material which would disgust a hardened sensualist in one decade might be viewed with indifference by a Sunday school teacher in the next.

A further complication was added by the inclusion in the law of a 'public interest' defence, to protect works of scientific or literary merit. It was this consideration which had led to the spectacular collapse of the *Lady Chatterley* trial of 1960, when the defence produced thirty-five witnesses (including clergymen) ready to exaggerate the literary qualities of D.H. Lawrence's novel. In itself, this case did not make the Act unenforceable against the printed word; after all, Lawrence was a well-known author with eminent admirers, and his publisher, Penguin Books, had plenty of allies in literary circles. But after 1960 it became increasingly difficult to persuade jurors that any book could 'deprave and corrupt' its readers. In January 1976 prosecutors failed to ban *Inside Linda Lovelace*, which purported to relate the sexual adventures of an American porn actress. The case caused a stir in the most elevated circles; the verdict even forced a dissenting judgment from *The Times*, in an editorial under the heading 'The Pornography of Hate'.[7] In the House of Lords the Earl of Halsbury (1908–2000) suggested that the sale of pornographic magazines should be restricted to special shops, and that they should carry a prominent government warning: 'Pornography corrupts and depraves.'[8] *Deep Throat* (1972), the film which had made Lovelace famous, had been banned in Britain and twenty-three US states. If anything, the film deserved the gentler treatment; it had a few comical moments, some of them intentional. But it was the book rather than the film which passed the legal test, and duly received critical acclaim from thousands of giggling schoolboys.

At best, by 1977 the Obscene Publications Act was capable only of selective enforcement, apparently at the whim of police, prosecutors and juries. Something clearly had to be done, but it was difficult to see how a satisfactory compromise could be negotiated when participants in the debate were so polarised. The Labour government's response was to set up the Committee on Obscenity and Film Censorship. There had already been a freelance operation on this subject, established in 1971 by the former Labour minister and penal reformer Lord Longford. Longford's committee, which included the journalist Peregrine Worsthorne, the disc jockey Jimmy Saville and the misogynistic novelist Kingsley Amis, had recommended much tighter laws. But the earnest endeavours of Longford's group were overshadowed by the appearance of the anarchist Alex Comfort's manual *The Joy of Sex: A Gourmet's Guide to Lovemaking* (1972), which proved a runaway worldwide best-seller in spite of its preponderance of bearded protagonists. Comfort's book would have been condemned as pornographic at any time before 1960; its popularity confirmed the suspicion that Longford's report was an echo of outdated prudishness.

By 1977 the British government was already cutting back on public spending; it had no wish to be seen as an enemy of a pleasure which, while not exactly free, was at least difficult to bring within the ambit of value added tax. It signalled its stance by appointing Professor Bernard Williams (1929–2003) as the committee's chairman. Williams was one of the few notable British moral philosophers of his time. The former husband of Shirley Williams – who was currently serving in the cabinet as education secretary – he differed from most of his profession in his belief that philosophy could be relevant to practical questions. However, his outlook was unflinchingly liberal.

Appointing a forceful character with these views to chair a committee on pornography was rather like asking a fox to advise on the safety features of chicken coops. When the Williams committee reported, it recommended that the obscenity laws should concentrate on the protection of children, while adults were allowed freedom of choice. This decision was based on the liberal litmus test of proven harm. The error of people like Lord Longford, Williams argued, was 'to get the problem of pornography out of proportion with the many other problems that face our society today'. In reality, 'given the amount of explicit sexual material in circulation, and the allegations often made about its effects, it is striking that one can find case after case of sex crimes and murder without any hint at all that pornography was present in the background'.[9]

This was a startling claim. It was one thing to deny that pornography was the primary motivator of most sex crimes, but according to Williams in 'case after case' it was not even a background factor. Yet he had admitted that there was a considerable amount of 'explicit sexual material in circulation'; indeed, his committee felt that there was so much pornography around in 1977 that it would be futile to guess its extent. The most reasonable conclusion was that even if pornography had not acted as the decisive trigger for many sex crimes, it was extremely likely to have formed part of the mindset of sex offenders. However, it proved possible for liberals to take an opposite view, and to argue that many sex crimes in Britain must have occurred because the perpetrators were *deprived* of access to pornography. The idea that pornography offered its consumers a harmless way of releasing their sexual frustrations was becoming increasingly familiar, and had been canvassed during the *Linda Lovelace* trial.

One telling flaw in Williams's argument was his failure to recognise that hard-core pornography was itself illegal. The production and distribution of such material was thus a 'sex crime' in itself, and even Williams would have been hard-pressed to argue that pornographers were not influenced in some way by pornography. Instances of people being coerced into such activities were not difficult to find in the 1970s. For example, in January 1975 a court was told of how a vicar, a doctor and a teacher had taken indecent pictures of young boys supplied to them by a child-care officer.[10] In the same month, while press attention focused on the errant MP John Stonehouse, who had been tracked down to Australia, a British doctor who had fled to Queensland killed himself in his hotel bedroom. The police had a warrant for his arrest, on charges relating to indecent assaults and the organisation of a 'porn ring' back home.[11]

These incidents pointed to additional serious problems with the Williams report. In true liberal style Williams assumed that 'rational' people (like himself) were unlikely to commit sexual crimes after watching smutty films or salivating over dirty magazines. Yet vicars, doctors and teachers were supposed, on the whole, to be rational, and clearly some of them were driven into criminal activity by their lust. Also, by focusing on the *consumer* of pornography, Williams down-played any effect on the people who worked in the 'industry'. In this respect Longford had been much wiser. His committee defined pornography as 'that which exploits and dehumanizes sex so that human beings are treated as things and women in particular as sex objects':[12] Longford was ridiculed by liberals and scoffingly dubbed 'Lord Porn'; with his other-worldly, professorial air, it was certainly unwise of him to allow journalists to witness his research trip to a Copenhagen sex club. Such antics allowed Roy Jenkins to conclude that Longford had 'made an absolute ass of himself'.[13] But Longford's approach was much more consistent with the key liberal principle of respect for others. Williams could reply that he was only willing to tolerate pornographic publications which featured consenting adults, but from Longford's perspective it could be argued either that such productions were not pornography at all – because only material which 'exploits and dehu-manizes sex' satisfied his definition – or that participants who were happy to be displayed as mere objects might not be aware of the possi-bility that their actions would cause subsequent harm to themselves and others. In this respect, the testimony of Mary Millington would have been of interest to the Williams committee. Just two months before it finally reported, Millington was found dead after taking a fatal dose of paracetamol, washed down with gin. The reasons for her suicide were complicated, but it is reasonable to think that she would not have taken that step if she had never been involved with the sex trade.

One reason for Millington's depression was the realisation that her shelf life as an actress was coming to an end as she approached her mid-thirties. But after her trial she had also alluded to the fact that Britain's (relatively) restrictive laws were putting home-based pornographers at a disadvantage. The appetite for hard-core films and magazines was being satisfied by material brought in from overseas. British sex films, like the risible *Come Play with Me* (1977) in which Milligton starred, were lamentably poor. The jocular *Confessions of a Window Cleaner* (1974) was successful enough to inspire several sequels, along with an imitative exercise by the *Carry On* team. But *Carry On Emmanuelle* (1978) was such an embarrassment that it brought the long-running series of low-budget comedy capers to an end. At his first sight of the script Kenneth Williams characterised it as 'monotonous and unfunny ... It's all about a nymphomaniac who does it with all kinds of people in all kinds of situations.'[14] Thanks to the general availability of video recorders by the end of the 1970s, Britons would soon be able to borrow or buy copies of the original, French-made *Emmanuelle*, and to view it at home without having to muffle themselves in raincoats for a visit to the local cinema. In itself, the arrival of home videos transformed the nature of the porn industry. Thus technology had made the earnest deliberations of the Williams committee redundant even before the appearance of its report.

Among those eager to investigate the potential of home videos was a Gloucester-based handyman and petty thief, Frederick West (1941–95). The semi-literate West was brought up in a household where sexual abuse was common, but his later career as a perverted mass murderer was clearly inspired by pornography. As one of his biographers has written, his house, 25 Cromwell Street, 'was full of blue magazines and blue movies. Dirty books and dirty films. There was hard-core pornography in magazine and video-cassette form all over the house.'[15] Whatever a liberal philosopher might think, Fred obviously believed that this material had a tendency to 'deprave and corrupt'; he forced his children to watch pornographic films while training them for a life of sexual slavery. He also acted as a freelance video librarian for the local perverts, happily handing out tapes from his collection. This had also been a common practice for the Cambridge rapist, Peter Cook. During his trial in 1975 his legal team admitted that Cook was addicted to pornography.[16]*

While it took almost a year to catch the Cambridge rapist, his methods made him vulnerable to early detection. He was an opportunist, who had actually begun his career of sex crime during a bungled burglary. Fred West was much more cunning, and kept his work closer to home. Between the autumn of 1973 and the spring of 1975 he raped, tortured and killed five girls and young women in 25 Cromwell Street. Before the Williams committee reached its conclusions about the marginal effects of pornography, West had butchered three more women, including one who was expecting his child – the second time he had killed a pregnant 'lover'. In one respect, at least, West's history provides some backing for Williams's findings. British society in the 1970s was clearly faced with many serious problems besides pornography. Initially it was presumed that several of West's victims had simply disappeared without trace and without noticeable lamentation. It was not until November 1992, when West and his wife were charged with sexual offences against one of their daughters, that anyone in a position of authority began to wonder if there was something unorthodox about his domestic arrangements. Even then charges were dropped because his brutalised, petrified children were unwilling to give evidence against him. Only in February 1994 did the local police begin to make a connection between the allegations of incest and the disappearance of West's daughter Heather back in 1987. Less than a year later West finally put his manual dexterity to a laudable purpose and hanged himself in prison awaiting trial.

In the aftermath of West's suicide it was easy to focus on the failings of the police and the legal system. Back in January 1973 West and his peculiar wife Rosemary were fined a total of £100 and advised to seek psychiatric help after subjecting a seventeen-year-old girl to a savage sexual ordeal. Fred had already been in trouble with the law on several occasions, for sex crimes as well as his habitual thievery, but the court was persuaded that the most recent victim had helped bring her misfortune on herself – a prejudice which was all too common in those days. The failure to incarcerate West at an earlier stage was

---

*Bizarrely, the members of the Williams committee decided that they knew Cook better than he did himself, and rejected the idea that pornography had helped in any way to motivate his crimes.

indeed worrying, but the authorities were not the main culprits. West remained at liberty for more than a quarter-century after his first murder because many people around him shared his 'depravity and corruption', at least to some degree. While Ian Brady could be regarded as the evil genius behind the Moors Murders of the 1960s, West was the malignant moron of the 'House of Horrors'. Far from concealing his true self, he advertised it, flaunting pornographic pictures of his wife and inviting workmates, family members and casual acquaintances to share her dubious charms. Any of these people could have reported the unsavoury environment at 25 Cromwell Street to the police, but they did not, because it was congenial to their own porn-crazed tastes. The people who could be forgiven for failing to register a complaint were the numerous women who survived West's assaults. In such a poisonous social context they could only expect the police to believe the lies of the aggressor.

The 'House of Horrors' was demolished in 1996, a year after Rose West had been sentenced to life imprisonment for her presumed role in the murders; the authorities were afraid it would become a house of homage. They destroyed most of the contents in the well-founded expectation that they would otherwise attract an army of souvenir hunters. In itself, the reason for these decisions provided an eloquent commentary on Britain in the 1990s.

II

The Thatcher government's refusal to act on the Williams report was widely regarded as a missed opportunity. The mourners were not just liberals like Professor Williams – who was later knighted. For anyone who considered themselves left wing, support for free sexual expression was compulsory, in the 1970s and for long afterwards. For some this was a self-serving argument; Howard Kirk, the anti-hero of Malcolm Bradbury's novel *The History Man* (1975), certainly used revolutionary rhetoric as an aphrodisiac. But when it was sincere, the notion that sex was invariably a progressive force arose from a faulty analysis of British society and politics – not surprisingly, since it was inspired by non-British sexual sages like Wilhelm Reich (1897–1957) and Herbert Marcuse (1898–1979). The *Lady Chatterley* trial had been lauded as a significant blow against the Establishment and the class system. This was true to an extent; some members of the Conservative government had been genuinely anxious to prevent the publication of Lawrence's book, and they were demoralised by the defeat. The prosecuting counsel also contrived to highlight an element of class prejudice in the case by asking whether *Lady Chatterley* was a book which could safely be entrusted to one's servants.

However, the left was quite wrong to think that the depiction of sexual activity in words or pictures was a central concern for Britain's rulers. Recent research has revealed the extent to which the Conservative government of Harold Macmillan (1957–63) was divided on moral questions.[17] Macmillan himself favoured relaxation of the law in certain areas. Some prominent ministers in this and later governments of both main parties were as liberal as Bernard Williams himself. The problem was that moving too fast in the repeal of remaining Victorian legislation was likely to alienate core party supporters – for Labour no less than the Conservatives. As a result, governments tended to offer clandestine support for private members' bills on questions like abortion or homosexuality, rather than openly sponsoring liberalising measures affecting sexual conduct. For the same reason they also felt it necessary to pass restrictive laws like the 1959 Obscene Publications Act, which was amended, though hardly clarified, in 1964. Attempting to enforce such laws was accepted as a duty by successive governments, but they had much more important work on hand in the early 1960s – like preventing the British public from having a say in the modernisation of Britain's 'independent' nuclear deterrent, and attempting to gain entry into the EEC without a popular mandate.

The left continued to believe that sexuality was one subject where the Establishment was on the run – and that idea was the more tenacious because progress in other respects was so limited in the 1960s and 1970s. Elsewhere, the most significant advances were in the field of womens' rights; the Equal Pay Act, passed in 1970, came into force in 1975, when the Sex Discrimination Act also reached the statute book. There were new laws against domestic violence, and in 1976 victims of rape were guaranteed anonymity. Successive relaxations of the divorce laws after 1969 were of disproportionate benefit to women; in 2005 they registered 69 per cent of divorce petitions, and more than half of these cited the unreasonable behaviour of the husband. But in the economic sphere results were mixed. Women became more active within the workforce, but by 2001 56 per cent of working women were in part-time jobs, while 91 per cent of men were working full time. Notoriously, employers continued to exploit career breaks for child rearing as an excuse to pay women less than the full rate for a job. But the change was still significant enough for many commentators to insist that the erosion of the traditional bread-winning role had plunged British men into a crisis. In truth, the new situation was critical for both sexes. Most men were now confronted with a more complex situation when they embarked on serious relationships, and many found the challenge unsustainable. Equally, though, women were faced with the theoretical illusion of unrestricted choice – the ideal of 'having it all' – while having to accept that economic and sexual freedom were rarely compatible with a fulfilling family life.

In any case, none of these legislative advances could ensure that women were granted equality of respect at a time when this quality was in ever-shorter supply across the range of human relationships. On this count, the sexual revolution was working at cross-purposes with legislative reforms. The improvement in women's economic rights was even regarded in some quarters as a licence for men to exploit them sexually, with an easier conscience. In this context the provision of free oral contraceptives by the NHS (announced in 1974) brought new complications as well as obvious and important advantages. Social conservatives were right to argue that the overall effect was deeply equivocal; as Melanie Phillips put it in 1999, sex in Britain had now become little more than 'a recreational sport', and men and women were now 'behaving irresponsibly, to the ultimate disadvantage and unhappiness of both'.[18]

The growing popularity of premarital hen nights acted as a further excuse for men to persevere with their most demeaning habits. It suggested that men were not wrong to visit strip clubs, because women would do exactly the same if they had the financial resources and a plausible pretext to sample such entertainments. In the mid-1970s attempts by the authorities to suppress these events only exposed the double standards of the male-dominated establishment. In August 1975 a judge tried his best to direct the jury towards a conviction in the case of two men who had hosted hen nights in their hotel at Wimborne, Dorset. The judge was clearly of the opinion that only a conviction could save Britain from a deluge of filth. 'You may think there are differences between men and animals,' he declaimed, 'at least for people who want to belong to a civilized country. For one thing, animals do not exhibit their sexual organs deliberately.' Zoologists in the courtroom might have dissented from this opinion, though they would have been hard pressed to find another species which did it for money. As it was, the defence counsel argued that the women who watched the strip show – featuring a performer clad only in a luminous Viking helmet – came away happily refreshed and were 'no doubt better wives and mothers' for the experience.[19] Given the dubious quality of the arguments on both sides, the trial ended in a rare triumph for British justice – the jury was unable to reach a verdict.

In 1979 there was at least one symptom of a more enlightened view, when the BBC decided to drop the woeful Miss World competition from its schedules. But compared to the kind of material available in other media outlets, this was the most token of triumphs. Political radicals should have been aware from an early stage that while they were cheering the permissive society, the wrong kind of people were turning it to concrete advantage. One distinctly unprogressive individual who benefited from the more relaxed ambience was Rupert Murdoch, who bought and transformed the *Sun* newspaper in 1969. Semi-naked women appeared regularly on page three from November 1970, but the *Sun*'s obsession with sex began on day one, along with a new, jeering brand of hypocrisy which no Victorian could have hoped to match. In a typical early campaign the newspaper sneered at Lord Longford and his report, thus aligning itself with people who exploited women. Nevertheless, it cheerfully denied that its pin-ups were anything to do with pornography. It lingered over every lurid detail of sex crimes – helping to deter rape victims from reporting attacks – while managing to reassure its readers that they were not the kind of people who would indulge in such activities. In the mid-1970s this formula was easily coupled with a pro-Tory message which became increasingly blatant, although a majority of readers somehow failed to notice it. A context was developing in which Conservative supporters could have their cake and eat it; they could enjoy the benefits of the permissive society, while blaming their political opponents for its perceived excesses.

By 1975 the Labour-supporting *Daily Mirror* had been forced to fight back in the circulation war by including topless models for the first time.[20] But the Labour Party itself was slow to respond. It regarded the *Sun*, and the *Daily Star* which began to feed at the same trough in 1978, as squalid nuisances, but the kind of liberal arguments which led people to deny a link between pornography and crime could be extended to the political propaganda of these scandal sheets. If a picture of a naked woman in a degrading pose was not in itself corrupting, then a *Sun* editorial lambasting Labour was unlikely to persuade anyone to vote Conservative. As Professor Williams might have put it, to concentrate fire on the right-wing tabloids was 'to get the problem of media influence out of proportion'.

Labour's attitude changed dramatically after the 1983 general election, when its policy platform was subjected to wild distortions in the tabloid press and its internal divisions gleefully exaggerated. Whether justified or not, Labour's complaint that the breakaway SDP owed its popularity to positive media coverage also implied belated recognition that the unassisted power of argument was unlikely to win elections. But the first real sign of a reaction against the tabloids did not come until after Murdoch's newspapers had made their union-busting move to Wapping. Clare Short's Indecent Display (Newspapers) Bill was debated in the House of Commons just two months later, in March 1986. Short was utterly sincere in her desire to prevent newspapers (not magazines) from publishing pin-ups, but it was surely not co-incidental that her speech only made reference to Murdoch and the *Sun*, rather than the more offensive (but less political) *Star*.

Although the stillborn Williams report was ancient history by March 1986, Short's arguments represented a systematic rejection of his liberal position. 'I agree,' she said, 'with the women who think that there is some connection between the rising tide of sexual crime and page three. Obviously, that is unprovable, but the constant mass circulation of such pictures so that they are widely seen by children must influence sexual attitudes and the climate towards sexuality in our society. Those pictures portray women as objects of lust to be sniggered over and grabbed at, and do not portray sex as something that is tender and private.'[21]

In other words, like Lord Longford, Short had identified the real problem with pornography of all kinds: namely that it undermined any attempt to equalise the life chances of men and women at a tolerable level, because it propagated the notion that individuals were objects rather than people with a right to be respected. Short's proposed legislation – which failed, in common with all private members' bills which lack at least tacit government support – provoked thousands of letters from men and women. The overwhelming majority were strongly positive, although a few dozen correspondents sent pornographic pictures with Short's head superimposed and suggested that she had only spoken out because she was too ugly to be raped.[22]

Judging by the Conservative contributions to the debate in March 1986, some of these poison-penmen might have been Tory MPs. Short's speech was repeatedly interrupted by laughter from the government benches, as the honourable representatives of the party of the family exposed their true feelings. One of their number, Robert Adley, did draw attention to the party-political motivation lurking behind Short's proposal, but the remainder of his speech was a disgrace to Parliament and his profession, complete with double entendres which would have been rejected with scorn at a *Carry On* script conference. 'Of all the measures that have been proposed to the House during this session,' quipped the elected representative for Christchurch, 'this Bill deserves the booby prize.' The list of MPs who turned up to vote makes instructive reading. The fifty-six who voted against Short included notorious buffoons and publicity hunters. One of these, Sir Nicholas Fairbairn, had been sacked as solicitor-general for Scotland after justifying his decision not to prosecute three alleged rapists on the grounds that women who said 'No' often mean 'Yes'. Other opponents, like Steven Norris, Edwina Currie, Tim Smith and Neil Hamilton, would later be involved in sexual or financial scandals.

The *Sun*'s response to this exercise in parliamentary democracy was predictable. An editorial comment protested that page three pictures were 'no more provocative than a statue in the park'. Actually for the most part this was close to the truth, but it made the inclusion of the pictures seem all the more gratuitous. Short was dubbed 'Crazy Clare' or 'Killjoy Clare'; the picture researchers were ordered into the archives to seek out any unflattering photographs of the MP. The newspaper's editorial team was well aware that Short's bill had no chance of becoming law, so it turned the incident into a publicity drive. The star of its campaign for press freedom was its current favourite, Samantha Fox – a new Mary Millington, but with a much bigger bust and a thong to conceal what remained of her modesty – who had first posed topless back in 1983, just a few days after her sixteenth birthday. The fact that Fox's breasts had been (flimsily) concealed in newspaper photographs prior to the date on which it became legal for her to have sex was all that an impartial observer needed to know about the newspaper branch of the porn industry.[23]

Despite its triumph over Clare Short, the incident was not without its dangers for the *Sun*. The scoffing attitude of Tory MPs – and a subsequent intervention in support of page three by the party chairman

Norman Tebbit – sent out a signal to would-be rivals of the news-paper. Having laughed at the idea that the sight of semi-naked women at the family breakfast table could adversely affect the outlook of children, the governing party would find it difficult to legislate against any publication which decided to outbid the *Sun* by pushing the boat further out into the pornographic swamp. Six months after Short presented her bill for the first time, the *Sunday Sport* duly hit the newsstands. Although it was issued in tabloid format, this was a (poor quality) soft-porn magazine masquerading as a newspaper. Its publisher was David Sullivan, the one-time lover and enthusiastic business associate of Mary Millington. Although the *Sport* made only a meagre contribution to his coffers, in time Sullivan's publishing interests would make him one of Britain's richest men and chairman of Birmingham City football club. In keeping with its self-proclaimed role as a 'family newspaper', the *Sun* refused to emulate the fleshy exposure of the *Sport*. However, its advice column ('Dear Deirdre') became increasingly open-minded, publishing amateuristic ventures into the world of erotic literature even if the 'problems' described were obviously made up.*

After the 1987 general election, when Labour lost for the third time in a row, an interesting article appeared in *The Times*. The author, Tony Blair, had taken the trouble to vote for Short's bill – unlike the majority of his colleagues, who had found other things to do on the day of the debate. In the article Blair was addressing the same topic, but unlike Short he concentrated his fire on the *Star*. This was a prudent precaution, since the proprietor of *The Times* also had the honour of owning the *Sun*. Nevertheless, the fact that Blair's critical reflections were allowed to appear quite regularly in *The Times* suggests that Rupert Murdoch already regarded the young MP as a person who should be kept onside. In this article Blair established an explicit connection between sexual exploitation and politics, arguing that the tabloids exemplified the Thatcherite ethos of '"grab what you can, when you can"'. 'Like the new generation of city slickers hankering after the latest BMW, Blair thundered, the tabloids were 'all about self, greed, acquisition, whether of people or of things'.[24]

---

* To take a random example, one reader complained that his Italian girlfriend 'with the body of a goddess, perfect breasts and great all-over tan' was making his life a misery with her incessant demands for sex. 'I don't want to finish with her because I love her,' he confided, 'and I can't tell my mates because they would laugh'; *Sun*, 8 November 2003.

Blair's well-argued case led to the conclusion that the existing Press Council should be beefed up into a statutory body 'armed with real powers'. A regulatory authority of this kind could at least act as 'a brake on the more obvious excesses', which also included gross intrusions into private matters and stories which were just 'plain fabrication'. Unfortunately, after Blair became Labour leader in 1994 the proposal to establish a more potent press watchdog slipped from his mind.

On the eve of the 2005 general election, the *Sun* published a fawning interview with Blair, but instead of discussing policy it focused on a throwaway remark of the prime minister about being a 'five times a night' man. The headline was 'Why Size Matters', and the text explained that 'Cherie says that Tony needs a big one . . . a big majority'. Blair, who had made the notion of 'respect' into a key campaigning theme, lodged no complaint against this demeaning treatment, even with the existing, toothless press regulatory body.[25]

III

Although by the mid-1980s most Labour supporters could agree that the *Sun* was an influential pestilence, it still took political courage to speak out against its most famous feature. Those who did so, like Short and Blair, ran the risk of being associated with the campaigning housewife Mary Whitehouse (1910–2001). This was indeed an embarrassment for anyone who wanted to retain a shred of credibility on the left. If Mrs Whitehouse had not existed, the left would have tried to invent someone very like her; but they could hardly have improved on the original. Whitehouse was the moral equivalent of Margaret Thatcher; like the prime minister, her sense of irony was as underdeveloped as her faculty of artistic appreciation, and she was equally certain that her views were always right. A former schoolteacher, Whitehouse had set up the National Viewers and Listeners Association (National VALA) in 1965. In the abstract this was a worthy initiative which aimed to make broadcasters accountable to their licence-payers. But although Whitehouse was a publicist of genius, too often she seemed anxious to promote herself rather than her cause. She claimed to abhor contemporary media mores, but became a regular on downmarket television chat shows and loved being photographed in celebrity company. Only an inflated sense of self-importance could have prompted her to write three separate autobiographies.* This fixation with transient, worldly things was a sign of frailty in Mary, who claimed to have been charged with her mission by the ultimate A-lister – God himself.

In themselves, her combined traits of egomania and excessive religiosity were sufficient to make Whitehouse a divisive figure. If British broadcasting was really in the parlous state that she described, National VALA required a leader who could maximise support for a drive to clean it up. But Whitehouse revelled in her notoriety, except when the impudent David Sullivan started publishing a magazine called *Whitehouse* – featuring a former prostitute who changed her name to Mary Whitehouse for her modelling assignments – and set up the Whitehouse Society in order to campaign on behalf of pornography. In 1974 the real Mary tried to instigate a prosecution for criminal libel.[26] Again like Margaret Thatcher, she despised the idea of consensus. She was undertaking a personal crusade, and if her actions served to augment enemy ranks, this simply made the task into a more fitting trial of her Christian faith.

Mrs Whitehouse certainly felt there was no point seeking an accommodation with the British libertarian Left. In her eyes, the increasing sexualisation of British society was a major element in a covert attempt to undermine traditional values. The agents of the left had infiltrated the schools and polluted the classrooms with lessons which were specifically designed to promote premature sexual activity in the young. They had also realised the indoctrinating power of television, and harnessed it to corrupt the morals of unsuspecting adults. In Whitehouse's view, the British Establishment itself was gradually falling under the influence of subversives. Hence the chief enemy obviously had to be the state-funded BBC rather than its commercial rival ITV. None of the BBC's output was safe from her censure. She even discovered moral impurity in *Doctor Who*, a programme which invariably portrayed good triumphing over alien evil.[27]

Whitehouse's ideological fanaticism made it difficult even for intelligent right-wingers to take her seriously. In 1974 the barrister Geoffrey Robertson heard her elaborating on her thesis at a meeting of Young Conservatives; her attempts to link pornography and communism, Robertson noted, 'met with their free-market mirth'.[28] Ironically, the people

---

* The title of the first – '*Who Does She Think She Is?*' (1971) – gives the flavour of their contents.

who were most inclined to agree with her were members of the left who
fantasised that the sexual revolution was transforming the country in
accordance with their ideals; the fact that Whitehouse shared their analysis
should have given them sufficient reason for a rethink. Others were more
clear-sighted. Just before the fall of the Heath government, for example,
the Home Secretary Robert Carr had complained that relaxation of
censorship 'has been used not to broaden freedom but to exploit for
commercial gain'.[29] In January 1976, the (pre-Murdoch) *Times* published
an editorial which denounced pornographers as 'sick-minded commercial men who sell images of hatred, and particularly of hatred of women,
for vast profit'.[30] In 1980, when the House of Lords debated the Williams
Report, Lord Nugent of Guildford noted that 'pornography is being
exploited today by powerful financial interests, both national and international'.[31] But Whitehouse's conspiracy theory was integral to her world
view, and only towards the end of her life did she show signs of wavering.
In the last of her autobiographies she wrote that 'It has been the attack
of materialism upon the quality of character and upon faith, which has
permeated the thinking and affected the actions of the West, an attack
that has soaked deep into the essence of how we live and think.'[32] Even
then, Whitehouse was always capable of blaming the rise of materialism
on the followers of Karl Marx rather than Adam Smith.

Whitehouse's chastened mood probably reflected the disappointment
of her hopes for a moral renaissance under the leadership of Mrs
Thatcher. The first Thatcher government might have earned some gratitude from the moralists when it ignored the Williams report, but it
had no intention of arresting the market forces which were removing
vestigial Victorian values in this sphere. A few months after Thatcher
became prime minister, a Plymouth bookshop manager was sacked for
refusing to display lucrative soft-porn magazines.[33] As Geoffrey
Robertson noted, despite declarations of mutual admiration between
Whitehouse and the prime minister, in practice the Conservative governments after 1979 'encouraged sexual profiteering – from the groaning
porn shelves in every corner newsagent to dirty talk on phone lines
leased from the privatized British Telecom'.[34] In practice, Mary
Whitehouse was more distant from Thatcherite values than Mary
Millington – a brazen tax evader whose brother acknowledged that
'Her main aim in life, towards the end, was to make as much money
as possible.'[35] At least Thatcher had consistently opposed the extension of homosexual rights. Early in 1993 Whitehouse extracted a

promise from John Major that he had 'no plans' to alter the existing age of consent for homosexuals. Soon after, Parliament voted to reduce it from twenty-one to eighteen.[36]

Although Whitehouse's influence began to wane in the late 1970s, it would be a mistake to underestimate the popularity of her views in the middle of the decade. In January 1975 Whitehouse herself claimed a membership of 15,000 for National VALA, and although this figure was dwarfed by the muster roll of other voluntary organisations like the RSPCA, every member of National VALA was a redoubtable campaigner, fizzing with zealous indignation. It was little wonder that successive home secretaries tried to deflect Whitehouse's protestations with polite words, and anyone who accepted the post of BBC director-general knew that angry visitations were part of the package. It might have been difficult to secure convictions in the courts, but in the mid-1970s many senior figures within the legal system shared Whitehouse's mixture of social conservatism and muddle-headedness. In the same month as the Millington and McKinney cases, for example, Nottingham magistrates ruled on the public display of the Sex Pistols' album *Never Mind the Bollocks* in the window of the King's Street branch of Virgin Records. The chairman of magistrates would have liked to convict the shop, but he was bound by the terms of the legislation. However, he was not gagged, and he recorded a howl of impotent rage against the infernal album, telling the court that he deplored 'the vulgar exploitation of the worst instincts of human nature for the purpose of commercial profit'.[37] The sentiment was admirable, but how the word 'bollocks' could exemplify 'the worst instincts of human nature' was a mystery to everyone except devoted followers of Mary Whitehouse, who believed that bad language was as corrupting as pornography or on-screen violence.

In later years Mrs Whitehouse's attacks often rebounded on her, giving free publicity to the intended victim. She tended to concentrate her fire on literary productions which married sex and politics. *The Romans in Britain*, for example, was an allegorical critique of Britain's more recent role in Northern Ireland. When the play was performed at the National Theatre in 1981 Whitehouse herself was not in attendance, but she was enraged by an eyewitness account and launched a prosecution for gross indecency. In fact, the play was a less subtle and far less entertaining version of Aristophanes' *Lysistrata* – a play which never raised Whitehouse's hackles, presumably because the issues were less topical. The prosecution raised attendances for a time, but after

the case ended in shambolic failure *The Romans in Britain* disappeared
from the stage for more than two decades.[38] It was very much like the
earlier attempt to suppress *Lady Chatterley's Lover*; the only way ordinary people could possibly be depraved and corrupted by the content
was if it was drawn to their attention, and the best way of doing this
was to prosecute it. In 1987 Whitehouse acted as an unwitting publicist for a more noteworthy production, Tony Harrison's long poem *v*.
Channel 4 had broadcast it, but the audience was relatively small. But
when the programme was attacked by Whitehouse and her ally, the
Times columnist Ronald Butt, it was guaranteed much wider circulation. The *Independent* newspaper published the poem in full.

Although Whitehouse's pronouncements were rarely free from
absurdity, she was capable of being at least half-right, even on crucial
issues. She had never been against sex education in itself – indeed,
before her rise to media stardom she had given lessons in the subject.
But by the time of her death there was a case for scrapping this part
of the curriculum entirely – on the safe assumption that pupils were
already better informed than their teachers – and using those hours to
teach children the connection between loving relationships and respect
for self and others. Nostalgic commentators spoke of childhood as an
age of innocence which ought to be protected. There was no way of
submitting this proposition to a fair test, in a country where sex was
slapped in the face of all youngsters from the time they had any
comprehension of their surroundings. Few newsagents bothered to
conceal pornographic magazines from the eyes of the young – there
was little point, when scantily clad models appeared on so many glossy
publications, covering subjects from cars to computers. Advertisements
for lingerie were a regular feature on giant billboards. By 2001 high
street shops were selling sexually provocative clothing for very young
girls. Melanie Phillips wrote bluntly of a 'culture of paedophilia'
emerging in Britain.[39] It was difficult to counter her argument and
ironic that those who dressed their youngsters like experienced volup-
tuaries were often the same people who would happily commit arson
if they felt a 'sex monster' had moved into their neighbourhood.
Prominent retail outlets like Asda and Next recognised the profit potential of lacy black underwear for nine-year-olds, and T-shirts aimed at
even younger girls which proclaimed, 'So many boys, so little time'.[40]
Blatant sexual imagery undoubtedly helped to make children more
conscious of body image, so that anorexia became almost as serious a

hazard as obesity among prepubescent girls. In 2004 doctors were told to look out for symptoms of eating disorders in girls as young as eight.[41] Constant exposure to sexual images, in short, was causing children both physical and emotional harm, on any reasonable definition of that contestable term. For most other people – even those who deliberately sought out depictions of sex in magazines, newspapers and the Internet – the whole subject was in danger of becoming a deadly bore.[42]

IV

If she had ever wanted a break from her attempt to clean up British TV, Mrs Whitehouse could have spared some time for the denizens of the House of Commons. In any assemblage of more than 600 people there is sure to be a sprinkling of unorthodox individuals. But certain aspects of a British MP's life – long hours, loneliness, a yearning to be loved – readily lend themselves to modes of conduct which can give rise to scandal. Given the obsessive interest of the media, the amazing thing is that politics continues to attract people who are neither monogamous nor monkish.

In the period since 1975 the first incident to hit the headlines was also the most sensational, involving the leader of the Liberal Party. Although there was little chance that Jeremy Thorpe could ever have become prime minister, he had played a central role in his party's revival and could have held high government office if the Liberals had helped the Conservatives build a coalition government after the inconclusive general election of February 1974. Nothing was ever proved against Thorpe; it is not even certain that he had an affair with his accuser, Norman Scott, who was an unstable character prone to fantasy. But Thorpe's career was finished by the disclosure in May 1976 of a letter in which the MP had referred to Scott as 'Bunnies'. He resigned from the Liberal leadership the following day. Three years later he stood trial for conspiracy to murder Scott; his acquittal left many observers unconvinced.

It is often argued that the British media persistently intrudes into the private lives of politicians because – unlike many of their continental counterparts, for example – their readers have an insatiable appetite for sex stories, particularly when they are obtained without consent. But this interpretation downplays the creative role of the British media in fostering that interest in the first place and providing it with a plausible justification. Obscure MPs hounded by the media in the

coming years had reason to regret the Thorpe affair. To the satisfaction of the media, at least, the incident had reinforced the lesson of
the Profumo scandal in the previous decade, establishing a clear connection between politics, sex and the public interest.

During the 1970s, though, media intrusion was relatively restrained.
At Westminster rumours often circulated about the private conduct of
Thorpe and his fellow party leaders, Edward Heath and Harold Wilson.
Heath never married, which was easily explained since he held most
of his fellow human beings in roughly equal contempt. But others were
happy to put a very different construction on his preference for music
and yachting over the delights of matrimony. Wilson, by contrast, was
alleged to have conducted at least one serious extramarital affair.
According to Mary Millington, even this was not enough to satisfy the
predatory prime minister. On her testimony, Wilson had met and
bedded her (somewhat roughly) on the night of 27 February 1975, in
a Glasgow hotel. Earlier that day the cabinet had held a heated discussion about the EEC referendum, but even a prolonged argument on
that vexatious topic could hardly have affected Wilson's judgement so
adversely as to make him work off his frustrations with one of the
most controversial and indiscreet women in Britain.[43]

Whatever the truth of such stories, Wilson and Heath's successors
as party leaders, Margaret Thatcher and James Callaghan, were never
likely to be accused of masking seething libidos. The next big scandal,
which became public knowledge shortly after the 1983 general election, involved Cecil Parkinson (born 1931), who had overseen the
victorious Conservative campaign as party chairman. Mrs Thatcher
had wanted to reward the affable Parkinson by making him foreign
secretary, but when he confided that he had made his secretary pregnant these plans were put on hold.

Politicians who are tempted to stray from the marital fold fall into
two categories: some opt for affairs with people who share their obsession with party intrigue, while others are attracted by the prospect of
casual encounters with those who have no interest in the 'Westminster
village'. According to the satirical magazine *Private Eye*, the latter
approach was taken in February 1981 by the left-wing Labour MP
Allan Roberts (1943–90). It was alleged that Roberts had attended
Buddy, a notorious Berlin club, equipped with a studded dog collar.
He had voluntarily subjected himself to a whipping from a fellow
reveller sporting an SS uniform.[44] Roberts denied the story, although

he had certainly sought hospital treatment for suspicious-looking weals. Notwithstanding lingering doubts, he remained an MP until his death. Cecil Parkinson, by contrast, was forced to resign as trade secretary when details of his affair with Sara Keays became public knowledge, and although he returned to the cabinet after the 1987 general election his prospects were permanently blighted.

Parkinson's story was a media sensation because of his prominent role within the Conservative Party. The dilemmas faced by everyone involved would be recognised by many Britons; indeed, there were complications which demanded that the story be handled with special sensitivity. But the next sexual scandal to affect the 'party of the family' was very different. Harvey Proctor, Conservative MP for Billericay, was widely disliked as a representative of a new breed of hard-line Tory MPs. In April 1987 his flat was raided by the Metropolitan Police; the visit resulted in four charges of gross indecency, which he later admitted in court. Instead of asking people in fascist uniforms to whip him, Proctor had paid rent boys (some of them, unknown to him, under the age of consent) to submit to a spanking.[45] To opponents of the Conservative Party at the time, his case was of genuine national importance although he was hardly ministerial material. Apart from illustrating the yawning gulf between Thatcherite rhetoric and practice on the subject of personal morality, it also seemed to confirm a link between extreme right-wing politics and sexual exploitation.

Oddly enough, the Proctor case came to light at a time when the Thatcher government was demonstrating a much more constructive attitude on sexual matters. In November 1986 – just a few months after the disgraceful attack on Clare Short's page three bill – the cabinet established a subcommittee on HIV and AIDS. The government's serious intent was confirmed by the fact that the deputy prime minister, Willie Whitelaw, took an active part in proceedings. During the following year a series of advertisements was produced to advise the public on the causes of infection and the ways it could be avoided. Edwina Currie, who had become a junior minister at health since voting against Short's bill, later hailed it as 'one of the most successful campaigns in the field of public health that this nation had ever seen'. Research showed that hardly anyone had been offended by the government's advertisements. However, a small minority was outraged. James Anderton, the Chief constable of Greater Manchester Police, claimed that practising homosexuals were 'swirling around in a human cesspit of their own making'. In his view, instead of telling them how to make love safely, the government should be trying to stop their activities. Like Mary Whitehouse, Anderton believed that he was speaking with the authority of God. From a less lofty perch, the *Sun* merely claimed that the prattling policeman had spoken on behalf of most ordinary Britons.[46]

Anderton's outburst created a serious dilemma for the government. On the one hand, its AIDS advertising was consciously aimed at educating male homosexuals, who were most at risk of infection. Yet in carefully avoiding a moralistic line, ministers could be said to be condoning homosexuality; and this, to campaigners like Whitehouse, was much the same as actively promoting it. At the time the right-wing tabloids were spouting a stream of distorted stories about Labour local authorities which spent a small proportion of their budgets on educational material about homosexuality. This was merely part of a wider tabloid campaign to discredit local government, which was continuing to resist Thatcherism. But for Whitehouse and her allies, any evidence that homosexuality was being promoted – particularly among children – triggered the familiar fantasy that left-wingers were using unconventional sex to sow the seeds of revolution.

In order to achieve the dual purpose of saving their AIDS campaign while retaining their reputation as guardians of the family, the Conservatives adopted a crude stratagem. Before the 1987 general election Whitehouse's eccentric ally the Earl of Halsbury introduced a bill in the House of Lords which would have prevented local authorities from promoting homosexuality. Although Mrs Thatcher was known to be sympathetic, the measure attracted insufficient support in the House of Commons. But after the election it was suddenly revived as an amendment to one of the government's many local government bills. Even David Wilshire, the Tory MP who proposed the amendment at committee stage, was 'flabbergasted' when the minister, Michael Howard, suddenly offered government support. After all, the measure (which became notorious as Clause 28) was a legal nonsense which would be difficult to enforce since it was so difficult to distinguish material that 'promoted' homosexuality from well-meaning advice on the subject, or classic literary depictions of same-sex relationships. Indeed the government spokesman in the Lords had said as much in response to Halsbury's original bill. But opposition MPs were caught off guard and offered minimal resistance.[47]

Ministers might have thought Clause 28 was a harmless sop to

divinely inspired crusaders like Anderton and Whitehouse, and significantly Michael Howard made sure that material relating to AIDS was
exempt from the terms of the legislation (thus making it even less
coherent). But members of Britain's gay community were understandably infuriated. The 1967 Sexual Offences Act had (partially) legalised
sex between men over the age of twenty-one. But since that time, as
we have seen, remaining restrictions for heterosexuals had been whittled away by powerful sections of the media and other commerical
interests. By contrast, the Whitehouse lobby had utilised every remaining
weapon in its battle to discredit homosexuality and make sure the
existing laws were rigorously enforced. In November 1976 the magazine *Gay News* published a poem which suggested that Jesus had not
been the most robust of heterosexuals. Mrs Whitehouse launched a
private prosecution under the blasphemy laws, and Denis Lemon,
editor of *Gay News*, was convicted. He was given a suspended sentence
and a fine. The circulation of *Gay News* (founded 1972) was about
20,000 – not much, considering the scarcity of direct competition at
the time, but rather more than the membership of National VALA.
While Whitehouse offered her thanksgiving prayers to God for the
verdict – but surely if God had taken an active interest in the case he
would have been hoping for a slightly stiffer sentence – she might have
wondered if her action would have the slightest effect in diverting the
straying 20,000 back to the path of righteousness.

Yet the *Gay News* case was not the most spectacular instance of a
prosecution which publicised unorthodox activities that otherwise would
have remained obscure. In December 1990 fifteen defendants were found
guilty of a variety of offences after a police operation codenamed Spanner.
The accused included a lawyer, a retired pig breeder, an ice-cream seller,
a missile designer, a retired fire officer, an antiques restorer and a lay
preacher. Some assiduous detectives had stumbled across an advertisement which this miscellaneous group had placed in a magazine. Further
inquiries revealed videotaped evidence of an orgy which made Allan
Roberts's alleged adventures in Berlin seem like a meeting of National
VALA. Several participants had undergone sexual torture – at their own
request and, apparently, very much to their satisfaction. In court these
voluntary victims were found guilty along with their accomplices. The
maximum sentence handed out was four and a half years.

The prosecution was certainly justified, since underage boys and
animals were involved. It was thus wrong to suggest, as some commen-

tators did, that Operation Spanner was a complete waste of police
time, on the grounds that the activities had been private (at least until
the court case earned them widespread coverage). Yet if the police had
paid equal attention to similarly dubious heterosexual orgies, the British
judicial system would have been overwhelmed. Thus the case only re-
affirmed that, given the radical disparity between moral norms as
reflected in law and the real attitudes of many Britons in the last quarter
of the twentieth century, prosecutions could only be launched on a
selective basis. The result of Operation Spanner and the fate of Harvey
Proctor proved that the chances of facing a jury because of sexual
activity were infinitely greater for homosexuals.

V

In hindsight, the scandals of the Thatcher years added up to no more
than the kind of indiscretions which could be expected in a heavily
sexualised age. Indeed, on the face of it Britain's legislators could still
be regarded as a fairly abstemious group, given their unusual working
conditions. But there were plenty of stories which the media missed at
the time. The hopelessly tangled private life of Alan Clark, the reckless, charismatic Conservative MP for Plymouth Sutton, would never
have featured in his obituaries if he had not decided to publish the
first volume of his diaries in 1993. Edwina Currie's affair with John
Major in the late 1980s hit the headlines when her own jottings were
serialised in 2002 – five years after Major had been voted out of office.

The protracted downfall of Major's government is usually traced to
events which happened after he led the Conservatives to their fourth
successive electoral victory, in 1992. That result looked like a personal
mandate for the prime minister rather than a parting gift from the voters
to his predecessor Margaret Thatcher. However, before the end of 1994
the Major government was in terminal decline, waiting for the electorate
to finish its miserable existence. The Conservative Party's reputation for
economic competence had been blown apart in September 1992 by Britain's
ejection from the Exchange Rate Mechanism of the European Monetary
System. On its own this debacle might have proved fatal to the
Conservatives at the next election; but the party's integrity was also
shredded after 1992 by a succession of financial and sexual scandals.

In fact, the first link in the chain of events which led to the association between Conservatives and sleaze was laid down while Mrs Thatcher

was still in office. In December 1989 David Mellor (born 1949), then a junior Home Office minister, was provoked by intrusive newspaper stories to warn that the British press was 'drinking in the last chance saloon'. The following June a Home Office report recommended much tougher regulation of the press, on the lines suggested by Tony Blair back in 1987. Actually, the new body which emerged in 1991 (the Press Complaints Commission) was no great improvement on its supine pre-decessor the Press Council. But Mellor's sabre-rattling had been noted by the tabloid press. The *Sun* in particular hoped for a chance to strike back because Mellor had explicitly singled out its notorious coverage of the Hillsborough disaster as the main evidence for the need to tighten restrictions on the press. This example was more dangerous to the tabloids because the victims of Hillsborough had been ordinary people, and thus more likely to win public sympathy than celebrities like Elton John and the England cricket captain Mike Gatting, who had also been subjected to gratuitous intrusion in recent years.

In April 1990 Mellor was promoted to the cabinet, as secretary of state for national heritage. His advancement hardly placed him at the epicentre of power, but his new rank did give the tabloids a greater incen-tive to cut him down if he stepped out of line. Shortly after the 1992 general election the *Sunday People* revealed that he had been having an affair with an actress who had performed in pornographic films. This much was true, but many of the embellishing stories were fabricated. They were published in order to make Mellor – who had previously been dubbed the 'minister for Fun' – to reflect the nature of his official respon-sibilities – into an object of ridicule, to make his position untenable just in case tabloid readers were prepared to forgive the bare fact of his infi-delity. Thus the *Sun* falsely claimed that Mellor had made love to his mistress while wearing the shirt of his favourite football team, Chelsea.

This lie could have been counter-productive, adding an endearing touch to Mellor's priggish public persona. But the minister had himself tried to manipulate the media by arranging for his family to be photographed in an unconvincing tableau of unity and mutual forgiveness. He had already offered to resign, but received strong backing from his close friend John Major. However, while the tabloids were still trying to oust Mellor on the basis of sexual tittle-tattle, it emerged that he had enjoyed a holiday in Spain as the guest of someone with connections to the Palestine Liberation Organisation (PLO). It was doubtful whether this friendship could adversely affect Mellor's current ministerial duties, but it was now

obvious that the tabloids would never rest until they had scalped their
enemy, and the affair was becoming a serious distraction for a government which was in trouble for other reasons. On 23 September 1992 –
just a week after Britain's ignominious ejection from the ERM – Mellor
counterattacked, asking, 'Who decides who is to be a member of the
British Cabinet – the Prime Minister or the editor of the *Daily Mail*?'
There could only be one answer, at a time when the Conservatives were
desperate to appease even fair-weather friends in the media. Two days
after his show of defiance Mellor resigned.[48]

In a subsequent parliamentary statement Mellor compared the atmosphere created by the tabloids to life in a totalitarian state and complained
about 'an alternative criminal justice system, run by the media'.[49] The
tabloids dismissed the speech as a display of sour grapes, but the fallen
minister had raised an interesting point. Sex was proving subversive after
all, but not in the way which idealists had hoped for. In the hands of
an irresponsible media it was stifling individual freedom not increasing
it. Ministerial fortunes now depended on the dictatorial whims of newspaper editors; and since it was increasingly difficult to dislodge them for
professional incompetence, unconventional sex was the best way to bring
them down. The stock response was that those who sought public office
had tacitly accepted that their lives could no longer be private. But people
who had no connection with politics, or even with the entertainment
industry in its various forms, could now expect a visit from a journalist
if their sexual preferences were deemed to be sufficiently titillating. If an
unaccountable press could harass a minister and his family night and
day, bugging telephones and bribing 'witnesses', it was the democratic
system itself which seemed to be in the last chance saloon. With Mellor's
head in their trophy cabinet, the press proprietors had little to fear from
Britain's legislators, who had to reconsider their views on tighter regulation in case the newspapers published material relating to their own
sexual exploits. Despite a well-argued report by a Home Office committee
headed by the eminent lawyer Sir David Calcutt, the government decided
that the press could continue to regulate itself.[50]

John Major, who had staked his reputation on Britain's continued
membership of the ERM, remained in office after the policy had failed;
his discredited chancellor Norman Lamont survived until May 1993
despite media innuendo about his own private life. By that time David
Mellor had offered his talents to the media – not so much a case of
poacher turned gamekeeper, as fox turned huntsman. As a BBC radio

presenter, his tendency to be tactless and opinionated was no longer a handicap. Few people had ever questioned his ministerial aptitude, and many members of the arts establishment had rallied to his support when the vultures of the press descended. A similar showing had saved *Lady Chatterley* from the censors; but twenty-five years later there was no chance that it could keep David Mellor in the cabinet.

At the 1993 Conservative Party conference Major decided to rally his wavering supporters by calling for a 'return to the old core values'. He had been searching for a theme which would distract his ageing audience from the government's problems. Despite all the subsequent ridicule of 'Back to Basics', it is easy to see why the new slogan was considered a good idea at the time – it was sure to raise a cheer in the hall and hopefully rouse spirits among the party faithful throughout the country. However, Major could have chosen his words more adroitly when he elaborated on his chosen theme. He referred to the need for 'self-discipline' and 'responsibility for yourself and your family'.[51] Although he was trying to avoid the impression of preaching about sexual morality – for reasons which became clear years later – listeners could be forgiven if they regarded this thorny subject as an integral part of his programme for national regeneration.

Back in 1986, when Major had been an under-secretary in the Department of Health and Social Security, he had attended the government's committee on AIDS. According to Edwina Currie, at one point he stressed the importance of defining one's terms. What, for example, did 'promiscuity' mean? Currie's contribution to the ensuing discussion arose from her memory of student life in the 1960s; in order to be promiscuous, she ventured, one had to have slept with more than five people per year.[52]*

By a curious coincidence, one of Currie's oldest political friends was Steven Norris, who had attended the same school. At the time of Back to Basics Norris was a junior minister in the Department of Transport. According to a story which broke at the end of the 1993 conference, he was also enjoying the simultaneous favours of five mistresses. As usual, the story contained serious distortions, but there was sufficient

---

* In 1994 the character played by Andie MacDowell in the successful British film *Four Weddings and a Funeral* owned up to having slept with thirty-three men. The scriptwriters evidently calculated that this would make her look experienced, but not shop-soiled; as the character put it, her list of conquests was 'Less than Madonna, more than Princess Di – I hope.'

truth in it to make Major's reference to self-discipline seem infelicitous
– especially since the former minister Alan Clark had only recently
divulged his own serial adultery (with three members of the same family)
in the first published volume of his *Diaries*. Norris survived the scandal
probably because he was a genial politician who had forged many
parliamentary friendships. But if he had been conducting a monogamous relationship with a man, his fate would have been very different.

Just after the 1992 general election the Liberal Democrat leader
Paddy Ashdown had given a masterclass in political survival in the
face of a ravenous media. Knowing that a story about Parkinsonian
activities with his secretary was about to break, he made a straightforward admission and was rewarded with a boost in public esteem.
However, by comparison most Tory MPs were at a relative disadvantage. Ashdown knew that his short-lived affair would create a sensation,
even among the tabloids which constantly assured their readers that
the Liberal Democrats were politically irrelevant. But when Tory MPs
were involved there was no way of knowing where, or how heavily,
the press would strike. The most obscure backbencher could be exposed
for behaviour which was odd but innocent, and the story justified as
'in the national interest' because the MP belonged to the governing
party. Thus, for example, David Ashby, MP for Leicester North-West,
was drawn into an unsuccessful libel action against the *Sunday Times*,
which claimed that he had shared a bed with a male friend on holiday.
Ashby argued that this had been a money-saving arrangement. Later
he was deselected by his constituency party.

Once Ashby had served his purpose as a bit player in the developing
media narrative about Tory sleaze, the pack moved on to its next victim.
But the incident had caused considerable personal distress for Ashby and
his family. In such a climate complications in the private lives of politicians were always likely to escalate into devastating personal tragedies.
The Ashby 'scandal' broke in January 1994; the same month the wife
of Lord Caithness, another junior minister at transport, committed suicide.
Caithness had just admitted that he was having an affair. Rather than
persuading the tabloids to pause, this catastrophe only acted as a stim-
ulant. A few days later Rupert Murdoch's *News of the World* revealed
that Gary Tucker, a Tory backbencher who had never previously figured
in the national media, had fathered a 'love child'.[53]

On 9 January 1994 the Tory MP Stephen Milligan had joined in
the Westminster tea room gossip about the Caithness tragedy.[54] Within

a month, Milligan was dead. This time there was no tearful spouse to be persecuted by the press; the unmarried Milligan had died from accidental asphyxiation during a solitary sex game. The media were alerted to the discovery of the body and the circumstances surrounding the death with remarkable speed; Milligan's father had not been notified by police before he heard the news on the radio.[55] To compound the list of ghastly coincidences, before Milligan had even been buried the House of Commons voted on Edwina Currie's proposal to reduce the age of consent for homosexuals to sixteen. Not surprisingly, the motion was defeated; in the frenzied context of those days in February 1994 it is remarkable that MPs overwhelmingly accepted a compromise. During the debate the bibulous Sir Nicholas Fairbairn interrupted a speech by the shadow home secretary Tony Blair to remind the House that 'putting your penis in another man's arsehole' was not 'natural'.[56]

The new consenting age of eighteen came too late to save the career of the Conservative MP Michael Brown, a junior whip who had enjoyed a holiday with a twenty-year-old man. He resigned immediately, rather than trying to hold on while Parliament completed its deliberations on the bill which would legalise such relationships. Brown was exposed by the *News of the World*, which had recently ended the careers of the chief of the Defence Staff Sir Peter Harding, and Hartley Booth, Mrs Thatcher's successor as MP for Finchley, thanks to 'kiss-and-tell' allegations. The paper's new and youthful acting editor, Piers Morgan, had promised Murdoch he would freshen its image and 'break more big stories', yet he maintained the familiar formula of muckraking and chequebook journalism. After printing the Brown story, he enthused that 'We're on a roll and it feels fantastic.' Apparently Murdoch agreed, making Morgan's appointment permanent in June 1994 with an annual salary of £125,000. At the time, the prime minister's total remuneration was less than £90,000.[57] Labour's landslide victory in the 1997 general election meant that John Major was free to make more money in the private sector but new stories of sexual sleaze plagued him almost to the end. On 29 March 1997, for example, the chairman of the Scottish Conservative Party resigned after revelations about 'past indiscretions' in his personal life. In the election the party lost all of its remaining seats in Scotland, where it had returned twenty-one MPs as recently as 1983.

VI

'He lay flat on his back in his bed, not noticing the chill of the sheets, his body still warm with the feel of her, the muscles in his arms still carrying the imprint of her, where he had held her so long and so tight.'[58]

It could have been an extract from a Mills & Boon novel or a candidate for the *Literary Review*'s Bad Sex Award.* In fact it had come from the pen of Pasternak – not the acclaimed Boris, but his greatniece Anna, in cooperation with a former army officer, James Hewitt. It was from a book published in October 1994, briefly distracting the press from their pursuit of sleaze within the Conservative Party. In the prose style of romantic fiction, it purported to tell the true story of Hewitt's three-year relationship with the Princess of Wales.

Pasternak's *Princess in Love* was noteworthy for its format rather than the content, which could have appeared as a newspaper story if the *News of the World* had improved its £500,000 offer to Hewitt.[59] The public had been hearing about infidelity among junior members of the royal family for years. The difficulties in the marriage between Diana and Prince Charles had been laid bare in Andrew Morton's book *Diana: Her True Story*, which was published in June 1992. Six months later John Major announced that the couple were to separate. In the meantime the tabloid press had got hold of tape recordings which had apparently been picked up by amateur radio enthusiasts. On 23 August 1992 the *Sun* published selections from a conversation between Diana and her long-time friend James Gilbey, who repeatedly referred to the Princess of Wales as either 'darling' or 'squidgy'. A thirty-minute tape recording was made available to *Sun* readers on a special phone line. Those hoping to hear heavy breathing and lascivious language were disappointed, although in expressing her views on the royal family Diana deployed a range of invective which would have dismayed Mary Whitehouse.

The *Sun* scoop has been the subject of numerous conspiracy theories, and there can be little doubt that subterfuge was involved. The original

* This prize – set up in 1993 'to draw attention to the crude, tasteless, often perfunctory use of redundant passages of sexual description in the modern novel, and to discourage it' – was itself a sign of growing boredom with examples of the genre.

conversation had taken place in January 1989 – three and a half years before publication. The impression that royal telephones had been bugged by the secret services and private calls rebroadcast much later in the hope that a member of the public would pick them up was increased when another tape materialised shortly afterwards. Once again, the original recording had been made in the late 1980s. This time the speakers were the Prince of Wales and his mistress Camilla Parker-Bowles. Their conversation was much more racey. At one time people had joked that the Queen was so distant from ordinary life it was impossible to imagine her using a toilet. In the 'Camillagate' tape her son embarked on a light-hearted fantasy about being a tampon. This was the section that most people remembered, along with Prince Charles's claim that being in love with him was Mrs Parker-Bowles's 'great achievement'. However, as an example of romantic dialogue the tape knocked the efforts of Anna Pasternak into a cocked hat. The couple were clearly too besotted to bring the conversation to a close, and at one point Prince Charles declared that 'I'd suffer anything for you. That's love. It's the strength of love.'

At least the accounts of 'Squidgygate' and Camillagate were not accompanied by photographs. The Duchess of York was less fortunate, thanks to the telescopic lens. Already separated from the duke, in August 1992 the former Sarah Ferguson was caught canoodling with her financial adviser, the balding Texan businessman John Bryan. In the heat of St-Tropez she had wisely discarded much of her clothing, and she was bestowing affectionate kisses on Bryan's foot. Appearing in the press just a few days before the intercepted royal phone calls, the photographs conveyed less complicated emotions. The duchess had been quite deeply involved with a previous American lover, but according to a 'friend', 'With John, it was more a case of having sex for the sake of having sex.'[60] The *Daily Mirror*, which published the pictures, was elated; its circulation rose by around 500,000 on the days when the story was running.[61]

'Fun-loving Fergie' had thus made it official: the last bastion of propriety had been stormed, and lust was at large within the royal family. But while the duchess had caused general embarrassment in 1987 through her enthusiastic participation in the televised *It's A Royal Knockout!*, her toe-sucking antics in 1992 actually brought the monarchy into closer contact with a nation which was obsessed with sex. The worst cases of excess remained hidden, to be investigated by journalists like Nick Davies, who was left feeling 'like an outsider in my own country' after researching a series of articles in 1993. On a subsequent investigative journey Davies encountered two boy prostitutes, aged no more than thirteen, who related their experiences over a meal at McDonald's in Nottingham. One of the boys told Davies of the time when a customer who 'looked like a rich man' had given him £50 in return for 'hand relief'. This transaction had occurred when he was ten years old.[62]

If Nick Davies had read the newspapers of 1975, he might not have felt such a sense of recent moral decline. Child prostitution was probably equally common at that time – especially among youngsters who had decided to run away from home for one reason or another. Since then, people had become more willing to believe allegations concerning the sexual abuse of children – hence the easy acceptance of stories about rampant paedophilia in the English county of Cleveland (1987) and the Orkney Islands (1990). In the new climate inaccurate diagnoses of child abuse could be made by paediatricians too ready to dismiss innocent explanations for suspicious symptoms. Equally, there was a danger that people with a score to settle would suddenly come forward with false stories about abuse in the distant past. But when such testimony was persuasive enough to convince a jury, it underlined the fact that the systematic abuse of children was nothing new. In November 2001, for example, the 'pop impresario' Jonathan King was jailed for seven years for offences which dated back to the 1980s.* The Paedophile Information Exchange (PIE) had been set up in 1974 to campaign for a reduction in the age of consent, and the 1978 Protection of Children Act included special provisions which acknowledged the existing risks of abuse. Ten years later one of the numerous criminal justice Acts introduced during the years of Conservative rule made the possession (as opposed to the production and distribution) of child pornography an offence for the first time.

With paedophilia firmly established as the last taboo by the early 1990s, almost any other kind of activity could now be regarded as part of the mainstream. Publicly, the new mood was marked in May 1994 with the appearance of *Loaded* magazine. Apart from its sexual connotation, the title recalled Harry Enfield's Loadsamoney. It was a clever concept, appealing to young men who regarded themselves as lovable rogues, like the main characters in the popular comedy series

---

*In May 2007 a vicar was jailed for five and a half years for a string of sexual offences against boys, dating back to 1975. Although the Church of England had been warned on two separate occasions, nothing had been done to prevent the offender from working with children.

Men Behaving Badly (1992–8). Every month *Loaded* featured a semi-naked model on the front; and it was certainly a magazine which could be judged by its cover. The models never went quite as far as their hard-core counterparts, so copies could be bought without blushing at the local newsagent (which was more than could be said for the *Sport*, which produced a daily edition from October 1991). The textual material in *Loaded* had none of the pretentions of publications like *Playboy*; the articles were unlikely to overtax even the most gormless reader. In the wake of *Loaded* came a blizzard of tosh of a similar stripe. Some of the magazines, like *FHM*, already existed, and were simply relaunched in the more demeaning 'laddish' form. By the middle of 1996 *Loaded* had a circulation of 238,000 per monthly issue, while *FHM* cleared almost 200,000 copies. In combination, the readership of these two magazines alone was greater than the number of Labour Party members, at a time when Tony Blair's popularity was at its height.

The real genius of magazines like *Loaded* was that their celebration of sex was increasingly difficult to attack from the feminist flank. In some respects it was less explicit than *Cosmopolitan* – launched in Britain in 1972 – which by the early 1990s was invariably crammed with 'frank' hedonistic advice for its female readership. These magazines had a strangely symbiotic relationship, guaranteed to maximise sales: one genre told women how to please their men in bed so that they would never be unfaithful, while the other advised men on the best way to secure the services of a succession of women, all of whom would be trying their hardest to provide satisfactory bedroom service. A similar rationale explained the success of the Ann Summers sex shops, purveyors of lingerie and sex toys to the mildly adventurous. Starting in 1981, a network of stores gradually spread throughout the UK. Each new branch invariably opened to a fanfare of free publicity, thanks to the protests of offended local residents. Women also had their own version of *Men Behaving Badly* – the US import *Sex and the City*, with leading characters who exhibited a mixture of smugness and sleaze which would not have been tolerated if they had been men. Meanwhile younger girls were being introduced to the 'liberated' adult world by the enervating, manufactured Spice Girls, who provided advice on how to get 'what you really, really want' (sex). While their elders spoke of sexual allure as a means of 'empowerment', the fans of the group referred to 'girl power'. In practice, it amounted to the same thing.

With fears of AIDS subsiding, these attitudes meant that the average 'lad' was in heaven by the mid-1990s. No evening on the town could be complete without a visit to a strip club. In 1996 Peter Stringfellow (born 1940), son of a Sheffield steelworker, introduced table-dancing clubs into London. First established in the US in the early 1970s, table-dancing was the live equivalent of *Loaded*; as long as they paid, customers could expect a close-up view, but touching was supposedly forbidden and the artistes were instructed to retain a shred of clothing. However, over time the local laws which forbade more explicit displays were circumvented, and table-dancing gave way to even more intimate lap-dancing. Ironically, at least in part this was a result of the Thatcher government's attack on local authorities, which now regarded themselves as businesses rather than campaigning political bodies. Having a lap-dancing club in the locality had become a useful source of revenue rather than a reason for councillors to feel abashed.

Once the lads had exhausted their funds at the lap-dancing club, they could always stumble home to loll in front of the television with one last lager. In 1990 TV had been brought under the terms of the Obscene Publications Act, but this move was of dubious value since the Act had always been so difficult to enforce. Children were supposed to be protected from sexual content on television by a 9 o'clock 'watershed', but this was increasingly a token safeguard, since so many were now equipped with TV sets in their bedrooms. The advent of satellite television brought a new influx of 'adult' material which was almost impossible to regulate. In response, the terrestrial channels ran increasingly explicit programmes of their own. Female actresses in every 'challenging new drama series' were permitted to keep their clothes on, but only if the scripts really demanded it, and, increasingly, they didn't. Mary Whitehouse was particularly exercised by Channel 4's 1992 dramatisation of Mary Wesley's novel *The Camomile Lawn*, and a complaint was upheld by the Broadcasting Standards Council. But this was a rare victory for the social conservatives; in future, the fate of programmes would be decided by their viewing figures, not by any tendency to deprave and corrupt. In October 2004 a TV 'celebrity' show featured a female contestant – who had become famous only because of an alleged affair with the footballer David Beckham – giving energetic assistance to a sperm-donating boar.

If the crusade to clean up British life had turned into a gradual retreat punctuated by a few pyrrhic victories, by the time of her death in November 2001 Whitehouse's opponents had gained access to the moral equivalent of the hydrogen bomb. For pornographers, the combination of the credit card and the Internet offered limitless moneymaking potential. In accordance with the laws of the free market, the highest profits accrued to the sexual entrepreneurs who purveyed the most 'depraved' pictures. There was, of course, a risk of detection; but as the volume of material increased, the likelihood of prosecution diminished. For overstretched police forces, there was a danger that concentrating on one porn ring would allow others to go free. The advent of Internet porn also focused attention on the plight of abused children, further encouraging the existing assumption that adults were incapable of being harmed in the production of pornography. Thus, for example, the conviction of a Texan computer consultant in 2002 triggered Operation Ore – the investigation of more than 7,000 Britons who had paid to look at children being abused. By March 2005 there had been over 1,000 convictions but also at least thirty-three suicides. Those arrested included teachers, social workers, soldiers, surgeons and fifty police officers. Some suspects, like The Who's Pete Townshend, were merely cautioned after providing plausible explanations for their conduct.[63]

The proliferation of pornography on the Internet can be said to mark the death of sexual imagination; for a few dollars it gave consumers a chance to see their deepest-rooted fantasies being enacted in virtual reality. Those who preferred a more tangible realisation of their desires could now become citizens of the world, exploiting cheaper air travel to seek a small corner of the globe where the authorities might be persuaded to wink at their predatory predilections. In the mid-1970s high taxation had induced many Britons to join the brain drain. Now, low fares encouraged many of them to become sex tourists. As so often, it took a celebrity to draw attention to this increasingly common phenomenon. The most notorious example was Paul Gadd (born 1944), better known as Gary Glitter. In 1999 he was convicted on fifty-four charges of possessing child pornography and jailed for four months. Released early, he first tried Cuba before moving to Cambodia. Although he was never convicted of any crime in that country, he was permanently expelled in December 2002. In March 2006 he was convicted of sex offences in Vietnam and sentenced to three years in prison. Glitter's biggest hits in the early 1970s included *Do You Wanna Touch?* and *The Leader of the Gang* (1973). In 2006 he looked sure to be a social pariah after his release – one of the world's untouchables – but if not exactly a leader, he was certainly a member of a sizeable and ever-growing gang of Britons who sought a perverted retirement in sunnier climes.[64]

VII

When Tony Blair took office in 1997, he became the most moralistic
British prime minister since Gladstone. His 1987 article about sexual
exploitation had not been a stunt; his sincerity is suggested by the fact
that, on this rare occasion, he obviously wrote the piece himself. But
after becoming leader of the Labour Party in 1994 he thought it
prudent to reach an accommodation with Rupert Murdoch. To
symbolise his liberation from outdated prescriptions in the sexual sphere,
he appointed Alastair Campbell – who had once been a paid contributor to Fred West's favourite magazine *Forum* – as his director of
communications. Later, Blair's Labour Party would accept donations
from Richard Desmond, the proprietor after November 2000 of the
Daily Star, which had certainly not become more enlightened since
Blair had attacked it in his *Times* article. Although Desmond furiously
denied he was a pornographer, his companies also controlled magazines such as *Asian Babes, Horny Housewives* and *Big Ones*, as well
as some 'adult' satellite television channels.*

   Almost certainly, Blair would rather not have done business (even at
arm's length) with people who had profited from sexual exploitation.
But the boundaries of the acceptable had shifted dramatically since 1987,
effectively silencing the voices of complaint from both left and right. A
remarkable example came in the year of Labour's landslide victory, when
the most popular British film was *The Full Monty*. It was the story of
unemployed steelworkers from Peter Stringfellow's home town who take
up stripping as their way of making ends meet. The film cashed in on
the current popularity of male disrobers like the Chippendales, whose
antics embodied the fantasies of *Cosmopolitan* readers. At the time
observers were noticing that women in real rather than fictional strip
clubs were becoming more blatant in their behaviour – to the extent that
they were getting away with conduct which would have been condemned
if men had been responsible.[65] Even so, *The Full Monty* was regarded
as a harmless piece of fun for all the family. Tony Blair claimed that it
reflected 'a great sense of confidence and adventure, and greater ease
and comfort with ourselves', while Alastair Campbell was even reported

---

* Desmond argued that his publications did not count as pornography because they
were not illegal; see *Guardian*, 27 October 2003.

to have cried after watching it.[66]* In 1975 the film would hardly have been regarded as a fit subject for a piece of entertainment, whether the central characters had been male or female, but that was not the only sign that things had changed. *The Romans in Britain* had caused genuine outrage in certain quarters as a sexually explicit metaphor for the British attitude to Ireland. Hardly anyone saw it, and only a small minority would have known of its existence had it not been for the clumsy intervention of Mary Whitehouse. By comparison, *The Full Monty* was shown at cinemas throughout the country without noticeable protest; and far from being an allegory, it reflected the unpalatable contemporary reality that many Britons were being forced into the sex trade because they had no prospect of finding a 'respectable' job. As such, there can be no better illustration of the link between lust and apathy than the unmerited success of *The Full Monty*.

As with the 'Sex in Chains' episode, the reversal of expected gender roles explains and partly excuses the absence of serious complaints about *The Full Monty*. In 2003, though, the formula was revisited in another British-made film, *Calendar Girls*. This was based on a true story about some 'mature' members of the Women's Institute who had agreed to take their clothes off for a charity publication. The success of the calendar established a trend which became so pervasive that in 2006 the satirical magazine *Private Eye* ran a spoof advertisement for a sensational charity production in which the contributors kept their clothes *on*.[67] Since the nudity and sex references were judged to be 'mild', the film was granted a certificate which allowed anyone over the age of twelve to see it in a cinema. It was certainly as rude as *Carry on Emmanuelle*, which had offended Kenneth Williams back in 1975. But compared to media products which children could now expect to see in their everyday lives – unless they dedicated their lives to their avoidance – its content was indeed mild. Whatever else it did, the subject matter of *Calendar Girls* showed that, in essentials, the British attitude to sex had not moved on since 1975. Sex was still the best way of selling things, even if the cause was charitable and the organs of procreation were carefully concealed behind items of furniture or stray pieces of foliage.

---

* David Blunkett's reaction to the film showed a much greater awareness of the real issues, probably because he was a Sheffield MP. He recorded that he found it 'sad rather than funny, as it depicted not just unemployment but a breakdown in social and family relationships, and a decline in manhood and the standing of craftsmen'; *The Blunkett Tapes*, 61.

7

APATHY

The [Conservative] Government are perfectly willing to appeal only to comfortable Britain ... and the rest must go hang ... Ultimately, a Government who are so careless of the inequality in our society are a threat to democracy.

Tony Blair, 1984[1]

Jeremy Paxman: Do you believe that an individual can earn too much money?
Tony Blair: I don't really – it is not – no, it's not a view I have.

Newsnight, BBC television, 4 June 2001[2]

I

ON 7 June 2001 the Labour government led by Tony Blair was re-elected. Its overall majority was 167 seats – just twelve fewer than its margin of victory after the landslide election of 1997. Only twenty-nine of Britain's 659 constituencies changed hands. As one of Labour's satisfied spin doctors reflected, 'It was almost as if the election had never happened.'[3]

For two fifths of the UK's registered voters that judgement was literally true; they had decided not to take part in the contest. As a result, turnout in June 2001 was lower than at any British election since the introduction of universal franchise in 1928. Since that time levels of participation had never fallen below 70 per cent. The 2001 figure – 59.1 per cent – thus made the election into the most significant non-event in post-war British political history. Some of the detailed figures were startling. In the 1997 election no single constituency had recorded a turnout of less than 50 per cent. By contrast, in 2001 the turnout fell below 50 per cent in 65 constituencies – and in three seats it was less than 40 per cent. Liverpool Riverside, which had recorded the lowest turnout in 1997, repeated the feat four years later with 34.1 per cent. At the other end of the scale, in 1997 453 seats had attracted a turnout of more than 70 per cent. Four years later, only eleven constituencies reached that level.[4]

Straight after the election, the gravity of the situation was acknowledged by David Blunkett (born 1947), who had co-written a book entitled *Democracy in Crisis* as long ago as 1987.[5] Before the 2001 general election, as education secretary, Blunkett had championed compulsory school courses in citizenship. The turnout figures implied that such lessons were sorely needed. 'People are switched off politics,' Blunkett confessed. 'They are disenchanted with representative democracy.' Having defied disability to carve out a successful career in politics, Blunkett was regarded by the public with more respect than most of his colleagues. He certainly sounded sincere when he promised after the election that the government would 'draw breath and decide how to re-engage with people ... it would be very foolish indeed if we didn't note the signals and we didn't take that message very seriously'.[6]

But what exactly could politicians do to make the voters 're-engage'? This was one area in which sex was unlikely to provide the necessary stimulation. In the 2001 general election Jordan, an anatomically augmented 'glamour model', contested a Manchester constituency. In an uncharacteristic flop she netted just 2 per cent of the vote, and the turnout (55 per cent) was below the national average. On the evidence of the overall campaign it was pretty clear that flattery would never work, either. The main party leaders had already taken that tactic beyond the limits of credulity. In the Labour manifesto Tony Blair assured his fellow Britons that 'We are not boastful. But we have real strengths. Great people. Strong values. A proud history.'[7] Despite the trouncing handed out to the Tories in 1997, four years later their leader William Hague was prepared to write off that result as a temporary lapse, applauding the 'wisdom, decency and enterprise of British citizens' in his own party's manifesto.[8] Anyone who took these tributes at face value would be left wondering if the country really needed political leadership; they might even draw the unwelcome conclusion that politicians were the cause of its remaining problems. At least the Liberal Democrats hinted that

government could play a useful role, as a kind of catalyst. Their leader
Charles Kennedy argued that 'The United Kingdom has huge potential.
Unlock the energies, skills and talents of its people, and its rich ethnic
and cultural diversity, and there is nothing that cannot be achieved.'[9]

Since these lavish appeals had left the electorate unmoved, pundits
seeking an explanation for the dismal turnout turned their attention
to the mechanics of the democratic process. The most popular suggestions for reform included lengthening voting hours, holding elections
at weekends, allowing voting on the Internet and even introducing
ballot boxes into shops. The underlying rationale for all these proposals
was that a significant number of non-participants would have entered
the fray in June 2001 if only it could have been made a little easier
for them. But as long ago as 1975 a pioneering study of electoral
abstention had concluded that 'voting demands from the British citizen
only the minimum of individual initiative or effort'.[10] And even before
the 2001 debacle some steps had been taken on behalf of citizens
lacking in 'individual initiative'. There had been a concerted drive, for
example, to encourage postal voting. Yet these reforms were notable
mainly for the technical difficulties and allegations of fraud that followed
their introduction. The fact that the most voter-friendly electoral
arrangements had resulted in the lowest turnout on record was an
inauspicious precedent for anyone who hoped that frenzied voters would
flock around the ballot boxes if only they could be located beside
supermarket checkouts. The proposed changes, in fact, were concessions to an increasingly blubbery Britain, where 20 per cent of the
population was already clinically obese. The *Guardian*'s Hugo Young
considered these measures, which included an expensive reorientation
of BBC political coverage, degrading and pointless: they implied that
'"youth" must be embraced, complexity must be trivialised, personality incessantly [emphasised] above policy, and "popular" opinions
given more airtime than professional debate'.[11]

Not for the first or last time, David Blunkett had been speaking out
of turn by emphasising the need for 're-engagement' after four years of
New Labour government. His remarks reinforced claims that his party
had failed to secure a fresh mandate from the electorate as a whole,
since less than a quarter of registered voters had actually made the minimal
effort required to endorse the government's record. But a very different
interpretation was available, and other government spokespeople were
quick to deploy it. On this view, the voters were not disengaged at all:

on the contrary, they had been following politics with keen interest, and decided to abstain because they were so happy with Labour's performance in office since 1997. If they had thought that the government might lose, they would have rushed out to record their gratitude. It was true that participation among young people had been particularly disappointing – about 39 per cent among 18–24-year-olds – but, as one minister put it, nowadays the young were distracted by a wider variety of 'lifestyle choices'. The distractions must have increased considerably since 1992, when more than two thirds of people from that age group had voted.[12] By implication, overall turnout had only reached as high as 59.1 per cent in 2001 because older citizens had much less to do with their time, and would themselves turn into abstainers if they ever stumbled upon the delights of computer games and Internet chat rooms.[13] In this context the 61.1 per cent turnout at the 2005 general election could actually be presented as a modest success, rather than a cause for soul-searching on the Blunkett model.

Although the media caravan soon moved on, political scientists continued to debate the implications of the 2001 election. Professor Ivor Crewe of Essex University, who had been one of the first to study non-voting in Britain, argued that the phenomenon was best understood by dividing it into four different categories. 'Apathetic abstainers' were uninformed and uninterested; 'indifferent abstainers' knew that the policies of the main parties were broadly similar, so that the outcome didn't really matter; 'instrumental abstainers' recognised that their individual votes would make little difference either nationally or in individual constituencies; while 'alienated abstainers' had a great deal of knowledge but disliked all of the electoral choices laid before them.[14]

Crewe's typology showed that although commentators tended to discuss non-participation under the umbrella term 'apathy', it was in fact a complex phenomenon. Those who failed to vote were not necessarily people with a limited interest in politics; on the contrary, they could be very well informed and highly principled. Crewe also corrected the idea that non-voting had suddenly emerged in 2001 as a problem for British democracy. Turnout had been falling since 1992, in parliamentary by-elections and local government contests. Although the general election of 1997 had produced a reasonable turnout of 71.5 per cent, this had marked a drop of more than 6 per cent since 1992. Admittedly the 1992 election had seen the biggest numerical turnout in British history (33.6 million); even so, 1997 witnessed the largest percentage decline between any two post-war elections despite the fact that the single-issue Referendum Party, which wanted to reopen the question of EU membership, added a novel ingredient that year.[15]

A Gallup poll of December 1996 suggested that a third of Britons considered membership of the EU to be a 'bad thing' – the highest level since Mrs Thatcher delivered her Euro-sceptical Bruges speech in September 1988.[16] This degree of discontent was not enough to win the Referendum Party a single parliamentary seat, let alone secure its overall objective. But one would have expected that public misgivings about the EU would be registered at the next relevant opportunity. To some extent, they were. At the 1999 elections to the European parliament the Euro-sceptical UK Independence Party (UKIP) managed to win three seats. However, less than a quarter of the electorate bothered to vote; the turnout had dropped by nearly 13 per cent since the previous European poll, in 1994. In England, where UKIP concentrated its campaign, participation was lower than in any other part of Britain; the turnout within the parliamentary constituency of Liverpool Riverside was less than 10 per cent. It was not as if the overall outcome of the 1999 Euro-elections had been a foregone conclusion. They actually resulted in a heavy defeat for the Labour Party less than two years after the landslide which brought Tony Blair into office.

These figures challenged the most benign explanation for the low turnout in 2001 – namely that people had failed to register a vote because the general election of that year had been uniquely dull and uncompetitive. The only incident which had caught the public's attention was the punch landed by John Prescott, the hefty deputy prime minister, on a protestor who had hit him at close range with an egg. Whatever the underlying reasons for both actions, the throwing of the egg and the punch were gestures of genuine feeling, which set them apart from most features of the campaign. A second Labour victory had been regarded as a near certainty ever since the polls had closed in 1997, and in the last few days before the 2001 poll the Conservatives tacitly admitted defeat by urging people to vote in order to keep the government's majority within reasonable bounds. This was an overt attempt by William Hague to give Ivor Crewe's 'indifferent abstainers' a reason for turning out after all. Hague's desperate appeal failed in 2001; but if indifferent abstainers really constituted a significant proportion of non-participants, there was still some reason to expect that they would make their voices heard in future, more closely contested elections. This optimistic view was supported by the fact that in 2001 the correlation between turnout and the marginality of specific constituencies was more marked than ever before.[17] However, most seats had overwhelming majorities for one party or another, and it was difficult to see how voters in these areas could be cajoled.

Survey data on the subject of non-voting is particularly untrustworthy; people are dubious witnesses to their own motives when asked why they plumped for a particular party, and this reservation applies with even more force when the question at issue is their failure to vote at all. Clearly in 2001 some people did stay away from the polls because Labour was sure to win an overall parliamentary majority, and a proportion of these were probably 'instrumental abstainers' broadly content with the inevitable outcome. Other non-voters must have felt unable to choose between Labour and the Conservatives – after all, the real policy differences between them were vanishingly small by post-war standards. By the same token, though, some regarded Labour's impending victory with dismay, and refused to take part because they found the whole process pointless and distasteful. The veteran Conservative MP Kenneth Clarke reported after the 2001 contest that 'I have never known an election when so many sensible, intelligent young people would speak to me and make it clear that they had no intention of taking part.[18]

In this respect things had not improved by 2005, despite the emergence of the Iraq War as an issue which generated widespread political interest. One *Times* columnist argued that people had more reasons for discontent in 2005 than in 2001, 'And anger – like hatred – certainly gets out the vote.' From this perspective, the small increase in turnout in 2005 has to be regarded as a bitter disappointment. Even worse, anecdotal evidence suggested that many of the people who voted in 2005 were reaching the end of their endurance. In her former constituency of Redcar Mo Mowlam guessed that rather than abstaining this time round many of her old supporters were reconciled to 'holding their noses and voting Labour'. 'This is the first election I have ever known,' the dying ex-minister wrote, 'when almost everyone will have reservations about whoever they vote for.'[19]

Underpinning all of these views was a sense that, whatever their personal circumstances or level of political knowledge, it was no longer a citizen's duty to cast a vote. In itself, the tendency of commentators to talk of the duty rather than the *right* to vote represented a significant and strongly negative terminological shift. Inconclusive as it is in some respects, the survey evidence does indicate a sharp decline in the acknowledgement of any moral obligation to vote. One post-election study in 2001 found that the largest proportion of non-voters (21 per cent) abstained because voting was 'inconvenient'. In this context, the word seems like a euphemism for 'couldn't be bothered'; the act of voting was, after all, easier than ever, and the survey provided separate categories for those who had been 'away' (16 per cent) and 'too busy' (6 per cent).[20] Previous generations would not have been deterred from participating by nameless 'inconveniences'.

It is dangerous to select a specific time as the starting point for electoral disengagement in Britain. Long-term structural changes, notably the weakening of the traditional link between social class and political allegiance, played a crucial part. This 'class dealignment' made it more difficult for political scientists to explain voting behaviour and to predict future results, but it also made a decline in turnout more likely. According to academic research, in 1964 almost all voters expressed a feeling of 'identity' with a specific party. Identification implied something more than a transient preference; indeed, David Butler and Donald Stokes claimed that 'many electors have had the same party loyalties from the dawn of their political consciousness'.[21] Usually this sense of partisan identity arose from non-political causes, notably the influence of family and friends. Peer pressure not only forged a persisting bias towards particular parties; it also fostered the feeling that one should turn out to back the favoured side, regardless of its recent record or policy programme. Thus while this tendency prevailed, the leaders of the two main parties could feel assured of respectable support at every election. Once it had begun to erode, the level of participation was likely to decrease; every individual would have to be given a positive reason for voting. In this context an era of disillusion with politics in general would be seriously damaging in its long-term effects. The rising generation of British citizens, who were no longer taught how to vote by parents or their peers, would learn instead that politics was a mug's game: they would have been *socialised* into incipient apathy.* Rather than having to make voters feel that on balance electoral participation was a reasonable idea, future politicians hoping for a tolerable

---

*Two young residents of Liverpool Riverside interviewed before the 2005 general election showed how apathy could become hereditary, as well as being a conscious individual choice. A twenty-year-old woman had no intention of voting because 'my mum says it's the same whoever gets in'. By contrast, her friend reported that 'My mum and dad always vote Labour but I'm not really interested;' *The Times*, 6 May 2005

turnout would have to convince them that it would be a national disaster if they stayed at home.

From this perspective the mid-1970s emerges as a key period in the story of British apathy. The public discourse of 1975 betrays a growing sense of weariness with democratic activity – not just because there had been three important national polls within eighteen months, but because the minority of voters who actually paid attention to political developments had so little faith that these contests would haul Britain out of its economic difficulties. Those who referred to apathy at the time were not concerned about the overall level of turnout, which remained relatively healthy; they meant that it was increasingly difficult to vote with any enthusiasm unless one had been preprogrammed into loyalty by half-forgotten social influences. Young people who were becoming conscious of politics at this time learned to regard election campaigns as periods of tedious futility; they were more likely to wonder why their parents continued to vote, in spite of all their grumbling, than to wish that they were already old enough to join them at the polling station.

This context makes the creative tactics of the professional strategists hired by the Britain in Europe campaign before the 1975 referendum look remarkably astute and far-sighted. In that poll those in favour of membership were not merely looking for a considerable percentage lead; the level of overall turnout was as important as the size of the majority. Drafting in celebrities was the only way to guarantee that a reasonable number of younger voters would pay any attention to the referendum; it might also persuade some of their seniors to deliver a verdict on a campaign which, if not exactly scintillating, had at least been a bit different from the usual partisan slanging match. Gyles Brandreth, himself later a celebrity MP, made the point explicitly when he characterised the recruits to his 'People for Europe' group: 'many of them famous, lots of them young'.[22]

On the basis of this evidence, the precipitate decline in electoral turnouts after the contest of 1992 looks like a delayed reaction to previous demographic shifts, more than an overt protest against the politics of those years. Death was reducing the ranks of those who had, when they themselves were young, developed the voting habit and retained it even through the miserable mid-70s. Gradually their place within the electorate was taken by people who could never be made to fall for the illusion that their individual partipication might make a difference to the overall outcome or to feel any respect for political leaders. However, this is not to say that Britain's politicians were the blameless victims of social changes and economic difficulties which lay outside their control. Rather, the inflationary effects of the oil shock in the mid-1970s exposed existing defects to an audience which was already less likely to take a charitable view of its politicians. Public-spirited as they were, in their different ways Harold Wilson and Edward Heath had both played politics, exaggerating their differences even when cooperation seemed the more rational course.

After the 1975 referendum party politics became increasingly polarised, as if to mock the well-meaning advocates of a national coalition, like *The Times* newspaper. Although there were several reasons for the eclipse of consensus politicians, both left and right derived considerable benefit from the decline of faith in the democratic process. The left took advantage of a lack of combative spirit among Labour moderates, and although they never took control of their party they exerted a powerful influence over policymaking after 1979. Meanwhile, having secured the leadership of their own party, right-wing Conservatives exploited apathy among the electorate as a whole, imposing an eighteen-year programme of radical reform on a country which – according to the opinion polls at least – showed a limited appetite for Thatcherism. In 1975 *The Times* had claimed that most Britons were broadly 'social democratic' in outlook, and a series of surveys continued to support this view. But when in 1981 the Social Democratic Party (SDP) was established specifically to cater for this constituency, it could not sustain its initial surge of support. Although Britain's victory in the Falklands War is often cited as the main reason for its failure to break the mould of British politics, the SDP interlude is more plausibly seen as a premature attempt to persuade voters that, having loosened their long-term loyalties, they should shop around for a more congenial brand. For understandable reasons this worked better with lukewarm Labourites than with Conservatives still uncertain about Mrs Thatcher. Thus it only plunged the new party (and its Liberal allies) into a bitter scrap with Labour for second place. If the SDP–Liberal alliance had emerged as runners-up, the political scene might still have been transformed. As it was, the 1983 general election reinforced the idea that – love her or loathe her – Thatcher was the only party leader really equipped to hold office.

This impression dominated British politics for the rest of the decade. When Thatcher finally left office in 1990 it was at the behest of disgruntled Tory MPs rather than the electorate. The subsequent years have been a sore trial for long-standing supporters of both main parties.

Between 1992 and 1994 the Conservatives became mired in allegations of sleaze and lost their reputation for economic competence. These damaging episodes dismayed Tory supporters who had been willing to give John Major a chance, even if they hankered after a return to Thatcher's crusading approach. As for Labour supporters, in 1992 they saw their leader Neil Kinnock acclaiming victory at a pre-election rally, only to find that the Tories had sneaked in once again. For the political satirist John O'Farrell, the realisation of another defeat for Labour was 'like having the inside of your stomach kicked out'.[23] Up to May 1994 most Labour supporters consoled themselves with the thought that their prolonged wait would soon be over, and that even if the party had changed many of its key policies it still had a recognisable social conscience and a leader with firm beliefs. But then John Smith died, and Tony Blair took his place.

II

Labour's desperation for office ensured that many supporters swallowed their reservations about Blair, at least until the 1997 election. They had accepted that the party would have to broaden its appeal if it were ever to form another government, and were prepared to believe that further changes were necessary. In particular, they acquiesced in the dropping of Labour's long-standing commitment to nationalisation. By 1994 no one seriously imagined that the party would restore state ownership to its pre-1979 limits; but many activists hoped at least that failing concerns like the privatised railways would be renationalised. Blair's insistence on scrapping Clause IV of the party's constitution thus had more than symbolic importance. It underpinned his subsequent insistence that, in all cases, private provision was superior to state-run services. At the time, though, it looked as if Blair was a pragmatist who wanted a free hand to judge every case on its merits, rather than the free-market ideologue he turned out to be.

Whether or not people agreed with Blair's ideas, his sincerity seemed unquestionable. In Labour's 1997 election manifesto he had expressed his desire 'to renew faith in politics by being honest . . . Our aim is no less than to set British political life on a new course for the future.'[24] The extent to which Blair was believed suggests that, despite their recent experiences, many British voters were still prepared to re-engage with the political process. Between his elevation to the Labour leadership and the election of May 1997 Blair's opinion poll rating was almost invariably higher than 50 per cent. At his party's annual conference a few months after New Labour's election victory he announced that his would be 'a government of high ideals' which would turn Britain into 'a beacon to the world'. The British character was 'creative, compassionate, outward-looking'. 'We can never be the biggest, we may never again be the mightiest,' he conceded. 'But we can be the best.'[25]

Although the Blairites always had a weakness for high-sounding epithets, this tribute evoked a suspicion that the prime minister regarded praise for his country as an excuse to savour some reflected glory. Just a few weeks after igniting his 'beacon' he was involved in sleaze allegations which ranked alongside any misdeed of the preceding eighteen years of Conservative rule. The Formula 1 motor-racing chief Bernie Ecclestone had given £1 million to Labour before the election, although his previous commitment to socialism had been tepid at best. A different reason for his donation was suggested when the Labour government exempted Formula 1 racing from a ban on advertisements by tobacco manufacturers, generous sponsors of Ecclestone's sporting interests. If this incident were not damaging enough in itself, Blair compounded the problem by appearing on television to protest that he was 'a pretty straight sort of guy' who would never do anything 'improper.'[26] Even those members of the public who continued to think that Blair was a fairly honest individual could only wonder how he had got himself mixed up in such a dirty business. Instead of rescuing the democratic damsel, the handsome young prince had jumped off his white horse and thrown himself into a mud-wrestling contest.

The Ecclestone incident showed the limits of the New Labour commitment to a cleaner style of politics, just as the party's traditional supporters were digesting the fact that there would only be limited changes in the substance of policy. The centrepiece of Labour's election campaign had been a 'pledge card', listing five modest policy goals covering education, law and order, the National Health Service, job creation and economic management. The pledges were intended to secure the allegiance of Conservative voters who were already tempted to switch to Labour. However, on the night of the 1997 election there was still a chance that Blair would take his massive parliamentary majority as a cue to explore more imaginative measures, and perhaps to reverse some Thatcherite reforms in areas like privatisation and the taxation of the rich. This prospect seemed doubtful when, in the immediate aftermath of victory,

Blair announced that his party would 'govern as New Labour'. The exact meaning of the remark was obscure – no less than it had been back in March, when he had used it to reassure *Sun* readers – but it was clearly intended to quench any radical expectations. For his part, the brooding and ambitious chancellor, Gordon Brown (born 1951), was determined to work within the spending constraints laid down by his Conservative predecessor Kenneth Clarke. By the time of the Ecclestone affair it had already become clear just how far New Labour was prepared to go in pursuing this goal – even though Clarke himself had never intended to keep within his self-decreed limits. Ignoring criticism from its own back-benches, the new government prepared a package of welfare reforms which included cuts in benefits for lone parents. In December 1997 this was forced through Parliament; at that stage, only forty-seven Labour MPs were bold enough to rebel against a measure which their leaders would have condemned as callous if it had been a Tory proposal.

Ostensibly, the government could justify such measures on the grounds that it wanted to avoid being seen a soft touch. While it would not allow a return to the days of economic boom and bust under the Tories, it was equally determined to dissipate memories of Labour's own mismanagement in the 1970s. But, ironically, the long years of Conservative rule had extinguished the latter possibility, at least in the short term; even the most militant trade unionists of 1997 would have been lambasted as capitalist lapdogs in the mid-1970s. A more pressing motive for distressing the left was the Blairite anxiety to appease vested interests in the City of London. This was an ignoble aim in itself, but it was also unnecessary. In their long foreknowledge of a Labour win, financiers had been given ample opportunity to factor in the possibility that Blair would attempt to mollify the people who had stayed loyal to the party through almost two decades in the political wilderness. Hard-nosed City analysts certainly expected a rise in the higher rate of income tax to 50 per cent, without making plans to leave the country, and senior accountants thought that a return to the pre-1988 rate of 60 per cent would be accepted if it was targeted at the fattest cats.[27] The only sensible conclusion is that the hard-line policies of Labour's first year formed an integral part of an ideological purge of the Labour Party – the counterpart of the coup which Tony Benn's supporters had tried to conduct after the 1979 general election.

Blair and his allies knew that it was safe to proceed with their putsch because traditional supporters would much rather abstain than vote for any other party. Their aim, in effect, was not just to nullify the supposed threat from the Labour left – which was quickly dubbed Old Labour in an attempt to discredit it with a label rather than a rational argument. It was a concerted campaign to rob left-wingers of any chance of meaningful participation in democratic politics. Over time, the Blairites would take more direct action: exploiting loopholes in the party's rule book in order to block parliamentary candidates who were unacceptable to the leadership; parachuting a millionaire ex-Tory, Sean Woodward, into a safe working-class seat; and going to ludicrous lengths in their failed bid to derail Ken Livingstone's attempt to become London's first elected mayor. In contrast to his attitude towards radical members of his own party, the prime minister went out of his way to emphasise his sympathy for public appointees of the Conservative years who (for good reasons) were hated by the left. Chris Woodhead, the chief inspector of schools, was kept in post for three more years and awarded a substantial pay rise although David Blunkett had serious doubts about his attitude.[28] Woodhead's ability to infuriate teachers had earned Blair's lasting gratitude, which endured even after his astonishing claim that affairs between teachers and their pupils could be 'educative on both sides' and damaging allegations about his own private life. Even when it emerged that he was hoping to receive a peerage from the Conservatives, and write lucrative articles in anti-government newspapers, it was considered imprudent to dismiss him.[29] The director-general of the BBC, John Birt, had alienated many of the Corporation's employees with his maladroit management style and penchant for meaningless prose, satirised by *Private Eye* as 'Birtspeak'. He departed voluntarily (with a peerage) in January 2000. Later he was re-recruited by the government, to engage in unpaid 'blue skies thinking'. Although his influence was widely regarded as 'disruptive and pernicious', he retained this mysterious role for five years.[30]

Blair's early decisions in government raised the question of why he had joined Labour in the first place. At the 1995 party conference, after persuading them to drop their historic commitment to nationalisation, he told Labour loyalists that 'I was not born into this party; I chose it.' In fact his father, Leo, had been brought up by fervent communists; he perversely switched to the Conservatives when Labour was at its most innovative under Clement Attlee. But this did not mean that Tony's choice was based purely on principle. In 2002 he was candid enough to reveal that he had given up his love of 'popularity for its own sake', implying that until fairly recently this desire had been a major motivation for his political decisions.[31] Almost certainly he joined Labour under the influence of Cherie Booth, a more gifted lawyer who subsequently became his wife. If Cherie had been selected for a safe Labour constituency before Blair was adopted at Sedgefield, he would certainly not have entered Parliament for any party; the couple had agreed that it would be too great a sacrifice of potential earnings for both of them to give up the Bar, so the first to win a seat would enjoy financial support from the other.[32] Despite this background of materialistic calculation, Blair had quickly won favourable attention after entering Parliament at the 1983 general election. Although the 1992 defeat must have been a serious disappointment to anyone with a desire to put his talents to constructive use, he was already a member of his party's front bench team, with excellent prospects of further advancement. However, it seems that he toyed with the idea of leaving politics at this point, presumably in the hope of financial gain in other fields. Colleagues of his generation felt similar twinges of thwarted ambition. They were impatient with the leadership of John Smith, who had experienced government in the 1970s and was prepared to hold a principled line until the electorate turned towards Labour, rather than rushing to meet its perceived demands. Smith's premature death handed the leadership of the party to the modernisers just at the point when rank-and-file Labour members were most desperate for electoral victory – and most likely to achieve it, given the terminal problems of the Major government.

Yet although Labour would have won the 1997 general election under John Smith – or indeed just about any other conceivable leader – Blair's allies were determined to use the remaining years in opposition to complete Margaret Thatcher's project of making socialism irrelevant in Britain. The strategy's centrepiece was Tony Blair's wooing of Rupert Murdoch, which became a priority as soon as he was elected party leader.* Ditching the commitment to nationalisation in 1995 was Blair's way of proving himself to the media mogul, just three months after he had flown thousands of miles to reassure a meeting of Murdoch

---

* 'I want a good relationship with your newspaper,' Blair told the editor of Murdoch's *News of the World* in September 1994. A few months later he privately characterised Labour's courtship of the right-wing tabloids as 'sensible' and 'adult'; see Piers Morgan, *The Insider*, 47, 82.

employees that he had no plans to tighten press regulation. Presumably the Labour leader was astute enough to realise that Murdoch's newspapers would have backed Labour anyway, to avoid alienating their readers. The likelihood of this development had been apparent to any clear-sighted observer since John Smith's death, when the *Sun* had tried to lead the mourning for Britain's 'lost leader'. It could be argued that Blair was covering all of his bases in the run-up to the election, but it would be difficult to deny that at least part of his purpose in cultivating Murdoch was to infuriate the left.

In these ways New Labour added to the growing army of abstainers, but the Blairite vanguard was a *product* as well as a cause of apathy. Long before 1997 senior members of the Labour Party had begun to suspect that the majority of the public was disloyal and selfish; even its best members were inattentive, but most were simply ignorant.* The public, after all, had elected the hated Conservatives in 1979 and failed to dislodge them in three subsequent elections up to 1992. To Blairite eyes this made the average voter preferable to Old Labour traditionalists, but only just. Anyone who had entered politics with an idealistic sense of mission would have tried to shrug off this negative view of the electorate; Blair's predecessor John Smith, for example, was talking with sincerity about his mission to serve the British public the night before his death. But when Tony Blair spoke of New Labour as 'servants of the people', the words seemed hollow even at the height of his popularity. This was not surprising, since Blair's coterie of aspirant office-holders and advisers based their electoral appeal on a crudely materialistic view of human nature which left little room for idealism. As one of them put it, Labour's natural constituents were 'aspiring, consuming, choosing what was best for themselves and their families. They had outgrown collectivism and left it behind in the supermarket car-park.' Whether or not this was true, only a desperate salesperson could claim that it was an honour to do business on behalf of such a constituency.[33]

While the drive to disenfranchise the left was deliberate, after becoming prime minister Blair also reinforced the case for 'instrumental abstention' among the people who remained most faithful to the ideals of representative democracy – namely, those who wanted to see the

---

* As the New Labour supporter Polly Toynbee accepted in a *Guardian* column before the 1997 election, the party leaders had 'abandoned their view of the voter as a decent sort and adopted the Tory model of the voter as selfish, lying bastard'; quoted in Peter Oborne, *The Rise of Political Lying*, Free Press, 2005, 47.

election of the best candidates, regardless of ideology or party labels. He made no attempt to disguise his contempt for Parliament, seeing it at best as a rubber stamp rather than a forum for meaningful debate on great national questions. Apart from the weekly ritual of prime minister's question time, he was hardly ever glimpsed in the House of Commons. As a decision-making body, the cabinet was also eclipsed. Blair preferred to address issues in bilateral meetings with relevant ministers, to minimise the opportunities for dissent. None of his colleagues had any experience of government, and they were ready to give way to Blair whenever the prime minister expressed his own preference. In a surreal meeting shortly after the 1997 general election the cabinet agreed not to abandon the lottery-funded Millennium Dome, although many ministers had serious and well-founded misgivings. On Blair's own account, 'The Cabinet thought long and hard and talked long and hard about whether to go ahead with the Dome.' But the rational discussion was not followed by a vote, which Blair would have lost; and the dissenting ministers subsequently allowed themselves to be stampeded into agreement.* As Nick Cohen has written, 'the discussion of 19 June 1997 showed that Cabinet government was as feeble as parliamentary democracy'.[34] If both of these institutions were now to be overridden by the will of a single individual, it hardly seemed worthwhile for ordinary members of the public to cast a vote – except, perhaps, in the prime minister's constituency of Sedgefield, which is in the north-east of England even though it was hardly typical of a region which had suffered badly during the Thatcher years.

According to one account, when Neil Kinnock congratulated Blair on his 1997 election victory the prime minister replied, 'OK, wise guy. What do we do now?'[35] But Kinnock himself had never held a ministerial post so he was hardly in a position to supply a constructive answer. There was, though, at least one person close to Blair who had experienced high office. Although Roy Jenkins (Lord Jenkins of Hillhead after 1987) was the child of working-class parents with close ties to Labour, he had never

---

* In February 1998 Blair informed the public that the Dome would be one of the greatest landmarks in British history. 'We will say to ourselves with pride: this is our Dome, Britain's Dome. And believe me, it will be the envy of the world.' The celebrations would confound 'the cynics who have rubbished the idea'. It would work because the British were 'by nature adventurous, innovative, pioneering, creative' and was certain to 'turn a profit for Britain'; see full text of speech, 'Why the Dome is Good for Britain', 24 February 1998, www.number10.go.uk.

been fully accepted by the party because of his penchant for aristocratic companions. He could thus regard Blair as a more fortunate version of himself – a semi-outsider who had taken advantage of circumstances to seize the leadership of a party which was no longer freighted with socialist baggage. Yet by 1997 Jenkins was an anachronism. He belonged to a generation of politicians which had always hoped to elevate the tone of public debate – albeit with mixed success in practice. A master of English prose, he was ill-attuned to the era of the *Sun* and the cynical sound bite. Despite their much-advertised friendship, the contrast between Jenkins and Blair was symbolised by their (much-criticised) social activities. While Jenkins consorted with lords and ladies, Blair tried to establish his credibility by mingling with pop stars and footballers. Although commentators regarded Jenkins as Blair's mentor, in reality their views only coincided in a shared interest in the game of tennis and a belief that the Conservative Party had prospered during the twentieth century because progressives had been divided. Their mutual hatred of the Conservatives obscured the fact that they had very different ideas about the nature of 'progressive' politics.

After the 1997 election Jenkins was put in charge of a semi-official commission of inquiry into possible reform of the voting system. The adoption of proportional representation (PR) promised to achieve several progressive goals at one stroke. The Conservatives would no longer be a serious electoral threat, provided that Labour and the Liberal Democrats could work together in reasonable harmony after winning a majority of the votes between them – as they had done at every general election since 1964. Even when the Tories recovered from their 1997 debacle, the two progressive parties in combination could expect comfortably to out-poll them, so that they could form an endless succession of coalition governments; at some point, they might even merge. No future prime minister would even have to pretend to fear Rupert Murdoch – after all, his fervent support for Margaret Thatcher during the 1980s had never pushed the Conservative vote-share close to the 50 per cent which would ensure their victory under PR.

But although the outcome of general elections would be predictable in the short term, PR also had the potential to reanimate Britain's moribund democratic culture. Individual votes would still not count for very much, but they would be of more equivalent value across the country, and well-informed citizens were less likely to think that their choices were completely irrelevant. Minority parties would have a better chance of winning parliamentary seats, thus providing their views with more publicity and increasing the range of meaningful electoral options. Of Ivor Crewe's categories, only the 'apathetic abstainers' – those who were not even bothered to find out if politics could be interesting – would be unaffected by the change.

Had Blair regarded the health of British democracy as an urgent priority – as his friend David Blunkett undoubtedly did – he would have given full backing to the Jenkins commission when his prestige was highest. However, the 1997 general election result had handed him an irresistible motive for inaction. Contemplating his massive majority – which, thanks to Britain's disproportional system, bore scant relation to the scale of the Labour vote – he began to think that the existing system had much to recommend it after all. Bold enough to defy powerful dissenters when he was Opposition leader, after gaining the additional prestige of the premiership Blair resorted to the excuse of internal differences in order to block reform. Conscious of the new realities, Jenkins produced a compromise proposal which was far removed from the strictly proportional system approved by his fellow Liberal Democrats. When the report was unveiled in October 1998 Blair agreed that it made 'a well-argued and powerful case for the system it recommends'.[36] This was Blairspeak for 'Thanks, but no thanks.' The Jenkins report was dead on delivery; even after the 2001 election reinforced its 'well-argued and powerful case', no one bothered to revive it. Those who remembered 1975, when *The Times* had presented an equally cogent argument for PR, would not have been surprised by this dismal saga. It was a catch-22 situation: the public as a whole was too apathetic to agitate on behalf of a reform which promised to reduce the level of apathy. If that had been the outcome in 1975, things were unlikely to be any different more than two decades later, under a regime which had based its whole approach to government on the assumption that apathy was here to stay.

III

'We insist that no community be written off,' Labour proclaimed in its 2001 election manifesto. 'Our reforms will build a strong and inclusive society.'[37] An attack on 'social exclusion' had been a central theme of Blair's campaigning back in 1997. He had used his first major speech after becoming prime minister to complain that 'For eighteen years, the poorest people in our country have been forgotten by government,' and in a newspaper article a few months later he called attitudes to exclusion 'the defining difference' between New Labour and the Conservatives.[38] A Social Exclusion Unit, reporting directly to the prime minister, was set up before the end of the government's first year.

There was, though, reason to doubt whether social exclusion troubled Blair any more than the fall in electoral turnout. For example, the 1997 Labour Party manifesto had included a section which quoted the famous mission statement (coined by Gordon Brown and cashed in by Tony Blair): 'Tough on crime, tough on the causes of crime'. On the basis of the proposals listed in that section, it emerged that the only causes of crime were criminals, so that being tough with them would cure both the symptoms and the disease. In the 1980s Labour spokespeople had incurred the displeasure of the tabloid press by connecting certain forms of lawbreaking – particularly large-scale social disorder – to adverse economic circumstances. When he became shadow home secretary in 1992 Tony Blair had been determined to ditch this approach. Like Margaret Thatcher – another undistinguished-barrister-turned-politician – Blair thought that poor people had no excuse if they turned to crime. Once he had become prime minister he came to believe that people no longer had any excuse for being poor.*

The Labour manifesto of 2001 boasted about the government's success in reducing the numbers of people sleeping on the streets and children brought up in poverty. New Labour's achievements in these fields after 1997 were often underplayed, as if the party's general lack of ambition should prevent it from receiving credit in the specific areas where it really did take effective action.[39] However, during the 2001 election campaign it became clear that some parts of Britain had remained impervious to the ministrations of the Social Exclusion Unit. On Saturday 26 May long-simmering racial tensions in Oldham led to a weekend of serious clashes between local Asians and racist thugs. In one incident the house of a pregnant Asian woman was targeted. In

---

*In one of his first speeches after the 1997 general election Blair actually used the link between poverty and crime as a rationale for *harsher* punishments for those who continued to offend once his social policies were in place. 'Don't be surprised,' he warned, 'if the penalties are tougher when you have been given the opportunities but you didn't take them' (quoted in Elliot and Atkinson, *The Age of Insecurity*, 215).

retaliation, a large group of Asians attacked a pub well known as a rendezvous for racists. The pub might have been chosen by someone with a sardonic sense of humour; it was called The Live and Let Live. The offices of the local newspaper were also petrol-bombed, suggesting an element of planning among the Asian community. But this was hardly surprising. According to one local resident who condemned the violence, racially motivated provocation had been stepped up over several weeks, after a visit from some hooligans who claimed to support Stoke City football team.[40]

On the face of it, the timing of the riots seemed to be a crushing blow for the Blair government. Originally it had planned to hold the general election on 3 May 2001, but the poll had to be put back because of a serious outbreak of foot and mouth disease in cattle. In the past serious social disturbances had invariably provoked searching political questions; an outbreak in one of the country's most deprived areas in the last few days of an election campaign should have been a disaster for the governing party. But this old-fashioned logic was inoperative in New Labour's Britain. Race rather than poverty was held to be the cause of Oldham's troubles, and race was an issue which all three main parties were desperate to avoid. Indeed, for a time the Oldham riots looked most likely to damage the Conservative opposition, which had been accused of fomenting racial tension in its desperate search for a populist election message.

There was, though, at least one political party which was keen to talk about race and its effects on Britain. The British National Party (BNP) was even prepared to discuss the link between racial conflict and poverty. In places like Oldham, its supporters alleged, recent immigrants were given preferential treatment over the British-born poor in the allocation of local government services like housing. Whatever the role of party activists in provoking them, the riots of May 2001 constituted a propaganda coup for the BNP. In Oldham East and Saddleworth – a seat which the party had not even bothered to contest in 1997 – its candidate received more than 11 per cent of the vote at the 2001 election. The result showed New Labour that its preferred target audience of partially informed people was not as reliable as it had supposed. The angst among government strategists was increased by the fact that the BNP had adopted its own techniques of media manipulation, so that the party's leader, Nick Griffin, presented Powellite policies with all the panache of the young Tony Blair.

Just two days before the general election there was another night of rioting, this time in the Harehills district of Leeds. Trouble had flared after the police arrested a man of Bangladeshi origin, using methods which local residents considered heavy-handed. Any links to the Oldham outbreak were played down, both by police and community leaders. But before the end of June there was trouble in Burnley, after a racially motivated attack on an Asian taxi driver. Significantly, Burnley was another place where the BNP had performed well in recent elections. A subsequent report into the rioting presented a complex picture, attributing the violence to drug dealing as well as racist agitation and 'grinding poverty'.[41]

The most serious trouble of that summer, though, broke out in Bradford a month after the election. For three nights white and Asian gangs battled with each other and with police, who sustained more than a hundred injuries. At least a thousand youths were involved, and as in other incidents during that summer petrol bombs and bricks featured in the violence. The Manningham area of the city was badly damaged. As in Burnley and Oldham, racism certainly played a part in reigniting a conflict which had broken out, at a lower level, in May; and as in those cases, subsequent investigation identified social deprivation as an underlying factor.

Most people living south of the River Trent forgot the riot season of 2001 fairly quickly. Thanks to the bias of the British media towards events in the south of England, many were barely conscious of the trouble in the first place. To some extent, though, the relative lack of publicity reflected a more laudable intention to minimise the chance of copy-cat outbreaks; to this extent, at least, the police and the media had absorbed the lessons of 1981. Even so, the disorder would almost certainly have left a more lasting impression had it not been overshadowed by the destruction of the World Trade Center in New York, just two months after the Bradford riot. As a result, it was rarely noted that three of the four participants in Britain's own terrorist outrage – the attack on London's transport system in July 2005 – came from areas which had experienced rioting in 2001.

Were the 2001 riots really different in character from the outbreak of 1981? In each instance the political response was roughly the same: the riots were depicted by the government and its media supporters as inexcusable acts of mass criminality. But the rioters of 1981 had attracted some sympathy from a sizeable constituency in Britain. Many people in their late teens or early twenties – those who had been aware from 1975 onward that they were likely to experience indefinite unemployment, or had already spent years on the dole – could understand the anger and despair that underlay the disturbances, whatever their proximate causes. This, rather than the extensive media coverage, explains why the battles in Bristol and Brixton were re-enacted in so many English towns and cities. The 1981 riots also had a soundtrack, thanks to groups like the Specials and The Clash; far from being a minority taste, their anthems for doomed youth were extremely popular. By contrast, in the summer of 2001 many young people in Britain's run-down estates were being brought up by parents who had only ever known the condition of welfare dependency. Far from urging constructive resistance to this depressing plight, the most popular artists in Britain were either manufactured bands or former actors in soap operas. Their inane lyrics were an incitement to self-harm rather than a call for subversive action on the streets. Few of the rioters of 2001 would have gone about their business humming 'Pure and Simple', the best-selling debut single by the short-lived group Hear'Say. Some might have been acquainted with the more challenging work of bands like Radiohead, but their songs tended to dwell on current disenchantment rather than suggesting that improvement was possible. Popular music no longer included menacing lines like 'The people getting angry', in The Specials' 'Ghost Town'.

Thus the rioters of 1981 could feel a loose attachment to a wider constituency, and saw themselves as the vanguard of a counter-attack against powerful forces which deliberately aimed to stultify their initial expectations of a meaningful life. By contrast, the participants in 2001 were authentic representatives of social exclusion, in the full sense of that term. If anything, the white racists were even more alienated from mainstream society than the Asian youths who confronted them; and their feelings spilled over into violence because they felt that they had been betrayed by their own kind. As they probably expected, their actions evoked no sympathy from the comfortable classes, who turned away from the scenes in Oldham, Burnley and Bradford with a shudder.

A more apposite precedent for the events of 2001 was the social disorder of 1991/2. The major incidents of the 1991 riot season were geographically dispersed – Cardiff, Oxfordshire and Tyneside – but they took place over a couple of weeks, between the end of August and the middle of September. The venue in each case was a socially deprived housing estate. There were other common themes in much of the unrest. On the Blackbird Leys estate near Oxford trouble was connected to the phenomenon of joy-riding; in the Meadow Well area of North Shields violence began after two young men died in a stolen car which had been chased by the police. Apart from showing their defiance of the authorities, local youths also singled out Asian-owned retail premises for arson attacks. Even before the riots the reputation of the Meadow Well estate was so bad that around a quarter of the housing stock was vacant. The troubles at the Ely estate on the western side of Cardiff arose out of a dispute between an Asian grocer and the local newsagent. The following year rioting in Bristol broke out after two white men died in another high-speed crash. They had stolen a motorcycle, and were being pursued by police. In the summer of 1992 there were also clashes in run-down areas of Coventry, Salford, Carlisle, Huddersfield, Burnley and Blackburn.[42]

If in any respect the rioters were inspired by the hope of drawing sympathetic attention to their situation, they were to be disappointed. No Conservative minister seized on the incidents to burnish a reputation for compassionate dynamism, as Michael Heseltine had done in the early 1980s. The Labour Party now knew better than to risk any association with lawbreakers. Its leader, Neil Kinnock, emulated his old sparring partner Margaret Thatcher by declaring that there was 'absolutely no excuse' for the incidents in North Shields. When the Bishop of Newcastle tried to link the unrest with 'the feeling of help-lessness and hopelessness' the Labour-supporting *Daily Mirror* (political editor, Alastair Campbell) accused him of talking 'twaddle'.[43]

The 1991–2 riots showed that parts of the UK, especially housing estates with high rates of unemployment, were suffering from a kind of *social* apathy intimately related to political disengagement. Beatrix Campbell has noted that by the end of the 1980s 'a large cohort of young men and women found themselves not only on the edge of poli-tics, but exiled from the social world. They were neither legitimate citizens nor consumers.'[44] Such areas also included some of Britain's most active citizens – people who recognised the impact of social exclu-sion and tried to work against it without losing their own sense of grievance against a society which preached meritocracy while treating so many as something far less than second-class citizens. However, in what Beatrix Campbell called 'Britain's dangerous places' these coura-geous activists were an embattled minority. When people living in squalor were constantly exposed to contrasting media images of afflu-ence, it was difficult to sustain the case for civic pride. Such arguments were unlikely to impress many residents of Moston, Manchester, where the sixteen-year-old Suzanne Capper was tortured by a street gang over eight days in December 1992 and finally burned to death.

The miserable fate of Suzanne Capper attracted much less national attention than the murder of James Bulger just two months later. This contrasting coverage provides a glaring insight into British social attitudes in 1992. Genuinely harrowing as it was, the Bulger case became a national talking point because a child had been abducted in one of the most sacred sites of British civilisation – a shopping centre. The helpless toddler was led away to his death under the impotent surveillance of closed circuit television, causing understandable anguish to all caring parents. But if Suzanne Capper had been killed off camera in the Surrey stockbroker belt rather than a deprived area of Manchester, it is reasonable to suppose that her murder would still have created a media sensation. Thus, in the supposed British meritocracy of 1992 the lives of young people were accorded different values on the basis of the context in which they died. As a rule, the most barbaric killings among the poor attracted fleeting coverage on the inside pages of newspapers; they were rarely reported in the national television news. By contrast, the murder of any affluent individual was a virtual guarantee of banner headlines and anguished discussion about the breakdown of law and order.

As if to compensate, the authorities offered the children of the poor one last desperate excuse for misconduct. During the 1990s it became increasingly common for doctors to accept that troublesome young people were suffering from illness rather than factors reflecting their upbringing. An impressive AIDS-like acronym – ADHD (attention deficit hyperactive disorder) – was applied to its victims. The controversial drug Ritalin, which had been available since the 1960s, was prescribed in such cases, which were said to affect around one in twenty of British children. In 2004 more than 350,000 prescriptions were issued in the UK to induce the chemical calm promised by Ritalin's manufacturers. For reasons which invited obvious speculation, ADHD was much more likely to affect children from the poorest households. The official explanation was that ADHD was in large part a genetic condition. Thus, it seemed, the majority of ADHD cases confirmed that the poor were poor because of their genes, rather than a lack of meaningful life opportunities. Continued class divisions were therefore inevitable.[45] On this view, the marginalised found themselves in their plight due to factors outside the control of governments, and well-meaning/hard-working/law-abiding citizens could be securely inactive in the knowledge that nothing short of genetic intervention could save the poor from their predetermined fate.

IV

The media's cursory treatment of the Capper case reflected a more general tendency which first emerged in the early 1990s. Violent outbursts among the marginalised still attracted some media interest, but unlike the riots of 1981 they were no longer seen as suitable subjects for national discussion. Increasingly, they were regarded as problems affecting specific areas beyond the consumerist pale, so that debate about the marginalised was also localised and (hopefully) medicalised. Although the Bulger murder aroused the protective instincts of parents across Britain, the incident itself was widely interpreted as an indictment of Liverpool – a city which had been badly affected by unemployment and suffered several tragedies in these years. The idea that riots were no longer considered a serious problem for law-abiding Britons is reflected in the memoirs of senior politicians. While Lady Thatcher had to devote a couple of pages to the Brixton riots for the sake of historical completeness, John Major – who had embarked on his period of office promising to build a nation 'at ease with itself' – overlooked the incidents of 1991–2 in his own auto-biography. The 2001 riots occupy half a sentence in the semi-authorised biography of David Blunkett, even though they were an urgent priority during his first days at the Home Office.[46]*

The 1991–2 riots, of course, took place soon after a spectacular success for the advocates of direct action. The poll tax riots of March 1990 had helped to induce a change of government policy, and the participants could even claim that they had contributed to Mrs Thatcher's departure from Downing Street. One reason for the success of this protest was its geographical location; the image of a burning car near Trafalgar Square proved far more arresting for the national media than brick-throwing mobs on the Meadow Well estate. But

*The events are briefly mentioned in Blunkett's published diary. After congratulating himself on the tough rhetoric he had used in response to the Bradford riot, he noted that 'we were not prepared to tolerate mindless violence and the counterproductive undermining of all our efforts, and that we would take any action necessary to stop it'; *The Blunkett Tapes*, 280.

under New Labour even London lost its lustre as a venue for protest. In July 1999 around 5,000 people gathered there for a Carnival Against Capitalism – part of a worldwide plan of action to coincide with the meeting of the affluent G8 group of nations in Cologne. Although the march was peaceful at first, some demonstrators in the City of London began to smash windows, and a group broke into a building associated with the Stock Exchange before being apprehended.

The following year anti-capitalist protestors descended on the capital for a May Day rally. This time the police were prepared for trouble; holiday leave was cancelled, and about 5,000 officers were on duty. However, this show of force proved insufficiently intimidating. Protestors in Parliament Square engaged in some 'guerilla gardening' – digging up turf and planting seeds – while the pugnacious statue of Sir Winston Churchill was daubed with graffiti. Around 1,000 people proceeded to the Strand, which had been a hub of the 1990 poll tax protest. They smashed the windows of a McDonald's burger bar, before clashing with police. Nearly a hundred activists were arrested on the day.

The former soldier who defaced Sir Winston's statue did a grave disservice to his cause. This action aroused the most negative publicity and provided a pretext for more 'interventionist' police tactics in future. The 2001 protests occurred on 2 May – the day before the general election would have been held, if the foot and mouth outbreak had been contained. Whether or not the police changed their plans to reflect the new electoral timetable, they were ready to prevent any new affronts to Sir Winston and the other august political figures on Parliament Square. In the capital's biggest police operation for over thirty years, more than 6,000 officers were on duty on 2 May 2001. After a series of peaceful and good-humoured protests, around 1,000 demonstrators converged on Oxford Street for what was rather ominously billed as The Sale of the Century. The crowd, which included tourists and avidly pro-capitalist shoppers, was penned in for hours by police cordons. Before leaving the area, all of these people were photographed by agents of the state. Despite this drastic action, the minority which had turned up looking for trouble got its way eventually: several shops were attacked. However, there were few injuries, and the government offered hearty congratulations to the police on a job well done.[47]

The images of 2 May 2001 provided a vivid snapshot of Britain at the end of Tony Blair's first term. The road which best symbolised the country's consumerist ethos had been turned into a temporary detention centre. But although a few representatives of the 'mainstream majority' had suffered serious inconvenience along with the militant hard core, the government clearly calculated that the electoral cost would have been much higher if they had not acted firmly. The overall impression created by the May Day scenes was that law-abiding people simply did not demonstrate, whatever the cause. The government's defenders could claim that there was no room for dialogue with the protestors on that specific occasion, but in other instances New Labour's policies created aggrieved minorities who felt that no one would listen unless they took direct action. For example, the pressure group Fathers 4 Justice opposed the operations of the Child Support Agency (CSA), as well as feeling that the courts too readily found in favour of the mother in contested custody cases. Although the CSA (founded in 1993) had aroused controversy under the Conservatives, its performance deteriorated under New Labour. The semi-autonomous government agency underlined the difficulty of holding ministers to account in the modern era. After a typical New Labour rebranding in June 2001, the Department of Work and Pensions took responsibility for the agency, but few members of the public would have been able to guess who was in overall charge. In May 2004 two exasperated members of Fathers 4 Justice breached security at the House of Commons and threw condoms filled with purple-dyed flour at the prime minister.

While the government could at least argue that it had inherited the CSA mess from the Tories, its handling of the hunting fraternity was a mess of its own making. Given that a hunting ban would be difficult to enforce and that many cruel 'sports' were left unaffected, the passage of legislation on this subject has to be counted as an example of the gesture politics which New Labour was supposedly against. The response was predictable. In September 2002 a London demonstration attracted at least 400,000 supporters of the newly-formal 'Countryside Alliance'. This passed without serious incident but two years later at least 10,000 pro-hunting demonstrators battled with police in Parliament Square. There were numerous complaints about aggressive police tactics from people who had only recently felt assured that the law would always favour them. On the face of it, the hunting fraternity was now as marginal to society as the denizens of Blackburn and

Burnley, or people who objected to the dehumanising effects of capitalism.*

Such events implied that although the Blair government passed the Human Rights Act in 1998 it had always taken a qualified view of its provisions. Civil libertarians lamented the apparent apostasy of politicians who had previously attacked the Conservatives for authoritarian attitudes; two of Blair's ministers, Patricia Hewitt and Harriet Harman (the wife of Jack Dromey, who had taken a leading role in the Grunwick protests of the 1970s), had actually been prominent in the National Council for Civil Liberties (NCCL). Before the 1992 general election Gordon Brown had identified himself with this trend within the Labour Party, telling the pressure group Charter 88 that the unwritten British constitution reflected 'the Hobbesian assumption that the function of government is to empower leaders, unbounded by any limitations, to deal with the threat to security posed by those who must be led'. Arguing that 'It is time to escape from that bleak view,' Brown put forward the case for 'entrenched rights' to protect the individual from the state. He also welcomed a resurgence of interest in PR at the time, arguing that 'a modern constitution must ensure the fullest possible public consultation'.[48] But an intolerance of dissent had been inherent in the Blair project from the start. Famously, New Labour MPs were badgered to 'stay on message' at all times by media managers. While this tendency originated in fear of the right-wing press, it coincided with a more general aspect of New Labour culture. The party went out of its way to create the impression that, while people were entitled to disagree with its policies, no respectable individual could possibly doubt its good intentions and open-mindedness. Thus, those who went as far as to demonstrate against the government must be irresponsible agitators, determined to impose their own views in defiance of the freely given mandate of the British people.

This 'control freakery' reached its apogee in 2005, when a veteran activist and refugee from fascism, Walter Wolfgang, was ejected from the Labour conference after heckling the foreign secretary, Jack Straw. In typical New Labour style, fulsome apologies were subsequently offered when it became clear that the media was interested in the story. Two very different demonstrations, from the early days of the New Labour era, indicated the extent to which non-believers would be marginalised. The first

---

* In July 2005 there was another serious clash between anti-capitalists and police, this time in Edinburgh just before the start of the G8 Summit at the Gleneagles Hotel.

was the stage-managed reception for Blair as he arrived in Downing Street on 2 May 1997. The following day even the crusty Conservative-supporting *Daily Telegraph* admitted that 'The television pictures of Mr Blair's young children entering Number 10 . . . somehow caught the national mood.'[49] In reality, New Labour's strategists had allowed a reliable group of party workers into Downing Street to wave their flags. More than anything else, it was this phoney image which inspired the uncritical media assertions about the 'national mood', rather than the authentic enthusiasm of people outside the iron gates, like the woman in her seventies who claimed that 'If I live to be a hundred there'll never be a day like it!' A decade later one columnist recalled scenes 'like the liberation of Paris' on London's South Bank, when Blair spoke in the immediate aftermath of victory: 'People were climbing lampposts, hugging each other, giddy with joy.' But such images conflicted with New Labour's concern to dampen expectations.[50]

The second demonstration was more spontaneous, but it was just as easy to turn it to New Labour's advantage. The car crash which killed Diana, Princess of Wales on 31 August 1997 was an indirect instance of 'Murder by Media', more than twenty years after John Stonehouse had proposed to write a book with that title. Naturally, Tony Blair decided not to dwell on the circumstances; instead he spoke as if the Lord had intervened to terminate the earthly toils of a sanctified being. His choice of reading at Diana's funeral – the verses in 1 Corinthians 13 which contain the injunction to 'bestow all my goods to feed the poor' – was slightly unfortunate, since not even the late princess had ever intended to go quite that far. But Blair's overall message throughout those days was that he and Diana enjoyed overwhelming democratic support, in contrast to the unelected Queen and her uncaring heir. The grief tourists who choked the Mall with 'floral tributes' in the days after Diana's death were his true subjects, whether or not they had voted Labour in the general election. The government's approval rating, which had declined quite steeply in July and August 1997, climbed back above 70 per cent in the wake of the funeral. This reversal of fortune mirrored that of Diana herself, whose public reputation had been under a cloud for some time before her death. Those who refused to plunge into ostentatious mourning were now the marginalised. Two elderly European visitors were jailed for two months (reduced on appeal) for the blasphemous act of pinching teddy bears from the pile of votive offerings. A Sardinian who committed a similar theft was fined £100 and beaten up after the court case.[51]

Blair's instant tribute to the 'People's Princess' had been a master-stroke from his own perspective. But it lent encouragement to people who presented much more of a threat to the British constitution than the rioters on the Meadow Well estate, or even the anti-capitalists who planted seeds in Parliament Square. Diana's death, and its anarchic aftermath, provided an unprecedented opportunity for enemies of the monarchy to exploit the public hunger for scapegoats. The cynical *Sun* placed itself at the head of the mob, commanding the Queen to demon-strate her compassion by ordering the flag on Buckingham Palace to be flown at half-mast. She had no choice but to comply, and to reas-sure the desolate nation with a broadcast which included the rather slighting but accurate description of Diana's devotees as 'millions of others who never met her, but felt they knew her'.

Although the monarchy scraped through the crisis, it was widely believed that it owed its survival to the sapient advice of Blair's media machine. Certainly Downing Street had given a public display of consti-tutional supremacy over Buckingham Palace in a way which Margaret Thatcher had never quite managed. In these circumstances it was much more difficult to resist a reform which brought the United Kingdom closer to dissolution. Less than a week after Diana's funeral the resi-dents of Scotland and Wales voted in referendums to establish devolved institutions. In both countries the turnout was unimpressive – 60 per cent in Scotland and 50 per cent in Wales, where the proposal for an assembly without tax-raising powers won a minuscule majority. The timing in fact was coincidental; Blair and his advisers would have tried to exploit Diana's death in the same fashion whether or not important constitutional questions were pending. Yet in tandem the incidents fostered the government's modernising image, while the Queen and the Conservatives were yoked together as unpleasant obstacles to change.

Devolution in Scotland and Wales would have proceeded under any Labour prime minister after 1997, but Northern Ireland presented a very different challenge; and in this field Blair's enhanced prestige was almost certainly a positive factor. On 10 April 1998, after protracted negotiations, most of the leading parties in Northern Ireland accepted proposals for a new elected assembly. Referendums in the North and in the Irish Republic subsequently endorsed this 'Good Friday agree-ment'. However, the vote among Unionists in the north was close, and support increased for Ian Paisley's Democratic Unionist Party (DUP), which had rejected the deal. The focal point of Unionist resentment was Drumcree, near Portadown in County Armagh. Every July since 1995 the UK government had been trying to prevent the local Orange lodge marching to Drumcree church through predominantly Catholic areas. For the first three years these attempts had failed, but in 1998, after the Good Friday agreement, the march was forcibly blocked for the first time. There was a violent reaction from some members of the Unionist community, and three young Catholic boys were killed in an arson attack in Ballymoney. The following month a car bomb in Omagh, County Tyrone killed twenty-nine men, women and children. The culprits were members of a group which had split from the IRA in protest against its renunciation of violence.

The horrified reaction to these atrocities suggested that the advocates of violence on both sides had finally been ostracised in Northern Ireland – the one part of the UK where an outbreak of apathy might have been a welcome development. The 1999 Unionist marching season passed off fairly quietly, even at Drumcree, but in 2000 there were renewed protests against the government's policy of rerouting the historic march of the Orangemen. Some areas of Belfast were brought to a standstill by barricades overseen by masked Unionist gangs. At Drumcree itself water cannon were used as a means of crowd control for the first time in thirty years. During the first two weeks of July 2000 nearly 300 people were injured – two thirds of them members of the security forces. In subsequent years the trouble receded, but Northern Ireland underlined its status as a place apart through its trend-defying electoral participation. Turnout in the 2001 general election was almost the same as it had been in 1992: just under 70 per cent. In 1992 that figure had been below the national average, but the 2001 turnout made Northern Ireland look like the UK's last outpost of democratic activism – even if its major parties were now Sinn Fein, which had until recently accepted the validity of violence as a political tactic, and the DUP, which continued to act as a roadblock against a negotiated settlement.

Tony Blair deserves considerable personal credit for his role in the Good Friday agreement. Although the elected Northern Ireland Assembly soon proved unworkable, at least this time the political stalemate was not accompanied by a general return to violence. The all-Ireland referendum took place on 22 May 1998. This was just two weeks after London residents had agreed in yet another referendum to set up an assembly of their own, with an elected mayor. This decision effectively reversed the Thatcherite abolition of the Greater London Council (GLC) back in 1986. Yet the turnout among Londoners was only 34 per cent. A similar proportion voted in the first assembly and mayoral elections, held in 2000. Blair and his allies had prevented the former GLC leader Ken Livingstone from standing as the official Labour candidate for mayor. In their eyes Livingstone was the epitome of Old, unelectable Labour. Livingstone effectively disproved the latter part of this proposition by standing as an independent and beating the official Labour candidate into third place. But given the dismal turnout in the election, he was left with even less democratic credibility than Blair.

New Labour's experiments with direct democracy brought mixed results; even if referendums went their way, they could not be sure what the voters would do next. Elections to the Scottish Parliament in May 1999 produced a coalition between Labour and the Liberal Democrats. The situation was similar in Wales, except that Blair's preferred candidate for first minister had to stand aside in favour of Rhodri Morgan, who was regarded as a renegade in the Livingstone mould. In the context of Westminster politics such setbacks were manageable, but Blair could not risk a rebuff from the UK electorate as a whole. He would have liked to call a poll on membership of the EU's single currency, and was advised by Roy Jenkins and others to grasp the nettle early in his first term while his popularity remained high. But the results of the devolution ballots, reinforced by the united opposition of Gordon Brown and Rupert Murdoch, persuaded him to back down. By October 1998 Blair and Brown had worked out a compromise formula under which the UK would only adopt the euro if five economic tests had been passed. Since the chancellor would be the judge, this meant in practice that Brown now enjoyed a veto over UK membership. Although the incident fuelled newspaper speculation about divisions at the top of New Labour, Brown had probably done Blair a considerable favour. In a referendum campaign the prime minister would have relied on his personal charisma to convert the less determined Euro-sceptics. After all, the same trick had been performed back in 1975, when Britain's most popular politicians had secured a vote in favour of continued EEC membership. Yet the task would have been considerably more difficult second time round. The public was no better informed about Europe, but the long years of relentless propaganda in newspapers like the *Sun* and the *Daily Mail* had hardened ignorant attitudes into saloon-bar certainties.

Additional evidence of apparent volatility and new-found recalcitrance among UK voters came in September 2000. As Anthony King has written, the fuel crisis of that month 'showed how quickly the British people as a whole could be turned against their government as a whole: "us" against "them" – in political rather than class terms. It also showed how much political tinder there was out there in the country, just waiting to be ignited.'[52]

Yet the fuel protests of September 2000 are open to a different interpretation. A small group of people – some estimates put the number at about 2,500 – almost brought the country to a standstill. Farmers, lorry drivers and other activists picketed oil refineries and deliberately dawdled on motorways, causing thirty-mile tailbacks. Ironically, among the many Tory policies which the government had retained, the protestors were targeting one of the few which had been far-sighted – the 'escalator', which from the early 1990s had raised the duty on fuel year on year in order to deter unnecessary motoring. However, the policy had been introduced when oil prices were low, and although Britain's own resources were running down it had been easy to assume that this situation would continue indefinitely. By the late summer of the year 2000, though, rising petrol prices had provoked a series of protests in France, where taxes on fuel were less onerous. British lorry drivers who made deliveries to continental Europe were badly affected by these actions, and when they finally struggled back to the UK – where fuel prices were much higher – a group of angry activists decided on direct action of their own.

When petrol was relatively cheap, the fact that almost three quarters of the cost consisted of duties and VAT was a fairly minor irritant. Yet as the price headed towards £4 per gallon – about 90p per litre – resentment among motorists in general inevitably focused on the government's imposts. Even so, far from demonstrating the quantity of 'political tinder' in the country, for most people the fuel crisis of 2000 was an entirely passive affair. They signalled their agreement with the protestors through opinion polls, and by the absence of vigorous objection as they queued before taking their turn at the petrol-pumps. Britain entered a period which, in its way, was just as surreal as the days of Diana hysteria. Although fuel supplies to emergency services were supposed to be guaranteed, the crisis had arisen too suddenly to accommodate contingency plans. Doctors on call certainly lacked any special provision. Less than a week after the protest began with the blockade of a refinery on Merseyside, only 300 out of Britain's 9,000 petrol stations still had fuel. Panic buying had begun in the shops, and preparations were made for declaring a state of emergency. Sensing an imminent change of mind among the fickle public and disorientated by the scale and speed of their success, the demonstrators began to relax their grip. Britain's motorists were soon back to their normal routine, frittering away fuel in motorway queues instead of waiting hours to refill their tanks on the forecourts.

At first sight, the 2000 fuel crisis seems to thwart any attempt to draw neat conclusions about the nature of protest in Britain since 1975. As a challenge to the authority of the state, the blockade of fuel depots across the country bears comparison with the miners' strike of 1984/5. On this occasion, though, the police just stood and watched. Far from trying to cross picket lines, as their counterparts had done at personal risk in previous disputes, the blockaded tanker drivers sat out the crisis and gloated over their swollen overtime payments. As one of them crowed, 'All we are doing is maintaining the vans, playing cards and drinking tea. But, best of all, we are being paid for it.'[53] The inactive drivers had the tacit support of their employers. The multinational fuel companies, as in the far graver situation of 1973/4, were siphoning profits from the crisis; and the longer it lasted the better for them.

Although there had been earlier stirrings of revolt with a 'Dump the Pump' campaign, the fuel crisis caught the government off guard. Loquacious ministers were suddenly unavailable for comment, although Blair himself made an unconvincing television appearance. The Conservatives actually surged ahead in the opinion polls, for the first time in more than eight years. The Opposition leader William Hague expressed guarded sympathy with the demonstrators. His party had stumbled into a rich vein of populist form; back in April it had championed the cause of a Norfolk farmer, Tony Martin, who was given a life sentence for shooting an intruder. Although this campaign was typical *Daily Mail* territory, it won backing from a much wider audience. When the BBC's prestigious *Today* programme asked its listeners at the end of 2003 to identify a new law that needed to be passed, the winning proposal, with more than a third of the votes, would have given householders the right to protect their property by any effective means.

The month before the fuel protests had also seen a spate of vigilante attacks against real or imaginary paedophiles. This outburst of millenarian madness was triggered by the murder in July 2000 of the eight-year-old Sarah Payne by Roy Whiting, who had already been convicted of child-sex offences. It was spurred on by Rupert Murdoch's *News of the World*, which was demanding a change in the law to notify local residents about any convicted paedophile living in their vicinity. Within two months a petition backing this reform had attracted more than 700,000 signatories. In the meantime, the newspaper published the names and supposed addresses of more than 100,000 child-sex offenders.

Over the years the *News of the World* had gradually been raising the stakes in its coverage, which included a 1994 exposé of a child porn ring including a retired major in the Irish Guards, a schoolmaster, an accountant, a weather forecaster for the RAF and the obligatory vicar. Colour pictures of all of the alleged offenders were included, but on this occasion the newspaper had at least done some homework on the individuals concerned.[54] During another campaign in 1997 a fourteen-year-old girl had died in a firebomb attack on the home of a suspected paedophile, and other innocent people were attacked. In that year, though, the law was tightened to prevent paedophiles from working with children and to increase the penalties for either taking or possessing indecent images. This followed a string of incidents like the random kidnapping, molestation and murder of a nine-year-old boy by two paedophiles in October 1994. Public outrage was understandable, particularly in a country where killers too often were released before they had served more than a fraction of their sentences; in this case, the idea of seizing and killing a young boy had apparently been hatched while the perpetrators were incarcerated together during the 1980s.[55] But on balance the press clamour against paedophiles undermined the purpose of the legal changes, making it more likely that serious offences would be committed in future. Potential offenders would now be far more reluctant to face up to their problem and seek help before they struck for the first time.

The *News of the World* should have been aware of the danger of inciting mob rule, whether or not its proposals were embodied in legislation. In February 2000 a convicted paedophile had been shot dead in the East End of London. In a local pub there had been no response to police inquiries about the likely culprits. As a regular explained, 'Everyone in here wants to buy them a big drink.'[56] During the *News of the World*'s campaign five months later cars were burned on Portsmouth's Paulsgrove estate and at least four families were forced to flee because of unfounded suspicions. One man, apparently, was targeted because 'he lived alone and often spoke of how much he loved his mother'. In Manchester a man's house was attacked by 300 local residents because he was wearing a neck brace; a similar surgical aid had been sported by one of the genuine paedophiles depicted in the *News of the World*. Mistaken identity was only to be expected, but some of these modern witch-hunters were also illiterate. Their most spectacular solecism occurred in south Wales, where the new custodians of public morality daubed 'paedo' on the home of a (female) specialist registrar in paediatric medicine. Such incidents were generally condoned by members of the public who thought that it was reasonable for innocents to suffer as long as the real child molesters knew that even after release from prison they would have to live in constant fear.[57] But apart from their direct contribution to several deaths, other aspects of the campaigns verged on child abuse. In Portsmouth, for example, very young children were encouraged to roam the streets chanting, 'Sex beast!' and, 'Hang him!'. In August 2002, children who witnessed the jeering of Maxine Carr, the partner of the Soham child-killer Ian Huntley, were visibly distressed.[58]

To its credit, the government did not give way to the *News of the World* over the public's identification of paedophiles. But its response to the vigilante violence was muted, compared to its unequivocal denunciation of any breakdown in public order which lacked the personal imprimatur of Rupert Murdoch. This context helps explain its supine attitude towards the fuel protestors, who emphasised their victory over the elected government by issuing a sixty-day ultimatum: if there was no action to reduce fuel prices before that time, the blockades would be back. There was no chance that Blair and Brown could comply with this deadline. They delayed their capitulation until the budget of the following March, when they poured out £1.7 billion of tax cuts for the gas-guzzlers.[59]

By then, New Labour's opinion poll lead had been restored. But an important lesson had been learned. In keeping with the general trend since 1975, protests which arose from an injured sense of self-interest were regarded as much more dangerous to governments than any collective expression of principle. The fuel crisis took this tendency to a new extreme. It had been an uprising of inert agitators – a mutiny of the immobile. State and society had been sent spinning into a sudden crisis because opinion polls showed majority support for the actions of a handful of angry people; the nation only returned to its senses when the effects of the protests became inconvenient. The immediate self-interest of being able to travel and to receive essential services finally overcame the selfish desire for cheaper petrol. In other words, whatever their current political allegiance, those who supported the protest were New Labour's target audience – the kind of people who had given Margaret Thatcher her disproportionate parliamentary majorities.

If the fuel protests underlined the power of unenlightened self-interest, the same month also marked a triumph for cultural bankruptcy. On 16 September 2000, while motorists replenished their thirsty vehicles, around ten million people seized their remote controls and punched the Channel 4 button. They were settling down to watch the last instalment of *Big Brother*'s first season. It is difficult to imagine a more effective deterrent for viewers than a television programme in which several attention-seeking young people are stuck together in a house, and encouraged to interact in order to fill several hours of broadcasting every night throughout the summer. Often the 'live' late-night episodes consisted entirely of uninteresting people asleep. Satirical comment seemed superfluous, although Ben Elton exploited *Big Brother*'s comic value in his novel *Dead Famous* (2001). Yet the show (based on a Dutch prototype) was very successful by Channel 4's standards, and that initial series in 2000 proved to be the first of many. The obvious reason was its appeal to the apathetic. It was a tacit recognition that millions of Britons were unable to inject anything which resembled entertainment into their own lives. It gave them something to talk about at work, and supplied the tabloids with pages of thoughtless commentary and speculation.

In view of these developments, it was hardly surprising that the turnout at the real general election just a few months later was so abysmal. If one could force a major government U-turn without bothering to protest, it was safe to leave the effort of voting to others; the result was unlikely to matter very much either way. The contrasting example of *Big Brother* underlined the predicament faced by politicians. It actually cost money to register a vote (via phone) in that contest, and no one could argue that the outcome would make the slightest difference to anybody, apart from the friends and relatives of the contestants. Yet, under relentless peer pressure and media insistence that 'everyone' was watching the show, young people (and even many older ones who should have been wiser) were able to convince themselves that this was a worthwhile exhibition, offering unique insights into contemporary society. In one respect this was true, but the interesting insights concerned the lasting popularity of the show, not its content.

The success of *Big Brother* under a Labour government would have reduced George Orwell to bitter tears. It seemed to verify the judgement of the journalist Peter Hitchens, who considered that Britain had bred 'the most conformist and least individualist generation in known history'.[60] The torrent of text votes cast an ironic light on research findings that depicted Britons as active citizens who had merely switched from collective enterprises, like voting in elections or joining political parties,* to individual forms of protest. According to one meticulous academic survey, although people were less likely to vote than they had been in the mid-1980s – or to contact politicians directly when they felt aggrieved – they were much more willing to boycott certain products or air their views through media outlets. 'Today's citizens,' concluded the authors of the study, 'are not alienated but atomised.' There were, though, more troubling findings in the same survey. Only 35 per cent were satisfied with the way British democracy was working, and more than half felt that they (and people like them) had no influence over government. In many cases the respondents who testified to a high level of activism were probably reporting what they *wished* they did rather than their actual behaviour. Certainly there was evidence that some respondents claimed to hold 'respectable' beliefs when their real attitudes were rather different. Recorded levels of public support for Tony Martin, for example, and the cool response to violence against paedophiles conflicted with the survey's finding that 66 per cent of Britons accepted that one should obey the law at all times.[61]

Amid talk of a crisis for Britain's main parties, research tended to focus on attitudes towards *political* engagement, albeit on a fairly wide definition of that term. While this task was difficult enough, it was almost impossible to get a genuine sense of the most pertinent *social* attitudes. Thus, for example, it was hard to admit to a researcher that, rather than intervening after witnessing a crime, one would avert one's eyes and make a dash for the domestic reassurances of home, a take-away meal and that evening's episode of *EastEnders*. But this was a key question about the psyche of consumerist society. Mrs Thatcher had answered it by saying that the Good Samaritan would not have been able to help the victim of robbery if he had been poor. This was true enough, but it was equally plausible to argue that his counterpart

---

* In 1975 membership of the Conservatives had been estimated at more than one million, but thirty years later it had fallen to around 300,000. Despite an initial rise in recruitment soon after Tony Blair became leader, individual Labour Party membership was less than 200,000 in the same year.

in contemporary Britain would have decided that it would be too much trouble to get involved. The feeling was vague and resistant to quantitive analysis, but to those who lived through the years after 1975 it seemed that Britain was dividing into two classes of passive bystanders: the well off, who were reluctant to jeopardise any of their prosperity, and the poor, who were aware that public-spirited actions could cost them everything.

In this context the initial response to the prospect of war in Iraq in 2003 was all the more remarkable. It certainly took the government by surprise, even more than the fuel protests of 2000. The conventional wisdom since 1975, after all, had been that the British were at their most apathetic when crucial decisions were pending. But on Sunday, 16 February 2003 more than a million people from around 250 cities and towns converged on London to protest against the long-plotted invasion. There were separate mass demonstrations in Belfast and in Glasgow, where the attendance was 100,000. It was possible to detect an undercurrent of individualism even in these vast gatherings – a common slogan, for example, was 'Not in my name', which implied that people were less bothered about the nature of the proposed action than the prospect of being held personally responsible for it. However, even if the protestors betrayed symptoms of 'atomisation', they gave a very convincing impression of unity in their opposition to the impending war. There were very few arrests in London, although it would be a mistake to call it a good-tempered demonstration. Among the speakers at the Hyde Park rally was the playwright Harold Pinter, who claimed that America was 'run by a bunch of criminal lunatics with Tony Blair as a hired Christian thug'.[62]

This evidence of public anger apparently presented Blair with a serious challenge. In the *Daily Mail* Richard Littlejohn referred to demonstrators as 'whistle-blowing Trots, mad women and excitable school children'.[63] But it was more difficult to dismiss the anti-war protestors as a mob of marginal malcontents. The numbers alone suggested that opposition to a war against Iraq must be widely spread, and the banners underlined the message. The London participants included the Eton George Orwell Society, Archaeologists Against War and a group of women barristers whose ranks presumably did not include the prime minister's wife.[64] However, after a little reflection Blair could conclude that the demonstration left his position unchanged. He was certainly taking a risk; despite the complacent military calculations of his US allies, there was a chance that the war would go badly. Whatever the outcome, it was unlikely that many of the marchers would be voting for New Labour next time round. But Blair knew that his prospects of a third term did not depend on people prepared to demonstrate on a matter of principle. The ones who mattered were those who stayed at home in front of their televisions and waited for events to tell them whether British involvement in Iraq had been wrong or right. They were the kind of people who would be more impressed by the views of a single celebrity than a million-strong march; and such individual initiatives were more likely to affect government decision-making. In February 2005 the 'celebrity chef' Jamie Oliver featured in the first instalment of a new series, *Jamie's School Dinners*. A month later 100,000 people had signed a petition demanding better meals for schoolchildren. Even before Oliver presented his petition in Downing Street, the government had decided that it could not resist such an impressive show of public support.

V

While Tony Blair presented himself as the embodiment of New Labour, his close friend Peter Mandelson was actually a more informative exemplar. Unlike Blair, Mandelson (born 1953) had strong family ties to the Labour Party, and in his youth his enthusiasm for radical causes had apparently brought him to the attention of the security services. After working in television, in 1985 he became Labour's director of campaigns and communications. In this role he gained a reputation for clever media manipulation. For example, he was credited with replacing Labour's red flag emblem with a red rose, although his role in this symbolic innovation has been disputed.[65] In fact, Mandelson's greatest achievement was to convince a swathe of Britain's media that he was exceptionally brilliant, if a little temperamental. Apart from his healthy self-regard and an ever-expanding list of useful contacts, tangible evidence of his prowess was difficult to pin down, but his reputation was strong enough to win selection for the safe Labour seat of Hartlepool in the north-east of England. Given Mandelson's outlook and high society associates, this was a bit like making Arthur Scargill MP for Tonbridge Wells.

After New Labour's 1997 election victory Mandelson certainly won himself an interesting footnote in political history. It is unlikely that anyone will match his record of being forced to resign from two different ministerial positions during the same parliament (in 1998 and 2001).* But even after his second involuntary departure Mandelson was not finished. Blair had a soft spot for him, not least because of dubious machinations which helped to win him the Labour leadership in 1994. In August 2004 the prime minister nominated Mandelson to serve as the EU's trade commissioner.

The latter appointment was the more breathtaking since both of Mandelson's resignations had raised serious doubts about his personal integrity. On the second occasion, in January 2001, he was accused of working to secure British passports for the billionaire Indian Hinduja brothers, who had been generous sponsors of the friendless Millennium Dome. If his previous record had been spotless, Mandelson would probably have avoided an involuntary career break over this incident; in itself it was far from being the most unsavoury episode in New Labour's protracted love affair with wealth, and the real culprits were the people who had foisted the Dome on an unwilling public in the first place. But his ministerial record was not particularly strong – after the second resignation the parliamentary sketch writer Simon Hoggart quipped that Mandelson was to government 'what Laurel and Hardy were to piano-moving' – and it was already obvious that personal considerations were capable of affecting his judgement.[66]

Mandelson had expensive tastes and was keen to experience social exclusion from the opulent end of the scale, living alongside those enviable individuals who are too rich to mingle with the unwashed multitude. Before the 1997 general election he had accepted the casual offer of a £373,000 loan from a fellow Labour MP, Geoffrey Robinson, to buy a house in Northumberland Place, between London's Bayswater and the newly fashionable Notting Hill. In itself, this was a serious mistake; apart from being associated with Mandelson's enemy Gordon Brown, Robinson's business activities were attracting official scrutiny. Possibly it was some calculation of this kind, rather than an accidental oversight, that excluded Robinson from the invitation list for Mandelson's house-warming celebration. By the time that news of the loan leaked out, in December 1998, Mandelson was secretary of state for trade and industry – the department investigating Robinson's financial affairs.

---

* He had begun as minister without portfolio, in which capacity he tried to rouse enthusiasm for the Millennium Dome. His efforts proved unsuccessful, despite his gushing praise of a game called surfball, which would be showcased in the Dome as 'The New 21st Century Sport'. Regrettably, no such game existed. See Peter Oborne, *The Rise of Political Lying*, Free Press, 2005, 3–5.

Mandelson's officials confirmed that he had not interfered with the inquiry. But he had failed to disclose the loan in Parliament's register of members' interests, and forgot to mention it to the building society which provided him with additional finance. When initially contacted by journalists, he claimed that the property had been purchased with 'family money'. More pertinently for his chances of survival, he had not even notified the prime minister of the true circumstances.[67]

At the height of the media hype about Mandelson, one serious commentator had gushed that this 'operator of genius' was 'impossible to dislike'.[68] In fact, almost exactly the reverse was the case. In one of his most puzzling comments Tony Blair had once said that his mission would not be complete until the Labour Party learned to love Peter Mandelson. After the 1998 loan it looked as if the party would not even have to pretend to tolerate him. Yet less than a year later he was back in the cabinet, as secretary of state for Northern Ireland. In a stunning insult to remaining party loyalists, Blair had re-hired Mandelson at the expense of Mo Mowlam, a person of independent character who had been more popular with many Labour loyalists than the prime minister himself.

Initial illusions about Blair and New Labour had dissipated even before Mandelson's first resignation. But Alastair Campbell, the shrewdest person in Downing Street, doubted that the government would ever recover its reputation once the Robinson loan became public knowledge. In the words of Campbell's hostile biographer, members of New Labour's inner circle were astonished that the negative impact in the opinion polls was so short-lived: 'the worst had happened – and nothing had changed'.[69] But the polls now reflected lack of confidence in the Opposition parties rather than enthusiasm for the government.

Mandelson was not the only minister to fall because of a fascination with the wealthy. In December 2004 David Blunkett was forced to resign from the Home Office after a series of stories arising from his affair with a rich American, Kimberly Quinn. The story contained elements of tragedy as well as the surreal. Blunkett was genuinely in love with Mrs Quinn, and as a divorced man his conduct could not be compared with that of his eminent predecessors like John Major. But apart from being married herself, Mrs Quinn was also the publisher of the right-wing magazine the *Spectator*. In the eyes of many Labour supporters this was a much greater offence than adultery. The liaison broke down amidst bitter recriminations and paternity claims. It subsequently emerged that Blunkett had indulged in Mandelsonian practices – trying to hurry through a visa application for a nanny who worked for his mistress.

When Blunkett finally resigned, Tony Blair said that he was departing without a stain on his integrity. If that was the case, it was asked, why had he been required to resign because of developments in his personal life? Blair's tacit answer was that Blunkett had not really resigned at all; he was just taking a temporary break before finding new employment. This, no doubt, explained why Blunkett was not asked to vacate his taxpayer-funded home in South Eaton Place, Belgravia – valued rather conservatively at £3 million. After the 2005 general election Blunkett finished his sabbatical and re-entered the cabinet as secretary of state for work and pensions. But within a few months he was out again, after revelations that he had taken a directorship in breach of ministerial guidelines. His offence showed that New Labour had inherited the financial laxity of previous governments, as well as their policies. It was a long-established custom for retired politicians to join the boards of prestigious companies, winning large handouts in return for minimal duties. But in the Thatcher years ex-ministers and former civil servants began to take up appointments with companies which they themselves had privatised. Despite muted public protests against this practice, it was not outlawed; ministers would just have to wait a few months before enjoying the real fruits of political office. By comparison, Blunkett's excursion into the private sector had not involved a major conflict of interest. But since he had been well aware that the prime minister wanted to bring him back he would have been well advised to avoid even the sniff of suspicion.

Although Blunkett and Mandelson epitomised a new breed of revolving-door ministers, they were not the only ones to behave erratically at this time. In June 2003 the unswervingly ambitious and ultra-Blairite health secretary, Alan Milburn, resigned in order to spend more time with his family. By the time of the 2005 general election the appeal of domestic life had clearly waned, and Milburn was hankering after a leading role in the campaign. These manoeuvres were not welcome to Chancellor Brown, and after the election Milburn returned to relative obscurity.

These comings and goings were bewildering enough for seasoned observers, let alone members of the general public, who had struggled to fit names to faces even in the old days when ministers took up posts and stayed there till their government fell. The incidents suggested that Blair disliked losing the services of dependable friends, but they also showed a significant relaxation in the standards expected from public servants, even since the sleaze-ridden 1990s and the introduction of tougher guidelines on conduct. It would have been bad enough if Blair had accepted resignations with reluctance, faced with overwhelming evidence of culpable conduct. As it was, the prime minister clearly did not consider that there had been any wrongdoing at all. The ministers only had to go because they generated a series of negative newspaper headlines, preventing New Labour from dictating the media agenda.

For ordinary voters, the message was clear. Ministers were no longer accountable, even in theory, to Parliament; their tenure of office depended on the favour of an untrammelled prime minister and an irresponsible media. Even then, they were not normally vulnerable solely on the grounds of professional competence. Ministers could face the sack for a variety of reasons, but now only succumbed if more than one difficulty was involved. In 1998 Mandelson was a victim of greed; but he had also been less than honest, and his unpopularity throughout the Labour Party had made him an accident waiting to happen. For his part, Blunkett had managed to dissipate a reservoir of public good-will through a combination of ill-judged affection, minor ministerial malpractice and finally financial impropriety.

Ironically, all these events happened at a time when, as Blunkett maintained in 2001, people were 'switched off' by politics, feeling that their representatives were 'out of touch'. The truth was very different. MPs and ministers were increasingly unpopular because they were no longer easy to distinguish from a considerable section of the electorate; and (unlike footballers and celebrity chefs) they were not interesting enough as people to deflect criticisms of their all-too-common frailties. Mandelson, for example, had coveted a property in a sought-after area of London while lacking the independent means necessary for the purchase. He fell from office (the first time) when the BBC was commissioning a stream of television programmes which catered for the growing army of property pornographers. Reality shows which followed the fortunes of would-be profiteers saturated the daytime schedules. Mandelson had bent the rules by failing to notify a building society that his Notting Hill purchase depended on another, much larger loan. But who in modern Britain would have behaved differently in his circumstances?

Blair's ministers should have been sensitive to allegations of personal avarice, given that they represented what had once been the workers' party. However, they were entirely unapologetic about their quest for wealth; even when caught cutting corners, they confined their regrets to the tactics they had used, not their ultimate aim of affluence. Thus, for example, in July 1998 one of Mandelson's associates who had become a private lobbyist was exposed for promising privileged access to ministers and inside information as long as the price was right. This 'cash for access' scandal was potentially more serious than its Majorite predecessor 'cash for questions'. It inspired Blair to reassert that 'We are on the side of ordinary people against privilege. We must be purer than pure.'[70] But a senior Downing Street adviser who was heavily implicated in the affair kept his position and was rewarded with a substantial pay increase.[71]

During Blair's second term the press turned its attention to his own property portfolio. In December 2002 the *Daily Mail* – still stubbornly off-message for all the government's wooing – revealed that the Blair family had bought flats in the elegant Clifton area of Bristol, where a son was attending university. This was a commonplace ruse for the rich; it allowed their children to live rent-free, and when their studies were over the property could either be sold at a handsome profit or rented out to the next generation of scholars. Thus the Blairs were trying to exempt themselves from the increasing financial burden imposed by higher education – a burden which the New Labour government substantially increased through the introduction of tuition fees. It was part of a pattern. The Blairs had also courted controversy by sending the same son to a grant-maintained school well outside their catchment area. But the story of the Clifton flats contained a further twist. According to the *Mail*, the asking price had been reduced after tough negotiations on behalf of the Blairs by a well-known Australian con man who was in a relationship with the former glamour model Carole Caplin.

Two years later the Blairs invested more than £3 million in 29 Connaught Square – within brick-throwing range of Hyde Park, the scene of the anti-war rally of February 2003. By most standards both Tony and Cherie were high earners, but not in the £3 million bracket. The taxpayer disbursed £179,000 per year for Tony's services, and although he was guaranteed a similar sum after retirement, he was obviously anticipating a regular supply of generous cheques from other sources once he had left Downing Street. Compared to the England football manager he had good reason to feel short-changed by public service. Back in 1974 the remuneration of the British prime minister and England's soccer supremo had been roughly the same (about £20,000 – although the prime minister received an additional £4,500 as an MP). But Sven Goran Eriksson's pay package was estimated to be worth around £4.5 million a year, and he was also able to sign up for a range of lucrative spin-offs. The England manager's name was even used to promote a recorded collection of classical music, which in the days of Don Revie would have been regarded as a feeble joke.

Eriksson's story was an updated version of the Revie affair of the mid-1970s with the sums involved on an entirely different scale, to reflect the rampant commercialisation of the game more than inflation. Revie had been a devoted husband at a time when personal morality was regarded as a relevant factor in a manager's life – in July 1977 Manchester United sacked Tommy Docherty because he was having an affair with the wife of the club's physiotherapist. By contrast, Revie's Swedish-born successor was a bachelor whose eye for physical talent provided additional material for the tabloids. Revie had been lured away by Middle Eastern money in an era when commentators were complaining that a brain drain was forcing talented Britons to leave the country; Eriksson was persuaded to move to England by the same inducements. When the appointment was announced in November 2000 some British newspapers were appalled that the country had to look abroad for a suitably qualified coach; the *Sun* called the decision 'a terrible, pathetic, self-inflicted indictment'.[72] These cries of patriotic pain died away after Eriksson's side beat Germany 5–1 – a result which kept alive English hopes of World Cup qualification, in addition to its xenophobic significance. Memories of this match allowed Eriksson to survive embarrassing revelations about his love life and (more relevantly) England's failure to win major international tournaments in 2002 and 2004. In the latter year, indeed, Eriksson was accused of negotiating a new job for himself, but unlike Don Revie the scandalous Scandinavian was rewarded by the FA with a pay rise. The public, which paid Eriksson's wages, was not consulted on the matter. The FA could ignore their feelings, safe in the knowledge that they were unlikely to withdraw their support from the national team whoever was in charge.

The contrast between Eriksson's treatment and the Revie case was a neat illustration of more general developments. In the intervening years British football had become a business rather than a sporting activity, yet its influence on society as a whole had grown enormously.

Footballers (or their female conquests) were now a regular feature on both the front and back pages of the tabloids. Now that most hooligans had been priced out of the all-seater stadiums, it was safe for Tony Blair and his friends to associate with successful teams. According to one delicious (but probably untrue) story, it was Alastair Campbell who first introduced Eriksson to one of his celebrity lovers, at a party hosted by a newspaper proprietor who was also a Labour Party donor.[73]

Like politicians, leading football teams had been sucked into a symbiotic relationship with the media. In the early twenty-first century managers were expected to talk like spin doctors, and players who were otherwise inarticulate were coached into using the same deceitful language. The uncritical media obsession with wealth and celebrity meant that overpaid footballers were no longer applauded merely for their performance on the pitch. Their lifestyles were held up as models for emulation, and many young people fell for the glamorous illusion. Even the joy-riders in estates like the Meadow Well probably thought that stealing a high-performance car and driving it much too fast would allow them to make fingertip contact with the same dream. Others took a more orthodox route to the same destination, funding their excesses with personal loans that they could never hope to repay. According to official figures, when New Labour won its landslide in 1997 UK consumers had totted up unsecured debts excluding mortgages of £88 billion. By 2005 this figure had more than doubled, to £193 billion. In 2004 Britain had more credit cards than people.[74]

In New Labour's Britain greedy footballers could still be criticised, but only when their teams were defeated. The stock response to moral objections was that astronomical salaries merely reflected the operation of the free market. Indeed, in many cases the residual feeling of revulsion was aroused not by the salaries but by their recipients – especially when they had originated in Britain's marginalised communities. By contrast, compared to the 1990s there was little comment about overpaid businessmen under Blair. In 2002 the average salary for a chief executive in one of Britain's top hundred companies was £1.7 million, excluding pension rights.[75] New Labour justified the maintenance of the Lawson/Thatcher top tax rate of 40 per cent for such individuals with the argument that it would be wrong for any government to penalise 'hard-working families'. While successive governments had forced the trade unions to adopt democratic procedures, there was little prospect that they would interfere in the internal affairs of businesses. It was assumed that excessive pay rises would be vetoed by shareholders, but the dominance of big, anonymous institutions invariably run by overpaid individuals meant that the average investor had no influence over boardroom decisions.

During the Thatcher years people like Sir Keith Joseph had heaped adulation on successful businessmen because of a genuine optimism about the dynamic potential of the entrepreneurial outlook. Long before Thatcher left Downing Street this feeling had begun to subside into a cynical worship of wealth, regardless of its origins. But many of Thatcher's ministers had experience of the business world, and could discriminate between different classes of crook to the extent that they usually avoided close contact with the ones who were sure to end up in prison. New Labour lacked this useful insight. Its leading figures were merely impressed by money, regardless of its provenance. Given the prevailing attitudes at the top, it is no surprise that individual ministers felt aggrieved when they were required to leave their posts because of financial transgressions which were vanishingly trivial when judged by the standards of private enterprise.

VI

After Britain joined the American adventure in Iraq, two ministers broke with recent tradition by resigning from the government on principle. Robin Cook (1946–2005) and Clare Short were not the only cabinet members with strong reservations about British policy, and purists argued that they should have left long before the conflict, given their general misgivings about New Labour. Yet by 2003 it could be said that, according to the criterion of integrity, the only people fit to serve in the British cabinet were the ones who were most willing to leave it. Nevertheless, two years later the electorate rewarded New Labour with a further period in office.

At least the 2005 general election saw a slight increase in turnout. However, as we have seen this was only achieved through new concessions to apathetic voters, who were now actively being encouraged to register a preference by post, whether or not they were away from home. And the detailed figures were more disturbing than ever. Among voters aged 18–24, turnout was only 37 per cent – a further decline of 2 per cent compared to the dire situation in 2001. The biggest increase was registered among the over-65s, who were most likely to respond to the suggestion that voting was a civic duty. This hardly augured well for the future. BBC Radio 4 listeners who successfully nominated apathy as the 'eighth deadly sin' in August 2004 had every reason to think that it would be a lasting phenomenon.* In March 2005 the chief executive of the Electoral Commission argued that 'Far from being a nation plagued by political apathy, people in the UK are feeling increasingly engaged.'[76] The reason for his claim was the unprecedented number of political parties which had registered with the commission before the 2005 general election. But the majority of new candidates were single-issue campaigners, standing in the hope of making a point – like Reg Keys, who opposed Tony Blair at Sedgefield in remembrance of his son who had been killed in the Iraq War.

Once again, in this election Labour secured the support of just over a fifth of the British electorate. Under an electoral system designed at a time when people actually voted, this still delivered a respectable overall majority of 66 seats. Keys mustered more than 10 per cent of the Sedgefield vote, but most of the other single-issue candidates sank without trace. There were, though, one or two upsets. Dr Richard Taylor, who had won Wyre Forest in 2001 as an independent trying to save the local hospital, retained the seat four years later. The constituency of Blaenau Gwent – sacred soil for Labour, as the old seat of Nye Bevan – was taken by a popular local figure who had resigned from the party in protest against an undemocratic selection process. The controversial anti-war campaigner George Galloway (born 1954), whose departure from the Labour Party had been involuntary, took Bethnal Green and Bow from Oona King, one of the ablest and most interesting of New Labour loyalists. Taking all the circumstances into account, this last result was probably the most sensational rebuke to British foreign policy in the era of universal franchise. But the government was able to shrug it off, and Galloway was reduced to trying to proselytise a wider audience by making a bizarre appearance on a celebrity version of *Big Brother*.

Thus even the outdated British electoral system could still administer some micro-shocks, but for those who resented the prolonged dominance of Labour and the Conservatives, the 2005 general election

* The rest of the top ten, in a poll run for the *Midsummer Sins* programme, were selfishness, hypocrisy, indifference, intolerance, ignorance, deceit, waste, cruelty and cynicism. Political correctness, spin, reality TV and celebrity worship were also-rans; *The Times*, 1 September 2004.

was uniquely dismal. There was an interesting contrast this time in the two sides' assessments of the state of Britain. On behalf of the Conservatives, their leader Michael Howard declared that 'Britain is a great country,' while Tony Blair more guardedly asserted that 'The British people have the capacity to make this a great country.' But on domestic issues the two parties were now virtually indistinguishable. A key theme of each manifesto was the importance of 'choice', but politics was the one arena in British society from which this was effectively excluded. Just as New Labour had tried since 1994 to give the electorate Thatcherism with a human face, now the Conservatives offered Blairism without Blair. Yet many New Labour candidates had already hit on the same idea, making sure that the prime minister's grinning visage was kept off their election literature. The Conservatives did try to distance themselves from the government's foreign policy. However, Michael Howard had been a strong advocate of action against Saddam Hussein long before the war broke out, and no one could seriously doubt that his party would have been just as subservient to the United States if it had returned to office in 2001.

Among Britain's major parties this left the Liberal Democrats. Once again, in his manifesto message their leader Charles Kennedy broke from the consensus, warning that 'Britain has real problems.' The party did reasonably well, winning 62 seats (up eight since 2001) with more than 22 per cent of the vote. But some leading Liberal Democrats had hoped for more, particularly since they had been well placed to benefit from opposition to the Iraq War. Within a few months they had ditched Charles Kennedy despite his personal popularity among Lib Dem activists and in the country as a whole. A drink problem was the main reason for Kennedy's downfall, although initially senior colleagues had tried to conceal this from the public. Kennedy's health only became an issue when members of his party grew impatient with his approach to the domestic policy agenda. In 2005 the Liberal Democrats were once again alone among the major parties in advocating higher income tax to pay for public services. They wanted to introduce a new top rate of 50 per cent. By post-war standards this was a timid proposal which would still leave the top rate below the level which had prevailed for most of Margaret Thatcher's premiership and it would start at a much higher income level. But some Liberal Democrats felt that the party would never make a decisive breakthrough if its policies deviated from the presumed demands of key voters. Kennedy's departure was seen as part of a campaign to reposition the Liberal Democrats in the 'middle ground of British politics', where they would fight for the favours of Britain's comfortable classes alongside Labour and the Conservatives.

The future shape of British politics was suggested by New Labour's slogan for the 2005 general election: 'Forward not back'. In May 2005 this just seemed starkly uninventive, but within two months Britons could be forgiven for looking back to the days before 1997 with nostalgia. Even the cold war seemed preferable to the fearful future which Tony Blair had heralded by agreeing to back George W. Bush's 'crusade' against the 'axis of evil'. On 7 July 2005 four bombs exploded in London's public transport network – three on Tube trains and one on a bus. Fifty-two people were killed and nearly 800 injured. The explosives were set off by British-born suicide bombers. For under-standable reasons the government tried hard to deny any responsibility, arguing with marginal relevance that the attacks on New York in 2001 had occurred before the Iraq invasion. The only logical conclusion was that the threat had been grave in 2001, and was now much worse thanks to Tony Blair's foreign policy.

In the ensuing blame game it was insufficiently remarked that the victims had included Muslims, Jews, Christians and agnostics from an astonishing variety of backgrounds. Whatever their origins or creeds, most of them would probably have thought of themselves as Londoners. This suggested that, in the capital at least, the general British attitude towards ethnic differences had improved beyond all recognition since the mid-1970s. From this poignant perspective, debates about the different approaches – multiculturalism, integration and the rest – seemed sterile. The existing approach, however ad hoc and even inco-herent, seemed to have been working. But away from London an underlying cause of unrest was a feeling of alienation from contem-porary British culture among many young Muslims. The rioting in towns like Bradford had given some indication of this problem, but a more telling early sign of the depth of feeling was the reaction in 1989 against Salman Rushdie's 'blasphemous' novel *The Satanic Verses*. The book had been burned in Bolton and Bradford; thousands marched in Leicester and London. The Iranian regime called on Muslims to kill the author and announced an additional financial inducement. The British government had provided Rushdie with armed protection, but apparently made little attempt to comprehend the nature of the backlash.

If it had done so, its conclusions would have unsettled its complacent assumption that serious disorder in Britain could only arise from the marginalised powerless poor, or from naive idealists whose ambitions encompassed no more than a few smashed windows and the planting of seeds on Parliament Square.

In its own way, the furore against Rushdie was a product of Islamic apathy. It was fairly safe to assume that very few demonstrators had leafed through the *Satanic Verses* and reached their own considered conclusions; unlike most members of the Church of England they were quite happy to follow the judgement of their religious leaders. Yet British Muslims were not alone in approving or tacitly accepting violent measures undertaken on the basis of other people's dogmatic opinions. Initially, Blair's decision to befriend the US President George W. Bush was a token of his desire to make a difference in global politics, made more urgent by the dominance of his rival Gordon Brown in domestic affairs. Yet Bush was elected for the first time in November 2000 – just a few weeks after the fuel crisis which had persuaded Blair to strengthen his appeal to right-wing populist sentiment at home. Bush's victory, narrow and bitterly contested as it was, gave an additional motive for Blair to move away from the progressive platform he had shared with the previous president, Bill Clinton. In any case, if the prime minister played hard to get with the new leader of the democratic world, there was a danger that William Hague would rush over to Washington and lap up all the photo opportunities before the next election.

Although he had sided so openly with Bush for tactical reasons, there was no way Blair could spin himself out of the role after the terrorist attack on New York in September 2001. Before the end of that month he had flown across the Atlantic and received two standing ovations during a speech by Bush in which the president told a joint session of Congress, 'either you are with us or you are with the terrorists'. After that emotional display of appreciation – so different from the receptions he could expect in Britain, at least without concerted stage management – the British prime minister would always actively seek reasons for giving the US wholehearted support when a cooler head would have dictated caution.[77]

Undoubtedly Blair believed intelligence reports about Saddam Hussein's accumulation and concealment of weapons of mass destruction. Back in November 1997 he had told the then Liberal Democrat leader Paddy Ashdown that Saddam Hussein was 'pretty close to [developing] some appalling weapons of mass destruction . . . We cannot let him get away with it.'[78] But it was clear from that conversation that Blair enjoyed his intimate contact with the intelligence community, which gave him access to information denied to others. The pleasure of being privy to big secrets – whether or not they were true – was one of the few meaningful perks of office. In his first term Blair had championed controversial but broadly successful military interventions in the Balkans and Sierra Leone. These conflicts strengthened his belief in his own judgement, and the antiquated British constitution meant that he could exercise prerogative powers over questions of war and peace. As a consequence, when Bush asked for his support, Blair could offer personal assurances with the confidence of his monarchical predecessors in pre-democratic days.

However, it would be helpful if Britain could be committed to war with majority backing from public opinion, and concrete proof of Saddam's deadly stockpiles was lacking. In February 2003 the respected US secretary of state, Colin Powell, had presented satellite pictures of suspicious Iraqi activity to the UN, but to the dismay of the British government the images contained nothing sinister. Powell's ill-starred performance followed closely on the production of a dossier by the British government. This had sounded more alarming, but turned out to be plagiarised from a PhD student, with superficial editing from government spin doctors.

There had been a more serious attempt to use intelligence reports to the same end in September 2002, and at the time no one could be sure that those reports were mistaken. But the production of a second dossier suggested a degree of panic among ministers, as it was becoming clear that Blair would have to allow a Commons vote before joining Bush's war. 'Either Tony knows something the rest of us don't know, or he's insane,' confided one of Blair's colleagues.[79] Presumably Blair was alone among members of the cabinet in knowing why a security alert sent troops and tanks to Heathrow Airport just before the Commons vote; to most objective observers it looked like a transparent attempt to link Iraq to al-Qaeda, and even the home secretary thought that the show of force was 'way over the top'.[80] The government's desperation was all too obvious to Labour backbenchers. When the vote was held, on 26 February 2003, 121 MPs rebelled against a three-line whip. However, the government's gargantuan majority coupled with the compliance of most Tory MPs made it look to casual observers as if Blair had secured a convincing mandate to make war. Once he had crossed this hurdle and the bombing had started, he could rely on British apathy to endorse his fait accompli. At the time of the London demonstration in February opinion polls suggested that more than half of the public was against war. Four days after the conflict started – when the principles at stake were unchanged and Saddam's regime had failed to retaliate with any of its 'appalling weapons of mass destruction' – dissent had dwindled to just 30 per cent. Sales of the *Daily Mirror*, which stood alone among the tabloids in articulating a robust anti-war case, began to fall by 80,000 per day. Before the war only a third of voters said that they endorsed the moral case for intervention. By May 2003, when it seemed that the campaign had been swift and virtually costless in terms of British lives, almost six in ten Britons accepted the justice of the cause.[81]

On 18 July 2003 Blair received more plaudits from his admirers in Washington after the award of a congressional medal in recognition of his services. But just before he delivered his speech of acceptance he had received some disturbing news. Dr David Kelly, who had served as a weapons inspector in Iraq, had committed suicide the previous day. Kelly had been exposed as the main source for a claim, put forward in a BBC broadcast at the end of May, that the government had built its case for war on information which it probably disbelieved. Breaking with usual practice, ministers had allowed Dr Kelly to appear before the parliamentary Foreign Affairs Committee, which had handled him roughly just two days before his disappearance. One MP had claimed with justice that Kelly was being set up as the 'fall guy'. Subsequently it was hinted that he had been affected by a variety of problems to make it seem that his exposure was merely the tipping point for a troubled man. In a sign of the money-grubbing attitudes which had supplanted the old public service ethos in the Whitehall of 2001, Kelly's personnel director at the Ministry of Defence had noted that 'The poor chap hasn't had a pay rise for three years.' At the time of his death Kelly's salary was 'only' £61,000 per year.[82] In hindsight, ministers probably thought that a few more thousand would have kept his mouth shut.

Renewed pressure after Dr Kelly's death forced the government to concede an inquiry, overseen by the experienced judge Lord Hutton. As it turned out, Hutton's experience was of the wrong kind. Much of it had been gained in Northern Ireland, where it was impolitic for the judiciary to ask too many relevant questions. At a cost to the taxpayer of £1.7 million, the inquiry exposed unacceptable practices in government, particularly in its dealings with the security services. But while Hutton could not control the flood of incriminating evidence, as judge and jury in this case he could draw conclusions according to his personal whim. When he reported in January 2004 he duly found that the BBC was to blame for everything. In an echo of old-style eastern European dealings with the media, Greg Dyke, the Corporation's director-general and a former donor to Labour Party funds, was forced to resign. Hutton's conclusions had been leaked in advance to the government's favourite mouthpiece, the *Sun*. This triggered another six-month inquiry, which failed to track down a culprit who would have been as easy to unmask as Dr Kelly himself had the pursuit been equally vigorous. No minister or civil servant left the government as a direct result of Hutton's findings; indeed, in some cases involvement in the scandalous affair proved no barrier to promotion.

For those with a medium-term memory, the Hutton inquiry suggested parallels with an earlier investigation. In February 1996, when Sir Richard Scott published his 1,800-page report on the sale of arms to Iraq in defiance of the government's own rules, the leader of the Opposition had been incredulous at the lack of accountability. 'On virtually every page of the report,' Tony Blair had stormed, 'there are details of answers that are untrue, inaccurate, misleading. Is no one going to take responsibility for that?'[83] In 1996 Blair had said that until the Major government answered Scott's criticisms, it would remain 'knee deep in dishonour'. From his phraseology it seems that Hutton, at least, had taken his cue from the Scott report. He even borrowed a word from his predecessor's rather lame conclusion, which had cleared ministers of 'any duplicitous intent' over the arms sales. Hutton's cut-and-paste version was that Blair had not conducted a 'dishonourable, duplicitous or underhand strategy' in his approach to the Kelly affair.

Between 1996 and 2004 politicians had learned some crucial lessons about the handling of public inquiries. The first task, of course, was to find a suitable person to preside. Sir Richard Scott had caused nothing but trouble, which could have been predicted from his previous track record. Once it became clear that Scott's findings would be inconvenient, 'Ministers and Whitehall mandarins had mounted an insidious campaign of denigration and intimidation against him.'[84] This was a disagreeable and time-consuming exercise which was never likely to get very far when even one of the implicated ministers, Alan

Clark, was willing to concede that Scott was 'a splendid man – cool, clear-headed and witty'.[85] There was no need for a similar campaign in 2004/5. At the time of his appointment Lord Hutton was depicted even by reasonably impartial journalists as a fearless truth-seeker, but the government must have been aware that the reality was somewhat different. Hearing of Hutton's appointment, one QC remarked that 'If I was a government and wanted a conservative judge to do what he's told to do, no more, no less, and keep it within very narrow confines, he would be my first choice.'[86] To reassure ministers who were worried that he might develop Scottite tendencies in the course of the inquiry, Hutton adopted highly restrictive terms of reference. As Simon Jenkins put it after Hutton had announced his findings, 'He was like a man seeking the causes of the Great War in the driving ability of Archduke Franz Ferdinand's chauffeur.'[87]

The deflating effect of the Hutton report on remaining British dissenters can hardly be exaggerated. As well as being exhaustively reported in the media, the evidence (running to 10,000 pages) was made available online as it emerged. On this basis a damning verdict followed by a humiliating public apology from the government was the least that could be expected. In September 2003 the Liberal Democrats had won Ken Livingstone's old constituency of Brent East on an anti-Labour swing of almost 30 per cent. David Blunkett had conceded that Iraq was a major factor in this result. Pre-Hutton surveys showed that less than half of the public now trusted either the BBC or the government to tell the truth.[88] In combination with the pre-war demonstrations, this amounted to the kind of scenario that had preceded Margaret Thatcher's departure from office in 1990. Yet in hindsight, since Britain's democratic institutions had failed to prevent participation in the conflict, it seemed over-optimistic to expect an unelected judge to regenerate confidence in the political system by condemning the way in which the government had manipulated its case for war. Once the report was published, phone-in polls conducted by the BBC and Channel 4 suggested an overwhelming feeling that Hutton had presented a whitewash. Those who had persisted in their opposition to the war despaired all the more because they sensed that there was no other way to hold the prime minister to account. Few people regarded either of the main opposition parties as viable alternatives to the existing party of government, and of course Blair could hold the next general election at a time of his choosing.

As Peter Oborne has written, 'when politicians lie they change their relationship with the electorate from one of equals to one of master and servant'.[89] Even on the kindest construction, Blair and his colleagues had argued the case for war on the basis of claims which turned out to be seriously exaggerated. If the government escaped without chastisement, the concept of public accountability in one of the world's oldest democracies would be exposed as a sham. At least after a comparable foreign policy misadventure – Britain's involvement in the Suez episode of 1956 – the prime minister, Anthony Eden, had been supplanted before the Conservatives were re-elected three years later. On that occasion the predemocratic processes of Eden's party had ensured his quiet removal. No similar informal mechanism existed within New Labour, which was the creation of the current prime minister. After Hutton it seemed that there was only one tribunal that could hold Blair to account. After committing Britain to the war, he had referred to his willingness to justify before God any of the deaths and maimings that resulted from his decisions.[90]

There was, though, one last line of earthly resistance. In the month after Hutton's report the government set up a new committee under the former cabinet secretary Lord Butler. This body had a much wider remit and could appraise the quality of intelligence on Iraq which had never been available to the public. Public expectation was low this time, reflecting the Hutton effect but also the patchy record of civil servants in previous inquiries of this kind. Ironically, back in 1996 Butler himself had been criticised by Sir Richard Scott for his role in the arms to Iraq affair. Yet when the findings of his committee were published in July 2004, they proved to be a stinging critique of the whole Blairite system of government. Although New Labour was dazzled by private industry, its decision-making process reflected its true exemplar: the media. Weighty matters of state were discussed informally, as if the ministers and their assorted aides were taking part in an editorial conference before a television chat show. Although the government habitually accused its critics of focusing on 'froth' instead of the substance of policy, the report proved that for New Labour presentational concerns *were* the substance. Butler knew all about Blair's attitude to collective decision-making from his brief service (1997–8) under New Labour. As the seasoned mandarin had reported to Paddy Ashdown at the time, on one occasion Blair remarked, 'I find it intensely boring having to consult with people, when the outcome is just common sense.'[91]

In short, the Butler inquiry confirmed what many had suspected – that behind its veneer of slickness and spin the government was a ramshackle outfit. Yet in spite of Butler's searching analysis, his constitutional position made it impossible for him to land the decisive blow without outside help. As he subsequently told the House of Commons Public Administration Committee, it would have been 'improper for [his committee] to say we think that the Government should resign on this matter'.[92] The former mandarin was clearly implying that Parliament had failed to take the broadest of hints.

At the beginning of October 2004 Tony Blair announced that he intended to fight the next election as prime minister but would stand down towards the end of the parliament. He claimed that he wanted to quell speculation about his position, but the real purpose was to dissuade anyone who wanted to turn the rampant speculation into an active attempt to accelerate his exit. Blair was tacitly saying to his critics that they would get their way before too long without running the risk of looking disloyal, if only they would exercise a little patience. At Labour's 2004 party conference he had fought grimly to stave off a critical motion on the Iraq War, and a minor heart problem required the kind of hospital treatment which so often prompts anxious colleagues to prescribe a well-earned rest. Once again, Mrs Thatcher's example was in Blair's mind. After spurning the opportunity of leaving Downing Street on the tenth anniversary of her first victory, she had given the impression of wanting to continue indefinitely. That prospect had been enough to convince some waverers that an involuntary change of leadership might be the lesser of two evils. If she had taken the Blair approach, she could have stayed on at least for another year.

Blair's announcement was a typical New Labour gambit, which contrasted with a famous Old Labour precedent. Harold Wilson had known before the February 1974 election that he would not serve another full term, but he had kept this information to himself until a few months before his retirement in April 1976, and even then only confided in a few people. In comparison, Blair's declaration could seem like a triumph for transparency. But from a longer perspective it brought the British democratic process into greater discredit. Despite Blair's protestations, in setting his own timetable for departure he was taking two constituencies for granted – Labour MPs, who still enjoyed the constitutional right to depose him if he lost their confidence in the interim, and the electorate as a whole, who might decide to eject his party from office before the appointed time. By October 2004 Blair's policies had made him many enemies within both constituencies – and few friends who could defend his record on principled grounds. In that context his revelation that he would leave Downing Street some time before 2010 was an eloquent comment on the state of British democracy, from someone who had studied the nature of public opinion more than most.

Yet even if things had never been all that good, it was clear from the perspective of 2005 that there had been a process of decline over the last three decades. Causes and effects were almost impossible to disentangle. For example, had politicians begun to inspire contempt because they were truly contemptible? Or had the electorate, spurred on by a disrespectful media, started to judge politicians by unrealistic standards? Did a selfish public get the politicians it deserved? Or had selfish demands been encouraged by irresponsible political campaigning?

The most depressing conclusion was that the original defects lay in the system of choosing Britain's leaders – in democracy itself, not just the archaic first-past-the-post British variant. On this view, New Labour was the logical culmination of the democratic process. A party whose only principle was the need to be popular, and which regarded electioneering, rather than government, as the main business of politics, had ended up persuading millions of voters to stay away from the polls. It might be argued that voting in general elections is an irrational activity. In a brilliant pamphlet written before the 2001 election, the academic Colin Crouch argued that democracy can only thrive 'in the early years of achieving it or after great regime crises'.[93] But on balance the act of voting is easier to defend on rational grounds than other modern pastimes – like travelling miles to London to add one more bouquet to Diana's leafy tributes; supporting local football teams whose players are all mercenary imports; waiting for a space to become free next to a supermarket in a half-empty car park; or helping to choose the winning housemate in *Big Brother*. It was only under New Labour that the exercise of a hard-earned citizenship right suddenly began to look eccentric amidst a fast-expanding range of non-rational undertakings.

Blair certainly deserves to be blamed for working hard to transform a party which had resisted consumerism in the 1980s and early 1990s into an unquestioning champion of 'flexible labour markets' and a compliant host for dubious multinational concerns. Along with his supposedly 'prudent' chancellor Gordon Brown he presided over a regime which frittered away billions of pounds of taxpayers' money on spurious management consultancy exercises and unworkable information technology systems. In December 2006, the National Audit Office found that government consultants had been paid £7.2 billion over the previous three years 'with no proof of any benefits'.[94] Blair's government also approved numerous private finance initiative (PFI) schemes which provided new hospitals and schools at grotesquely inflated costs, boosting the profits of private companies whether or not the work was done well.[95] Even when such abuses of public trust were not unique to the Blair government, they were taken to new extremes. But Blair's main offence was shared with his predecessors, Margaret Thatcher and (to a lesser extent) John Major. All three took pains to flatter the good sense and unflagging virtues of the British public while consciously cultivating the support of individuals who were presumed to be ignorant and selfish. In particular, they targeted the kind of people who not only bought the *Sun*, but also read it and absorbed its unsubtle message on social and political issues. They were prepared to overlook that newspaper's obvious defects because they took at face value its claims to represent the true voice of the British people. With a formula which derived profit from the negative aspects of human nature – anger, greed, fear and lust – it had truly captured the spirit of the age.

During Tony Blair's last months in office fear was certainly the predominant emotion. After the criminal outrage of July 2005 Britons were told to brace themselves for further terrorist attacks. The government assured them that additional incidents were inevitable; the only remaining question was the choice of target. Even if the terrorists were unable to lay their hands on nuclear material, the threat of indiscriminate carnage was reminiscent of cold war fears. Blair used the crisis as justification for the proposed introduction of identity cards, to enable the state to keep its citizens under tighter control. Voters were entitled to ask themselves if it was sensible to hand more powers to a government which had done so much to make Britain a prime target for fanatical killers. However, opinion polls suggested that the proposal was popular. Fear also helped the acceptance of closed circuit television, which had become so ubiquitous by 2004 that the government's own information commissioner warned about the danger of 'sleepwalking into a surveillance society'.[96]

This willingness to accept the snooping state was not created by the terrorist threat. Indeed, despite the arguments of right-wing critics, it

long predated New Labour. According to some observers, historic stereotypes about Britain's obstinate resistance to all forms of external
direction were already becoming redundant in the late 1970s. In 1977,
for example, Winston Churchill's former private secretary Lord Colville
had noted that 'even if the public are unimpressed by the paternalism
of their rulers, too often expressed in mealy-mouthed terms at which
their ancestors would have rebelled, they suffer it with a detachment
new to the British character'.[97] From a very different viewpoint, E.P.
Thompson protested in 1980 that 'The freeborn Englishman has been
bred out of the strain, and the stillborn Englishman has been bred in.'[98]
Despite the ideological gulf between them, there was a thread of perception common to both communicators. Undoubtedly the change they
perceived owed much to economic circumstances – the mixture of affluence and insecurity which took a lasting hold in the second half of the
1970s. But this was compounded by a dramatic loss of confidence in
the nation's governors at a time when members of the public were
beginning to realise that they had very little chance of affecting the
biggest decisions, which were taken above their heads. The result was
a mood aptly characterised by David Aaronovitch as 'indignant passivity'.[99] Equally, in view of the new disdain for politicians, it could be
described as 'contemptuous subservience'.

Blair's government was not even the first to take advantage of this
new British outlook, which had helped Margaret Thatcher and Michael
Heseltine to override objections during the cruise missile controversy.
Thatcher, it could be argued, had precipitated her own downfall by
miscalculating the extent of apathy and pressing ahead with the unpopular poll tax despite widespread signals of incipient rebellion. But her
policy had been seen by most voters as a direct attack on their living
standards, which was the best way to stir up residual anger in the
British public. Despite its own slip-up with fuel taxes, New Labour
was usually careful not to provoke the backlash which could be expected
to arise from injured self-interest. But Gordon Brown's abstention from
1970s-style economic interference and 'punitive' taxation did not mean
that Labour MPs lacked any outlet for their old interventionist itches.
There was still plenty of scope for a programme of disciplinary paternalism, with the overall aim of moulding a modernised workforce
which could meet the challenges of a globalised economic order.[100]

In pursuit of this goal, under New Labour government activity became
a mirror image of the 1960s, when the state played a fairly intrusive

role in economic matters while allowing and even encouraging greater social freedom. After 1997 the British people were subjected to a rash of targets, regulations and diktats, even on such matters as diet, personal hygiene and the amount of homework schoolchildren should undertake. The public, on balance, seemed grateful for this detailed attention to what used to be regarded as their personal business. Even smokers were anxious for government restrictions, in the hope that legislation would provide them with the necessary willpower to ditch their habit. When the government introduced measures which simultaneously condoned and condemned activities like drinking and gambling there was mild consternation.* But the most serious reservations applied to revenue-raising speed cameras, which were deployed to enforce a law that almost every motorist infringed at one time or another.

Although disciplinary paternalism was widely accepted, it was unlikely to raise public esteem for politicians or encourage higher levels of electoral participation. For a quarter of a century both of the main parties had won elections on the promise that they would get the state off people's backs and allow 'hard-working families' to proceed with the task of enriching themselves. The general elections of 2001 and 2005 proved that this strategy no longer generated any excitement, even among its intended beneficiaries. Some prosperous people were too complacent to vote; others belatedly discovered that the accumulation of wealth was not making them happy, and used politicians as the most convenient scapegoats for their tarnished illusions. New Labour's answer was to offer more of the same in a more earnest tone of voice. During the 2005 general election campaign Tony Blair called for a restoration of 'respect' throughout society, which was rather like a serial adulterer upholding the sanctity of marriage. In February 2006 the prime minister's ally, the erstwhile socialist Alan Milburn, argued that the party still had not done enough to 'come to terms with the "me generation", people who are more aspirational than ever and want to exercise control over their own lives'.[101] It was difficult to see what more could be done to appease this constituency. Whatever else had been achieved by the agenda of economic liberalism, most people felt less control over their own affairs than ever before. This important fact seemed to have bypassed the ambitious ex-communist health secre-

---

* New Labour relaxed licensing hours despite delivering repeated homilies against 'binge drinking', and agreed to the spread of casinos while deploring 'problem gambling'.

tary John Reid, who before the 2005 general election set out his credentials as a possible successor to Tony Blair by advocating 'a politics of consumerism which does not detract from the enjoyment of that experience, but ensures that the consumer, who is determined to shape her own life, is also aware of her potential contribution to the wider systems on which she depends'.[102]

Something new was urgently needed, at a time when political parties could only continue to finance their activities by selling honours to rich individuals or asking the taxpayer to subsidise their unappealing activities.* David Blunkett's citizenship courses might help to convince some young people that voting is worth a little personal 'inconvenience', even to the consumer 'who is determined to shape her own life'. However, the teachers would have to be truly inspirational if they were to overcome the range of social influences which were deterring newly qualified voters; the effect would probably be limited even if the courses were extended to the whole adult population. Voting itself could be made compulsory, but this was one area in which New Labour knew it would have to curb its authoritarian instincts, allowing the carrot to prevail over the stick. An alternative was suggested by an inventive US Internet campaign – Votergasm – which urged volunteers to cajole reluctant electors to the ballot box with offers of sex. But the response in America was surprisingly flaccid. Although lust was an inadequate incentive, there was always the reliable standby of material greed. Before long, supermarket shoppers might be invited to cast their votes at the checkouts in return for a free ticket in the National Lottery.

---

* Tony Blair, who in July 2004 had revealed a 'personal crusade' to ensure that 'those that play by the rules do well; and those that don't, get punished', became in December 2006 the first serving prime minister to be questioned by police as part of a criminal investigation as a result of the 'cash for honours' scandal.

CONCLUSION: APATHY AND ANGER

On 10 May 2007 Tony Blair travelled from London to his Sedgefield constituency in order to make his long-expected resignation speech. He was, in fact, staying in office until late June; but the party would need time to select a new leader and prime minister, even though everyone knew that this would be Gordon Brown. The content of Blair's speech was no less predictable. It was an attempt to justify his premiership, peppered with flattering references to the British public who would judge his record.

'I have been very lucky and very blessed,' Blair acknowledged. 'This country is a blessed nation. The British are special. The world knows it. In our innermost thoughts, we know it. This is the greatest nation on earth. It has been an honour to serve it.' The nation was 'comfortable in the twenty-first century, at home in its own skin, able not just to be proud of its past but confident of its future.' Modern Britons, he claimed, were 'open-minded about race and sexuality, averse to prejudice and yet deeply and rightly conservative with a small "c" when it comes to good manners, respect for others, treating people courteously'.[1] Taken at face value, Blair's oration suggested that New Labour had fulfilled John Major's broken promise of 1990 – to bring closure to the turbulent Thatcher years and build a country 'at ease with itself'.

There was, though, one aspect of national life which remained imperfect after ten years of New Labour. A month after giving notice of his abdication Blair delivered a lecture on public life, in which he compared the media to 'a feral beast, just tearing people and reputations to shreds'. He had no intention of blaming specific individuals; as he acknowledged, there was a time in the early days of New Labour when even he probably made mistakes in his dealings with the media. However, he singled out the *Independent* newspaper as a 'metaphor' for the new, destructive journalism. Instead of giving its readers the unvarnished facts, it constantly intruded opinion into its reporting, making it more of a 'viewspaper' than a newspaper. Not content with criticising government decisions, it was always ready to attribute venal motives to individuals in responsible positions. Increasing public cynicism about political life was the inevitable result.

Blair's speech said more about the condition of his own mind than the state of the nation. The suggestion that control and manipulation of the media agenda had been a short-lived phase for New Labour was breathtaking in itself. Blair, of course, owed his own position to the presumed demands of the media age: otherwise Gordon Brown would certainly have been elected party leader in 1994. Having once been a media darling who benefited from the personalisation of politics, Blair could hardly complain about his treatment once his image had been tarnished. He had spun his way through his ten-year stint in Downing Street, while a small army of verbal conjurors performed the same role on behalf of ministers and government departments. Spin was involved even in his lecture to the press, which included the lament that 'If you are a backbench MP today, you learn to give a press release first and a good Parliamentary speech second.'[2] If this course of action was necessary for a publicity-hungry backbencher, a retiring prime minister giving a speech to the news agency Reuters was likely to attract plenty of publicity without releasing his text in advance. However, Downing Street made sure that it was available for discussion on the airwaves long before Blair had opened his mouth.*

Even more remarkable was Blair's assault on the *Independent*. It was obvious that the newspaper's chief offence was its passionate opposition to British foreign policy in the Middle East, rather than its alleged inability to distinguish fact from opinion. Indeed, one passage in Blair's lecture seemed to point the finger at other publications. He claimed that the media's methods had resulted in coverage where 'Things, people, issues, stories are all black and white.' Rather than applying to the *Independent*, this was an excellent characterisation of the *Daily Mail* and the *Sun*. Yet Blair did not mention either of these, because he was

---

* It was also claimed that Blair's earlier Sedgefield speech had been composed spontaneously on his journey north, but journalists knew him too well to fall for this line.

still frightened of the first and the second was owned by Rupert Murdoch. Three days after Blair's lecture the *Sun* epitomised its balanced, factual reporting by splashing the headline 'Seven days to save Britain'.[3] The nation's existence, it turned out, was threatened by developments within the European Union, which was hell-bent on destroying the political independence and cultural identity of the country which had saved Europe so often. The *Sun* had issued so many similar warnings of the kind that even its Europhobic readers must have wondered if the situation really justified such alarmist rhetoric. Instead of lashing out against this juvenile treatment of a serious issue, Blair merely took steps to reassure the public that he would not betray British interests.

Blair thought it demonstrable that media standards had declined since 1997. But although he was right to suggest that newspapers had changed because of the threat from 24-hour, 'rolling' television news, this did not mean that things had changed for the worse in recent years; it just felt that way to him, because the non-Murdoch papers were more hostile than they had been in the early days of 'Teflon Tony'. The deterioration in general standards had actually begun long before, starting to go downhill in the late 1970s, plunging under Thatcher before hitting rock bottom under Major. At that time it was indisputable that Britain had the most irresponsible media in the world; and Tony Blair's New Labour had been the chief beneficiary. A single anecdote will suffice to illustrate the change since the beginning of our period. In July 1975 the Press Council upheld a complaint against the *Daily Express* for its reporting of the Guildford pub bombings in the previous year. The Council sternly declared that one of its headlines 'overstated the facts and should have been corrected'.[4] In those days such a rebuke was a fairly serious matter, implying that the *Express* had let the side down and should mend its ways in future. By 2007 it had become a newspaper with a two-track mind, anticipating every twist of the housing market with apocalyptic headlines and displaying a morbid fascination with the death of Princess Diana a decade earlier. A return to the days of merely 'overstating the facts' would have marked a stunning renaissance for the *Express*. But although that paper was in a class of its own, hardly any edition of the tabloids published between 1992 and 2007 would have escaped censure from the Press Council of 1975.

It was understandable that Blair's lecture on public life concentrated on the relationship between the media and politics. But if he had widened his focus and examined the impact of the media on society as a whole he might have been forced to revise his claim that Britain was 'comfort-able in the twenty-first century, at home in its own skin'. Over the years, the media had fashioned a stock response to claims about its adverse effects. Journalists habitually argued that it was all too easy to blame the media, when Britain's problems clearly arose from a range of complex factors. Yet blaming the media was only easy because, among all the deleterious influences, its culpability was the most obvious. Just three days after Blair's lecture the point was underlined by an advi-sory group funded by the Department of Health, which argued that constant exposure to the celebrity culture had fostered promiscuity among teenagers, leading to a crisis in sexual health.[5] The implication was that the media should either tone down its coverage of celebrities, or at least seek out more wholesome individuals for attention. It was most unlikely to do anything of the kind, since stories of celebrity misbehaviour always seemed to boost the ratings.

Driven to desperation, a British journalist could always resort to the cliché about the public getting the media it deserved. By 2007 the public as a whole had allowed itself to be duped and exploited by the media for so many years that the self-serving phrase had become more accurate than ever before. The media, in short, had helped to create the kind of public which deserved to be treated with contempt.

Back in 1975, an energetic soldier-turned-entrepreneur, John Hoskyns, had impressed several leading Conservatives, including Margaret Thatcher, with his argument that Britain was heading for economic ruin because of systematic flaws in the political system, notably high taxa-tion and the power of the trade unions.[6] Hoskyns's identified a radical rupture between economic goals and political decisions, so that politi-cians who hoped to widen prosperity were constantly taking decisions which resulted in general impoverishment. Thanks to their efforts the British economy had become dysfunctional, and in the gloomy global context of the mid-1970s reform could no longer be postponed.

Like many observers of the time, Hoskyns assumed that the British people had been let down by the politicians of both main parties. In itself, as we have seen, this view implied a degree of apathy among the voting population, which had allowed itself to be misled for too long. But Hoskyns could be confident that the public was basically sound, and would respond readily if provided with robust leadership. By 2007 it was no longer possible to build ambitious programmes for reform on such optimistic presuppositions. The British economy was performing reasonably well, although its success seemed precarious since the country was no longer a major manufacturing force and was again reliant on imported fuel. But far from being inherently sound, society had become so decadent that it was itself dysfunctional, riddled with self-contradictions which could not be resolved by government intervention.[7]

New evidence of deep-rooted social problems emerged at the time of Blair's lecture on public life. It was reported, for example, that treatment for obesity was being offered to one-year-old children. The obvious answer to childhood obesity was more exercise; but fears of sexual predators and violent bullies meant that parents were increasingly reluctant to let their children walk home from school, let alone enjoy hours of unsupervised activity in public playgrounds. In any case, 'prudent' financial stewardship since the Thatcher years had ensured the sale for development of much land previously reserved for recreation. Supposedly the government was taking firm action in response to exaggerated fears of sexual abuse of children by strangers rather than family members. In part, this explained why at the time that Blair lectured on public life the prison population had established a new record figure, about to top 81,000. Yet on the day before the speech it emerged that over the past five years almost 8,000 sex offenders had been cautioned by the police rather than sent to jail; more than 1,500 of the offences were inflicted on children, and 230 were cases of rape. Successful prosecutions which led to prison sentences only revealed the true extent to which Britons were in thrall to illicit sex. On 18 June came the revelation that police had broken up an internet porn ring, run by a British man based in Suffolk. Of more than 700 suspects involved in the abuse, around 200 were living in the UK, a world-leader in the field.[8]

These snapshots of life in 2007 contrasted sharply with Blair's complacent generalisations about British attitudes to sexuality. Everyday experience also cast serious doubt on his claim about people being 'deeply and rightly conservative with a small "c" when it comes to good manners, respect for others, treating people courteously'. There probably were millions of Britons who at least hoped to behave well towards others. But even they found it difficult to stick to these standards amid the hurry and harassments of contemporary life. Many others seemed to have no conception of good manners, respect or courtesy; and despite Blair's introduction of anti-social behaviour orders their conduct rarely incurred even informal sanctions. The steady erosion of social trust meant that honesty now really was the worst policy in all but the most trivial interactions, even with close relatives and supposed friends but especially with colleagues at work.[9] Perhaps wisely, in view of the ongoing investigation into 'cash for honours', Blair made no reference in his speech to these essential ingredients of a truly harmonious society. Instead, he seemed to believe that the qualities of the average Briton had played a key part in persuading the International Olympic Committee to plump for London as host for the 2012 summer games. The prospect of this fillip for the south-east of England – announced on the day before the terrorist attacks on London in July 2005 – was not enough to detain the growing number of people who now wished to leave other parts of Britain. In the mid-1970s, many people emigrated because of 'punitive' taxation; now, they were leaving at an estimated rate of 1,000 per day because life abroad just seemed more attractive. Even those with strong emotional ties to the UK began to wonder if it was time to jump ship.[10]

Some of New Labour's decisions in government did make life better for specific groups. Blair was right when he claimed that Britons, taken as a whole, were less prone to unthinking prejudice in 2007 compared to the situation ten years earlier. Homosexuals and ethnic minorities could still be subjected to abuse and assault, but the worst examples of ill-treatment and discrimination were greeted with genuine abhorrence. Although the status of women was still unstable, blending real economic advance with exploitation in most other fields, the beneficial effect of previous measures was increasingly felt. It was more difficult to give New Labour credit for the country's economic performance, which apparently owed most to the government's decision to relinquish control of interest rates. But some threatening episodes in the global economy had been weathered, and there had been no return to the giddy oscillations of the Thatcher years. Although personal bankruptcies were becoming increasingly common this was in part because the traditional stigma had largely been removed, thanks to the Blair government's Insolvency Act of 2000 which encouraged the overcommitted to settle their affairs through Individual Voluntary Arrangements. Gordon Brown's attempts to alleviate poverty through the Working Families Tax Credit was dogged by administrative blunders, but was at least well-intentioned. While the impact of the minimum wage was questionable at such a low level, Labour had established a principle which could bear fruit in future. In the last days of the Blair premiership there were even signs that action might be taken against the super-rich, although the main demand was for the closure of tax-loopholes which had been created by that iron-fisted antagonist of greed, Gordon Brown.[11]

Labour's remaining media friends often complained that the government received insufficient credit for its achievements. Yet this was easily explained, because the advances were overshadowed by the disastrous mistake of Iraq; and in most cases the constructive reforms merely papered over a few of the cracks in society which had developed before 1997. In 1975, Geraldine Norman had expressed the view that human beings tend to be unhappy, regardless of their material circumstances, when they feel unable to control their own destinies. By that standard, she judged that in 1975 the British were not particularly 'blessed'. In this crucial respect the situation had certainly deteriorated over nearly two decades of Tory rule, and if anything the situation worsened afterwards. The fear of unemployment had subsided, although the problem was not negligible and in some notorious cases workers were dismissed by text-message, without warning. The time when the daily routine could seriously be disrupted by industrial action seemed to be over for ever. Yet the balance of power in the workplace had been redressed in a way which left most employees dissatisfied with their lot, either because of bullying management, widening inequalities in financial rewards, long hours, unpleasant exchanges with customers, or repeated government edicts imposing new and more onerous duties. The general feeling of financial well-being, which Blair underlined in his Sedgefield speech, owed much to the fact that both adults in Britain's remaining two-parent families were now forced to be economically active, regardless of their circumstances or private wishes. The predictable result has been an unmistakable increase in domestic strain, which among other things played a considerable part in fuelling Britain's crazy housing market. People were just finding it more difficult to share a common space – or even live in proximity to each other.

Far from being 'at home in its own skin', the Britain of 2007 was stressed out, full of troubled people who had turned inwards to brood over real problems or imagined inadequacies. Perhaps the worst aspect of the situation was the tendency of misery to multiply: even those who resolved to remain cheerful could hardly do so when so much of their life was absorbed by shallow encounters with lugubrious people.

When it becomes so widespread, unhappiness is sure to prove contagious – even compulsory, for anyone who spends much time in the
company of others. This phenomenon certainly helps to explain the
new prevalence of apathy. Anger could still be momentarily aroused
by public scandal. But the attention span was briefer than ever, and
the fleeting outrage of the citizen was easily trumped by the ingrained
preoccupations of the private individual. This context was distinctly
unpromising even for passionately-argued plans for reform, like Simon
Jenkins's proposal for a dramatic switch of power from central institutions to local government.[12] Institutions are obviously important, and
national politicians have certainly helped to foster apathy in Britain.
But a stage had been reached, for a variety of reasons, when the British
public rather than the political system stood in need of reformation:
and until that happened, it seemed unlikely that the country could be
well governed.

Thus democratic revival in Britain depended upon an upsurge in civic
spirit amongst its citizens – a development which, if achieved, would
feed through into an improvement of government performance at all
levels. The present survey has suggested that generational change might
provide some slender grounds for optimism. If the first thirty years after
the Second World War should be regarded as a period in which Britons
clung on to illusions against the odds, subsequent developments have
seen them stripped away. This process culminated under the Blair
government, when the right to host a future renewal of the Olympic
Games – at ever-escalating cost – was trumpeted as the nation's main
reason to feel pride in itself. By contrast, people born after 1975 have
at least a theoretical chance of growing to full maturity with a clearer
perspective; they might even adopt the 'post-materialist' views which
have been more talked about than realised in practice since the early
1970s.[13]

Yet a more sober assessment of practical experience leads to a less
optimistic outlook. Left to themselves, the citizens of the future might
have been able to throw off the well-founded cynicism which has
pervaded British life for the past two decades. But the views of young
people are being shaped by the generations which have created the
country's problems. A study of 1993 established that the parenting
skills of materialistic people left something to be desired; emotional
disturbance among children under ten rose by almost 50 per cent
between 1985 and 1990.[14] When 'Thatcher's children' themselves

became parents, they were unlikely to fare much better. On 20 June 2007 the *Daily Mail* gleefully disclosed that more than a million young-sters were now suffering from a variety of mental and emotional problems. The paper noted that 'experts blamed a damaging mix of family breakdown, junk food diets, marketing, binge-drinking, increasing availability of drugs, sexy images projected by magazines and mounting exam pressure for the trend'. It was interesting that the *Mail*, which itself lost no opportunity to print 'sexy' images to illus-trate news stories or perk up its 'fashion' pages, considered that only magazines were capable of corrupting the young. But the findings appar-ently confirmed the message of an earlier UNICEF report which suggested that British children were far less happy than their counter-parts in many less prosperous countries.[15]

The 'quality of life' had forced its way onto the political agenda at an inauspicious time. Unlike the political generation which helped Britain to improvise its way through the crises of the mid-1970s, the senior policy-makers of 2007 were open to serious question on the grounds of motivation and aptitude. Among many contenders for the title, Britain's current education system is probably the starkest example of the combined effect of decadent people and muddle-headed government intervention. Tony Blair was not the first product of a public school to lead Labour, but his posh predecessors (like Clement Attlee) had wisely refrained from meddling too much where their own first-hand experiences had been so misleading. Blair was more impul-sive, and despite Gordon Brown's glowering presence at the Treasury he had a relatively free hand in education which he had prioritised before the 1997 election. The main result of his endeavours was a steep increase in demand for school places outside the state system.

Optimists could claim that this trend was merely a side-effect of growing prosperity: thanks to Labour's sound economic stewardship, more parents could now make the necessary financial sacrifices to give their children a head-start in the independent sector. The same could be said for the tendency of middle-class parents to pay massively inflated sums for houses within the catchment areas of the best-reputed state schools. But in reality, most parents chose to pay the price one way or another because of a violent 'push' rather than the 'pull' of something better than adequate. They were fearful that exposure to the 'bog standard' state system would cause lasting intellectual, emotional and/or physical damage to their children. The latter assumption was openly acknowledged by the government in its 2006 Violent Crime Reduction Act, which gave teachers the right to search their tender charges for concealed weaponry. Although many British schools were unsavoury places in 1975, such a legislative measure would have been quite unthinkable at that time. The new dispensation to frisk the kids came into force just after Blair's resignation speech; the Professional Association of Teachers responded by pointing out that stab-proof vests would have to be provided for the pedagogues who undertook the task. A survey published in June 2007 suggested that two-thirds of Britain's teachers had been physically or verbally assaulted over the previous year, and that almost a fifth had been threatened with a weapon.[16] Teachers were also rightly protesting against the state-imposed culture of tests and league tables, which threatened to squeeze out any remaining relish for life among pupils who had somehow retained their integrity and innocence. Citizenship courses were most unlikely to repair the damage incurred by young people in their formative years, in school or at home.

From many of his pronouncements in his final term of office it seemed that Tony Blair was not entirely ignorant of the troubles which faced ordinary Britons, whatever stage they had reached in that unpredictable consumerist adventure called 'life'. But as Margaret Thatcher had also found, the tenure of high office is an isolating experience which can give rise to inaccurate impressions of the public mood. Blair's resignation speech opened a surreal period in which he toured the world at taxpayers' expense, promoting his future career as a globetrotting post-prandial raconteur for the powerful rich. In the speech he implied that his departure from office had been entirely voluntary, in keeping with the ancient ideals of civic republicanism. 'Sometimes,' he declared, 'the only way you conquer the pull of power is to set it down.' Evidently he had been less successful in conquering the seduction of spin. Lurking beneath his finely-honed and honeyed phrases was a strong impression that he would not be spending much time with his fellow-Britons, unless he happened to meet them on his speaking and book-signing tours abroad. He closed his Sedgefield speech with the words 'Good luck'; and the people he was leaving behind in Britain were certainly going to need it.

NOTES

Introduction: Anger and Apathy

1 *Daily Telegraph*, 2 June 1979.

2 Penguin edn, 1985, 149.

3 Tim Jackson, *Chasing Progress: Beyond Measuring Economic Growth*, New Economics Foundation, 2004.

4 Quoted in *The Times*, 24 May 2005.

5 *The Times*, *Guardian*, 13 September 2003.

6 *Observer*, 28 January 2007.

7 See for example Layard's article 'The Secret of Happiness', *New Statesman*, 3 March 2003.

8 Keith Middlemas, *Power, Competition and the State, Vol. 3, The End of the Postwar Era – Britain since 1974*, Macmillan, 1991, 3.

9 *New Statesman*, 3 January 1975.

10 *The Times*, 26 May 1975.

11 *Hansard*, Vol. 779, col. 909, 9 April 1976.

12 *The Times*, 25 August 1975.

13 Christopher Booker, *The Seventies: Portrait of a Decade*, Allen Lane, 1980, 4.

14 Zoe Williams, *Guardian*, 19 April 2005.

15 Richard Sennett, *The Fall of Public Man*, Faber and Faber, 1993 edn, 259.

16 For important exceptions to this trend, see Dave Haslam, *Not ABBA: The Real Story of the 1970s*, Fourth Estate, 2005, and Howard Sounes, *Seventies: The Sights, Sounds and Ideas of a Brilliant Decade*, Simon & Schuster, 2006.

17 Tony Blair, speech at Aylesbury Estate, Southwark, 2 June 1997.

18 Giovanni Arrighi, *The Long Twentieth Century: Money, Power, and the Origins of Our Times*, Verso, 1994; Eric Hobsbawm, *The Age of Extremes: The Short Twentieth Century, 1914–1991*, Michael Joseph, 1994.

19   'White Man in Hammersmith Palais', CBS single.

20   Simon White of Menswear, quoted in John Harris, *The Last Party: Britpop, Blair and the Demise of English Rock*, Fourth Estate, 2003, 208.

21   *House of Lords Debates*, Vol. 361, col. 353-4, 11 June 1975.

22   *The Times*, 24 January 1975.

23   *The Times*, 11 July 1975.

24   *The Times*, 27 January 1975.

25   Bob Geldof, *Is That It?*, Penguin edn, 1986, 150.

26   *Things Can Only Get Better: Eighteen Miserable Years in the Life of a Labour Supporter, 1979–1997*, Black Swan edn, 1999.

27   Tony Blair, speech at Aylesbury Estate, Southwark, 2 June 1997; www.socialexclusion.gov.uk/news.

1. Britain in 1975

1   Eva Harazsti Taylor (ed.), *Letters to Eva, 1969–1983*, Century, 1991, 273.

2   Bernard Donoughue, *Downing Street Diary: With Harold Wilson in No. 10*, Jonathan Cape, 2005, 503.

3   See Harold Wilson, *Final Term*, Weidenfeld & Nicolson, 1979, 113 and note.

4   *The Times*, 8 May 1975.

5   *The Times*, 2 January 1975; Robert J. Wybrow, *Britain Speaks Out, 1937–87: A Social History as Seen through the Gallup Data*, Macmillan, 1989, 161.

6   Taylor, 223.

7   *Leicester Mercury*, 2, 25 January 1975.

8   Taylor, 247.

9   David Bowie, quoted in *The NME Rock 'n' Roll Years*, BCA, 1992, 279.

10   Barbara Castle, *The Castle Diaries 1974–76*, Weidenfeld & Nicolson, 400–1 (22 May 1975).

11   *The Times*, 10 May 1975.

12   Sir Leo Pliatzky, *Getting and Spending: Public Spending, Employment and Inflation*, Blackwell, 1982, 161.

13   *Spectator*, 4 January, 14 June 1975; Maurice Corona in *The Times*, 2 September 1975.

14   Lord Chalfont, 'Our Security Menaced' in Patrick Cormack (ed.), *Right Turn: Eight Men Who Changed Their Minds*, Leo Cooper, 1978, 41–2.

15   *House of Lords Debates*, Vol. 357, col. 823.

16   *House of Lords Debates*, Vol. 357, cols 820–36.

17   *House of Lords Debates.*, Vol. 357, cols 896, 914, 26 February 1975.

18   *The Times*, 12 December 1975.

19   Ian Gilmour, *Inside Right: Conservatism, Policies and the People*, Quartet edn, 1978, 218.

20   See minutes of meeting on taxation, 18 May 1975, in CRD 4/4/144, CPA, Bodleian Library.

21   Blake Baker, *The Far Left: An Exposé of the Extreme Left in Britain*, Weidenfeld & Nicolson, 1981, 24–5.

22   *The Times*, 10 January 1975.

23   Francis Wheen, 'Strange Days Indeed', in *Hoo-Hahs and Passing Frenzies: Collected Journalism, 1991–2001*, Atlantic Books, 2002, 91–6.

24   *Hansard*, Vol. 873, col. 127, 7 May 1974.

25   *Daily Mail*, 28 November 1974; Tony Benn, *Against the Tide: Diaries 1973–6*, Arrow edn, 1990, 272–3; PRO PREM 16/587.

26   Bernard Levin in *The Times*, 21 January 1975.

27   Richard Crossman, *Diaries of a Cabinet Minister*, Vol. 3, *Secretary of State for Social Services*, Hamish Hamilton/Jonathan Cape, 1977, 339.

28   Donoughue, 271.

29   Robert Armstrong to Harold Wilson, 9 January 1975, in PRO PREM 16/587.

30   John Stonehouse, *Death of an Idealist*, W.H. Allen, 1975, 184.

31   *The Times*, 26 May 1975.

32   Stonehouse to Edward Short, 26 January 1975, PRO PREM 16/587.

33   *Guardian*, 11 April 1995.

34   A.H. Warren to Harold Wilson, 17 January 1975, in PRO PREM 16/587.

35   Stonehouse, 153.

36   *The Times*, 13, 28 June 1975.

37   *The Times*, 19 July 1975.

38   Stonehouse, 158.

39   Woodrow Wyatt, *What's Left of the Labour Party?* Sidgwick & Jackson, 1977, 120–9; 111–12.

40   David Butler and Uwe Kitzinger, *The 1975 Referendum*, Macmillan, 1976, 166.

41   *The Times*, 28 May 1975; SCAN (Lancaster students' newspaper), 3 June, 1975.

42   Donoughue, 401.

43   Butler and Kitzinger, 256.

44   *Leicester Mercury*, 2 January 1975.

45   Donoughue, 393–4.

46   Ben Pimlott, *Harold Wilson*, HarperCollins, 1992, 105.

47   Stephen Dorril and Robin Ramsay, *Smear! Wilson and the Secret State*, Grafton edn, 1992, 333.

48   Collins, 1979.

49   The classic academic exposition of this view is Anthony King, 'Overload: Problems of Governing in the 1970s', *Political Studies* (1975), 284–96.

50   Gabriel Almond and Sidney Verba, *The Political Culture*, Little, Brown, 1965 edn, 361.

51   *The Times*, 16 May 1975.

52   *The Times*, 13 May 1975.

53   Jad Adams, *Tony Benn: A Biography*, Pan edn, 1993, 327–30; Tony Benn, *Office Without Power: Diaries 1968–72*, Arrow edn, 1989, 421.

54   *Hansard*, Vol. 889, col. 1030, 8 April 1975; *Times*, 1 May 1975.

55   *The Times*, 19 May 1975.

56   *The Times*, 12 May 1975.

57   *The Times*, 4 May 1975.

58   Butler and Kitzinger, *Referendum*, 256.

59   *The Times*, 2 June 1975.

60   *Castle Diaries*, 408.

61   *The Times*, 2 June 1975; Hugo Young, *This Blessed Plot: Britain and Europe from Churchill to Blair*, Macmillan, 1999, 287.

62   Russell Davies (ed.), *The Diary of Kenneth Williams*, HarperCollins, 1993, 493–4, 469.

63   Philip Goodhart, *Full-Hearted Consent*, Davis-Poynter, 1976, 168–9.

64   For the statements of both sides, see Mark Baimbridge (ed.), *The 1975 Referendum on Europe, Vol. 1, Reflections of the Participants*, Imprint Academic, 2006, Appendices 2 and 3.

65   Don Watson, 'Leeds United 1974/5' in Nick Hornsby (ed.), *My Favourite Year: A Collection of New Football Writing*, H.F. & G. Witherby, 1993, 204.

66   Goodhart, *Full Hearted Consent*, 169.

67   *The Times*, 8 July 1975; *Political Quarterly*, Vol. 41 no.2, April–June 1970, 146–51.

68   *The Times*, 11 July 1975.

69   Record of meeting on 15 September 1975; Foot to Wilson, 17 November 1975, in PRO PREM 16/381.

70   Roy Jenkins, *A Life at the Centre*, Macmillan, 1991, 374.

71   *The Times*, 8 February 1975.

72   Robert Shepherd, *Enoch Powell: A Biography*, Hutchinson, 1996, 462.

73   *The Times*, 12 July 1975.

74   Quoted in Margaret Thatcher, *The Path to Power*, HarperCollins, 1995, 281.

75   *The Times*, 19 May 1975.

76   *The Times*, 7 May 1975.

77   *The Times*, 4 August 1975.

78   Peter Calvocoressi, *The British Experience 1945–75*, Pelican edn, 1979, 253.

79   *The Times*, 14 January 1975.

80   *The Times*, 31 December 1975.

81   *The Times*, 31 July 1975.

82   *The Times*, 3 February 1975.

83 *The Times*, 23 January, 22 April 1975.

84 *The Times*, 18 August, 1975.

85 *The Times*, 4 February 1975.

86 *The Times*, 27 June 1975.

87 *The Times*, 14 June 1975.

88 *The Times*, 28 June 1975.

89 *The Times*, 21 June, 28 January 1975.

90 *The Times*, 9 April, 19 August 1975.

91 *The Times*, 8 May 1975.

92 See, for example, the case reported in *The Times*, 9 January 1975.

93 *The Times*, 7 March 1975.

94 *The Times*, 22 July 1975.

95 *The Times*, 20 August 1975.

96 *The Times*, 17 February 1975.

97 *The Times*, 1 February 1975.

98 *The Times*, 19 August 1975.

99 See memo of 18 March 1975, PRO PREM 16/490.

100 *The Times*, 16 August 1975.

101 *The Times*, 8 July 1975.

102 *The Times*, 22 August 1975.

103 *The Times*, 21 June 1975.

104 Letter of 3 June 1975 in papers of Baron Shore of Stepney, BLPES, Shore 10/54.

105 Peter Hitchens, *The Abolition of Britain: From Lady Chatterley to Tony Blair*, Quartet, 1999, 142.

106 *Kenneth Williams Diaries*, 505. Williams also found fault with *The Good Life* – 'tasteless and unpleasant': ibid., 492.

107 *The Times*, 11 April 1975.

108 Ray Monk, *Bertrand Russell: The Ghost of Madness, 1921–1970*, Vintage, 2001, 501.

109 See Keith Jacka, Caroline Cox and John Marks, *The Rape of Reason: The Corruption of the Polytechnic of North London*, Churchill Press, 1975.

110 *The Times*, 9 April 1975.

111 *The Times*, 30 August 1975.

112 C.B. Cox and R. Boyson (eds), *Black Paper 1975*, J.M. Dent, 1975, 3.

113 *The Times*, 3, 5 February, 7 April, 6 May, 12 June 1975.

114 Iris Murdoch, 'Socialism and Selection', in *Black Papers 1975*, 9.

115 *The Times*, 19 August 1975.

116 *The Times*, 6 August 1975.

117 *The Times*, 16 October 1975.

118 Donoughue, 503 (19 September 1975).

119 SCAN, 4 March 1975.

120 *The Times*, 17 July 1975.

121 *The Times*, 31 December 1975.
122 W.G. Stonehouse to Merlyn Rees, 26 November 1977; memo of 11 September 1978, in PRO PREM 16/589.
123 *The Times* obituary, 15 April 1988.
124 Stonehouse, *Idealist*, ix.

2. Anger

1 Quoted in Neil Nugent, 'The National Association for Freedom', in Roger King and Neil Nugent (eds), *Respectable Rebels: Middle Class Campaigns in Britain in the 1970s*, Hodder and Stoughton, 1979, 82.
2 Ibid.
3 Sir Walter Walker in *The Times*, 7 March 1975.
4 The character, Jimmy (played by Geoffrey Palmer), inspired an unsuccessful Channel 4 spin-off, *Fairly Secret Army* (1984).
5 On this subject, see Stephen Dorril and Robin Ramsay, *Smear! Wilson and the Secret State*, Grafton, 1992 edn, 264–9.
6 *The Times*, 29 November 1975.
7 *Hansard*, Vol. 901, cols. 1189, 1190, 28 November 1975.
8 *The Times*, 5 November 1975.
9 *Hansard*, Vol. 901, col. 1193, 28 November 1975.
10 Rhodes Boyson, *Speaking My Mind*, Peter Owen, 1995, 125–7.
11 Jonathan Dimbleby, *The Prince of Wales: A Biography*, Little, Brown, 1994, 266.
12 Peter Taylor, *Brits: The War Against the IRA*, Bloomsbury, 2001, 222–4.
13 Zig Layton-Henry, *The Politics of Immigration*, Blackwell, 1992, 58–60.
14 Enoch Powell, speech at Brussels, 28 September 1972, reprinted in *The Common Market: Renegotiate or Come Out*, Elliott Right Way Books, 1973, 104.
15 *The Times*, 28 February 1975.
16 Richard Clutterbuck, *Britain in Agony: The Growth of Political Violence*, Faber and Faber, 1978, 152–6.
17 *The Times*, 25 May 1975.
18 Layton-Henry, 92.
19 Jonathan Dimbleby, 273.
20 Patricia Hewitt, *The Abuse of Power: Civil Liberties in the United Kingdom*, Martin Robertson, 1982, 126–7.
21 *Daily Telegraph*, 24 April 1979.
22 Jan Morris, *A Writer's World: Travels 1950–2000*, Faber and Faber, 2003, 221–2; Clutterbuck, 215; Martin Walker, *The National Front*, Fontana, 1977, 197.
23 *Kensington News and Post*, 29 August 1975.

24   Reports of 16 October and 5 September 1975 in PRO MEPO 2/10891.

25   Sir Robert Mark, *In the Office of Constable: An Autobiography*, Collins, 1978, 222.

26   Pat Gilbert, *Passion is a Fashion: The Real Story of the Clash*, Aurum Press, 2005 edn, 100–1; Jon Savage, *England's Dreaming: Sex Pistols and Punk Rock*, Faber and Faber, 1992 edn, 234.

27   Quoted in Jonathon Green, *Them: Voices from the Immigrant Community in Contemporary Britain*, Secker & Warburg, 1990, 340.

28   Clutterbuck, 240 (author's italics).

29   Phillip Whitehead, *The Writing on the Wall: Britain in the Seventies*, Michael Joseph, 1985, 235.

30   Nugent, 84, 87.

31   Ibid., 82.

32   Peregrine Worsthorne, 'The Trade Unions: New Lads on Top', in R. Emmett Tyrell, Jr (ed.), *The Future That Doesn't Work: Social Democracy's Failures in Britain*, Doubleday & Co, 1977, 6.

33   Worsthorne, 19–20.

34   *The Times*, 4 February, 11 January 1975.

35   Patrick Hutber, *The Decline and Fall of the Middle Class – and How It Can Fight Back*, Penguin edn, 1977, 121.

36   Ibid., 117, 156, 123.

37   *The Times*, 16 June 1975.

38   King and Nugent (eds), 88.

39   Joe Rogally, *Grunwick*, Penguin, 1977, 85.

40   Keith Joseph, speech at Doncaster Racecourse Restaurant, 24 June 1977.

41   For evidence at Scarman inquiry, see PRO PREM 3923/1, 3923/2.

42   Clutterbuck, 210.

43   Mark, 245, 299.

44   Michael Crick, *Scargill and the Miners*, Penguin, 1985, 61.

45   Minden Blake and H. J. Weaver, *Suicide By Socialism*, Springwood Books, 1979, 3.

46   Richard Littlejohn in *Daily Mail*, 24 November 2006.

47   Austin Mitchell, *Four Years in the Death of the Labour Party*, Methuen, 1983, 52.

48   Robert Harris, *The Making of Neil Kinnock*, Faber and Faber, 1984, 164.

49   Margaret Thatcher, *The Downing Street Years*, HarperCollins, 1993, 341.

50   Margaret Thatcher, *Let Our Children Grow Tall: Selected Speeches 1975–1977*, Centre for Policy Studies, 1977, 35.

51   Andrew Shonfield, *The Use of Public Power*, Oxford University Press, 1982, 107.

52   Charles Townsend, *Making the Peace: Public Order and Public Security in Modern Britain*, Oxford University Press, 1993, 147.

53   Michael Crick, *Michael Heseltine: A Biography*, Penguin edn, 1997, 227.

54 Ian Jack, *Before the Oil Ran Out: Britain in the Brutal Years*, Vintage, 1997 edn, 141. For other responses to unemployment in this period, see Paul Bagguely, *From Protest to Acquiescence? Political Movements of the Unemployed*, Macmillan, 1991.

55 Crick, *Heseltine*, 229.

56 Baker, *The Far Left*, 148.

57 Tony Benn, *The End of an Era: Diaries 1980–90*, Arrow edn, 1994, 106.

58 Mitchell, 51; Giles Radice, *Diaries 1980–2001: From Political Disaster to Electoral Triumph*, Weidenfeld & Nicolson, 2004, 87.

59 Peter Chippendale and Chris Horrie, *Stick It Up Your Punter! The Rise and Fall of the Sun*, Mandarin edn, 1992, 118–20.

60 For MacKenzie, see Chippendale and Horrie, 85–107.

61 *The Times*, 10 May 2005.

62 Andrew Neil, *Full Disclosure*, Macmillan, 1996, 20.

63 William Shawcross, *Murdoch*, Simon & Schuster edn, 1993, 190.

64 Neil, 71–3.

65 Ibid., 80.

66 Nigel Lawson, *The View from No.11: Memoirs of a Tory Radical*, Bantam, 1992, 157.

67 *The Times*, 28 November 1977.

68 Philip Bassett, *Strike Free: New Industrial Relations in Britain*, Papermac edn, 1987, 36.

69 Chippendale and Horrie, 175–7.

70 *Independent*, 5 March 2004.

71 *Sunday Times* Insight Team, *Strike: Thatcher, Scargill and the Miners*, Andre Deutsch, 1985, 214.

72 *Daily Mail*, 25 June 1985.

73 Benn, *End of an Era*, 356.

74 Quoted in Thatcher, *Downing Street Years*, 352, 371.

75 Robert Harris, 25, 34.

76 Chippendale and Horrie, 221.

77 O'Farrell, *Things Can Only Get Better*, 200.

78 Ian Jack in *New Statesman*, 6 December 1999.

79 O'Farrell, 200.

80 Bill Bryson, *Notes from a Small Island*, Black Swan edn, 1996, 56, 52.

81 Benn, *End of an Era*, 448–50.

82 O'Farrell, 124.

3. Fear

1 *The Times*, 15 April 1975.

2 Wybrow, *Britain Speaks Out*, 144.

3   CND ADD 5/3, BLPES.

4   Martin Amis, *Einstein's Monsters*, Penguin edn, 1988, 15, 3.

5   Ken Livingstone, *If Voting Changed Anything, They'd Abolish It*, Collins, 1987, 233.

6   See, for example, 'Our Capability of Godlike Reason', in David Martin and Peter Mullen (eds), *Unholy Warfare: The Church and the Bomb*, Basil Blackwell, 1983; Roger Jowell and Sharon Witherspoon (eds), *British Social Attitudes: The 1985 Report*, Gower, 1985, 103.

7   *The Church and the Bomb: Nuclear Weapons and Christian Conscience*, Hodder & Stoughton, 1982, 154.

8   John Minnion and Phillip Bolsorer (eds), *The CND Story*, Allison & Busby, 1983, 130.

9   Duncan Campbell, *The Unsinkable Aircraft Carrier: American Military Power in Britain*, revised edn, Paladin, 1986.

10   Powell in Martin and Mullen (eds), 8.

11   Campbell, 13.

12   See Michael Heseltine, *Life in the Jungle: My Autobiography*, Hodder Headline, 2000, 245–6.

13   Crick, *Heseltine*, 247–8.

14   George McKay, 'DiY Culture: Notes towards an Intro', in George McKay (ed.), *DiY Culture: Party & Protest in Nineties Britain*, Verso, 1998, 28–9.

15   Crick, 253.

16   Jowell and Witherspoon (eds), 103.

17   See, for example, Chalfont's unconvincing attempts to discredit the CND position in *The Shadow of My Hand: A Memoir*, Weidenfeld & Nicolson, 2000, 196–8.

18   Philip Gould, *The Unfinished Revolution: How the Modernisers Saved the Labour Party*, Little, Brown, 1998, 70.

19   For an excellent discussion of Kinnock's dilemmas on this issue, see Paul Hirst, *After Thatcher*, Collins, 1989, 83–112.

20   Taylor, *Brits*, 280–5.

21   Ibid., 182–3.

22   Ibid., 229.

23   *Hansard*, Vol. 86, col. 682, 14 November 1985: 'The penalty for treachery is to fall into public contempt.'

24   John Cole, *As It Seemed to Me: Political Memoirs*, Phoenix edn, 1996, 291.

25   Thatcher, 447.

26   Ian R. Taylor, 'Soccer Consciousness and Soccer Hooliganism', in Stanley Cohen (ed.), *Images of Deviance*, Pelican, 1971, 131.

27   Alan Clark, *The Last Diaries: In and Out of the Wilderness*, Weidenfeld & Nicolson, 2002, 264 and note.

28   Colin Ward and 'Chubby' Chris Henderson, *Who Wants It?*, Mainstream, 2000, 51, 54–5, 122.

29 John Campbell, *Margaret Thatcher*, Vol. II, *The Iron Lady*, Jonathan Cape, 2003, 573–4.

30 Wybrow, *Britain Speaks Out*, 125; Mark Garnett and Ian Aitken, *Splendid! Splendid! The Authorized Biography of Willie Whitelaw*, Jonathan Cape, 2002, 275–6.

31 *The Times*, 4 October 1975.

32 Matthew Colin, *Altered State: The Story of Ecstasy Culture and Acid House*, Serpent's Tail, 1997, 77–8.

33 Chas Critcher, *Moral Panics and the Media*, Open University Press, 2003, 55.

34 Drew Hemment, 'Dangerous Dancing and Disco Riots: The Northern Warehouse Parties', in George McKay (ed.), 208–27.

35 Critcher, 54.

36 *Daily Mail*, 21 November 1992.

37 *Guardian*, 26 April 1996.

38 Anthony King (ed.), *British Political Opinion 1937–2000: The Gallup Polls*, Politicos, 2001, 91–2.

39 Gould, *Unfinished Revolution*, 395.

40 *Guardian*, 22 October 2004.

41 *The Times*, 16 January 2006.

42 *The Times*, 26 November 2003.

43 Joanna Bourke, *Fear: A Cultural History*, Virago, 2005, 336.

44 *The Times*, 20 May 2004.

45 *The Times*, 23 January 2004.

46 Richard Ingrams, *Muggeridge: The Biography*, HarperCollins, 1995, 243.

47 *The Times*, 25 November 2005; *Guardian*, 27 February 2002; *The Times*, 28 April 2005.

48 Young, 461.

49 Alvin Toffler, *Future Shock*, Pan edn, 1971, 43.

50 Radice, *Diaries 1980–2001*, 454.

51 See Mark Garnett, 'Win or Bust: The Leadership Gamble of William Hague', in Mark Garnett and Philip Lynch (eds), *The Conservatives in Crisis: The Tories after 1997*, Manchester University Press, 2003, 59.

52 *The Times*, 10 March 2005.

53 *Daily Mail*, 25 November 2003.

54 See, for example, *Guardian*, 23 October 2006.

55 *The Times*, 9 September 2004.

56 *The Times*, 22 September 2005, 7 April 2004.

57 *The Times*, 7 December 2005.

58 See Beatrix Campbell and Judith Jones, *Stolen Voices*, The Women's Press, 1999, 156–62, for an insightful discussion of the Bulger case.

59 King (ed.), *British Political Opinion*, 269–73.

60 See Shamit Saggar, 'The dog that didn't bark? Immigration, race and the

general election', in Andrew Geddes and Jonathan Tonge (eds), *Labour's Landslide: The British General Election 1997*, Manchester University Press, 1997, 147–64.

61   Andrew Adonis and Stephen Pollard, *A Class Act: The Myth of Britain's Classless Society*, Hamish Hamilton 1997, 176–7.

62   Basset, *Strike Free*, 15.

63   Wybrow, 162, 135; Kevin Hawkins, *Unemployment*, Penguin, 1987 edn, 19.

64   Dorothy Rowe, *Living with the Bomb: Can We Cope without Enemies?* Routledge, 1985.

65   Dorothy Rowe, *Beyond Fear*, Fontana, 1987, 392.

4. Charity, Faith and Hope

1   Quoted in Nicholas Kochan, *Ann Widdecombe: Right from the Beginning*, Politicos, 2000, 99.

2   Interrupting a *Vanity Fair* interview of Tony Blair; see *Daily Telegraph*, 4 May 2003.

3   Quoted in Terry Coleman, *Thatcher's Britain: A Journey through the Promised Lands*, Bantam Press, 1987, 107.

4   John Lahr (ed.), *The Diaires of Kenneth Tynan*, Bloomsbury, 2002 edn, 291.

5   *House of Lords Debates*, Vol. 361, cols 1418–23, 25 June 1975.

6   Ibid., col. 1418.

7   The Duke of Edinburgh, 'Intellectual Dissent and the Reversal of Trends' in Arthur Seldon (ed.), *The Coming Confrontation*, IEA, 1978, 208–17.

8   Andrew Morton, *Diana: Her True Story*, Michael O'Mara Books, 1993, 138.

9   Dimbleby, 281–3. Diana's mother, Frances Shand Kydd, rightly protested against the media harassment of her daughter, but to no avail.

10   Morton, 54; Dimbleby, 205.

11   Geldof, *Is That It?*, 388, 378.

12   *The Times*, 15 July 1985.

13   Nigel Fountain in *Observer*, 27 July 1997.

14   *Daily Mirror*, 20 October 2003.

15   Simon Jenkins, *Accountable to None: The Tory Nationalisation of Britain*, Penguin edn, 1996, 213.

16   Ibid., 214.

17   Anthony Thwaite (ed.), *The Selected Letters of Philip Larkin*, 1940–1985, Faber and Faber, 1992, 662–3.

18   Bernard de Mandeville, *The Fable of the Bees* (1724), Pelican edn, 1970.

19   Raymond Snoddy and Jon Ashworth, *It Could Be You: The Untold Story of the National Lottery*, Faber and Faber, 2000, 47.

20   Adonis and Pollard, *Class Act*, 266.

21   John Major, *The Autobiography*, HarperCollins, 1999, 411.

22   Adonis and Pollard, 174.

23   Ibid., 266, 273, 276.

24   Bill Murphy, *Home Truths: A Jaunt around the Decaying Heart of England*, Mainstream, 2000, 217.

25   Snoddy and Ashworth, 177–8.

26   See David Blunkett, *The Blunkett Tapes*, Bloomsbury, 2006, 388.

27   *Daily Express*, 11 February 2004.

28   Snoddy and Ashworth, 155–6; *Daily Express*, 11 February 2004; *Guardian*, 9 January 2002.

29   Polly Toynbee in *Guardian*, 11 July 2003.

30   Hobson, 910.

31   On attitudes to begging and the *Big Issue*, see Michael Adler, Catherine Bromley and Michael Rosie, 'Begging as a challenge to the welfare state' in Roger Jowell et al. (eds), *British Social Attitudes: The 17th Report*, Sage, 2000, 209–38.

32   *Daily Mail*, 6 September 1997.

33   Simon Critchley, 'Di and Dodi Die' in Jeffrey Richards et al. (eds), *Diana: The Making of a Media Saint*, I.B. Tauris, 1999, 158.

34   *Sun*, 15 September 1997.

35   *Guardian*, 1 November 1997.

36   Radice, *Diaries*, 397.

37   *The Times*, 28 March 2005.

38   West, 65.

39   Dominic Hobson, *The National Wealth: Who Gets What in Britain*, HarperCollins, 2001, 919. For the donations of specific individuals and companies, see 920, 922. According to those figures, in 1994 Richard Branson – one of Princess Diana's personal favourites – gave 0.2 per cent of his fortune to charity.

40   *Guardian*, 25 November 2002.

41   Hobson, 917–18.

42   *The Times*, 15 February 2005.

43   Dimbleby, 535.

44   Humphrey Carpenter, *Robert Runcie: The Reluctant Archbishop*, Hodder and Staughton, 1996, 220–5.

45   See John Colville, *The New Elizabethans, 1952–1977*, Collins, 1977, 211–25.

46   Hobson, 153.

47   Nan Dirk De Graaf and Ariana Need, 'Losing Faith: Is Britain Alone?', in Roger Jowell et al. (eds), *British Social Attitudes: The 17th Report*, National Centre for Social Research, 2000, 123.

48   *Guardian*, 23 December 2006.

49   *Guardian*, 21 October 2001.

50   *The Times*, 27 January 1975.

51   Mary Whitehouse, *Quite Contrary: An Autobiography*, Pan edition, 1994, 67–70.

52   Hobson, 144.

53   *The Times*, 16 April 1975.

54   *The Times*, 31 July 1975.

55   *The Times*, 15 March 1975.

56   *The Times*, 28 July 1982.

57   *The Times*, 27, 28 July 1982.

58   Sarah Curtis (ed.), *The Journals of Woodrow Wyatt*, Vol. 1, Macmillan, 1998, 22; Campbell, *Margaret Thatcher*, 390.

59   *Faith in the City: A Call for Action by Church and Nation*, Church House Publishing, 1985, 359.

60   Jeremy Paxman, *The English*, Michael Joseph, 1998, 106–7.

61   Interview with the late Lord Runcie.

62   *Crockford's Clerical Directory 1987–8*, Church House Publishing, 1987, 69, 75.

63   *Crockford's Clerical Directory*, 69.

64   Anthony Sampson, *The Changing Anatomy of Britain*, Hodder and Stoughton, 1982.

65   For the full text and an incisive critique, see Jonathan Raban, *God, Man and Mrs Thatcher*, Chatto & Windus, 1989.

66   Hobson, 161, 138.

67   *The Roy Strong Diaries, 1967–1987*, Phoenix edn, 1998, 198.

68   *The Scotsman*, 16 May 2003.

69   Francis Wheen, *How Mumbo Jumbo Conquered the World: A Short History of Modern Delusions*, Fourth Estate, 2004, 126.

70   De Graaf and Need, 123.

71   *Guardian*, 23 December 2006.

72   *Guardian*, 23 August 2005.

73   Dimbleby, 113–14.

74   Stephen Pollard in *The Times*, 7 July 2004.

75   Paxman, 188.

76   Tim Hames in *The Times*, 26 June 2006.

77   See Denis Healey, *The Time of My Life*, Michael Joseph, 1989.

78   Friedrich A. Hayek, *The Intellectuals and Socialism*, 1998 edn, IEA, 12.

79   Zachary Leader (ed.), *The Letters of Kingsley Amis*, HarperCollins, 2000, 840.

80   Shawcross, 57, 67.

81   Keith Joseph and Jonathan Sumption, *Equality*, John Murray, 1979.

82   Blake and Weaver, *Suicide by Socialism*, 155, 10.

83 Paul Johnson, *The Intellectuals*, Weidenfeld & Nicolson, 1988, 342.

84 E.P. Thompson, *Writing by Candlelight*, Merlin Press, 1980, 255–6.

85 In June 1988 the radical journals *New Statesman* and *New Society* had merged.

86 Cambridge University Press, 1981.

87 Matthew Arnold, *Culture and Anarchy* (1869), Cambridge University Press edn, 1960, 69.

88 For an impassioned attempt to rebuff the evidence for dumbing down, see Richard Morrison in *The Times*, 14 September 2004.

89 John Carey, *The Intellectuals and the Masses: Pride and Prejudice among the Literary Intelligentsia 1880–1939*, Faber and Faber, 1992.

90 John Maynard Keynes was another astonishing omission.

91 *Sunday Times*, 15 February 1976.

92 Christopher Bradley, *Mrs Thatcher's Cultural Policies: 1979–1990*, Columbia University Press, 1998, 281.

93 See Simon Jenkins, *Accountable to None*, 140–2.

94 For concise discussions of higher education under Thatcher and Major, see Peter Scott, 'Higher Education', in Dennis Kavanagh and Anthony Seldon (eds), *The Thatcher Effect: A Decade of Change*, Oxford University Press, 1989, 198–212, and Peter Dorey, 'The 3 Rs – Reform, Reproach and Rancour: Education Policies under John Major', in Peter Dorey (ed.), *The Major Premiership: Politics and Policies under John Major, 1990–97*, Macmillan, 1999, 147–64.

95 *The Times*, 29 November 2004.

96 *The Times*, 28 January 2004.

97 *Times Educational Supplement*, 1 February 1985.

98 Noel Annan, *Our Age: The Generation That Made Post-War Britain*, Fontana edn, 1991, 580.

99 *Daily Telegraph*, 31 October 2003.

100 The proportion of unemployed people voting Conservative was about 25 per cent; see David Willetts, *Modern Conservatism*, Penguin, 1992, 21.

101 *Guardian*, 20 May 2002.

102 See, for example, Onora O'Neill's ruminations on the decline of public trust, the Reith Lectures of 2002 (published by Cambridge University Press as *A Question of Trust*, 2002); and Bernard Williams's efforts to wrestle with the problem of pornography, discussed in Chapter 5 below.

103 Anthony Giddens, *The Third Way: Renewal of Social Democracy*, Polity Press, 1998.

104 Tony Blair, Introduction to Giles Radice (ed.), *What Needs to Change: New Visions for Britain*, HarperCollins, 1996.

105 See in particular Richard Hoggart, *The Way We Live Now: Dilemmas in Contemporary Culture*, Pimlico edn, 1996, for contemporary fears of cultural desolation.

106 Daniel Johnson in *Daily Telegraph*, 24 September 2004; *Guardian*, 1 July 2003.

107 Kingsley Amis, *Memoirs*, 319.

108 David Hare, *Writing Left-Handed*, Faber and Faber, 1991, 35.

109 *The Ripple* (Leicester University student newspaper), 25 October 2004.

110 Hare, 22–3.

111 Charles Drazin (ed.), *John Fowles: The Journals*, Vol. 2, Jonathan Cape, 2006, 411.

112 Tynan, 215, 317.

113 Palin, *Dairies 1969–1979*, 559.

114 Thomas Hobbes, *Leviathan* (1651), Basil Blackwell edn, n.d., 57.

5. Greed

1 *The World of Goods: Towards an Anthropology of Consumption*, Viking edn, 1979, 2.

2 Fontana, 1992, 24.

3 *The Times*, 13 July 1977.

4 Tom Bower, *Broken Dreams: Vanity, Greed and the Souring of English Football*, Simon and Schuster, 2003, 28.

5 Abraham H. Maslow, *Motivation and Personality*, 3rd edn, Longman, 1987, 22–3.

6 *The Times*, 13 July 1989.

7 *Guardian*, 16 November 2000.

8 *Guardian*, 5 September 2003.

9 Cantley's remarks were immediately lampooned by the comedian Peter Cook, in what his biographer rightly calls 'one of the finest satirical attacks in the history of British comedy'; see Harry Thompson, *Peter Cook: A Biography*, Hodder and Stoughton, 1997, 371.

10 *The Times*, 24 April 1975; *Leicester Mercury*, 2 January 1975.

11 Wybrow, *Britain Speaks Out*, 144.

12 http://www.nationalarchives.gov.uk/films/1964to1979/filmpage-vandalism.htm.

13 Paul Foot, *The Vote: How It Was Won and How It Was Undermined*, Viking, 2005, 396.

14 Paul Johnson, 'A Brotherhood of National Misery', in *New Statesman*, 16 May 1975.

15 Foot, 396.

16 Quoted in Whitehead, *The Writing on the Wall*, 284.

17 Ibid., 283.

18 See, for example, Stephen Haesler, *The Battle for Britain: Thatcher and the New Liberals*, I.B. Tauris, 1989, 46.

19 *Leicester Mercury*, 2 January 1975.

20 *The Times*, 18 January 1975.

21 Professor Hugh Clegg, quoted in *The Times*, 30 April 1975.

22 Hutber, *Middle Class*, 34–6.

23 *The Times*, 13, 18 January, 1975.

24 Jack, *Before the Oil Ran Out*, 83.

25 See Savage, *England's Dreaming*; Mick Brown, *Richard Branson: The Inside Story*, Headline edn, 1992, 191.

26 John Campbell, *Margaret Thatcher*, Vol. I, *The Grocer's Daughter* (Jonathan Cape, 2000), 287–9.

27 *The Times*, 6 January 1975.

28 Quoted in Campbell, 182.

29 *Saga* Magazine, May 2004.

30 Thatcher, *Path to Power*, 14; November 1985 interview with Miriam Stoppard, quoted in Campbell, 24.

31 Interview with Miriam Gross, in *Required Writing: Miscellaneous Pieces 1955–1982*, Faber and Faber, 1983, 52.

32 Hutber, 23.

33 Thatcher, 77–8.

34 Campbell, 24.

35 Andy McSmith in *Daily Telegraph*, 16 February 2002.

36 See p.214, above.

37 *Sunday Times*, 3 May 1981.

38 Paul Johnson, *The Recovery of Freedom*, Basil Blackwell, 1980, 92.

39 Centre for Policy Studies, 1977.

40 John Westergaard and Henrietta Resler, *Class in a Capitalist Society*, Pelican edn, 1976, 40. See also Frank Field, Molly Meacher and Chris Pond, *To Him Who Hath: A Study of Poverty and Taxation*, Penguin, 1977.

41 Digby Anderson, *All Oiks Now: The Unnoticed Surrender of Middle England*, The Social Affairs Unit, 2004, 10–13; Anthony Deane, *The Great Abdication: Why Britain's Decline is the Fault of the Middle Class*, Imprint Academic, 2005; *Guardian*, 12 September 2003.

42 Jack, 94–8.

43 Whitehead, 366.

44 John Casey, *Sunday Times*, 30 September 1984.

45 Martin Amis: *Money: A Suicide Note*, Penguin edn, 1985, 58, 64, 78.

46 Mark Hollingsworth and Paul Halloran, *Thatcher's Fortunes: The Life and Times of Mark Thatcher*, Mainstream, 2005, 144; *Daily Telegraph*, 10 October 1994.

47 Hollingsworth and Halloran, 86, 147.

48 Edgar Wilson, *A Very British Miracle: The Failure of Thatcherism*, Pluto Press, 1992, 93.

49 See Rodney Tyler, *Campaign! The Selling of the Prime Minister*, Grafton Books, 1987.

50 'Values: The Crusade that Failed', in Kavanagh and Seldon (eds), *The Thatcher Effect*, 239–50; see also John Rentoul, *Me and Mine: The Triumph of the New Individualism?*, HarperCollins, 1989.

51 John Nott, *Here Today, Gone Tomorrow: Recollections of an Errant Politician*, Politicos, 2002, 347.

52 Editorial, *Sunday Telegraph*, 7 June 1987; Peregrine Worsthorne, *The Politics of Manners and the uses of inequality*, CPS, 1988, 9.

53 William Keegan, *Mr Lawson's Gamble*, Hodder & Stoughton, 1989, 221.

54 *Hansard*, Vol. 129, cols 1116, 1268, 16, 17 March 1988; Vol. 130, col. 106, 21 March 1988.

55 *Guardian*, 30 December 2005.

56 Thatcher, *Downing Street Years*, 674.

57 Hollingsworth and Halloran, 269–70.

58 Hutber, 153.

59 Sarah Curtis (ed.), *The Journals of Woodrow Wyatt*, Vol. 1, 629.

60 Quoted in Campbell, *The Iron Lady*, 249–50.

61 See Richard Bellamy, 'The Anti-Poll Tax Non-Payment Campaign and Liberal Concepts of Political Obligation', *Government of Opposition*, Vol. 29, no. 1, Winter 1994, 22.

62 Major, *The Autobiography*, 200–1.

63 Roger Jowell, Sharon Witherspoon and Lindsay Brook (eds), *British Social Attitudes: The 7th Report*, Gower Publishing, 1990; Rentoul, *Me and Mine*, 170.

64 For the Westland saga, see David Leigh and Magnus Linklater, *Not with Honour*, Sphere, 1986.

65 Gould, *Unfinished Revolution*, 144.

66 For an excellent analysis of the policy review, see Eric Shaw, *The Labour Party since 1979: Crisis and Transformation*, Routledge, 1994, 81–107.

67 'Thatcherism – Breaking out of the Impasse', in Stuart Hall and Martin Jacques (eds), *The Politics of Thatcherism*, Lawrence and Wishart, 1983, 53.

68 *Guardian*, 1 October 1990.

69 Mistrust of the 'modernised' Labour Party was detected in post-election analysis by the Fabian Society; see *Qualitative Research amongst Waverers in Labour's Southern Target Seats*, Fabian Society, 1992.

70 Christopher Johnson, *The Economy under Mrs Thatcher, 1979–90*, Penguin, 1991, 12.

71 O'Farrell, *Things Can Only Get Better*, 278 (italics in original).

72 Tom Bower, *Maxwell: The Final Verdict*, HarperCollins, 1995, 49–57.

73 Chippendale and Horrie, *Punter*, 239–40.

74 Snoddy and Ashworth, *It Could Be You*, 153.

75 *Guardian*, 20 October 1994.

76 For a lively account of this period, see David Leigh and Ed Vulliamy, *Sleaze: The Corruption of Parliament*, Fourth Estate, 1997.

77 *Financial Times*, 28 October 1991; Sampson, *Who Runs This Place?*, 333.

78 Hobson, *The National Wealth*, 562.

79 Quoted in Harris, *The Last Party*, 272.

80 On the 1992 ERM crisis, see Philip Stephens, *Politics and the Pound: The Tories, the Economy and Europe*, Macmillan, 1996.

81 David Conn, *The Football Business*, Mainstream, 1998 edn, 70.

82 Ibid., 76.

83 Ibid., 67.

84 Ibid., 224, 228.

85 Nick Hornby, *Fever Pitch*, Indigo edn, 1996, 187.

86 Quoted in Bower, *Broken Dreams*, 144–5.

87 *Blueprint for the Future of Football*, quoted in Conn, 145.

88 Jimmy Greaves with Normen Giller, *Don't Shoot the Manager: The Revealing Story of England's Soccer Bosses*, Boxtree, 1994 edn, 87.

89 Quoted in *The Definitive History of Leeds United*, www.mightyleeds.co.uk.

6. Lust

1   *House of Lords Debates*, Vol. 369, col. 695, 24 March 1976.

2   Whitehouse, *Quite Contrary*, 214–15.

3   Quoted in Roy McCloughry, *Belief in Politics*, Hodder & Stoughton, 1996, 127.

4   Picador edn, 1997, 20.

5   *The Times*, 24 November 1977.

6   Simon Sheridan, *'Come Play with Me': The Life and Films of Mary Millington*, FAB Press, 1999, 104.

7   *The Times*, 30 January 1976.

8   *House of Lords Debates*, Vol. 369, col. 698, 24 March 1976.

9   *Report of the Committee on Obscenity and Film Censorship*, Cmnd 7772, 1979, 63.

10 *The Times*, 15 January 1975.

11 *The Times*, 21 January 1975.

12 *Pornography: The Longford Report*, Coronet, 1972, 412.

13 Peter Stanford, *Lord Longford: An Authorized Life*, William Heinemann, 1994, 414–16, 424.

14 Davies (ed.), *Kenneth Williams Diaries*, 557.

15 Gordon Burn, *Happy Like Murderers*, Faber and Faber, 1998, 341.

16 *The Times*, 4 October 1975.

17 See Mark Jarvis, *Conservative Governments, Morality and Social Change in Affluent Britain, 1957–64*, Manchester University Press, 2005.

18 Melanie Phillips, *The Sex-Change Society: Feminised Britain and the Neutered Male*, Social Market Foundation, 1999, 23, 28.

19 *The Times*, 8 August 1975.

20 Chippendale and Horrie, *Stick It Up Your Punter*, 38–40.

21 *Hansard*, Vol. 93, col. 938, 12 March 1986.

22 See Short's introduction to *Dear Clare . . . This Is What Women Feel about Page 3*, Radius, 1991.

23 Chippendale and Horrie, 201.

24 Tony Blair, 'Licence to print anything', *The Times*, 13 October 1987.

25 *Sun*, 4 May 2005.

26 See PRO DPP 2/5541 for details of this case, including a police interview with the incredulous David Sullivan and Mary Millington.

27 Dominic Sandbrook, *White Heat: A History of Britain in the Swinging Sixties*, Little, Brown, 2006, 545–6.

28 Geoffrey Robertson, *The Justice Game*, Vintage edn, 1999, 57.

29 *Hansard*, Vol. 864, col. 329, 13 November 1973.

30 *The Times*, 30 January 1976.

31 *House of Lords Debates*, Vol. 404, cols 121–2, 16 January 1980.

32 Whitehouse, 195.

33 *Daily Telegraph*, 1 November 1979.

34 Robertson, *Justice Game*, 181. For the Conservative record in this sphere, see Martin Durham, *Moral Crusades: Family and Morality in the Thatcher Years*, New York University Press, 1991.

35 Sheridan, 104, 126.

36 Whitehouse, 216–17.

37 *The Times*, 25 November 1975.

38 See Robertson, 163–81, for an amusing account of this case.

39 Phillips, 24.

40 *Independent*, 21 February 2007.

41 *Daily Mail*, 28 January 2004.

42 See Matthew Sweet, 'No sex please; we're bored' in *Guardian*, 24 November 2006.

43 Sheridan, 94–5; Benn, *Against the Tide*, 329–31.

44 Matthew Parris, *Great Parliamentary Scandals*, Robson Books, 1995, 228–30.

45 Ibid., 249–59.

46 Edwina Currie, *Lifelines*, Sidgwick & Jackson, 1989, 89–90, 95.

47 Michael Crick, *In Search of Michael Howard*, Simon & Schuster, 2005, 209–12.

48 Parris, 287–91.

49 *Hansard*, Vol. 212, cols 139–41, 22 September 1992.

50 On the Calcutt report, see Richard Shannon, *A Press Free and Responsible:*

Self-Regulation and the Press Complaints Commission, John Murray, 2001, 98–133.

51 *The Times*, 9 October 1993.

52 Currie, 86–7.

53 Parris, 317.

54 Gyles Brandreth, *Breaking the Code: Westminster Diaries*, Phoenix edn, 2000, 227.

55 Parris, 318.

56 *Hansard*, Vol. 237, col. 98, 21 February 1994.

57 Piers Morgan, *The Insider*, Ebury Press, 2005 edn, 24, 38.

58 Anna Pasternak, *Princess in Love*, Bloomsbury, 1994, 62–3.

59 Morgan, 39–40.

60 Vasso Kortesis with David Leigh, *The Duchess of York: Uncensored*, Blake Publishing, 1996, 131.

61 Shannon, 105.

62 Nick Davies, *Dark Heart: The Shocking Truth about Hidden Britain*, Vintage edn, 1998, vii, 4–8.

63 Duncan Campbell in *Sunday Times*, 26 June 2005; *Guardian*, 18 December 2002.

64 Although the extent of the problem in each country can only be estimated; see Worldvision.org.uk.

65 Philips, 22, 25–6.

66 Hal Colebatch, *Blair's Britain: British Culture Wars and New Labour*, Claridge Press, 1999, 40; Peter Oborne, *Alastair Campbell: New Labour and the Rise of the Media Class*, Aurum Press, 1999, 201 note.

67 *Private Eye* 1172, 21 November 2006.

7. Apathy

1 *Hansard*, Vol. 62, cols 1234–6, 28 June 1984.

2 http://news.bbc.co.uk/1/hi/events/newsnight/1372220.stm.

3 Lance Price, *The Spin Doctor's Diary: Inside Number 10 with New Labour*, Hodder & Stoughton, 2005, 365.

4 David Denver, 'The results: How Britain voted (or didn't)', in Andrew P. Geddes and Jonathan Tonge (eds), *Labour's Second Landslide: The British General Election 2001*, Manchester University Press, 2002, 13.

5 David Blunkett and Keith Jackson, *Democracy in Crisis: The Town Halls Respond*, Hogarth Press, 1987.

6 *The Times*, 6 June 2001.

7 *Ambitions for Britain*, Labour Party manifesto, 2001.

8 *Time for Common Sense*, Conservative Party manifesto, 2001.

9   *Freedom. Justice. Honesty.* Liberal Democrats manifesto, 2001.

10   Ivor Crewe, Tony Fox and Jim Alt, 'Non-voting in British general elections, 1966–October 1974', in Colin Crouch (ed.), *British Political Sociology Yearbook*, Vol. 3, Croom Helm, 40.

11   *Guardian*, 24 October 2002.

12   *Guardian*, 28 August 2002.

13   Price, 362; Steven Fielding, '"No-one else to vote for?" Labour's Campaign', in Geddes and Tonge (eds), 39.

14   Ivor Crewe, 'A New Political Hegemony?', in Anthony King (ed.), *Britain at the Polls, 2001*, Chatham House, 2002, 225–6.

15   David Denver, 'The results: how Britain voted', in Andrew Geddes and Jonathan Tonge (eds), *Labour's Landslide: The British General Election 1997*, Manchester University Press, 1997, 17–20.

16   King (ed.), *British Political Opinion 1937–2000*, 301–2.

17   I owe this point to Professor David Denver.

18   *The Times*, 4 February 2003.

19   *Independent*, 4 May 2005.

20   www.mori.com

21   David Butler and Donald Stokes, *Political Change in Britain*, 2nd edn, Macmillan, 1974.

22   *The Times*, 2 April 1975.

23   O'Farrell, *Things Can Only Get Better*, 269.

24   *New Labour: Because Britain Deserves Better*, foreword.

25   *Guardian*, 1 October 1997.

26   *On the Record*, BBC, 16 November 1997.

27   *Guardian*, 11 May, 1996.

28   Stephen Pollard, *David Blunkett*, Hodder & Stoughton, 2005, 240; Blunkett, *The Blunkett Tapes*, 89–90, 212–16.

29   *The Times*, 6 February 1999.

30   Peter Riddell in *The Times*, 16 June 2006.

31   *Guardian*, 2 October 2002, 28 September 1995.

32   Francis Beckett and David Hencke, *The Survivor: Tony Blair in Peace and War*, Aurum Press, 2005, 76.

33   Gould, *Unfinished Revolution*, 4.

34   *Mail on Sunday*, 12 November 2000; Nick Cohen, *Pretty Straight Guys*, Faber and Faber, 2003, 139; Beckett and Hencke, 189,

35   Andrew Rawnsley, *Servants of the People: The Inside Story of New Labour*, Penguin edn, 2001, 17.

36   Quoted in Rawnsley, 206.

37   *Ambitions for Britain*, Labour Party manifesto, 2001, 29.

38   *Observer*, 23 November 1997.

39   See Polly Toynbee and David Walker, *Did Things Get Better? An Audit of Labour's Successes and Failures*, Penguin, 2001.

40   *Daily Telegraph*, 29 May 2001.

41   *Daily Telegraph*, 11 December 2001.

42   For a critical study of the 1991/2 riots, see Beatrix Campbell, *Goliath: Britian's Dangerous Places*, Methuen, 1995.

43   John Pilger, *Distant Voices*, Vintage edition, 1994, 29.

44   Campbell, *Goliath*, 95.

45   On the persistence of class divisions see Adonis and Pollard, *Class Act*, and Ferdinand Mount, *Mind the Gap: The New Class Divide in Britain*, Short Books, 2004.

46   Pollard, *David Blunkett*, 275.

47   David Beetham, Iain Byrne, Pauline Ngan and Stuart Weir, *Democracy under Blair: A Democratic Audit of the United Kingdom*, Politicos, 2002, 50.

48   Gordon Brown, 'The Servant State', *Political Quarterly*, Vol. 63, no. 4, October–December 1992, 400–1.

49   *Daily Telegraph*, 3 May 1997.

50   Toynbee and Walker, 1; Fraser Nelson in *News of the World*, 4 May 2007.

51   Colebatch, *Blair's Britain*, 92.

52   Anthony King, 'Tony Blair's First Term', in King et al. (eds), *Britain at the Polls, 2001*, 38.

53   *The Times*, 13 September 2000.

54   *News of the World*, 16 January 1994.

55   *Guardian*, 8 May 1996.

56   *Independent*, 6 May 2000.

57   Patrick West, *Conspicuous Compassion: Why Sometimes It Really Is Cruel to Be Kind*, Civitas, 2004, 16–17.

58   *Guardian Unlimited*, 4 February, 2001; West, 16.

59   Stephen Ward, 'Environment and Transport: A Conspiracy of Silence?', in Geddes and Tonge, 169.

60   Hitchens, *Abolition of Britain*, 214.

61   Charles Pattie, Patrick Seyd and Paul Whiteley, 'Civic Attitudes and Engagement in Modern Britain', *Parliamentary Affairs*, Vol. 56, no. 4, 2003.

62   David Aaronovitch in *Guardian*, 18 February 2003.

63   *Daily Mail*, 25 March 2003.

64   Euan Ferguson in *Observer*, 16 February 2003.

65   See Andy McSmith, *Faces of Labour: The Inside Story*, Verso, 1996, 247–8.

66   *Guardian*, 22 May 2003.

67   See Rawnsley, 219–31, and Oborne, 80–1.

68   Brian Appleyard in *Sunday Times*, 19 May 1991.

69   Oborne, *Alastair Campbell*, 201.

70   Rawnsley, 211–12.

71   Greg Palast, *The Best Democracy Money Can Buy*, Robinson edn, 2003, 295.

72   Quoted in Joe Lovejoy, *Sven Goran Eriksson*, HarperCollins, 2002, 41.

73   Ibid., 275–6.

74 *The Times*, 3 November 2004.

75 Sampson, *Who Runs This Place?* 317.

76 *The Times*, 30 March 2005.

77 Christopher Meyer, Britain's ambassador to the US at the time, has given a flavour of the head-turning adulation Blair received on this visit in his *DC Confidential*, Phoenix edn, 2005, 204–6.

78 Paddy Ashdown, *The Ashdown Diaries 1997–1999*, Vol. 2, Allen Lane, 2001, 127.

79 Quoted in *Guardian*, 26 April 2003.

80 *The Blunkett Tapes*, 447.

81 Alan Travis in *Guardian*, 26 April 2003; Piers Morgan, 391; Paul Whiteley in *Guardian*, 6 May 2003.

82 Patrick Lamb, quoted in Sampson, 166.

83 Quoted in Richard Norton-Taylor, Mark Lloyd and Stephen Cook, *Knee Deep in Dishonour: The Scott Report and its Aftermath*, Victor Gollancz, 1996, 7.

84 Ibid., 10.

85 Clark, *The Last Diaries*, 177.

86 Quoted in *Guardian*, 22 July 2003.

87 *The Times*, 30 January 2004.

88 *Guardian*, 19 August 2003.

89 Oborne, *Political Lying*, 224.

90 Quoted in Peter Stothard and Nick Danziger, 'A Portrait of Power', *The Times*, 3 May 2003.

91 Ashdown, 144 (16 December 1997).

92 *Independent*, 22 October 2004.

93 Colin Crouch, *Coping with Post-Democracy*, Fabian Society, 2000, 4.

94 *The Times*, 15 December 2006.

95 See, for example, *Guardian*, 21 September 2006.

96 *The Times*, 16 August 2004.

97 Colville, 301.

98 Thompson, 255.

99 *The Times*, 27 June 2006.

100 On this subject see Elliott and Atkinson, especially 208–15.

101 *Guardian*, 21 February 2006.

102 *The Times*, 28 January 2005.

Conclusion: Apathy and Anger

1 *Guardian*, 10 May 2007.

2 'Our Nation's Future – Public Life', speech delivered at Canary Wharf, London, 12 June 2007.

3   *Sun*, 15 June 2007.

4   *The Times*, 14 July 1975.

5   http://news.bbc.co.uk/1/hi/health/6755247.stm.

6   See John Hoskyns, *Just in Time: Inside the Thatcher Revolution*, Aurum Press, 2000, 1–21.

7   On this subject see Mark Garnett, *The Snake that Swallowed its Tail: Some Contradictions of Contemporary Liberalism*, Imprint Academic, 2004.

8   http://news.bbc.co.uk/1/hi/england/6717997.stm; http://news.bbc.co.uk/england/suffolk/6744655.stm.

9   For an insightful discussion of the problem of trust in the Internet age, see Kieron O'Hara, *Trust*, Icon Books, 2004.

10 The dilemma was examined in a book by George Walden, a former Tory minister and one of the most independent-minded parliamentarians of his generation: see *Time to Emigrate?*, Gibson Square Books, 2006.

11 *Guardian*, 6 June 2007; *Private Eye*, 22 June 2007.

12 Simon Jenkins, *Big Bang Localism: A Rescue Plan for British Democracy*, Policy Exchange, 2004. The same remarks, of course, applied with even more force to the ambitious reform proposals announced by Gordon Brown less than a week after succeeding Blair. In themselves, Brown's ideas represented a tacit critique of the Blair government in which he had played such a central role.

13 See, for example, Ronald Inglehart, 'The Silent Revolution in Europe: Intergenerational Change in Post-Industrial Societies', *American Political Science Review*, Vol. 65, no. 4 (December 1971), 991–1017.

14 Cited in Robert E. Lane, 'The Road Not Taken', in David A. Crocker and Toby Linden (eds), *Ethics of Consumption: The Good Life, Justice, and Global Stewardship*, Rowman & Littlefield, 1998, 220.

15 *Daily Mail*, 20 June 2007.

16 http://news.bbc.co.uk/1/hi/education/6692091.stm; *Guardian*, 28 June 2007.

BIBLIOGRAPHY

Primary Sources

British Library of Political and Economic Science (BLPES), London School of
  Economics
Conservative Party Archives (CPA), Bodleian Library, Oxford
National Archives, Kew

Official Publications

Hansard
House of Lords Debates
Report of the Committee on Obscenity and Film Censorship, Cmnd. 7772, 1979

Newspapers and Magazines

*Daily Mail; Daily Mirror; Daily Telegraph; Guardian; Independent: Kensington
News and Post; Leicester Mercury; New Statesman; Observer; Private Eye; Saga
Magazine; The Spectator; Sun; Sunday Telegraph; Sunday Times; The Times*

Student Newspapers

Ripple (Leicester University); *SCAN* (Lancaster University)

Books and Articles

Adams, Jad, *Tony Benn: A Biography*, Pan edn, 1993
Adonis, Andrew, and Pollard, Stephen, *A Class Act: The Myth of Britain's
  Classless Society*, Hamish Hamilton, 1997
Almond, Gabriel and Verba, Sidney, *The Political Culture*, Little, Brown, 1965
  edn

Amis, Kingsley, *Memoirs*, Penguin edn, 1992

Amis, Martin, *Success*, Penguin edn, 1985

Amis, Martin, *Money: A Suicide Note*, Penguin edn, 1985

Amis, Martin, *Einstein's Monsters*, Penguin edn, 1988

Anderson, Digby, *All Oiks Now: The Unnoticed Surrender of Middle England*, Social Affairs Unit, 2004

Annan, Noel, *Our Age: The Generation That Made Post-War Britain*, Fontana edn, 1991

Arnold, Matthew, *Culture and Anarchy*, Cambridge University Press edn, 1960

Arrighi, Giovanni, *The Long Twentieth Century: Money, Power and the Origins of Our Times*, Verso, 1994

Ashdown, Paddy, *The Ashdown Diaries*, Vol. 2, 1997–1999, Allen Lane, 2001

Bagguely, Paul, *From Protest to Acquiescence? Political Movements of the Unemployed*, Macmillan, 1991

Baimbridge, Mark (ed), *The 1975 Referendum on Europe*, Vol. 1, *Reflections of the Participants*, Imprint Academic, 2006

Baker, Blake, *The Far Left: An Exposé of the Extreme Left in Britain*, Weidenfeld & Nicolson, 1981

Bassett, Philip, *Strike Free: New Industrial Relations in Britain*, Papermac edn, 1987

Beckett, Francis, and Hencke, David, *The Survivor: Tony Blair in Peace and War*, Aurum Press, 2005

Beetham, David, Byrne, Ian, Ngan, Pauline, and Weir, Stuart, *Democracy under Blair: A Democratic Audit of the United Kingdom*, Politicos, 2002

Bellamy, Richard, 'The Anti-Poll Tax Non-Payment Campaign and Liberal Concepts of Political Obligation', *Government and Opposition*, Vol. 29, No. 1, Winter 1994

Benn, Tony, *Office without Power: Diaries 1968–72*, Arrow edn, 1989

Benn, Tony, *Against the Tide: Diaries 1973–6*, Arrow edn, 1990

Benn, Tony, *The End of an Era: Diaries 1980–90*, Arrow edn, 1994

Blake, Minden, and Weaver, H.J., *Suicide by Socialism*, Springwood Books, 1979

Blunkett, David, *The Blunkett Tapes: My Life in the Bear-Pit*, Bloomsbury, 2006

Blunkett, David, and Jackson, Keith, *Democracy in Crisis: The Town Halls Respond*, Hogarth Press, 1987

Booker, Christopher, *The Seventies: Portrait of a Decade*, Allen Lane, 1980

Bourke, Joanna, *Fear: A Cultural History*, Virago, 2005

Boyson, Rhodes, *Speaking My Mind*, Peter Owen, 1995

Bower, Tom, *Maxwell: The Final Verdict*, HarperCollins, 1995

Bower, Tom, *Broken Dreams: Vanity, Greed and the Souring of English Football*, Simon and Schuster, 2003

Bradley, Christopher, *Mrs Thatcher's Cultural Policies: 1979–1990*, Columbia University Press, 1998

Brandreth, Gyles, *Breaking the Code: Westminster Diaries*, Phoenix edn, 2000

Brown, Gordon, 'The Servant State', *Political Quarterly*, Vol. 63, no. 4, October–December 1992

Brown, Mick, *Richard Branson: The Inside Story*, Headline edn, 1992

Bryson, Bill, *Notes from a Small Island*, Black Swan edn, 1996

Burn, Gordon, *Happy Like Murderers*, Faber and Faber, 1998

Butler, David, and Kitzinger, Uwe, *The 1975 Referendum*, Macmillan, 1976

Butler, David, and Stokes, Donald, *Political Change in Britain*, Macmillan, 1974 edn

Calvocoressi, Peter, *The British Experience 1945–75*, Pelican edn, 1979

Campbell, Beatrix, *Goliath: Britain's Dangerous Places*, Methuen, 1995

Campbell, Beatrix, and Jones, Judith, *Stolen Voices*, Women's Press, 1999

Campbell, John, *Margaret Thatcher*, Volume 1, *The Grocer's Daughter*, Jonathan Cape, 2000

Campbell, John, *Margaret Thatcher*, Volume 2, *The Iron Lady*, Jonathan Cape, 2003

Carey, John, *The Intellectuals and the Masses: Pride and Prejudice among the Literary Intelligentsia 1880–1939*, Faber and Faber, 1992

Carpenter, Humphrey, *Robert Runcie: The Reluctant Archbishop*, Hodder and Stoughton, 1996

Castle, Barbara, *The Castle Diaries 1974–76*, Weidenfeld & Nicolson, 1980

Chalfont, Lord, *The Shadow of My Hand: A Memoir*, Weidenfeld & Nicolson, 2000

Chippendale, Peter, and Horrie, Chris, *Stick It Up Your Punter! The Rise and Fall of the Sun*, Mandarin edn, 1992

Church of England, Board for Social Responsibility, *The Church and the Bomb: Nuclear Weapons and Christian Conscience*, Hodder & Stoughton, 1982

Church of England, *Faith in the City: A Call for Action by Church and Nation*, Church House Publishing, 1985

Clark, Alan, *The Last Diaries: In and Out of the Wilderness*, Weidenfeld & Nicolson, 2002

Clark, Henry, *The Church under Thatcher*, SPCK, 1993

Clutterbuck, Richard, *Britain in Agony: The Growth of Political Violence*, Faber and Faber, 1978

Cockett, Richard, *Thinking the Unthinkable: Think Tanks and the Economic Counter-Revolution 1931–1983*, HarperCollins, 1994

Cohen, Nick, *Pretty Straight Guys*, Faber and Faber, 2003

Cohen, Stanley (ed), *Images of Deviance*, Pelican, 1971

Cole, John, *As It Seemed to Me: Political Memoirs*, Phoenix edn, 1996

Colebatch, Hal, *Blair's Britain: British Culture Wars and New Labour*, Claridge Press, 1999

Coleman, Terry, *Thatcher's Britain: A Journey through the Promised Lands*, Bantam, 1987

Colin, Matthew, *Altered State: The Story of Ecstasy Culture and Acid House*, Serpent's Tail, 1997

Colville, Jock, *The New Elizabethans, 1952–1977*, Collins, 1977

Conn, David, *The Football Business*, Mainstream, 1998 edn

Cormack, Patrick (ed.), *Right Turn: Eight Men Who Changed Their Minds*, Leo Cooper, 1978

Cox, C.B., and Boyson, R. (eds), *Black Paper 1975*, J.M Dent, 1975

Crick, Michael, *Scargill and the Miners*, Penguin, 1985

Crick, Michael, *Michael Heseltine: A Biography*, Penguin edn, 1997

Crick, Michael, *In Search of Michael Howard*, Simon & Schuster, 2005

Critcher, Chas, *Moral Panics and the Media*, Open University Press, 2003

Crocker, David A., and Linden, Toby (eds), *Ethics of Consumption: The Good Life, Justice and Global Stewardship*, Rowman and Littlefield, 1998

Crockford's Clerical Directory 1987–8, Church House Publishing, 1987

Crossman, Richard, *Diaries of a Cabinet Minister*, Vol. 3, *Secretary of State for Social Services*, Hamish Hamilton/Jonathan Cape, 1977

Crouch, Colin, *Coping with Post-Democracy*, Fabian Society, 2000

Crouch, Colin (ed.), *British Political Sociology Yearbook*, Vol. 3, Croom Helm, 1977

Currie, Edwina, *Lifelines*, Sidgwick & Jackson, 1989

Curtis, Sarah (ed.), *The Journals of Woodrow Wyatt*, Vol. 1, Macmillan, 1998

Davies, Nick, *Dark Heart: The Shocking Truth about Hidden Britain*, Vintage edn, 1998

Davies, Russell (ed.), *The Diary of Kenneth Williams*, HarperCollins, 1993

Deane, Anthony, *The Great Abdication: Why Britain's Decline is the Fault of the Middle Class*, Imprint Academic, 2005

Dimbleby, Jonathan, *The Prince of Wales: A Biography*, Little, Brown, 1994

Donoughue, Bernard, *Downing Street Diary: With Harold Wilson in No. 10*, Jonathan Cape, 2005

Dorey, Peter (ed.), *The Major Premiership: Politics and Policies under John Major, 1990–1997*, Macmillan, 1999

Dorril, Stephen and Ramsay, Robin, *Smear! Wilson and the Secret State*, Grafton edn, 1992

Douglas, Mary, and Isherwood, Baron, *The World of Goods: Towards an Anthropology of Consumption*, Viking edn, 1979

Drazin, Charles (ed.), *John Fowles: The Journals*, Vol. 2, Jonathan Cape, 2006

Durham, Martin, *Moral Crusades: Family and Morality in the Thatcher Years*, New York University Press, 1991

Elliott, Larry, and Atkinson, Dan, *The Age of Insecurity*, Verso, 1998

Field, Frank, Meacher, Molly, and Pond, Chris, *To Him Who Hath: A Study of Poverty and Taxation*, Penguin, 1977

Fielding, Helen, *Bridget Jones's Diary*, Picador edn, 1997

Foot, Paul, *The Vote: How It Was Won and How It Was Undermined*, Viking, 2005

Garnett, Mark, *The Snake that Swallowed Its Tail: Some Contradictions of Contemporary Liberalism*, Imprint Academic, 2004

Garnett, Mark, and Aitken, Ian, *Splendid! Splendid! The Authorized Biography of Willie Whitelaw*, Jonathan Cape, 2002

Garnett, Mark, and Lynch, Philip (eds) *The Conservatives in Crisis: The Tories after 1997*, Manchester University Press, 2003

Geddes, Andrew, and Tonge, Jonathan (eds), *Labour's Landslide: The British General Election of 1997*, Manchester University Press, 1997

Geddes, Andrew, and Tonge, Jonathan (eds), *Labour's Second Landslide: The General Election of 2001*, Manchester University Press, 2002

Geldof, Bob, *Is That It?*, Penguin edn, 1986

Giddens, Anthony, *The Third Way: Renewal of Social Democracy*, Polity Press, 1998

Gilbert, Pat, *Passion is a Fashion: The Real Story of the Clash*, Aurum Press, 2005 edn

Gilmour, Ian, *Inside Right: Conservatism, Policies and the People*, Quartet edn, 1978

Goodhart, Philip, *Full-Hearted Consent*, Davis-Poynter, 1976

Gould, Philip, *The Unfinished Revolution: How the Modernisers Saved the Labour Party*, Little, Brown, 1998

Greaves, Jimmy, with Giller, Norman, *Don't Shoot the Manager: The Revealing Story of England's Soccer Bosses*, Boxtree, 1994 edn

Green, Jonathon, *Them: Voices from the Immigrant Community in Contemporary Britain*, Secker & Warburg, 1990

Haesler, Stephen, *The Battle for Britain: Thatcher and the New Liberals*, I.B. Tauris, 1989

Hall, Stuart, and Jacques, Martin (eds), *The Politics of Thatcherism*, Lawrence and Wishart, 1983

Hare, David, *Writing Left-Handed*, Faber and Faber, 1991

Harris, John, *The Last Party: Britpop, Blair and the Demise of English Rock*, Fourth Estate, 2003

Harris, Robert, *The Making of Neil Kinnock*, Faber and Faber, 1984

Haslam, Dave, *Not ABBA: The Real Story of the 1970s*, Fourth Estate, 2005

Hawkins, Kevin, *Unemployment*, Penguin, 1987 edn

Healey, Denis, *The Time of My Life*, Michael Joseph, 1989

Heseltine, Michael, *Life in the Jungle: My Autobiography*, Hodder Headline, 2000

Hewitt, Patricia, *The Abuse of Power: Civil Liberties in the United Kingdom*, Martin Robertson, 1982

Hirst, Paul, *After Thatcher*, Collins, 1989

Hitchens, Peter, *The Abolition of Britain: From Lady Chatterley to Tony Blair*, Quartet, 1999

Hitchens, Peter, *Monday Morning Blues*, Quartet Books, 2000

Hobsbawm, Eric, *The Age of Extremes: The Short Twentieth Century, 1914–1991*, Michael Joseph, 1994

Hobson, Dominic, *The National Wealth: Who Gets What in Britain*, HarperCollins, 2001

Hoggart, Richard, *The Way We Live Now: Dilemmas in Contemporary Culture*, Pimlico edn, 1996

Hollingsworth, Mark, and Halloran, Paul, *Thatcher's Fortunes: The Life and Times of Mark Thatcher*, Mainstream, 2005

Hornsby, Nick (ed.), *My Favourite Year: A Collection of New Football Writing*, H.F & G. Witherby, 1993

Hornby, Nick, *Fever Pitch*, Indigo edn, 1996

Hoskyns, John, *Just in Time: Inside the Thatcher Revolution*, Aurum Press, 2000

Hutber, Patrick, *The Decline and Fall of the Middle Class – and How It Can Fight Back*, Penguin edn, 1977

Inglehart, Ronald, 'The Silent Revolution in Europe: Intergenerational Change in Post-Industrial Societies', *American Political Science Review*, Vol. 65, no. 4, December 1971

Ingrams, Richard, *Muggeridge: The Biography*, HarperCollins, 1995

Jack, Ian, *Before the Oil Ran Out: Britain in the Brutal Years*, Vintage edn, 1997

Jacka, Keith, Cox, Caroline, and Marks, John, *The Rape of Reason: The Corruption of the Polytechnic of North London*, Churchill Press, 1975

Jackson, Tim, *Chasing Progress: Beyond Measuring Economic Growth*, New Economics Foundation, 2004

Jarvis, Mark, *Conservative Governments, Morality and Social Change in Affluent Britain, 1957–64*, Manchester University Press, 2005

Jenkins, Roy, *A Life at the Centre*, Macmillan, 1991

Jenkins, Simon, *Accountable to None: The Tory Nationalisation of Britain*, Penguin edn, 1996

Jenkins, Simon, *Big Bang Localism: A Rescue Plan for British Democracy*, Policy Exchange, 2004

Johnson, Christopher, *The Economy under Mrs Thatcher, 1979–90*, Penguin, 1991

Johnson, Paul, *The Recovery of Freedom*, Basil Blackwell, 1980

Johnson, Paul, *The Intellectuals*, Weidenfeld & Nicolson, 1988

Joseph, Keith, and Sumption, Jonathan, *Equality*, John Murray, 1979

Jowell, Roger, and Witherspoon, Sharon (eds), *British Social Attitudes: The 1985 Report*, Gower, 1985

Jowell, Roger *et al* (eds), *British Social Attitudes: The 17th Report*, Sage, 2000

Kavanagh, Dennis, and Seldon, Anthony (eds), *The Thatcher Effect: A Decade of Change*, Oxford University Press, 1989

Keegan, William, *Mr Lawson's Gamble*, Hodder and Stoughton, 1989

King, Anthony, 'Overload: Problems of Governing in the 1970s', *Political Studies* (1975), 284–96

King, Anthony (ed.), *British Political Opinion 1937–2000: The Gallup Polls*, Politicos, 2001

King, Anthony (ed.), *Britain at the Polls, 2001*, Chatham House, 2002

King, Roger, and Nugent, Neil (eds), *Respectable Rebels: Middle Class Campaigns in Britain in the 1970s*, Hodder and Stoughton, 1979

Kochan, Nicholas, *Ann Widdecombe: Right from the Beginning*, Politicos, 2000

Kortesis, Vasso, with Leigh, David, *The Duchess of York: Uncensored*, Blake Publishing, 1996

Lahr, John (ed.), *The Diaries of Kenneth Tynan*, Bloomsbury, 2002 edn

Larkin, Philip, *Required Writing: Miscellaneous Pieces 1955–1982*, Faber and Faber, 1983

Lawson, Nigel, *The View from No. 11: Memoirs of a Tory Radical*, Bantam, 1992

Layard, Richard, 'The Secret of Happiness', *New Statesman*, 3 March 2003

Layton-Henry, Zig, *The Politics of Immigration*, Blackwell, 1992

Leader, Zachary (ed.), *The Letters of Kingsley Amis*, HarperCollins, 2000

Leigh, David, and Linklater, Magnus, *Not with Honour*, Sphere, 1986

Leigh, David, and Vulliamy, Ed, *Sleaze: The Corruption of Parliament*, Fourth Estate, 1997

Letwin, Shirley Robin, *The Anatomy of Thatcherism*, Fontana, 1992

Livingstone, Ken, *If Voting Changed Anything, They'd Abolish It*, Collins, 1987

[Longford Committee] *Pornography: The Longford Report*, Coronet, 1972

Lovejoy, Joe, *Sven Goran Eriksson*, HarperCollins, 2002

Lydon, John, *No Irish, No Blacks, No Dogs*, Plexus, 1994

McCloughry, Roy (ed.), *Belief in Politics*, Hodder & Stoughton, 1996

McKay, George (ed.), *DiY Culture: Party & Protest in Nineties Britain*, Verso, 1998

McSmith, Andy, *Faces of Labour: The Inside Story*, Verso, 1996

Major, John, *The Autobiography*, HarperCollins, 1999

de Mandeville, Bernard, *The Fable of the Bees*, Penguin edn, 1970

Mark, Sir Robert, *In the Office of Constable: An Autobiography*, Collins, 1978

Martin, David, and Mullen, Peter (eds), *Unholy Warfare: The Church and the Bomb*, Basil Blackwell, 1983

Maslow, Abraham, *Motivation and Personality*, Longman, 1987 edn

Meyer, Christopher, *DC Confidential*, Phoenix edn, 2005

Middlemas, Keith, *Power, Competition and the State*, Vol. 3, *The End of the Postwar Era – Britain since 1974*, Macmillan, 1991

Minnion, John, and Bolsorer, Phillip (eds), *The CND Story: The First 25 years of CND in the Words of the People Involved*, Allison & Busby, 1983

Mitchell, Austin, *Four Years in the Death of the Labour Party*, Methuen, 1983

Monk, Roy, *Bertrand Russell: The Ghost of Madness, 1921–1970*, Vintage, 2001

Morris, Jan, *A Writer's World: Travels 1950–2000*, Faber and Faber, 2003

Morgan, Piers, *The Insider*, Ebury Press, 2005 edn

Morton, Andrew, *Diana: Her True Story*, Michael O'Mara Books, 1993

Mount, Ferdinand, *Mind the Gap: The New Class Divide in Britain*, Short Books, 2004

Murphy, Bill, *Home Truths: A Jaunt around the Decaying Heart of England*, Mainstream, 2000

Neil, Andrew, *Full Disclosure*, Macmillan, 1996

[*New Musical Express*] *The NME Rock 'n' Roll Years*, BCA, 1992

Norton-Taylor, Richard, Lloyd, Mark, and Cook, Stephen, *Knee-Deep in Dishonour: The Scott Report and its Aftermath*, Victor Gollancz, 1996

Nott, Sir John, *Here Today, Gone Tomorrow: Recollections of an Errant Politician*, Politicos, 2002

Oborne, Peter, *Alastair Campbell: New Labour and the Rise of the Media Class*, Aurum Press, 1999

Oborne, Peter, *The Rise of Political Lying*, Free Press, 2005

O'Farrell, John, *Things Can Only Get Better: Eighteen Miserable Years in the Life of a Labour Supporter, 1979–1997*, Black Swan edn, 1999

O'Hara, Kieron, *Trust*, Icon Books, 2004

O'Neill, Onora, *A Question of Trust*, Cambridge University Press, 2002

Palast, Greg, *The Best Democracy Money Can Buy*, Robinson edn, 2003

Palin, Michael, *Diaries 1969–1979: The Python Years*, Weidenfeld & Nicolson, 2006

Parris, Matthew, *Great Parliamentary Scandals*, Robson Books, 1995

Pasternak, Anna, *Princess in Love*, Bloomsbury, 2004

Pattie, Charles, Seyd, Patrick, and Whiteley, Paul, 'Civic Attitudes and Engagement in Modern Britain', *Parliamentary Affairs*, Vol. 56, no. 4, 2003

Paxman, Jeremy, *The English*, Michael Joseph, 1998

Pilger, John, *Distant Voices*, Vintage edn, 1994

Pimlott, Ben, *Harold Wilson*, HarperCollins, 1992

Pliatzky, Sir Leo, *Getting and Spending: Public Spending, Employment and Inflation*, Blackwell, 1982

Pollard, Stephen, *David Blunkett*, Hodder & Stoughton, 2005

Powell, Enoch, *The Common Market: Renegotiate or Come Out*, Elliott Right Way Books, 1973

Prentice, Reg, 'Not Socialist Enough', *Political Quarterly*, Vol. 41, no. 2, April-June 1970, 146–51

Price, Lance, *The Spin Doctor's Diary: Inside Number 10 with New Labour*, Hodder and Stoughton, 2005

Raban, Jonathan, *God, Man and Mrs Thatcher*, Chatto & Windus, 1989

Radice, Giles (ed.), *What Needs to Change: New Visions for Britain*, HarperCollins, 1996

Radice, Giles, *Diaries 1980–2001: From Political Disaster to Electoral Triumph*, Weidenfeld & Nicolson, 2004

Rawnsley, Andrew, *Servants of the People: The Inside Story of New Labour*, Penguin edn, 2001

Rentoul, John, *Me and Mine: The Triumph of the New Individualism?*, HarperCollins, 1989

Richards, Jeffrey et al. (eds), *Diana: The Making of a Media Saint*, I.B. Tauris, 1999

Robertson, Geoffrey, *The Justice Game*, Vintage edn, 1999

Rogally, Joe, *Grunwick*, Penguin, 1977

Rowe, Dorothy, *Living with the Bomb: Can We Cope without Enemies?*, Routledge, 1985

Rowe, Dorothy, *Beyond Fear*, Fontana, 1987

Sampson, Anthony, *The Changing Anatomy of Britain*, Hodder and Stoughton, 1982

Sampson, Anthony, *Who Runs This Place? The Anatomy of Britain in the Twenty-First Century*, John Murray, 2005

Sandbrook, Dominic, *White Heat: A History of Britain in the Swinging Sixties*, Little, Brown, 2006

Seldon, Arthur (ed.), *The Coming Confrontation*, IEA, 1978

Shannon, Richard, *A Press Free and Responsible: Self-Regulation and the Press Complaints Commission*, John Murray, 2001

Shaw, Eric, *The Labour Party since 1979: Crisis and Transformation*, Routledge, 1994

Shawcross, William, *Murdoch*, Simon & Schuster edn, 1993

Shepherd, Robert, *Enoch Powell: A Biography*, Hutchinson, 1996

Sheridan, Simon, '*Come Play with Me*': *The Life and Films of Mary Millington*, FAB Press, 1999

Shonfield, Andrew, *The Use of Public Power*, Oxford University Press, 1982

Snoddy, Raymond, and Ashworth, Jon, *It Could Be You: The Untold Story of the National Lottery*, Faber and Faber, 2000

Sounes, Howard, *Seventies: The Sights, Sounds and Ideas of a Brilliant Decade*, Simon & Schuster, 2006

Stanford, Peter, *Lord Longford: An Authorized Life*, William Heinemann, 1994

Stephens, Philip, *Politics and the Pound: The Tories, the Economy and Europe*, Macmillan, 1996

Stonehouse, John, *The Death of an Idealist*, W.H. Allen, 1975

Strong, Roy, *The Roy Strong Diaries, 1967–1987*, Phoenix edn, 1998

Sunday Times Insight Team, *Strike: Thatcher, Scargill and the Miners*, Andre Deutsch, 1985

Taylor, Eva Harazsti (ed.), *Letters to Eva, 1969–1983*, Century, 1991

Taylor, Peter, *Brits: The War against the IRA*, Bloomsbury, 2001

Temple, Mick, *Blair*, Haas Publishing, 2006

Thatcher, Margaret, *Let Our Children Grow Tall: Selected Speeches 1975–1977*, Centre for Policy Studies, 1977

Thatcher, Margaret, *The Downing Street Years*, HarperCollins, 1993

Thatcher, Margaret, *The Path to Power*, HarperCollins, 1995

Thompson, E.P., *Writing by Candlelight*, Merlin Press, 1980

Thompson, Harry, *Peter Cook: A Biography*, Hodder and Stoughton, 1997

Thwaite, Anthony (ed.), *The Selected Letters of Philip Larkin, 1940–1985*, Faber and Faber, 1992

Toffler, Alvin, *Future Shock*, Pan edn, 1971

Townsend, Charles, *Making the Peace: Public Order and Public Security in Modern Britain*, Oxford University Press, 1993

Toynbee, Polly, and Walker, David, *Did Things Get Better? An Audit of Labour's Successes and Failures*, Penguin, 2001

Tyler, Rodney, *Campaign! The Selling of the Prime Minister*, Grafton Books, 1987

Tyrrell, R. Emmett (ed.), *The Future That Doesn't Work: Social Democracy's Failures in Britain*, Doubleday, 1977

Walden, George, *Time to Emigrate?*, Gibson Square Books, 2006

Walker, Martin, *The National Front*, Fontana, 1977

Ward, Colin, and Henderson, Chris, *Who Wants It*, Mainstream, 2000

West, Patrick, *Conspicuous Compassion: Why Sometimes It Really Is Cruel to Be Kind*, Civitas, 2004

Westergaard, John, and Resler, Henrietta, *Class in a Capitalist Society*, Pelican edn, 1976

Wheen, Francis, *Hoo-Hahs and Passing Frenzies: Collected Journalism, 1991–2001*, Atlantic Books, 2002

Wheen, Francis, *How Mumbo Jumbo Conquered the World: A Short History of Modern Delusions*, Fourth Estate, 2004

Whitehead, Phillip, *The Writing on the Wall: Britain in the Seventies*, Michael Joseph, 1985

Whitehouse, Mary, *Quite Contrary: An Autobiography*, Pan edn, 1994

Wiener, Martin, *English Culture and the Decline of the Industrial Spirit 1850–1980*, Cambridge University Press, 1981

Willetts, David, *Modern Conservatism*, Penguin, 1992

Wilson, Edgar, *A Very British Miracle: The Failure of Thatcherism*, Pluto Press, 1992

Wilson, Harold, *Final Term*, Weidenfeld & Nicolson, 1979

Worsthorne, Peregrine, *The Politics of Manners: and the uses of inequality*, CPS, 1988

Wyatt, Woodrow, *What's Left of the Labour Party?*, Sidgwick & Jackson, 1977

Wybrow, Robert J., *Britain Speaks Out, 1937–87: A Social History as Seen through the Gallup Data*, Macmillan, 1989

Young, Hugo, *This Blessed Plot: Britain and Europe from Churchill to Blair*, Macmillan, 1999

INDEX